HOLLYWOOD HEROES

HOLLYWOOD HEROES

David Hofstede

MADISON BOOKS
Lanham • New York • London

Published by Madison Books
4720 Boston Way
Lanham, Maryland 20706

3 Henrietta Street
London WC2E 8LU England

Distributed by National Book Network

The paper used in this publication meets the minimum requirements of American National Standard for Information Sciences—Permanence of Paper for Printed Library Materials, ANSI Z39.48–1984. ♾™
Manufactured in the United States of America.

Library of Congress Cataloging-in-Publication Data

Hofstede, David.
Hollywood heroes : thirty screen legends from King Arthur to Zorro / by David Hofstede.
p. cm.
Includes index.
1. Adventure films—History and criticism. 2. Heroes in motion pictures. I. Title.
PN1995.9.A3H64 1994
791.43'652—dc20 94–10207 CIP

ISBN 1–56833–029–4 (cloth : alk. paper)

For my teachers and everybody's. . .the greatest of heroes.

TABLE OF CONTENTS

Preface

"Wherever the tyrant sets his hand there is a cry (if not from the housetops, then--more miserably--within every heart): a cry for the redeeming hero, the carrier of the shining blade, whose blow, whose touch, whose existence, will liberate the land."

--Joseph Campbell

This quote, from Campbell's book *The Hero With 1000 Faces*, was of great help when I began formulating the list of fictional and historical personages whom the reader will meet in the pages that follow. The title of "hero" can rightly be bestowed upon an infinite variety of men and women of laudable accomplishment, from the doctor who saves lives in the operating room to the mother who raises her children to become solid citizens. But one particular brand of hero has been celebrated in story and song since the beginning of civilization--the man or woman of action, who battles against insurmountable odds with gun, sword or just the sinew of muscle to save a family, a community, or a country, or perhaps even the world.

Such is the power and influence of motion pictures that many of these heroes, despite being centuries old, have been defined by Hollywood. In some cases the film adaptation is a straightforward rendering of the source material, but for the most part the movies have reinvented the subject to suit their own criteria. The facts are available in any number of books and documentaries, so it is preferable to just sit back and enjoy the movies rather than gripe about historical inaccuracies (though there were instances, as the reader will discover, when I could not resist).

I have tried to include every appropriate film and television adaptation, though some that are unworthy of serious consideration are mentioned only in passing for purposes of completion. The Italian sword and sandal adaptations of Hercules are all listed, for instance, but only those possessing some unique trait or unexpected quality are described in detail. Technical credits are as complete as possible.

Silent film treatments are recorded, but sadly, an estimated 70 percent of all silent cinema has been lost forever, and is therefore unavailable for review. I have not included all animated treatments, with the exception of feature films such as Disney's *Robin Hood.* Most are derivative of their live-action counterparts and add nothing of value. There are exceptions; the animated "Star Trek" series was voiced by the original actors and written by the same writers who made its predecessor a classic, and the Max Fleischer Superman cartoons are interesting and historically significant; all of these are specified.

Videocassette availability was as of publication. "Available on Videocassette" status may change in the future as previously unreleased movies become available. Films were only listed as available if they could be found at any reasonably well-stocked video store. Some that are not labeled as such can often be found from other sources, such as libraries, universities and stores that specialize in the rare and obscure. A list of these outlets can be found in the appendix.

And that's about all you need to know before turning the page, hopefully to get acquainted (or reacquainted) with the greatest movie heroes, and some great heroic movies.

RATINGS

5 stars...A Classic
4 stars...Excellent
3 stars...Respectable
2 stars...Worth a look
1 star....Bomb
0 stars...Worthless

Acknowledgments

For their assistance in locating and providing some of the films reviewed in this volume, the author wishes to thank Allen "Stokey" Stollerman, Wendy Bousman and the folks at Video Park in Las Vegas, and Eddie Brandt's Saturday Matinee. Other research was assisted by the staff of the libraries of UCLA and UNLV. For their inspiration, helpful encouragement, and constructive criticism, my thanks to the Niles North High School class of 1982, and Mom and Dad.

KING ARTHUR

"If King Arthur did not live, he should have."
--Sir Winston Churchill

Churchill's words express a sentiment that is held by all with romance in their hearts. It is preferable to believe that the wealth of poetry, prose and song devoted to Arthur, his knights of the Round Table, and their incredible adventures have some basis in fact. If they all emerged from the imagination of an inspired Dark Ages dramatist, the stories lose some of their magic.

This time, however, history does seem to have a heart. Yes, Virginia, there was a King Arthur, and a Queen Guinevere and a Sir Lancelot as well. Any detailed biographies, if they ever existed, are now lost forever, but enough reliable information has been unearthed by enough distinguished scholars to at least bring us past the first hurdle. The question is no longer "Was there a King Arthur?" but "Who was he?"

LITERATURE

It is tempting to begin with the best-known source of Arthurian lore, Sir Thomas Malory's *La Morte d'Arthur*, completed in 1470. However, this would be like starting *War and Peace* on page 500. So much was written of Arthur before Malory, and so much after, that his *Morte* is but one prominent link in a chain that began 600 years earlier.

Among the many texts that predate Malory are the ninth century *Historia Britonum*, written by Nennius, in which Arthur fights twelve battles against the Saxons. From the same period, the *Annales Cambriae* mentions Arthur's victory at a place called Mons Badonicus in 516, and the Battle of Camlann in 537, in which the king supposedly fell.

The most authoritative pre-Malory contribution was by the historian Geoffrey of Monmouth, who published the *Historia regum Britanniae*, or *History of Britain's Kings* between 1135 and 1139. Geoffrey drew upon Nennius and other early sources for his chapter on Arthur's conquests, and added the figure of Merlin, the sword Excalibur, and the island of Avalon to the saga. It was this version that paved the way for Arthur's emergence as a major figure in the European literature of the Middle Ages.

Published in 1155, Wace of Jersey's *Roman de Brut* introduced the Round Table into the mix. *The Vulgate Cycle* of 1225 was the first detailed coverage of Sir Lancelot. The Holy Grail became entwined with Arthurian lore in the twelfth century writings of Chretian de Troyes, and was a prominent feature in thirteenth century stories of the romance between Lancelot and Guinevere. The two stories were then joined through Sir Galahad, Lancelot's son and the "pure knight" who achieved a vision of God through the Grail that his adulterous father was denied. *The Merlin*, a thirteenth century romance by Robert de Borron, described Arthur's youth, including the "sword in the stone" legend; it also covered the war between Lancelot and Sir Gawain that followed Arthur's death at the hand of Mordred.

Sir Thomas Malory mined all the best nuggets from six centuries of material and published the first English prose account of King Arthur. The best-known edition dates to 1485, but a somewhat different manuscript edition was discovered in 1934 and now resides in the British Museum. Translation is still necessary with either version, since fifteenth century English bears only a passing resemblance to its contemporary counterpart. The best available now is by medieval literature scholar R. M. Lumiansky, who manages to modernize the language while preserving the tone and style of Malory's elegant prose.

Every contribution to Arthurian lore since owes something to Malory, though the consideration of historical accuracy had by this time been almost completely obliterated. The nineteenth century poetry of Alfred Lord Tennyson, though based on Malory, only pushed Arthur further toward the realm of the fanciful, as did T. H. White's 1958 novel *The Once and Future King*, which was adapted into the musical *Camelot*.. Arthur even became a comic book hero, in the outstanding 1982-83 miniseries *Camelot 3000* by Mike Barr and Brian Bolland.

Throughout the twentieth century reports of architectural excavations in England revived interest in the historical Arthur, but it was the brilliant detective work of historian and linguist Norma Goodrich that finally tilted the scale in favor of non-fiction. In her 1986 book *King Arthur*, Goodrich cross-references and clears up the inconsistencies in earlier translations of all the Dark Age sources, and eighteen more sources published between 1125 and 1250. She is also the first to make use of the information in the *Annals of Wales*, which date back centuries but were only published recently, and offer what Goodrich believes is "ample and precise verification of the historic King Arthur."

The complete results of her search are too lengthy even to summarize here, but among her most exciting discoveries is the strong possibility that Arthur was the son of the Roman Emperor Constantine. He was clearly a man of accomplishment who most likely did fight twelve battles as recorded by Nennius, the outcome of which changed the course of his country's history. Goodrich is also able to pinpoint the year of Arthur's death--542--and argue convincingly for Caerlaverock Castle near the city of Carlisle as his birthplace. The castle mound is still visible today. Goodrich has also found Avalon, which for years was identified with Glastonbury Tor in modern-day Somerset. With apologies to the still-brisk Somerset tourist trade, the actual location is the Isle of Man.

Although Goodrich conclusively disproves most of the more romantic aspects of Malory's *Morte*, she does confirm the existence of all the major figures in the stories. The life of Sir Lancelot, in fact, is better documented than that of Arthur. Goodrich has since written three more books devoted to Lancelot, Guinevere, and Merlin, which shed further light on the Dark Ages' most celebrated fellowship.

THE FILMS

They are fascinating reading, and preferable to almost every film adaptation of Arthurian literature. As one of the seminal heroic figures in recorded history King Arthur is worthy of several royal cinematic treatments, but two dozen attempts have only produced one classic, one classic farce, and an enjoyable musical--a less-than-regal performance from Hollywood.

The first three films to feature Arthur were all adaptations of Mark Twain's 1889 novel *A Connecticut Yankee in King Arthur's Court*, the story of a modern pragmatist cast adrift in a primitive, superstitious age. Twain strives to puncture the fairy tale image of Arthur's Britain with the cold, hard facts about life in the Middle Ages, while also managing to take some satiric shots at his own day and age. Indeed, the more progressive ideas and inventions that protagonist Hank Morgan introduces to Camelot, the more screwed up Camelot becomes. Hank sets himself up as a visionary and philanthropist, but ends up killing 25,000 people. Twain skewers the monarchy, but is somewhat sympathetic toward King Arthur; the well-meaning but headstrong monarch is as much a victim as a proponent of the society he rules.

Connecticut Yankee is often perceived as a book for children, but there are passages that describe the brutality of Arthur's time in graphic detail. These were the first to go when the cameras rolled. In 1921 Douglas Fairbanks rejected the Yankee role, which then went to Harry C. Myers, who would later play opposite Charlie Chaplin in *City Lights* (1931). King Arthur was played by Charles Clary. Today the film is either lost or hiding very cleverly, which certainly would not have happened if Fairbanks said yes.

Will Rogers starred in the 1931 version as Hank Martin, a radio shop owner who lands in Arthur's time and introduces the sixth century to telecommunications, cigarette lighters and roller skates. The king's daughter Alisande is kidnapped by Morgan Le Fay, and Arthur and Hank ride to save her. Merlin, jealous of Hank's closeness to the king, tips off Morgan about the attempted rescue. The would-be heroes are captured and about to be put to death when Clarence, Hank's assistant, leads a party of knights in cars, tanks and airplanes that reduce Morgan's castle to rubble. Hank is caught in an explosion and wakes up back in the twentieth century.

There is a tangible link between Mark Twain and Will Rogers, and some of the frontier humor for which both men were famous is preserved in the movie. The book was very much a product of its time, and this film version is no different, with plenty of amusing references to the Great Depression. *Connecticut Yankee*, incidentally, was the book from which President Franklin Roosevelt borrowed the term "New Deal."

However, besides the basic fish-out-of-water set-up and a few of the more memorable situations, little else from the book was retained, and the harshest satiric barbs were either softened or sliced. But it's fun to watch, with Rogers uttering lines like "Canst tell me where in the helleth I am?", and donning his cowboy hat to lasso a knight during a jousting tournament. There's an added bonus in the appearances of Myrna Loy as Morgan and Maureen O'Sullivan as Alisande.

The first movie King Arthur in the post-silent era also springs from Twain's book. William Farnum is very much the surface simpleton of the book, but he does not convey the inherent nobility that Twain also suggests. However, since that would not be in the spirit of the piece it's an unfair criticism.

The same story received a musical treatment in 1949, with Bing Crosby as the Yankee time-traveller. In this version Alisande is the king's niece, who is betrothed to Lancelot but falls for newcomer Hank Morgan. When Lancelot returns to Camelot he challenges Hank, dubbed "Sir Boss" by the king, to a joust. The

Boss wins, but Alisande is angered by Hank's embarrassing of a noble knight, and decides to marry Lancelot after all.

Hank convinces Arthur to embark on a road trip to meet his subjects, but while they're gone Merlin and Mordred conspire to steal the throne. Hank foils the plan and reconciles with Alisande just before he is returned to his own time.

It's a typical, though not distinguished forties musical, and has even less in common with the book than the Will Rogers version. There is no social commentary at all this time, and never any real sense of danger for the hero. However, the film wisely kept Twain's prologue, in which the Yankee visits the castle in today's England where his adventures occurred, to point out a bullet hole in a suit of armor and correct a tour guide on several points, before telling his story in flashback.

Arthur, as played by Sir Cedric Hardwicke, is a doddering old coot with a long white beard, who figures not very prominently in the story. Though king and Boss take a trip through the country as in the book, it is hardly the same life-altering experience here, nor should it be in this context. Watching the film it makes hard to remember how cynical the source material was. The task given to Hardwicke here wastes his considerable talent.

The sets are good but the tunes are forgettable, though enthusiastically performed by Bing and luscious Rhonda Fleming. The best scene has the Boss introducing swing music to Arthur's medieval minstrels--"Tomorrow, I may teach 'em the turkey trot!"

A serial entitled *The Adventures of Sir Galahad* invited audiences back to the theater for fifteen weeks in 1949, but I doubt there were many takers. Future Superman George Reeves plays the brave knight, but he looks far better in tights than he does in armor. He shows no sign of the ability to carry a heroic role, but the material certainly shares the blame. The minuscule budgets granted to serials were hardly sufficient to mount a convincing costume drama, but the fact that they tried anyway allows for some enjoyable games of spot the anachronism.

Galahad, who is not related to Lancelot in this saga, arrives in Camelot asking for a place at the Round Table. Arthur says he can pull up a chair, *if* he can successfully guard Excalibur for one night. But someone spikes his wine and the sword is gone the next morning. It takes Galahad twelve chapters to get it back, after fighting Merlin's spells, magic invisibility rings and the mysterious "Black Knight." But the sword is quickly lost again, and Galahad is aided by the Lady of the Lake and Merlin, who turns out to be a good guy after all, in recovering Excalibur just in time for Arthur to dispatch the Black Knight, unmasked as Mordred.

Anyone with even a passing interest in serials will recognize the names of director Spencer Bennet and writer George Plympton, who churned these potboilers out at a phenomenal rate for over a decade. This one has nothing to distinguish it from an already undistinguished crowd, except for a few okay swordfights and some unintentional laughs. As King Arthur, Nelson Leigh scores nearly as high as Reeves on the yuk-meter. His flat, hopelessly Midwest monotone delivery and tacked-on Brillo-pad beard are funny enough, but wait, there's more. My favorite scene is when the Lady of the Lake holds Excalibur aloft, an occurrence that should be greeted by the king with wonderment. But Arthur casually drifts by in a rowboat, and takes the sword as if it were a pizza delivery he had pre-ordered.

King Arthur appeared in three 1954 releases, starting with *Prince Valiant*, a first-rate adaptation of the Harold Foster comic strip and one of the unheralded gems of the swashbuckler genre.

The peaceful kingdom of Scandia is overthrown by a traitor named Sligon. Its ruler, King Aguar, escapes with his wife and son and is given sanctuary by King Arthur in a remote abbey. Aguar dispatches his son Valiant to Camelot, hoping he will become a knight and lead the battle to regain Scandia. During his journey Valiant overhears talk of a plot between Sligon's men and the infamous Black Knight to overthrow Arthur. He warns the king at Camelot, and is allowed to begin his journey toward knighthood as the squire of Sir Gawain.

Valiant falls in love with Aleta, daughter of the King of Ord. When the king offers her hand in marriage to the winner of a tournament, Valiant dons Sir Gawain's armor to compete but is defeated by Sir Brack, one of Arthur's most revered knights. The real Gawain then appears and wins the tournament, while Valiant is thrown in the dungeon for impersonating a knight of the Round Table.

When word reaches Camelot of Aguar's capture, Valiant escapes and rides into a trap set by Sir Brack, who is revealed to be the Black Knight. But with the help of a handful of loyal Scandia subjects, Valiant is able to defeat the usurper and restore Aguar to the throne.

Every attempt was made to create another classic in the mold of *The Adventures of Robin Hood* (1938), from the lavish production values to the all-star cast and creative team, including Oscar-winning screenwriter Dudley Nichols and *Lives of a Bengal Lancer* director Henry Hathaway. But Errol Flynn was past his prime (though sadly still trying) in 1954, so 20th Century Fox took a chance with relative newcomer Robert Wagner in the title role. Wagner, a debonair leading man in the Cary Grant mold, does not work comfortably in costume drama, and that pageboy haircut doesn't help.

James Mason is excellent as Sir Brack, Janet Leigh was never lovelier as Aleta, and the best character actors in Hollywood filled the supporting roles, including Victor McLaglen, Sterling Hayden and Debra Paget. Brian Aherne has only a handful of scenes as King Arthur, but he makes them count with a classy performance.

There is action aplenty throughout, and when all Scandia breaks loose in the last reel Valiant executes a series of maneuvers worthy of Indiana Jones as he is chased through Sligon's castle. Back in Camelot, the final duel between Brack and Valiant ranks with the best swordplay ever captured on film, and that's saying something.

Knights of the Round Table was loosely based on Malory, and was Golden Age Hollywood's only "A" list attempt at Arthurian lore. The Robin Hood and Zorro films of this era became definitive treatments of their subjects, but that is not the case here. All the right elements seem to be in place, but there's just no magic.

The story opens with the sword-in-the-stone incident, and with Morgan Le Fay and Mordred vowing to fight Arthur's coronation all the way. The king finds allies in Lancelot, Perceval, Gareth and Gawain, and together they rout Mordred's forces and secure the throne. However, Lancelot storms out of Camelot after Arthur shows mercy to his conquered foes.

When Lancelot returns to make amends, Arthur appoints him champion of the new queen, Guinevere. Bad move. Mordred catches on to the queen's affair and tells the king. Lancelot is banished, and Guinevere is dispatched to a nunnery. With Lancelot gone, Mordred's forces attack and kill Arthur. When word of the battle reaches Lancelot, he returns and slays Mordred.

This was MGM's first Cinemascope production, but the studio was sliding rapidly by this time without Louis B. Mayer and most of its top stars. In my opinion, it doesn't appear that anyone's heart was in this project. The cast just goes through the motions, and you never forget that you're watching actors reading lines. Everyone's emotions are at half-speed--when Lancelot proclaims, "Hail Arthur, King of Britain," after the battle with Mordred is won, there is no enthusiasm in the moment.

Robert Taylor gives one of his worst performances as Sir Lancelot, and Mel Ferrer's King Arthur does not rise above the general air of indifference. Ava Gardner, who plays Guinevere, never could act, but in this case and this company it doesn't stand out as much. The best performance in the film comes from Maureen Swanson, who as an unknown perhaps felt a need to try harder, as Lancelot's wife.The studio still knew how to make a period piece look good, with all the requisite scenery and pageantry, but among the lush settings there is no drama or excitement.

Also from 1954, *The Black Knight* starred Alan Ladd as John, a young peasant swordmaker with a crush on Linet, a noblewoman above his station. He is unfairly branded a coward after an attack on his master's castle, and goes into training to recover his reputation and prove himself worthy of Linet's love. He assumes the guise of the Black Knight, and uncovers a Saracen plot against King Arthur.

As in *Knights of the Round Table*, there is no shortage of beautiful Technicolor pictures--the location footage at Stonehenge is particularly captivating. The plot, a direct steal from a hundred westerns, has plenty of action and is played out by a solid cast. Alan Ladd always makes a stalwart hero, but as a Yank adrift in British accents, his voice is too conspicuous. He's also stretching a bit playing a youngish character one year after his classic portrayal of a veteran gunfighter in *Shane* (1953).

Anthony Bushell plays Arthur, and comes off a bit reserved for a famous warrior-king. Peter Cushing and Patrick Troughton supply expert villainy. This was director Tay Garnett's second foray into the period, after helming the Bing Crosby version of *Connecticut Yankee*.

Television's first coverage of the King Arthur stories debuted in 1956 and lasted only one season. "The Adventures of Sir Lancelot" starred William Russell as the brave knight and Ronald Leigh-Hunt as a kindly, patriarchal King Arthur. The series was filmed in England and took pride in its Oxford University–approved period settings and costumes. The stories, all light comedy/adventure fare, were aimed at a young audience, but were played straight and well by a talented British cast.

From 1963, *Sword of Lancelot* tells almost exactly the same story as *Knights of the Round Table*. However, the enthusiasm of the principles ranks it above the former, even without the MGM gloss. Cornel Wilde, ever the poor man's Errol Flynn, directed and starred as Lancelot, and it may be his best performance. Wilde's off-screen wife Jean Wallace plays Guinevere, and together they generate some respectable sparks.

The famous love triangle is simply and sincerely related, though the sets, costumes and by-the-numbers script are reminiscent of a school play version of Malory. Brian Aherne again does a credible job as Arthur (see *Prince Valiant*) and gets more screen time in his second attempt. Yugoslavia ably substitutes for Britain as a backdrop.

Walt Disney's *The Sword in the Stone* (1963) was the first major miscue from the studio's legendary animation wing. The story of Arthur as an awkward youth being trained by Merlin never takes off, and none of the characters are all that interesting. Richard M. and Robert Sherman, who wrote the magnificent scores to *Mary Poppins* and *The Jungle Book*, were off their form on this one, which has little to recommend outside of a cleverly-devised "wizard's duel" between Merlin and Mad Madame Mim.

In *Siege of the Saxons* (1963), King Arthur has a daughter named Kate who must flee Camelot after her father is murdered. In her absence the murderer, Edmund of Cornwall, announces that he is now King. But Kate returns to interrupt the coronation, and assumes her rightful place with help from Merlin and her heroic fiance` Robert Marshall.

Mark Dignam, who played Merlin in *Sword of Lancelot*, plays King Arthur, but he is not around long enough to have much impact. The largely unknown cast, led by Janette Scott and Ronald Lewis, do their best with a very predictable story.

Hollywood's adaptation of the hit Broadway musical *Camelot* (1967) was probably a disappointment to anyone who saw the stage version; it did not feature any of the original cast members--Richard Burton, Julie Andrews and Robert Goulet. Listen to the cast album today and the movie still runs a distant second, but is not without merit.

Arthur, a capable but reluctant king, marries his lady love Guinevere and sets about creating a new code of moral and ethical law. He sends invitations throughout the land to brave knights who will join his cause. Among the first to join is Lancelot, a mighty warrior eager to please but not lacking in ego.

At a tournament that Guinevere rigs to give Lancelot his comeuppance, the queen and the knight end up falling in love. Mordred exposes the affair and Arthur, who took great pride in his establishment of a trial by jury, must now abide by the decision to burn Guinevere at the stake. Lancelot rescues her, to Arthur's thinly disguised relief, but the Round Table is destroyed. Time passes and, while Mordred assembles an army to march on Camelot, Arthur ruminates on how his life and dream will end. He sees Lancelot and Guinevere once more and forgives their trespass. Before his final battle, the king meets a child who has heard the stories of Camelot, and wants to become a knight. Arthur now realizes that his accomplishments will not be forgotten.

Director Joshua Logan obviously made a concerted effort to avoid stiffly filming the stage production, but he overcompensates. The extreme close-ups used ad nauseum are clumsily executed, and distract from rather than embellish such musical numbers as, "I Wonder What the King is Doing Tonight?" The choreography is uninspired and one of the best songs, "Follow Me," is thrown away as background mood music.

But there is much to like here. The title song is charmingly staged and performed by Richard Harris as Arthur and Vanessa Redgrave as Guinevere, and the scene continues with a memorable monologue by Harris on Arthur's unique path to the crown. There are several such brief shining moments distributed throughout the three-hour running time, plus fine orchestrations of the Alan Jay Lerner-Frederick Loewe score that hits more than misses. When Camelot starts to collapse so does the movie, but by then you'll be in for the duration.

Harris does not possess the commanding timbre of Richard Burton, but the evolution of his portrayal, from a still somewhat playful young monarch to the crestfallen victim of adultery and subterfuge still ranks as the most in-depth interpretation to date. Harris has many splendid scenes, including his soliloquy on betrayal and the bittersweet final reprise of the title song.

Vanessa Redgrave cannot even approximate the pristine vocals of Julie Andrews, and you have to feel for Julie after being aced out of both her Broadway triumphs (Audrey Hepburn replaced her for the movie of *My Fair Lady*). When she's not singing, however, Redgrave is an appealing, vivacious Guinevere. Franco Nero starts out too clownish as Lancelot, but settles down later for a fine version of the show's big number, "If Ever I Would Leave You." David Hemmings makes the most of his few scenes as Mordred.

The fourteenth century poem *Sir Gawain and the Green Knight* is familiar to almost everyone from high school, but not until 1973 did someone turn the famous tale into a movie. In this low-budget British production, Murray Head plays Gawain, who accepts the Green Knight's offer of a complimentary swipe with an ax, with the agreement that the Green Knight can return the stroke one year later. Anthony Sharp plays King Arthur, who appears briefly at the beginning and at the close.

From France, *Lancelot du Lac* (1974) is a "revisionist" look at the legend, which means it takes great delight in draining out the romance for the sake of historic accuracy. Robert Bresson's film is actually no more accurate than Malory, but its thoughtful treatment of the love triangle is handled well.

In this movie, the Round Table Knights return empty-handed from the Grail quest, and pillage everything in their path out of spite. The defeat is particularly hard on Lancelot, who had never been on the losing side before. He is comforted by Guinevere, and they resume their affair. Arthur learns about the relationship from Mordred and imprisons Guinevere. When Mordred's forces attack, Lancelot remains loyal to his king, but even their combined might is unsuccessful.

Bresson's attempt to present a realistic look at life in the Middle Ages almost sinks the film. Between the dim light of oil lamps and the incessant clanging of armor, all we really learn is that Camelot was a dark, noisy place. The hypnotic quality of Bresson's visual style draws a viewer in, but the unsavory story and angst-laden performances are a bit much. Vladimir Antolek-Oresek plays King Arthur.

The antithesis to the Bresson treatment is *Monty Python and the Holy Grail* (1975). It's sort of about Arthur receiving a divine order to find the Holy Grail in Britain circa 932, but in reality the film is a series of individual skits with a common theme. Only in *Life of Brian* (1979) did Monty Python manage to work their insanity into a sustained, coherent storyline.

This is not so much an adaptation of King Arthur as adapting Arthur to fit Python. As played by Graham Chapman, the king is argumentative, befuddled and in general completely detached from rational behavior, a description that is applicable to most memorable Python characters, from the cheese shop owner who doesn't sell cheese to the drill sergeant who trains recruits in self-defense against bananas. Like all of their best work, *Monty Python and the Holy Grail* runs the comedic gamut, from slapstick to sophisticated wordplay, with anarchic brilliance. To describe what happens cannot do it justice, but the Camelot song, Arthur's battle with the Black Knight, the "Bring out your dead" wagon and the bridgekeeper's three questions are as funny as motion picture comedy gets, though admittedly it will play funnier to the already converted.

In 1975, the BBC again brought King Arthur to television in the short-lived series "Arthur, King of the Brittons." The series was then edited together for the feature film *King Arthur--The Young Warlord*. Arthur himself narrates this story of his early life as the leader of a Celtic tribe. Weary of the constant wars with other clans, Arthur dreams of uniting all of Britain's tribes under one ruler. With the help of his brother Kai he is able to forge such an alliance, just in time to route an invading army of Saxons. But when the threat is averted, Arthur must still struggle to keep the tribes together.

This little-seen film takes the novel approach of presenting the "truth" behind the legends. The look is authentic sixth century--shiny suits of armor and glorious castles are rightly replaced by animal-skin clothing and primitive huts and shelters. But the actual tales are as fictional as anything in Malory and, with the exception of Kai, do not incorporate any of the other prominent Arthurian figures.

The lackluster direction, overbearing musical cues and obvious morality lessons call to mind a BBC Afterschool Special. In this variation, for instance, Arthur rigs the sword-in-the-stone scenario in advance to place the other tribal leaders under his control. The legend is turned into a moral lesson--only when all the leaders worked together could the sword be removed. Arthur is played by Oliver Tobias as a thinker among savages, with lofty ideals that he is willing to achieve through practical and sometimes underhanded means. Brian Blessed, one of the UK's best character actors, is memorable as Arthur's occasional ally Mark of Cornwall.

Though bridged by narration, the episodic structure of the film betrays its source. As a TV series, this is still an above-average rendition, but as a film it cannot sustain its repeated beginnings and climaxes.

Perceval (1978) is director Eric Rohmer's adaptation of Chretian de Troyes's twelfth century romance about one of Arthur's greatest knights. The plot has Perceval, a dumb but honest country youth, dreaming about Round Table status but terminally confused about the nature of chivalry. Eventually he does join Arthur's court, but it does not bring the satisfaction he expected.

Rohmer is normally one of the most accessible foreign filmmakers to American audiences, and on the surface it would seem that *Perceval* would fit right into his very popular "Moral Tales" series. But the film has more in common with *Lancelot du Lac*--slow story development, highly stylized visuals and a calculated artificiality that is not for all tastes. Marc Eyraud plays King Arthur, who does not figure much in the saga. The cast includes many familiar faces to art-house patrons, such as Arielle Dombasle (*Pauline at the Beach*) and Marie-Christine Barrault (*Cousin, Cousine*).

Disney's second visit to Camelot was 1979's *Unidentified Flying Oddball*, which was yet another adaptation of *Connecticut Yankee*. But this live-action comedy did not fare any better than *The Sword in the Stone*.

Astronaut Tom Trimble and his android companion Hermes are sent on a mission to explore the stars, but end up back in the sixth century. Tom quickly runs afoul of Merlin and Mordred, but ends up saving the kingdom from their schemes. It is Disney at its most infantile, the kind of movie that makes *The $1,000,000 Duck* look like a classic. Having one of the worst titles in motion picture history doesn't help.

Dennis Dugan plays Trimble and his robot double (a needless plot complication) but fails to impress in either role. Sheila White has some nice moments as Alisande, who in this version returns with Trimble to the twentieth century, a departure from previous treatments. The role of King Arthur fell to

Kenneth More, whose flustered, over-the-hill leadership is reminiscent of Inspector Fenwick in the Dudley-Do-Right cartoons.

It was in 1981 that the king and his court finally received their due. All the famous stories, all the well-known characters, and all the timeless symbols were brilliantly brought to life by writer-producer-director John Boorman and a stellar cast in *Excalibur*. After getting bits and pieces in lesser efforts, here is everything a lover of Malory's prose could desire in a movie.

The story begins not with Arthur but with his father Uther Pendragon, whose lust for another man's wife sets events in motion that only Merlin, their principal architect, could perceive. Merlin gives Uther access to Igrayne, the object of his desire, in exchange for the child he knows they will produce. Uther would agree to anything at that moment, and nine months later the sorcerer returns to claim his fee.

The child grows up to be king of all England, after pulling his father's sword Excalibur from a stone. With Merlin as his adviser, Arthur unites his country. He marries Guinevere, and recruits a Round Table of knights, including the libidinous Lancelot. The seeds for Camelot's destruction are sown by Morgan Le Fay, first with her exposure of the queen's adultery and then with her supernatural tryst with the king, which produces Mordred. Arthur sends his knights on a quest for the Holy Grail, hoping to revive the spirit of his court, but when that fails as well he realizes the end is near. Lancelot returns for the final battle between Arthur and Mordred, and Merlin returns to settle up with friend and foe alike after being imprisoned by Morgan. When Arthur falls he is transported to Avalon, while Perceval carries out his last wish and tosses Excalibur into the sea. The Lady of the Lake retrieves the mighty sword, and holds it until the next man worthy of its power is crowned.

John Boorman's films typically deal with the raw primal emotions of humanity and the consequences of acting upon them (*Hell in the Pacific*, *Deliverance*). *La Morte D'Arthur* is ideal source material for such scrutiny, and not just for Lancelot and Guinevere. Arthur's birth resulted from Uther's raging passion for Igrayne, and the deed was witnessed by a young Morgan, whose consuming hatred of the Pendragons ruled her life and destroyed Camelot.

The extreme violence and sexual situations were always part of the legend, but this is the first film that doesn't turn the other way. The hacked-off limbs, the blood spurting through armor joints and one particular gross-out scene during Perceval's Grail search might be too intense for young children, but could not be considered gratuitous.

King Arthur, as played by Nigel Terry, knows that he was "not born to lead a man's life, but to be the stuff of future memory." His destiny decided at his conception, Arthur became the brave and noble ruler who forged England's path from savagery to civilization, though he was powerless to avoid his predestined downfall. Terry is the best Arthur we have on screen, but he is still somewhat overshadowed by the more flamboyant performance of Nicol Williamson. Williamson is the first to play Merlin as neither good nor evil, but as a force of nature who has the power to change history and realizes that when Christianity replaces paganism his mystic arts will no longer be in demand.

Cherie Lunghi and Nicholas Clay are ideal as the lovers Guinevere and Lancelot. There is also memorable early-career work by Helen Mirren (a marvelous Morgan), Gabriel Byrne, Liam Neeson and Patrick Stewart.

The breathtaking Irish locations demand to be seen on a theater-sized screen. The dazzling waterfall at Glendalough is a perfect backdrop to Arthur and Lancelot's first meeting. The production is no less attractive when it moves indoors--the Round Table assemblage and Arthur's wedding are equal to the millennium of descriptive poetry they inspired.

Excalibur received only one Oscar nomination, for cinematography, which is shocking when watching the film today. Boorman's direction and the intelligent script he cowrote with Rospo Pallenberg, Trevor Jones's music, which draws upon the Gregorian Chant of the period, the art direction and the costume design all deserved recognition. But in 1981 the Academy was preoccupied with stargazing at Robert Redford and Meryl Streep in *Out of Africa* and Jack Nicholson and Kathleen Turner in *Prizzi's Honor*, two films that have long since faded from memory as the reputation of *Excalibur* continues to grow.

Though *Knightriders* (1982) is not a King Arthur film in the strictest sense, this unusual and underappreciated film that transfers the age of chivalry to the twentieth century is definitely worth seeing. Ed Harris plays Eddie, the man in charge of a traveling medieval fair that stages jousting matches on motorcycles. Eddie and his troupe are not just acting--they have devoted their lives to recapturing the spirit and code of honor that flourished in Arthur's Camelot. But when Tom Savini, who plays the bad guy Morgan in the skits, starts to act a bit too villainous, Eddie wonders if the old ways are capable of surviving in the modern world.

This long but engrossing film was conceived and directed by goremeister George Romero, who again demonstrates how to infuse an overworked genre with new life. The performances are strong and the ending is sure to spark debate. Look for author Stephen King in a cameo.

Stuck on You (1982) is as bad a movie as appears in this entire book, a comedy of the lowest level that should be a profound embarrassment to anyone whose name is in the credits. The story has former lovers Bill and Carol suing each other in palimony court. The judge, a fallen angel looking to earn his wings, shows them through historical flashbacks that their problems are not unique. After learning about Adam and Eve, Arthur and Guinevere, and Napoleon and Josephine, Bill and Carol renew their romance and the judge gets his wings.

The shameless theft from *It's A Wonderful Life* is obvious, and all the more offensive in a film that seems to have been written by two snickering twelve-year-old boys in between remedial English classes. Every cheap and easy sight gag and bathroom joke is exhumed and ineptly performed. The cast is led by Professor Irwin Corey, whose sole contribution to film is ten adequate minutes in *Car Wash* (1976). Arthur is mercifully on screen for only a brief moment, and is played by an "actor" billed as Mr. Kent. Beyond pathetic.

Stephen Weeks, the director who filmed *Gawain and the Green Knight* in 1973, took a second stab at the same material ten years later, but *Sword of the Valiant* was not an improvement. Weeks had enough talent and resources at his disposal this time to create a classic, but after a mesmerizing set-up, his film is sunk by a change in tone that can only be described as maddening.

Sean Connery is brilliant as the Green Knight, whose challenge to Arthur's court as the film opens is superbly conceived and photographed by three-time Oscar winner Freddie Young. But after Gawain's fate is sealed and the Knight departs, the next scene has Gawain asking his companion "How do I relieve myself in this tin suit?" The shift from drama to silliness is near-instantaneous, and the film remains in nonsense mode right through the unsatisfying conclusion, which ignores the chivalric moral of the original material.

Connery returns twice, and with each appearance elevates everyone and everything around him. Lila Kedrova, an Academy Award winner in *Zorba the Greek* (1964), is wasted in a dead-end role. Miles O'Keeffe, formerly Bo Derek's Tarzan, plays Gawain, but his lines are dubbed by another actor. The wonderful Trevor Howard plays a distinguished King Arthur in his later years, and only appears in the film's outstanding opening scene, berating his knights for getting soft in times of peace. Howard then wisely departs before the buffoonery begins. But the indications in that moment of what might have been make *Sword of the Valiant* the most frustrating film on the list.

"Arthur the King" was originally broadcast on CBS over two nights in 1985 (after sitting on the shelf for three years), and was later cut in half for video release under the title *Merlin and the Sword.* It's a misfire in either form, so you're better off watching the shorter version because it's over quicker.

During a visit to Stonehenge, an insurance agent named Katherine falls down a rabbit hole and meets Merlin and his beloved Niniane, who have been trapped under the monument for centuries. Merlin tells Katherine stories about Camelot as he knew it, and of his desire to return and change what went wrong. Somehow with Katherine's help he gets that chance, and manages to undo some ancient damage.

This is King Arthur filtered through *Alice in Wonderland*, with a backstory cribbed from Chaucer's *Canterbury Tales*. Writer J. David Wyler borrowed from the best but couldn't adapt the elements into a cohesive whole. The prologue with Dyan Cannon as Katherine starts the piece off on a less-than-serious note, but is inappropriate since the rest of the film is played more or less straight. Cannon turns up throughout to comment on the proceedings, and while I can usually watch her in anything, this stretches my loyalty.

Malcolm McDowall is always an intriguing presence on screen, and his driven, low-key performance as Arthur is often better than the material. So is Edward Woodward as a vulnerable Merlin, who is a participant rather than an observer (or architect) in human events and emotions. There is also Candice Bergen, bedecked in a fright wig from the Bride of Frankenstein's garage sale, as Morgan Le Fey. Her performance is atrocious and light years away from the comedic skills she displays in "Murphy Brown."

In 1989, yet another paycheck was sent to the Mark Twain estate when *Connecticut Yankee* was dredged up once more, this time as a vehicle for ten-year-old Cosby kid Keshia Knight-Pulliam. There was ample opportunity to put some novel twists on the old chestnut--how would Arthur and his court react to a child who's smarter than they are? How would they react to an African-American?

Unfortunately, there were no such sociological insights in Paul Zindel's script. Instead, there are scenes of Arthur being fascinated by a Walkman and of Keshia teaching an aerobics class to Guinevere and her ladies-in-waiting. It's a kiddie show all the way, done with heart and an eye toward educating, but with nothing for the parents who are roped in by their offspring. Pulliam is an engaging lead, precocious without being cutesy, and the cast seems to be having fun playing dress-up. Michael Gross, head of the Keaton clan of "Family Ties," plays a likable but somewhat goofy King Arthur, Emma Samms is a regal Guinevere, and Jean Marsh is the epitome of family-hour villainy as Morgan.

Every version of Twain's story is appropriate for all ages, but the only one that will bring equal pleasure to children and adults is *Bugs Bunny in King Arthur's Court* (1977), in which Bugs tunnels for the Georgia Peanut Festival and ends up in Camelot. Daffy Duck is Arthur, Yosemite Sam is Merlin of Monroe, Porky Pig is side-splitting as Sir Loin of Pork (get ready to laugh when Bugs asks him for the date). Chuck Jones wrote and directed this thirty-minute gem which contains hilarious references to Ray Bradbury, Joan of Arc and *My Fair Lady*. All this plus Acme goes into the armor business. What more could you want?

THE FILMS

A Connecticut Yankee At King Arthur's Court (20th Century Fox, 1921, 90 minutes)
Directed by Emmett J. Flynn; Written by Bernard McConville, based on the novel by Mark Twain.
Cast
Harry C. Myers (Martin Cavendish), Pauline Starke (Sandy), Rosemary Theby (Queen Morgan Le Fey), CHARLES CLARY (KING ARTHUR), William V. Mong (Merlin)

A Connecticut Yankee (20th Century Fox, 1931, 95 minutes
Directed by David Butler; Written by William Conselman and Owen Davis, based on Twain.
Cast
Will Rogers (Hank), WILLIAM FARNUM (KING ARTHUR), Myrna Loy (Morgan), Maureen O'Sullivan (Alisande), Mitchell Harris (Merlin)
Rating: ***1/2
Available on Videocassette

A Connecticut Yankee in King Arthur's Court (Paramount, 1949, 106 minutes)
Directed by Tay Garnett; Written by Edmund Beloin, based on Twain; Produced by Robert Fellows; Music and lyrics by James Van Heusen and Johnny Burke
Cast
Bing Crosby (Hank Martin), William Bendix (Sir Sagramore), SIR CEDRIC HARDWICKE (KING ARTHUR), Rhonda Fleming (Alisande), Murvyn Vye (Merlin), Virginia Field (Morgan), Henry Wilcoxson (Sir Lancelot)
Rating: ***
Available on Videocassette

The Adventures of Sir Galahad (Columbia serial, 1949, 250 minutes)
Directed by Spencer Bennet; Written by George H. Plympton, Lewis Clay and David Matthews; Produced by Sam Katzman; Music by Mischa Bakaleinikoff
Cast
George Reeves (Sir Galahad), Charles King (Bors), William Fawcett (Merlin), Pat Barton (Morgan), Hugh Prosser (Lancelot), Lois Hall (Lady of the Lake), NELSON LEIGH (KING ARTHUR), Marjorie Stamp (Guinevere)
Rating: *

Knights of the Round Table (MGM, 1953, 115 minutes)
Directed by Richard Thorpe; Written by Talbot Jennings, Jan Lustig and Noel Langley, based on La Morte D'Arthur by Sir Thomas Malory; Produced by Pandro S. Berman; Music by Miklos Rozsa
Cast

Robert Taylor (Lancelot), Ava Gardner (Guinevere), MEL FERRER (KING ARTHUR), Anne Crawford (Morgan), Stanley Baker (Mordred), Felix Aylmer (Merlin), Maureen Swanson (Elaine)
Rating: **1/2
Available on Videocassette
Awards: Academy Award nominations for Best Art Direction/Set Direction and Best Sound

Prince Valiant (20th Century Fox, 1954, 100 minutes
Directed by Henry Hathaway; Written by Dudley Nichols, based on the comic strip by Harold Foster; Produced by Robert L. Jacks; Music by Franz Waxman
Cast
Robert Wagner (Prince Valiant), James Mason (Sir Brack), Janet Leigh (Aleta), Debra Paget (Ilene), Sterling Hayden (Sir Gawain), Victor McLaglen (Boltar), BRIAN AHERNE (KING ARTHUR)
Rating: ****
Available on Videocassette

The Black Knight (Columbia, 1954, 85 minutes)
Directed by Tay Garnett; Written by Alec Coppel; Produced by Irving Allen and Albert R. Broccoli; Music by John Addison
Cast
Alan Ladd (John), Patricia Medina (Linet), Andre Morell (Sir Ontzlake), Peter Cushing (Sir Palamides), ANTHONY BUSHELL (KING ARTHUR), Patrick Troughton (King Mark), Jean Lodge (Guinevere)
Rating: ***

Sword of Lancelot (Universal, 1963, 116 minutes)
Directed by Cornel Wilde, Written by Richard Schayer and Jefferson Pascal, based on Malory; Produced by Bernard Luber; Music by Ron Goodwin
Cast
Cornel Wilde (Lancelot), Jean Wallace (Guinevere), BRIAN AHERNE (KING ARTHUR), George Baker (Sir Gawaine), Mark Dignam (Merlin)
Rating: ***1/2
Available on Videocassette

The Sword in the Stone (Disney, 1963, 75 minutes)
Directed by Wolfgang Reitherman; Written by Bill Peet, based on a book by T.H. White; Music by George Bruns, songs by Richard and Robert B. Sherman
Cast (voices of)
RICKIE SORENSON (ARTHUR/WART), Sebastian Cabot (Sir Ector), Karl Swenson (Merlin), Junius Matthews (Archimedes), Alan Napier (Sir Pelinore), Martha Wentworth (Mad Madame Mim)
Rating: **
Available on Videocassette
Awards: Academy Award nomination for Best Score

Siege of the Saxons (Columbia, 1963, 85 minutes)
Directed by Nathan Juran; Written by Jud Kinberg and John Kohn; Produced by Jud Kinberg; Music by Laurie Johnson

Cast
Ronald Lewis (Robert Marshall), Janette Scott (Katherine), Ronald Howard (Edmund of Cornwall), MARK DIGNAM (KING ARTHUR), John Laurie (Merlin)
Rating: ** 1/2

Camelot (Warner Bros., 1967, 179 minutes)
Directed by Joshua Logan; Written by Alan Jay Lerner, based on the play by Lerner and Frederick Loewe and the book The Once and Future King by T.H. White; Produced by Jack L. Warner; Music and lyrics by Lerner and Loewe
Cast
RICHARD HARRIS (KING ARTHUR), Vanessa Redgrave (Guinevere), Franco Nero (Lancelot), David Hemmings (Mordred), Lionel Jeffries (King Pellinore), Laurence Naismith (Merlin)
Rating: ****
Available on Videocassette
Awards: Academy Awards for Best Art Direction/Set Direction, Best Score, Best Costume Design.

Gawain and the Green Knight (UA/Sancrest, 1973, 93 minutes)
Directed by Stephen Weeks; Written by Philip Breen and Stephen Weeks, based on a medieval poem; Produced by Carlo Ponti; Music by Ron Goodwin
Cast
Murray Head (Gawain), Nigel Green (Green Knight), Claran Madden (Linet), Robert Hardy (Sir Bertilan), ANTHONY SHARP (KING ARTHUR)
Rating: *** 1/2

Lancelot du Lac (Mara Films, 1975, 85 minutes)
Directed and written by Robert Bresson; Produced by Jean-Pierre Rassam; Music by Philippe Sarde
Cast
Luc Simon (Lancelot), Laura Duke Condominas (Guinevere), Humbert Balsan (Gawain), VLADIMIR ANTOLEK-ORESEK (KING ARTHUR), Patrick Bernhard (Modred)
Rating: ** 1/2

Monty Python and the Holy Grail (Python, 1975, 89 minutes)
Directed by Terry Gilliam and Terry Jones; Written by Graham Chapman, John Cleese, Terry Gilliam, Eric Idle, Terry Jones and Michael Palin; Produced by Mark Forstater; Music by Neil Innes
Cast
GRAHAM CHAPMAN (KING ARTHUR, others), John Cleese (Black Knight, Sir Lancelot, others), Terry Gilliam (The Bridgekeeper, the Green Knight, others), Eric Idle (The Dead Collector, others), Terry Jones (Sir Belvedere, others), Michael Palin (Dennis, Sir Galahad, others), Connie Booth (Witch), Carol Cleveland (Zoot, Dingo)
Rating: ****
Available on Videocassette

The Young Warlord (HTV, 1975, 90 minutes)

Directed by Sidney Hayers, Patrick Jackson and Peter Sasdy; Written by Terence Feely and Robert Banks Steward; Produced by Peter Miller; Music by Elmer Bernstein
Cast
OLIVER TOBIAS (KING ARTHUR), Jack Watson (Llud), Michael Gothard (Kai), Brian Blessed (Mark of Cornwall), Peter Firth (Corin), Gila (Rowena)
Rating: ***

Perceval (Gaumont/New Yorker Films, 1978, 137 minutes)
Directed and written by Eric Rohmer, based on the novel by Chretian de Troyes; Produced by Barbet Schroeder; Music by Guy Robert
Cast
Fabrice Luchini (Perceval), Andre Dussalier (Gawain), Arielle Dombasle (Blanchfleur), Michel Etchverry (Fisher King), MARC EYRAUD (KING ARTHUR), Marie-Christine Barrault (Guinevere)
Rating: ***1/2

Unidentified Flying Oddball (Disney, 1979, 93 minutes)
Directed by Russ Mayberry; Written by Don Tait, based on Twain; Produced by Ron Miller; Music by Ron Goodwin
Cast
Dennis Dugan (Tom Trimble, Hermes), Jim Dale (Sir Mordred), Ron Moody (Merlin), KENNETH MORE (KING ARTHUR), John Le Mesurier (Sir Gawain), Sheila White (Alisande)
Rating: **
Available on Videocassette

Excalibur (Orion, 1981, 140 minutes)
Directed and produced by John Boorman; Written by John Boorman and Rospo Pallenberg; Music by Trevor Jones
Cast
NIGEL TERRY (KING ARTHUR), Nicol Williamson (Merlin), Nicholas Clay (Lancelot), Helen Mirren (Morganna), Cherie Lunghi (Guinevere), Paul Geoffrey (Perceval), Robert Addie (Mordred), Gabriel Byrne (Uther), Katrine Boorman (Igrayne), Liam Neeson (Gawain)
Rating: *****
Available on Videocassette
Awards: Academy Award nomination for Best Cinematography

Knightriders (Laurel/United Film Distribution, 1981, 145 minutes)
Directed and written by George Romero; Produced by Richard P. Rubenstein; Music by Donald Rubinstein
Cast
Ed Harris (Eddie), Gary Lahti (Alan), Tom Savini (Morgan), Amy Ingersoll (Linet)
Rating: ***
Available on Videocassette

Stuck on You! (Troma, 1983, 88 minutes)
Directed by Michael Herz and Samuel Weil; Written by Stuart Strutin, Warren Leight, Don Perman, Darren Kloomok, Melanie Mintz, Anthony Gittleson, Duffy

Ceaser Magesis, Michael Herz, Lloyd Kaufman and Jeff Delman; Produced by Lloyd Kaufman and Michael Herz
Cast
Irwin Corey (Judge Gabriel), Virginia Penta (Carol), Mark Mikulski (Bill), MR. KENT (KING ARTHUR)
Rating: zero
Available on Videocassette

Sword of the Valiant (Cannon, 1984, 101 minutes)
Directed by Stephen Weeks; Written by Stephen Weeks, Philip M. Breen and Howard C. Pen; Produced by Menahem Golan and Yoram Globus; Music by Ron Geesin
Cast
Miles O'Keeffe (Gawain), Sean Connery (Green Knight), Cyrielle Claire (Linet), TREVOR HOWARD (KING ARTHUR), Peter Cushing (Seneschal), Lila Kedrova (Lady of Lyonesse)
Rating: *1/2

TELEVISION

"The Adventures of Sir Lancelot" (BBC series,1956-57)
Cast
William Russell (Sir Lancelot), Jane Hylton (Guinevere), RONALD LEIGH-HUNT (KING ARTHUR), Cyril Smith (Merlin)
Rating: **

"Arthur The King" (CBS movie,1985, 94 minutes)
AKA: Merlin and the Sword
Directed by Clive Donner; Written by J. David Wyler; Produced by Martin Poll; Music by Charles Gross
Cast
MALCOLM MCDOWELL (KING ARTHUR), Edward Woodward (Merlin), Candice Bergen (Morgan), John Smith (Narrator), Dyan Cannon (Katherine), Lucy Gutteridge (Niniane)
Rating: **

"A Connecticut Yankee in King Arthur's Court" (NBC movie, 1989, 120 minutes)
Directed by Mel Daniski; Written by Paul Zindel; Produced by Graham Ford
Cast
Keshia Knight-Pulliam (the Yankee), MICHAEL GROSS (KING ARTHUR), Emma Samms (Guinevere), Jean Marsh (Morgan), Hugo F. Blick (Mordred), Whip Hubley (Lancelot)
Rating: **1/2

Adam West as the Caped Crusader in the television series *Batman*.

BATMAN

In retrospect, one can better appreciate what an astonishing one-two punch it was. In 1938, DC Comics introduced Superman. In 1939, the same company introduced Batman. Today, more than fifty years later, these two heroes remain the most recognized characters to emerge from the pages of a comic book. The current comics market is dominated by Marvel mutants and Swamp Things and "For Mature Readers Only" vigilantes, but the Man of Steel and the Caped Crusader have long since moved beyond the month-to-month wars at the newsstand. Sales of their titles may rise and fall, but the characters themselves have been accepted into the pantheon of myths and legends with the likes of Robin Hood, Hercules and King Arthur--defenders of the weak, protectors of the poor, and the subjects of epic stories from several generations of writers and artists.

THE COMICS

The creation of Batman was a conscious attempt to follow up the success of the Superman series with another costumed crimefighter who would grab the public's fancy. But instead of presenting a pale imitation of an already established commodity (like Captain Marvel), writer Bob Kane developed a character who was practically the antithesis of its prototype.

Tragedy entered the lives of both Bruce Wayne and Kal-El early in childhood, but that is where the similarities in their origins end. Whereas Superman acquired his powers simply by landing on earth (a result, we are told, of our galaxy's yellow sun, as opposed to the red sun that orbited Krypton), Batman had to exercise to gain his physique, and study to learn the abilities that would aid his fight against crime.

He is not superhuman. Theoretically, anyone willing to devote fifteen or so years to martial arts and chemistry and weapons technology and gymnastics could eventually do what Batman does. It is inconceivable for most of us, but for Bruce Wayne we believe because of the impetus that began his quest--the brutal murder of his parents by a hold-up man.

It is not for purely altruistic motives that Batman battles the underworld. He is driven as much by the need to exorcise his own demons as by a desire to protect Gotham City. This grim obsession is perhaps the most fascinating aspect of Batman, and explains the dark, almost sinister persona he created for his mission.

These qualities were apparent almost from the beginning, in the relatively primitive 1940s comics with basic hero-villain-fight-resolution stories. In these early tales Batman was already a no-nonsense avenger, who even carried a gun on more than one occasion. The addition of Robin in 1940 brought a humanizing element to the character, and eventually more additions (Batwoman, Batgirl, Batmite and Ace the Bat-Hound) gradually lightened the tone of his adventures.

But in the 1970s, after the comic stopped emulating the campy "Batman" television series, the Caped Crusader started getting back to his roots, culminating in the groundbreaking *Dark Knight* limited series by Frank Miller in 1986. It was the Batman recreated here, and developed in Miller's superb *Batman: Year One* saga (issues #404-407) that inhabits the 1989 film.

THE FILMS

What a difference there is between Michael Keaton's interpretation and that of Lewis Wilson, the first actor to play Batman on the screen in a 1943 serial. Even by serial standards Batman's debut is pretty lame, though its wartime portrayal of the Japanese is perversely intriguing.

The action begins when Martin Warren, the uncle of Bruce Wayne's girlfriend Linda Page, is kidnapped immediately after being released from prison. He is taken to the headquarters of Dr. Tito Daka, leader of an underground organization dedicated to assisting in the Japanese victory and the "ultimate enslavement of America." Daka pumps Warren for the location of the Wayne Foundation's radium supply, which he hopes to steal and use to fuel a super atom smasher. When Warren refuses to cooperate, he is turned into a zombie.

Daka makes several attempts to obtain radium, but is repeatedly thwarted by the efforts of Batman and Robin. Bruce Wayne disguises himself as a mobster named Chuck White, and tries to infiltrate Daka's organization. His ruse is discovered, but he manages to escape with his life.

After deducing a connection between Batman and Linda Page, Daka abducts Linda and turns her into a zombie. Bruce receives a note from Linda arranging a meeting. Batman suspects a trap, but plays along and is captured. Just as Daka starts warming up the zombie machine, Robin bursts in and hogties the evil doctor. Daka is forced to restore Linda and the others to normal, but falls into his own alligator pit during an escape attempt. The police arrive to clean up what's left of the spy ring, and Linda is reunited with Bruce.

Dr. Daka is easily the most interesting presence in the serial, though I'd still have preferred the Joker or the Penguin. Durable character actor J. Carol Naish does what he can to suggest menace, but his exaggerated accent and the Asian makeup job seem horribly dated. However, his threat to end the war with a powerful atomic weapon is unsettlingly prophetic.

As the first man in the Bat-costume, Lewis Wilson plays up the contrast between "good-for-nothing playboy" Bruce Wayne and his heroic alter-ego. Neither performance is particularly memorable. As Robin, Douglas Croft doesn't embarrass himself, but that's about it. Loyal butler Alfred, played by William Austin, comes across as an effeminate dimwit.

The storyline is more sustained than most serials, and not as forgetful of characters and plot threads. But it's light on action and lighter on humor (at least the intentional kind). Despite its ineptness, however, *Batman*'s place in history is secure not only for being first to the screen, but also for creating the name "Batcave" to describe Batman's underground base of operations. The term was quickly adopted by the comic after the serial was released.

The Dynamic Duo's next appearance, in the 1949 serial *Batman and Robin*, could not even match the dubious heights achieved by its predecessor. Every cliche` common to serials is present and accounted for, but there's little evidence of any thrills, chills or excitement.

Our heroes are called into action when a "Remote Control Machine" is stolen from the laboratory of its inventor, Professor Hammil. The theft is masterminded by a mysterious hooded figure known only as the Wizard. Journalist Vicki Vale snaps of a photo of the Wizard's gang, and is shocked to learn that her brother Jimmy is among them. Batman uses the photo to capture one of the Wizard's men, and later attempts to infiltrate the villain's organization disguised as a mobster (sound familiar?). But the Wizard catches on and Bruce Wayne is captured, only to be rescued by Robin.

Vicki hears from her brother and agrees to a meeting. At first Jimmy seems to be baiting a trap, but later he turns against the Wizard and loses his life trying to save Batman. Professor Hammil, meanwhile, develops a neutralizer that will counteract the Remote Control Machine, but the Wizard steals it before it can be used.Using his skills as a detective, Batman discovers that the Wizard is actually Hammil's attendant, Carter. After being temporarily perplexed by the appearance of Carter's twin brother, Batman finally takes the villain into custody.

This one is truly a chore to sit through. When the best performance of the bunch is given by Lyle Talbot, you know something's wrong. Even serial veteran Spencer Bennet's normally brisk direction is listless. The cliffhangers are resolved with no imagination whatsoever; Batman simply falls down at the end of one chapter and gets up at the beginning of the next. The Batmobile, a Mercury convertible, is the same car used by Bruce Wayne--good thing the Wizard never checks license numbers.

Other aspects of the production are equally lame. When I was six years old I dressed up as Batman for Halloween, and *my* costume was better than Robert Lowery's. And any sense of camaraderie between Lowery and John Duncan's Robin is nonexistent. Instead of friends and allies they act like business associates in adjacent offices. It was nice to see the producers paying attention to the comic by adding Vicki Vale to the cast, but Jane Adams comes off as a poor man's Lois Lane in a poorly drawn role.

If you are driven to see every film adaptation of Batman, try to limit your viewing of this mess to Chapter Six, which is slightly less intolerable than the rest and contains Lowery's undercover portrayal of a thug.

In 1965, Columbia Pictures rereleased the two serials under the title "An Evening with Batman and Robin." Inexplicably, they played to packed houses on college campuses and ignited a new wave of Batmania. ABC Television was already developing a Batman TV series, and when the wave hit they rushed the series into production. It was an instant hit, and remains a cult classic.

I love this show. I know that some purists believe it demeans the character, and it's true that Adam West's Batman bears almost no resemblance to the very serious crimefighter of the comic books. But taken on its own merits, this ersatz Caped Crusader can be awfully entertaining, and repeat viewings reveal how cleverly written and well performed the series actually was.

Perhaps the biggest reason for "Batman" 's enduring success is its ability to engage both children and adults on two completely different levels. Kids, who know the word "camp" only as a place to go for two weeks in July, perceive "Batman" as a straightforward, colorful action series with lots of neat gadgets and bang-up fistfights (POW! BAM! OOF!). Those above the age of twelve are able to appreciate Adam West's hilariously wooden performance, Burt Ward's gee-whiz enthusiasm and Neil Hamilton's earnest but clueless turn as Commissioner Gordon.

And then there are the villains. Frank Gorshin is just about everybody's favorite, frenetically sending up both Kirk Douglas and James Cagney as the Riddler. I've always been partial to Julie Newmar as the Catwoman, but not just for the obvious reasons. Most of the Catwoman stories, written by the series's best contributor, Stanley Ralph Ross, were packed with inside Hollywood references and double entendres, and Newmar purred her lines with velvet venom.

"Batman" was quite the flavor of the month back in 1966, which explains the guest appearances of such luminaries as Otto Preminger, Tallulah Bankhead and Shelley Winters. When the joke started to get stale, producers brought in Yvonne Craig as Batgirl, which was great news for male viewers but couldn't save the show from cancellation in 1968. There was talk of a fourth season on CBS, but the Batcave set was too expensive to rebuild and had already been torn down at ABC.

While the show was still riding high, a film version of "Batman" was rushed into theaters, with the full cast plus Gorshin, Cesar Romero as the Joker, Burgess Meredith as the Penguin and Lee Meriwether as Catwoman. The story united the four dastardly arch-villains, who steal a "Total Dehydrator" and plan to use it on the nine ambassadors to the United World Security Council.

After a merry chase and several close calls, Batman and Robin foil their scheme, and are able to restore the diplomats thanks to the handy Super Molecular Dust Separator in the Batcave. When the voices are returned to the wrong bodies, Batman predicts that the result might be better relations among the countries of the world.

The budget was bigger, the Bat Boat and Bat Copter are pretty cool, but the script doesn't hold together as well as nearly any episode of the series (and Lee Meriwether is no Julie Newmar). Even camp has its limits, and the line between good-natured silliness and outright stupidity is crossed more than once. One sequence, though, in which Batman tries to dispose of a medicine-ball-sized bomb is hilarious.

Batman returned to the screen in 1989, and made the transition from motion picture to milestone within weeks of its initial release. It took a year for the dust to settle, but when it did the movie that became a phenomenon turned out to be just a movie after all--better than most, and the best handling of the character yet, but flawed beyond what its ticket sales would suggest.

Gotham City is approaching its two hundredth anniversary as the film opens, but a brutal crime wave has left its citizens with little to celebrate. Rumors of a six-foot human bat begin to circulate, particularly among the city's criminal element. Gotham Globe reporter Alexander Knox and photographer Vicki Vale begin looking into the story.

Gang leader "Boss" Grissom learns that the police are about to raid one of his chemical factories, and sends his associate Jack Napier to clean it out, fully aware that he will be captured. At the factory, the police, assisted by the mysterious Batman, subdue the criminals, and Napier is thrown into a vat of toxic chemicals and believed to be killed. Napier, however, emerges from the vat with his skin chalk-white and his face distorted into a hideous smile. Calling himself the Joker, Napier kills Grissom and declares war on Gotham City.

After a romantic dinner date, Vicki Vale becomes intrigued by millionaire Bruce Wayne, and asks Knox to look into his background. The Joker begins his crimewave by poisoning a shipment of cosmetics, and luring Vicki to an art museum with intentions of seduction and murder. Batman intervenes and, following a dramatic rescue, takes Vicki to the Batcave. He provides the astonished photographer with information on the Joker's activities to take to the press. The next morning, she wakes up in her apartment only to find the film she had shot of Batman's heroics destroyed.

Bruce Wayne drops by to apologize for neglecting her. They are interrupted by the Joker just as Wayne is set to reveal his dual identity. During their confrontation, Wayne realizes that Jack Napier is the mugger who killed his parents years earlier, the event that compelled Bruce Wayne to devote his life to crimefighting.

The Joker announces his intention to drop $20 million in cash on the streets of Gotham City during its anniversary festival, and challenges Batman to stop him. As the Caped Crusader prepares for battle, Bruce Wayne's butler Alfred brings Vicki into the Batcave and exposes his master's secret. Bruce tells Vicki that while he does have feelings for her, his work as Batman must come first. The Joker drops the cash as promised, along with several balloons filled with poison gas. Soaring over the city in his Batwing jet, Batman seizes the balloons and releases their deadly contents over the ocean. At Gotham Cathedral, the two combatants stage their showdown. After a fierce struggle the Joker falls from the belfry to his death.

When the casting of Michael Keaton was announced, there were screams of protest from Bat fans of all ages. Although the controversy dwindled after the film grossed a mint, the fact remains that Keaton was hardly an ideal choice for the role, and the fans' concerns indeed proven valid.

The intrinsic value of casting an unknown in a role like this is highly underrated. Look at *Superman* (1978), the standard for comic book movies. When the unfamiliar face of Christopher Reeve is first seen in the familiar red cape and costume of Superman, the experience somehow acquires an added dimension. In a world where characters of fantasy actually exist, one couldn't help but believe that Reeve could be Superman, for his appearance and actions fulfill every expectation of the Man of Steel that has developed over the past half-century.

Maybe it sounds frivolous but, after all, escapist entertainment is the whole objective of movies like this, and it's hard to escape while thinking, "Michael Keaton sure looks dumb in that Batman suit." Granted, it's an unfair criticism, but if this were the only drawback in the actor's performance it could conceivably be overcome. There are other problems, however, for which Keaton must take full responsibility.

As both Bruce Wayne and Batman, Keaton is a closed book. His intensity is right, but he never lets us inside the character. At the crucial moments when we should share his agony and understand his compulsion to live a double life, it just doesn't happen. The presence of a Robin, which could humanize the character as it did in the comic, is sorely missed.

The body-armor costume is also a bad idea. Keaton's face is engulfed by the cowl, and the chestplate (complete with built-in pectorals) is a poor substitute for a developed physique. But while Batman does at least hold your interest, Bruce Wayne is practically a noncharacter. Keaton underplays the role to such an extent that his personality, if indeed he has one, is a puzzlement.

On the positive side there is Jack Nicholson, whose casting also raised some eyebrows. But this time, the producers picked a winner. Nicholson is inspired as the Joker, moving with a mercurial grace that belies the fact that he is nearly twice his costar's age. His delightfully devastating dance through an art museum is the movie's unqualified highlight, and the all-important laughter, laced with a sinister edge that Cesar Romero never achieved, is stunning.

Other performances are also impressive. You'd think that if anyone could drag some emotion out of Keaton it would be Kim Basinger, but even her knockout presence has no effect. Robert Wuhl, Pat Hingle and Michael Gough form a solid supporting cast. Anton Furst's production design provides a mesmerizing backdrop for the too-few action scenes. Combining elements from *Metropolis* (the Fritz Lang film, not Lois Lane's hometown), 1940s film noir and dazzling futuristic cityscapes of his own devising, Furst has created a truly unique vision of urban hell.

The problem, of course, is that *Batman* should not be memorable only for Nicholson or Basinger or the way it looks. Remember, despite the familiarity of Gene Hackman and Marlon Brando in *Superman*, Christopher Reeve still held the spotlight. Michael Keaton's failure to command center stage means that *Batman* is a film worth seeing, but for all the wrong reasons.

A sequel was inevitable, and happily it corrects some of the problems in the original. Once again there are a plethora of individually brilliant though disparate elements that never quite gel into a satisfying whole, but *Batman Returns* (1992) is such a dazzler that its flaws don't seem obvious until the second viewing.

A monstrous-looking newborn baby is tossed into the sewers by his mortified parents in a flashback opening. Jump forward thirty-three years, as the now grown-up castaway prepares an assault on Gotham City. Called the Penguin by the newspapers, he kidnaps slimy industrialist Max Schreck for blackmail purposes. Schreck has a better idea--he's looking for a mayoral candidate for his back pocket, and the Penguin wants the respect of the society that abandoned him, so they agree to help each other.

After a few successful publicity stunts, the Penguin becomes a viable candidate for Gotham's highest office. Schreck discovers a threat to his operations in his mousy secretary Selina Kyle, who learns too much about his questionable business dealings. He pushes her out of a high-rise window, but Selina survives, physically sound but mentally unbalanced. She adopts the identity of Catwoman and begins prowling the nighttime in search of mischief.

The interference of Batman in their respective schemes forges an alliance between Penguin and Catwoman, who set out to frame Batman for a series of violent crimes. Meanwhile, a budding romance between Bruce Wayne and Selina Kyle is complicated when they learn each other's dual identities. After Penguin is exposed as a sociopath during a campaign rally, he plots to steal the children of every city official. When this fails as well, thanks to Batman, he straps missiles onto the backs of hundreds of real penguins and lets them loose in Gotham City. Batman saves the day and the penguins, but his love-hate relationship with Catwoman ends uncertainly.

Michael Keaton shows definite improvement in his sophomore outing; Bruce Wayne is given more screen time, which allows Keaton to flesh him out one film late as an important character. The relaxed scenes with Alfred are welcome breaks from the mayhem, and provide a necessary contrast to Batman's ice-cold demeanor.

The series continues to be inspired in casting its villains. Michelle Pfeiffer gives a performance of astonishing depth and agility as Catwoman and Selina Kyle. The comic book relationship between the characters is wisely preserved, with Selina acting as both nemesis and mirror to the Caped Crusader. Confronted with her sad, schizophrenic existence, he must face the tortured dichotomy of his own life. The scene in which they learn each other's dual identities is one of the movie's best.

Danny Devito was the only choice for the Penguin, and his delightfully depraved interpretation is a far cry from the almost buffoon-like Penguin of the comics. Christopher Walken completes the evil triumvirate as Max Schreck, a poorly drawn character who is frequently lost in the shuffle. His name is an inside joke for movie buffs, referring to the actor who first played Dracula in the 1922 silent film *Nosferatu.*

But *Batman Returns* is clearly Tim Burton's film more than it is Keaton's, Pfeiffer's or Devito's, and that's a mixed blessing. Burton's eye for stunning visuals is uncontested--every set, not just the big ones such as Gotham Zoo or Wayne Manor, is an eyeful. Selina's apartment, Max's office, even the storefront windows that line Gotham's streets each have a distinct personality.

Burton's world has grown darker and more cynical than in *Batman.* One of the film's recurrent images is the corruption of symbols and events that provoke happy memories for most children; members of the Penguin's gang appear in the guise of circus performers, and the Penguin himself rides around in a giant rubber duck. Even Christmas is not spared. This is clearly a reflection of the twisted childhoods of both the Penguin and Batman and represents the best clue to the director's overriding creative influence.

The best news is that Batman finally finds a sense of humor, manifested not just with dark, sardonic dialogue but with good healthy comic interaction that breaks up the gloom. There is absolutely delicious irony in Bruce Wayne's and Selina Kyle's both attending a costume party without a costume. What a smart moment! This is what the first film lacked.

However, the problems that do exist can be attributed to the director as well. The plot is a disjointed mess; the framing of Batman is never resolved, the subplot of Schreck's power plant goes nowhere, and the Penguin's three grand schemes, launched in rapid succession, are each foiled by Batman with only a modicum of effort. Burton also overdoes the Grand Guignol and the gadgets--just once I'd have liked to see a good old-fashioned slugfest.

Batman Returns is a vicious movie, and Burton had to know that the word of mouth about the brutality, body count and a suggested infanticide might provoke parents to keep their little bat-tykes away from the theater. In a way, he made an art-over-commerce decision that one must admire, even if there is still debate over whether his vision is worth protecting. This probably isn't the Batman that some folks hoped to see in pictures, and their distaste is understandable. But one finds much to applaud in *Batman Returns,* and every reason to believe that the next film may be the classic we've been hoping for since 1988.

THE FILMS

Batman (Columbia serial, 1943, 250 minutes)
Directed by Lambert Hillyer; Written by Victor McLeod, Leslie Swabacker and Harry Fraser, based on characters created by Bob Kane; Produced by Rudolph Flothow; Music by Lee Zahler

Cast
LEWIS WILSON (BATMAN/Bruce Wayne), Douglas Croft (Robin/Dick Grayson), Shirley Patterson (Linda Page), J. Carol Naish (Dr. Daka), William Austin (Alfred)
Rating: **
Available on Videocassette

Batman and Robin (Columbia serial, 1949, 250 minutes)
Directed by Spencer Bennet; Written by George H. Plympton, Joseph Poland and Royal Cole; Produced by Sam Katzman; Music by Mischa Bakaleinikoff
Cast
ROBERT LOWERY (BATMAN/Bruce Wayne), John Duncan (Robin/Dick Grayson), Lyle Talbot (Commissioner Gordon), Jane Adams (Vicki Vale), Eric Wilton (Alfred), William Fawcett (Professor Hammil)
Rating: *
Available on Videocassette

Batman (20th Century Fox, 1966, 104 minutes)
Directed by Leslie H. Martinson; Written by Lorenzo Semple, Jr.; Produced by William Dozier; Music by Nelson Riddle, Batman theme by Neil Hefti
Cast
ADAM WEST (BATMAN/Bruce Wayne), Burt Ward (Robin/Dick Grayson), Lee Meriwether (Catwoman/Kitka), Cesar Romero (The Joker), Burgess Meredith (The Penguin), Frank Gorshin (The Riddler), Alan Napier (Alfred), Neil Hamilton (Commissioner Gordon), Stafford Repp (Chief O'Hara), Madge Blake (Aunt Harriet)
Rating: ***1/2
Available on Videocassette

Batman (Warner Bros., 1989, 126 minutes)
Directed by Tim Burton; Written by Sam Hamm and Warren Skaaren, based on a story by Sam Hamm; Produced by Jon Peters and Peter Guber; Music by Danny Elfman. Songs by Prince
Cast
Jack Nicholson (The Joker/Jack Napier), MICHAEL KEATON (BATMAN/Bruce Wayne), Kim Basinger (Vicki Vale), Robert Wuhl (Alexander Knox), Pat Hingle (Commissioner Gordon), Billy Dee Williams (Harvey Dent), Michael Gough (Alfred), Jack Palance (Carl Grissom), Jerry Hall (Alicia)
Rating: ***1/2
Available on Videocassette
Awards: Academy Award for Best Art Direction

Batman Returns (Warner Bros., 1992, 126 minutes)
Directed by Tim Burton; Written by Daniel Waters, based on a story by Waters and Sam Hamm; Produced by Tim Burton and Denise Di Novi; Music by Danny Elfman
Cast
MICHAEL KEATON (BATMAN/Bruce Wayne), Danny Devito (Penguin), Michelle Pfeiffer (Catwoman/Selina Kyle), Christopher Walken (Max Schreck), Michael Gough (Alfred), Pat Hingle (Commissioner Gordon)
Rating: ****
Available on Videocassette

TELEVISION
"Batman" (ABC series, 1966—68)
Cast
ADAM WEST (BATMAN/Bruce Wayne), Burt Ward (Robin/Dick Grayson), Alan

Napier (Alfred), Neil Hamilton (Commissioner Gordon), Stafford Repp (Chief O'Hara), Madge Blake (Aunt Harriet), Yvonne Craig (Batgirl/Barbara Gordon)
Rating: ****
Awards: 1965–66 Emmy nomination for Outstanding Comedy Series and Best Supporting Actor (Frank Gorshin)

Tom Laughlin stars in *Billy Jack* (1971)

BILLY JACK

It was a 1970s thing, and is only a dim memory now, but there was a time when Billy Jack threatened to carve out a permanent place in modern American folklore. That is, until his creators lost the glimmer of actual inspiration they had and turned the character into a boorish hypocrite who landed off the scale for self-righteous smugness. Today he is grouped with disco music and Sheriff Buford Pusser, his antithesis on the political spectrum, as fads we're better off without, and a little embarrassed that we liked in the first place.

Funny thing about memory, though--it cheats on you both ways. The passage of time has made even Donna Summer and Chic sound pretty good, so another look at Billy Jack is required. Are there any discernible signs of what made him the antihero of a lost generation, or was he rightly discarded with the Village People on the trash heap of history?

On a visceral level, the films remain exciting, well-directed works, and ideologically their hearts are in the right place, even if the message is delivered with the subtlety of a pneumatic drill. The most oft-repeated criticism of the series is Billy Jack's oxymoronic "peace through violence" approach. What has been forgotten is that the paradox is acknowledged in the movies. Billy's wife, Jean, tells him repeatedly how foolish he is to resort to fighting, and when he starts philosophizing about how he doesn't want to be violent, she tells him "That's a load of crap!"

Jean's comment is also somewhat appropriate to the final two Billy Jack films, which helps account for the series' lingering bad aftertaste. But even in star-writer-director Tom Laughlin's worst moments, and there are lots of them in *Billy Jack Goes to Washington*, the characters and their utopian vision maintain a sincerity that is admirable, even when it borders on obnoxious.

Billy Jack made his first appearance as a supporting character in the 1967 film *Born Losers*. If the book *Son of Golden Turkey Awards* is to be believed, the movie emerged from a chance meeting between Laughlin and Elizabeth James on an airplane--he was a passenger, she was a stewardess. Together, they made what is now considered by many to be the best biker movie ever made, if you don't count *Easy Rider* (1969). The Born Losers, a motorcycle gang, ride into a rural California town and wreak havoc on the locals. Billy Jack, a Vietnam veteran recently returned to his backwoods home, confronts the gang while they assault a motorist. Billy shoots one of the gang and gets a stiffer sentence from the law than the bikers. His lawyer advises Billy to remember that next time he feels like helping someone.

Gang members rape four girls and then intimidate them into keeping quiet.

One of the victims is kidnapped again, and when the cops prove useless Billy Jack rides to the bikers' lair alone. He rescues the girl, but ends up accidentally shot by the late-arriving police.

The film's title refers to the gang but is also applicable to Billy Jack, a card-carrier in two of the most maligned groups of the century--Native Americans and Vietnam veterans. He's the only citizen willing to stand up to the bikers, but he ends up a loser again--first in the courts and later at the wrong end of an officer's bullet.

The bikers may be the villains, but the townspeople aren't much better. Doctors, policemen, and other authority figures are well-meaning but ineffectual, resorting to tired cliches` and homilies rather than actual involvement. Society as a whole is either hostile or apathetic. These themes pervade most biker movies of the era, but in *Born Losers* the performances and technical credits are a cut above the norm.

Tom Laughlin, who directed under the pseudonym T. C. Frank, shows a flair for the creative angle and fashions several memorable sequences. But his ability to tell a story with depth and economy eroded as the series continued. Billy Jack is a quiet character in his first appearance, and as an actor Laughlin communicates best with few words. Elizabeth James is a good foil for Laughlin, and her presence is missed in later films. The big casting shock is Jane Russell, in her penultimate role as the shrill, half-batty mother of one of the rape victims.

The success of *Born Losers* was primarily attributed to Billy Jack, so a sequel was made focusing on his further adventures. In *Billy Jack* (1971) the action centers on a progressive "freedom school" in the Arizona desert run by teacher Jean Roberts. Billy serves as handyman and unofficial "protector." Of course, the residents of a nearby town think the school is filled with long-haired weirdos, and harass the students at every opportunity. One of the worst offenders, the racist son of the town's most prominent citizen, rapes Jean and kills one of the students. Billy Jack kills the creep and then kills a sheriff's deputy in self-defense. After a long stand-off with the police, Billy turns himself in after securing promises that the school will not be shut down.

The scenes at the school have not aged gracefully, and represent the beginning of the end for Billy Jack. Every tired hippy-dippy sixties platitude is paraded out as obvious bait for the suburban rebels in the audience. Violence may not be the solution to America's ills--just look at how Billy ends up at the fadeout of the first three films--but songs such as "Rainbow Love," warbled off-key by one of the students, aren't going to do it either. The message I get from this, although Laughlin probably didn't intend it, is that little is accomplished on the fringes of society, no matter which fringe you're on.

The action scenes are poorly shot and choreographed, the skits by Howard Hesseman and the improvisational troupe The Committee are embarrassing, and no amount of good intentions can save Laughlin's spouting of Indian mysticism in his flat monotone.

Laughlin and his wife Delores Taylor (who plays Jean) insisted on making the film without any outside interference. They challenged Richard Zanuck, the head of 20th Century Fox, over the final edit, and ended up buying the movie back from him and releasing it at Warner Bros.. The finished product shows evidence of a genuine filmmaking talent, but also demonstrates the need for editors.

Billy Jack's first appearance already shows him campaigning for mythic status. He emerges on horseback from a misty forest, with the camera panning slowly from his boots to his trademark hat, and it is suggested that he appears by magic when needed to right an injustice. The climax, set in a church, contains obvious Biblical parallels as the Christ-like Billy is led down his final road to glory. The recurring image in *Born Losers* of animal carcasses devoured by vultures and insects is revived with scenes of wild mustangs being killed so their meat can be sold to a dog food company. One species feeds on another, heavy symbolism of what an awful place the world can be. Coven's anthem "One Tin Soldier" drives the point home once more.

But amidst all the overblown hyperbole is treasure. Delores Taylor's heart-wrenching performance, particularly after her character's rape, drew praise from no less than Pauline Kael. The scene in which B.J. drives a racist bully's car into a lake could not be better, and the city council meeting called to discuss the school's future is a fascinating neorealist document that contains dialogue as compelling as exists in films of this era. Next time you watch it, think about the L.A. riots and you'll be saddened at how little the country has changed.

Billy Jack seesaws between such transcendent moments and moments of shallow manipulation. It was as good as the series got. The best thing you can say about *The Trial of Billy Jack* (1974) is that it was not a quickly-made, half-hearted effort to capitalize on the unexpected success of the previous film. The Laughlins' sincerity is again apparent, but there is smugness in the mix as well.

The story is told in flashback by Jean, who is recovering in a hospital room from injuries suffered during a vicious attack on the Freedom School. Billy Jack was released from prison for his escapades from the last movie, and returns to Arizona. The school sets up a TV station, which begins reporting on suspicious government activity. Two federal agents are sent to investigate, and Billy Jack fights them off. The National Guard is called in, and someone starts shooting. An old Indian land treaty is found that forces the troops to vacate, but not before Billy, Jean and several students are wounded.

The anti-government message is forced into the movie by such ludicrous means as giving a ragtag hippy school its own television station. The once-quiet Billy Jack now makes speeches at the drop of a hat (though never his own), and the martial arts scenes seem obligatory. The musical numbers, performed by Laughlin's daughter Teresa, again date the film worse than anything else. Marlon Brando fans might be intrigued by the appearance of Sacheen Littlefeather, who accepted Brando's *Godfather* Oscar in 1973.

In *Billy Jack* the stand-off between "ordinary" citizens and the progressive school was an insightful look at the culture-clash of the time. This time Laughlin pits soldiers against students, which was already getting old in 1974, and rips off the tragedy of Kent State. There is also a stultifying sequence of Billy Jack taking a mystic Indian drug trip. The last thing this 170-minute film needed was more padding. But it was a hit.

The final series entry, *Billy Jack Goes to Washington* (1977), was never released and is almost impossible to find today. It should have been interesting to have the antihero try to achieve change by working within the system, but the premise and the blue-chip source material (*Mr. Smith Goes to Washington*) cannot withstand the weight of a D.O.A. script and another three-hour running time.

Billy is appointed by the governor to fill an unexpired term in the U.S. Senate. His injuries from the last movie and his criminal record are conveniently forgotten. After that, he more or less follows the road first traveled by Jimmy Stewart in *Mr. Smith*, though this journey pales by comparison. Laughlin's speeches in Congress are not very inspiring, and the humor that lifted the original is nowhere to be found. Delores Taylor, who has never exactly been a cut-up, and Lucie Arnaz divide the Jean Arthur role. E.G. Marshall emerges best as the cynical senator who first scoffs at Billy Jack and then comes to respect him.

When the film didn't make it into theaters Laughlin rampaged against the government, accusing it of an elaborate conspiracy designed to silence his message. The general consensus was that he was starting to lose it, and since then he has only appeared in one other movie (the disastrous *Legend of the Lone Ranger* in 1981). Billy Jack is both gone and forgotten now and so is Laughlin, but for awhile anyway there was merit in what they both had to say.

THE FILMS

Born Losers (AIP, 1967, 114 minutes)
Directed by T. C. Frank (Tom Laughlin); Written by E. James Lloyd; Produced by Donald Henderson (Tom Laughlin) and Delores Taylor
Cast
TOM LAUGHLIN (BILLY JACK), Elizabeth James (Vicky Barrington), Jane Russell (Mrs. Shorn), Jeremy Slate (Danny Carmody), Jeff Cooper (Gangrene)
Rating: ***
Available on Videocassette

Billy Jack (Warner Bros., 1971, 112 minutes)
Directed by T. C. Frank (Laughlin); Written by Frank and Teresa Christina (Delores Taylor); Produced by Mary Rose Solti; Music by Mundell Lowe, song "One Tin Soldier" by Coven
Cast
TOM LAUGHLIN (BILLY JACK), Delores Taylor (Jean Roberts), Clark Howat (Sheriff Cole), Bert Freed (Posner), Ken Tobey (Deputy), David Roya (Bernard)
Rating: ***1/2
Available on Videocassette

The Trial of Billy Jack (Taylor-Laughlin, 1974, 170 minutes)
Directed by Frank Laughlin; Written by Frank and Teresa Christina Laughlin; Produced by Joe Cramer; Music by Elmer Bernstein
Cast
TOM LAUGHLIN (BILLY JACK), Delores Taylor (Jean Roberts), Teresa Laughlin (Carol), Victor Izay (Doc), Sacheen Littlefeather (Patsy Littlejohn)
Rating: **1/2

Billy Jack Goes to Washington (Taylor-Laughlin, 1972, 155 minutes)
Directed by T. C. Frank; Written by Frank and Teresa Christina; Produced by Frank Capra, Jr.; Music by Elmer Bernstein
Cast
TOM LAUGHLIN (BILLY JACK), Delores Taylor (Jean Roberts), E. G. Marshall (Senator Joseph Paine), Teresa Laughlin (Staff Worker), Lucie Arnaz (Saunders McArthur), Sam Wanamaker (Bailey), Dick Gautier (Gov. Hubert Hopper)
Rating: **

JAMES BOND

At the time this book went to press it had been four years since *License to Kill*, the most recent James Bond film. This is the longest interval between entries since the series began in 1962, and has inevitably led to speculation as to whether Agent 007's time has finally passed.

Such speculation is ridiculous. Once the legal entanglements that have kept him away are resolved, Bond will be back on the world's movie screens, and no matter what other films open that week he will emerge on top. The reason does not require any library research; with few exceptions, each 007 movie offered a solid action-adventure story, a dashing hero admired by men and loved by women, exotic locations, good music, and stunt sequences that continually topped themselves in cleverness and spectacle.

Of course Agent 007's time has passed--it happened sometime around 1971. When the series began to lose its edge the producers could have pulled up stakes, but instead they just acknowledged that the character had begun to approach self-parody, and gave him a push over the top.

The occasional change of personnel was needed, but there was barely a nod to the changing social climate. Female characters may be doctors or scientists in later entries, but Bond treats them the same way he did beach bimbo Ursula Andress in *Dr. No.* And they love it. Of course, fantasy figures often exist in a vacuum and are not required to evolve. James Bond, as the ultimate male fantasy, has guaranteed lifetime immunity from such considerations.

The character first appeared in a series of novels written in the 1950s by British author Ian Fleming. The books sold well before being discovered by the silver screen, but after *Dr. No* was released, and after President John F. Kennedy ranked *From Russia With Love* on his list of favorite novels, the Bond phenomenon exploded. The real-life model for James Bond was Merlin Minshall, a Special Operations Agent who worked with Fleming in World War II. The name was taken from a textbook on birds written by an ornithologist named James Bond, who probably never slept with a Russian spy.

For most of us, though, Bond is no longer a Fleming creation. He is Sean Connery and, to a lesser extent, Roger Moore, Timothy Dalton and whoever inhabits the film role in the future. And the fact is that none of the actors match the description of 007 offered by his creator: "A dark, clean-cut face with a three-inch scar showing whitely. The eyes were wide and level under straight, rather long black brows. The longish nose ran down to a short upper lip below which was a wide and finely drawn but cruel mouth." Dalton comes closest, but it is Connery who will forever be identified with the role.

Like Doctor Who, another British hero, Bond changes personality with the actor who portrays him, with little regard for the source material. Most assessments of Bond's movie evolution have him starting out serious (early Connery), then becoming frivolous (late Connery), then becoming more frivolous (Moore), and then back to serious (Dalton), with the George Lazenby film an anomalous blip on the chart. The biggest problem with this picture is the disservice it does to Roger Moore, who accepted the daunting task of following the original and made the role his own.

Moore never even tried to break his typecasting dilemma, moving gracefully from Simon Templar (in the Bond-like television series "The Saint") to 007 to retirement. Sean Connery was a relative unknown when he won the role and, like Christopher Reeve in *Superman* (1978), audiences met the actor and the character at the same time, forging an identification that often proves indelible. Although Connery has continued to make movies since leaving the series in 1971, not until 1986's *The Name of the Rose* did he emerge completely from the shadow of Bond.

On October 21, 1954, CBS television presented a one-hour production of *Casino Royale*, the first James Bond novel, as part of its "Climax Mystery Theater" program. "Card-sense Jimmy Bond," as he is called here, is not in the Secret Service, and as played by Barry Nelson he is not even British! Because of the almost complete disregard for everything that we now associate with the character, most Bond filmographies begin with Sean Connery and *Dr. No* in 1962, but if you want to win a trivia contest remember it was Barry Nelson who first brought 007 to life.

Ian Fleming was not always happy with the way his creation was played in the movies, but he was smart enough to demand a percentage of all present and future box-office revenues. Producers Albert "Cubby" Broccoli and Harry Saltzman agreed to the author's terms, and signed a multipicture deal with United Artists. *Dr. No*, a huge hit despite lukewarm critical reception, inaugurated most of the trademark scenes that fans now expect in every series entry, and introduced audiences to British Secret Service Agent 007 (the number, for those who don't know, is a rank that signifies the license to kill).

We first meet James Bond, appropriately, at the baccarat table of a London casino. Sean Connery, in his first starring role, becomes Bond from his first appearance. He is handsome, but not in a male model way, and older than the average movie sex symbol, with a receding hairline and ears that are a bit too prominent. But Connery's poise and debonair charm made it easy to believe 007's ladykilling power.

Connery also conveyed an inner quality of controlled strength and perfectly captured Bond's most singular character trait--complete self-assurance in any given situation. From art museums to golf courses, from space stations to racetracks to restaurants in any country in the world, James Bond never looks or feels out of place. This is a quality we all would like to possess and, apart from the dangerous missions and the beautiful women, it is another key to his enduring popularity.

Filmakers still showed some concern about paying attention to the books here, and the script of *Dr. No* is somewhat consistent with its source material; A British Secret Service agent is murdered in Jamaica, and 007 is assigned to the case. Bond teams up with FBI agent Felix Leiter, who would become a recurring character in the series, and together they uncover a plot by the insidious Dr. No to divert missiles launched at Cape Canaveral from his island fortress. No plans to blackmail the U.S. government, but Bond says "no" to No and destroys the doctor's equipment. And the doctor.

Dr. No was one of the more realistic (as opposed to cartoon) violent Bond films, and Bond himself is still more of a human being than a superhero; 007 actually registers fear in the scene where he wakes up with a tarantula, and becomes sick afterward. Joseph Wiseman, by contrast, borders on inhuman as megalomaniac Dr. No, the prototypical Bond opponent. We are also introduced to Felix Leiter, who would be played by a different actor in almost every series appearance. Jack Lord was the first here, and the best.

More firsts: Bernard Lee and Lois Maxwell begin their stints as M and Miss Moneypenny, reliable presences for much of the series, and the superb John Barry theme perfectly underscores the action. Ursula Andress, emerging from the Jamaican surf in a white bikini, sets the standard for "Bond girls," in measurements if not in acting ability. Honey Rider was not Bond's first screen conquest, however--that honor falls to a lady named Sylvia, played by Eunice Grayson. Feel free to win a few more trivia contests.

Bond squares off against Ernst Stavro Blofeld and SPECTRE for the first time in *From Russia With Love* (1963), which also features the first appearance of Desmond Llewelyn as Q, the gadget man of the British Secret Service. Here he gives 007 an attache` case with more functions than a Swiss army knife.

This time Bond is off to Istanbul to fetch a Russian decoding machine. Making the task more difficult are two of SPECTRE's most memorable operatives, Red Grant (Robert Shaw) and Rosa Klebb (Lotte Lenya). Former Miss Universe contestant Daniela Bianchi may be the Bond girl of record, but Lenya, in her poison-tipped orthopedic shoes, is unforgettable. She is also a very cultured actress with a host of other distinguished credits, and this probably isn't the legacy she would have desired. Bianchi, as Russian agent Tatiana Romanova, cannot even rise to the acting heights of Ursula Andress and, like Andress in *Dr. No,* her voice was dubbed.

From Russia With Love is another first-rate outing, but *Goldfinger* (1964) is the classic of the Connery era. Although there were similar ties between the first two films, it is *Goldfinger* that sets the pattern for the entire series. Critic Roger Ebert deserves credit for laying this pattern out in print, but the elements are obvious: An exciting precredit sequence is followed exotic titles created by Maurice Binder, accompanied by a song that usually becomes a top-40 hit. Next, Bond exchanges quips with Moneypenny, gets his assignment from M and his new arsenal of gadgets from Q, who will usually utter in exasperated tones "Pay attention, 007!" The villain and his colorful henchmen (or women) are introduced, as well as an insidious deathtrap that will fail to work on Bond. Bond beds a beautiful woman (or two), storms the fortress of the bad guy and wins the battle that is always to the death.This structure is now predetermined from the opening shot of 007 in the gun barrel, and to deviate from it is to risk failure.

Goldfinger, who "loves only gold," has already bought up all the private stocks of his favorite metal and now wants the U.S. government's. But since he can't break into Fort Knox he plans to detonate an atomic device to contaminate the Fort's gold, thus making him the richest man in the world. Bond battles not only Goldfinger but his assistant Oddjob and his pilot Pussy Galore, his most difficult conquest yet. So many famous images--Shirley Eaton as Goldfinger's first victim, who suffocates after being covered in gold paint; Oddjob (Harold Sakata) and his razor-brimmed derby; Honor Blackman as Pussy Galore, still high-kicking as she did in "The Avengers"; Gert Frobe as the obsessed title character, gloating over Bond when the agent is at his mercy; the first appearance of the Aston-Martin; the thrilling climax. Shirley Bassey's rendition of the theme threw down a gauntlet for future entries.

Thunderball (1965) had been attended as the first James Bond film; years earlier Ian Fleming had written a script with Kevin McClory that he shopped around Hollywood to no avail. He then turned the script into the novel *Thunderball.* When the book was optioned for the now-successful Bond film series, McClory sued. The case was settled but not amicably--McClory would later remake the film as *Never Say Never Again.* This was the last film Fleming saw before his death one year later.

Another great opening, with the Aston-Martin showing off more tricks than the Batmobile, is followed by Tom Jones's bombastic theme and then we are clued in on SPECTRE's latest scheme; a NATO nuclear aircraft is stolen, and Bond trails the plot to the Bahamas and then back to Britain. The villain is Dr. Emilio Largo, played by Adolfo Celi. The ladies are Claudine Auger as Domino, a role which was almost played by Raquel Welch, and Luciana Paluzzi as Fiona Volpe.

The producers went for glitz over grit this time, and the bigger-is-better approach was greeted as a triumph and pushed *Thunderball* into the top-ten grossing films of all time. Later, the same approach would be criticized by Fleming purists as the series' major flaw. The extensive underwater footage is still impressive, but it tends to slow the pace of Bond's fourth mission.

Blofeld returned and tried to start World War III in *You Only Live Twice* (1967). With SPECTRE technology he abducts a spacecraft from both the Unites States and the Soviet Union, and waits for the accusations to fly. Bond fakes his own death to put Blofeld at ease and then heads for the villain's volcano fortress in Japan. The huge volcano headquarters set is the most amazing in the series, and blows up real good in the thrilling finale.

The film makes full use of its Japanese locations and, like every series entry, is rich in travelogue footage. If you watch every James Bond film, there will be few places in the world worth seeing that you haven't seen. This movie may be the most underrated of the Connery era; *You Only Live Twice* pleads guilty to being more light and gimmicky than previous entries, but it is no less entertaining for being so. Connery had vowed to leave after this film, but if he was already fed up it did not show in his typically dead-on performance. However, his attempt to become Japanese for a phony wedding with Bond girl Kissy Suzuki (Mie Hama) is pretty lame. It would not get past the political-correctness police today.

Although he was the chief baddie in *From Russia With Love*, Blofeld is seen for the first time here in the person of Donald Pleasance. You would think SPECTRE could afford a better wardrobe for its leader than that tacky beige jumpsuit.

Also from 1967, *Casino Royale* was the first James Bond film produced away from Cubby Broccoli and United Artists. It is a failure, but is one of the most intriguing failures in movie history. The credits for the film are almost comical--seven directors (including John Huston and Val Guest), eight writers (including Ben Hecht, Joseph Heller and Billy Wilder) and two producers toiled behind the scenes, along with a cast that includes such disparate talents as Orson Welles, Woody Allen, Deborah Kerr and Ursula Andress, plus William Holden, John

Huston, Charles Boyer, Peter Sellers and David Niven as Sir James Bond. Put these folks in a room together for a week and they could probably come up with a dozen movies better than this one.

The insensible plot has Bond coming out of retirement after M (Huston) is slain by SMERSH. Other stories are going on simultaneously, such as the Secret Service's attempt to abduct the man who finances SMERSH with his baccarat winnings, the shenanigans of Bond's nephew Jimmy, and the explosives in the Casino Royale. And then there's the spaceship, but chances are you will have given up by then.

There are plenty of other spoofs and spinoffs of the James Bond mythos--*Matt Helm*, *Our Man Flint* and *A Man Called Flintstone* come to mind. Bond also inspired two classic television series--"The Man From UNCLE" and "Get Smart." All of these are better than *Casino Royale*.

In the official series, meanwhile, Connery was true to his word and said goodbye to Bond, at least temporarily. The inevitable global search for a replacement followed,but most of the best choices on the globe must have been busy because the role was given to George Lazenby. The film was *On Her Majesty's Secret Service* (1969), and Lazenby is all that holds it back from being the best Bond film in the series bar none.

To this day his casting is a puzzlement. He is not a convincing actor, he's not particularly handsome or suave, and his Australian accent is far more pronounced than Connery's equally inappropriate Scottish brogue. What hurts more is that *OHMSS* delves deeper into the Bond character than any previous film, and we're stuck with the shallowest actor at the helm. To be fair, however, the change of personnel allows for the best line in the series, which closes the pretitle sequence: After dispatching several would-be assailants on a Portuguese beach, Lazenby loses the girl he rescued and quips "This never happened to the other fellow."

But you still have to question the reference to previous entries, which is echoed in the flashbacks to Connery's era in Maurice Binder's title sequence. Because when the torch is passed, it is dropped. Diana Rigg, already a star in her own right from "The Avengers," was brought in to compensate for the loss of Connery. She plays Tracy, a Spanish contessa whom Bond is hired to protect, and whom he later marries. She is outstanding, the best female lead in a James Bond movie, more polished than Lazenby in the action scenes, and the ideal choice to play 007's one true love. But this is the story of Bond's "great tragedy" according to the book, and indeed Tracy is killed by Blofeld's agents in the film's heartbreaking final scene.

OHMSS is still hailed by many Bondphiles as the best film and it does have many excellent features besides Rigg: the Louis Armstrong theme song, Telly Savales as Blofeld, and a breathtaking bobsled chase. But the nagging thought of what might have been if Connery had remained for one more film is unavoidable. Connery and Rigg would have been a dream team, and it is not an overstatement to say that had it happened, *OHMSS* would have launched Diana Rigg on the motion picture career that eluded her. After this film and "The Avengers" she was never at a loss for work, but with the exceptions of *The Hospital* (1971) and the camp horror film *Theater of Blood* (1973), the films she appeared in were not worthy of her considerable ability.

After Lazenby proved ineffective, Broccoli and Saltzman toyed with recasting the role again (among their choices: Roger Moore and Timothy Dalton) before luring Connery back with an offer he couldn't refuse; a $1.25 million salary, a percentage of the gross, and an agreement with the studio to bankroll two more films of Connery's choice, a commitment that could have amounted to another $20 million in risk. Lest you think that Connery was a money-grubbing ingrate, he actually donated his entire salary to the Scottish International Educational Trust.

Diamonds Are Forever (1971) introduced the Bond of the 1970s and 1980s; quick with a clever line and relying more on technology than ingenuity. Blofeld (Charles Gray) is back for his third straight appearance, stealing diamonds to power a laser that will be aimed at Washington, D.C., from outer space. Raquel Welch was an also-ran again for the role of Tiffany Case, which went to Jill St. John. Lana Wood plays the other Bond girl, Plenty O'Toole . Mr. Wint and Mr. Kidd, two erudite homosexual hit men, join the parade of unique series supporters, the car chase through the streets of Las Vegas is a hoot, and wouldn't we all love to have Q's device for beating the slot machines! Purists say the series goes south with *Diamonds*, but it's still fun.

Connery's second departure led to the casting of Roger Moore, whose performance in "The Saint" on television served as a perfect audition tape. *Live and Let Die* (1973) was the first of Moore's seven entries, and his super slick and smooth performance was ideal for the direction the series had embarked upon with *Diamonds are Forever*. But if Moore pushed the character a step further toward fantasy, he did so in a story grounded in the harsh reality of the times; Dr. Kananga (Yaphet Kotto), a Caribbean diplomat, develops a super-addictive form of heroin, which he plans to distribute free. Under his alter-ego of Mr. Big, he hopes to put the other drug dealers out of business and create a monopoly, to serve a rapidly multiplying number of addicts.

James Bond in an urban American ghetto is an intriguing dynamic in itself; the two worlds represented in the scene rarely meet, and provides one of the only moments in which 007 is out of his element. Fighting drug dealers instead of would-be world conquerors also makes for a nice departure. Unfortunately, the film overall does not provide Moore with the quality launch he deserved.

There are healthy doses of action; the boat jump during a water chase in Louisiana was actually a world record when it was achieved for the film, but the villains are too cartoonish to be taken seriously, and when Kananga literally blows up at the end the scene would not be out of place in a Warner Bros. *Merry Melody*.

On the plus side there is the Paul McCartney title song, the biggest hit yet for the series, and Jane Seymour as Solitaire, a tarot-card reader whose psychic power will disappear with her virginity. Bond forces her into another line of work. Seymour, far more than a pretty face, actually had a career after her Bond-girl stint.

The series took another step back with 1974's *The Man With the Golden Gun*. The film debuted just one year after *Live and Let Die* to further associate Moore with Bond for the moviegoing public. Unfortunately, *Golden Gun* was the worst entry to date, and the only film that can fairly be described as dull.

Scaramanga, the world's most proficient assassin, tries to eliminate M. Bond, already sent on the unusually pedestrian mission of tracking down a solar-energy converter to relieve the global energy crisis, uncovers a link between the converter and Scaramanga. He tracks the assassin to his private island and bests him in a showdown. The Western-style gunfight between 007 and Scaramanga just didn't measure up to the larger-than-life finales that audiences had come to expect, and there is very little to get excited about before the final confrontation.

Bikini-clad Britt Ekland is teamed with Bond as rookie agent Mary

Goodnight, allowing for all the old cliches` between veterans and greenhorns that turn up in every TV cop show at least once. Christopher Lee (Scaramanga) and sidekick Nick Nack (Herve Villechaize) are uninspiring villains, and the return from *Live and Let Die* of Clifton James as redneck sheriff J. W. Pepper is unneeded and unwelcome. Minor saving grace: Lulu's upbeat theme, an agreeable change from the usual grand orchestral ballads.

A third strike might have meant the end of the series, but *The Spy Who Loved Me* (1977) was a brilliant return to form, and the one true classic of Roger Moore's reign. It is also the first film not taken from an Ian Fleming story, though it's true that previous entries like *You Only Live Twice* borrowed little more than the title from their literary source. *The Spy Who Loved Me* is actually very similar in plot to *You Only Live Twice*--a brilliant but wacko troublemaker tries to ignite World War III by raising tensions between America and the Soviet Union. Instead of spaceship-swallowing like Blofeld, the nefarious Stromberg opts to steal nuclear submarines from both sides.

The pretitle sequence, once seen, is unforgettable; James Bond is pursued on the ski slopes by several armed assassins. After executing a stunning series of maneuvers he skis right off the edge of a cliff. He unhooks his skis, and freefalls for almost 30 seconds before pulling the cord on a Union Jack parachute. Stuntman Rick Sylvester was paid $30,000 for a feat that could have killed him about six different ways. Nothing that follows could top this opening, but the film never stops trying. The action is almost nonstop, culminating in a finale staged on the largest movie set ever built.

Roger Moore, bad puns and all, gives Bond more of a vicious streak than he's had in years. His "interrogation" of a bad guy before dropping him off a roof is wonderfully played. Curt Jurgens plays the criminal mastermind Stromberg, the best Bond baddie since Telly Savales's Blofeld, but the guy everyone remembers is Jaws (Richard Kiel), a seven-foot giant with razor-sharp metal teeth, who ranks with Oddjob and Rosa Klebb among the all-time audience favorites. Barbara Bach plays Anya,the Soviet agent and reluctant ally of 007. In a series renowned for presenting the world's most beautiful women, Bach (in this writer's opinion) wins the tiara and bouquet. Caroline Munro also appears, too briefly, as Stromberg's pilot. The Carly Simon theme song, "Nobody Does it Better," could not be more appropriate for one the series' gems.

For Your Eyes Only was originally scheduled to follow, but then *Star Wars* (1977) opened and grossed a mint, so the decision was made to send James Bond into space. The film that turned 007 from globehopper to planet-hopper was *Moonraker* (1979), another action-packed carnival ride of a movie that is far better than its reputation.

The U.S. space shuttle is loaned out to Great Britain, where it is abducted by Hugo Drax (Michael Lonsdale). Drax needs the shuttle to transport his followers--the best and the brightest earth has to offer--to a private space station. When that's finished he plans to douse the earth with lethal nerve gas. Jaws is back, at first as Drax's enforcer, but later he changes sides after learning that he doesn't fit the mold of his boss's master race. Lois Chiles plays Dr. Holly Goodhead, proving once again that Ian Fleming was even better at namedropping than Chester Gould. Holly is both a scientist and a CIA agent, the rare Bond girl who is given a brain. *Moonraker* marked the last appearance of Bernard Lee as M, and brought back Shirley Bassey to sing her third opening theme.

For Your Eyes Only (1981) became film number twelve, and represents the best blend of Fleming-style espionage with movie-Bond style action. The complicated plot, involving a device that sends encoded signals to activate nuclear submarines, combines elements of two Fleming novelettes--*For Your Eyes Only* and *Risco*, with a healthy dose of original material. Julian Glover as Kristatos is a refreshingly down-to-earth villain, and Carole Bouquet as Melina is given a more three-dimensional role than any Bond girl since Diana Rigg, though she is unequal to the task.

The movie opens with Bond visiting Tracy's grave, one of the few attempts at continuity in a series with four 007s and more than a half-dozen Felix Leiters. Bond is then attacked by a remote-controlled helicopter operated by Blofeld, and at last exacts his revenge on the man who killed his wife. The hit Sheena Easton theme then gives way to some of the very best stunts in the series, including a ski sequence that nearly rivals the one in *The Spy Who Loved Me*.

In 1983 two James Bond films opened, leading to a highly publicized box office battle between Sean Connery and Roger Moore. *Octopussy*, the next official series entry was pitted against Connery's third return appearance, appropriately entitled *Never Say Never Again*. The early favorite was Connery, so it was something of a surprise when the Moore film not only outgrossed *Never Say Never Again*, but was also better written and directed.

Octopussy was based on a Fleming short story, the plot of which comprises about ten minutes of the film's running time. Another incredible pretitle sequence, followed by a slick but bland Rita Coolidge theme, and then we meet the mysterious international smuggler known as Octopussy (Maud Adams). For reasons that should have been established more clearly, she links up with a renegade Soviet military man who likes the Cold War cold, and plans to detonate a nuke in Europe to keep it that way. Adams, with her earlier appearance in *The Man with the Golden Gun*, becomes the only actress besides Lois Maxwell to appear more than once in the series. She is ably supported by Louis Jourdan as the suave Kamal Khan and Kristina Wayborn, who leads an all-female tactical squad in impossibly tight uniforms into the film's final explosive battle. In the twenty-first year of the series, *Octopussy* became the highest-grossing Bond film yet, proving that James Bond was still a hot commodity.

Never Say Never Again, meanwhile, was a remake of *Thunderball* that could not stand up to the original. Irvin Kershner directed after helming *The Empire Strikes Back* (1980), bad guy Largo is played by the distinguished actor Klaus Maria Brandauer, and the Bond girl roles are ably filled by Barbara Carrera and Kim Basinger, but the finished product turns out to be much less than the sum of its parts. The film suffers from its legal inability to use all the Bond trademarks--John Barry's music, Maurice Binder's titles and the familiar office personnel of the British Secret Service. This creates a guilty conscience atmosphere that even Sean Connery cannot rise above. Sure it's fun to see him back in action, and winning underwater fights without losing his hairpiece, but once he bailed out he should have stayed bailed.

Roger Moore, likewise, should have quit with *Octopussy*, when he was still an effective, entertaining secret agent. His seventh and final entry, *A View to a Kill* (1985), proved to be one too many. Previous lesser entries such as *The Man with the Golden Gun* are still passable timekillers, but after a typically strong pretitle sequence everything that follows is just about unwatchable.

The list of series worsts achieved by *A View to a Kill* is formidable: the awful Duran Duran theme song; the atrocious performance of Tanya Roberts, who makes Carole Bouquet look like Greta Garbo, as Bond girl Stacey Sutton; the recycled *Goldfinger*-for-the-1980's plot, in which Christopher Walken as bad guy Max Zorin tries to wipe out California's Silicon Valley and corner the microchip market; even the action scenes are uncharacteristically slipshod. The chase through Paris is well executed, but the climax on San Francisco's Golden Gate Bridge was shot in front of a very obvious filmed backdrop. In *For Your Eyes Only* that really was Roger Moore dangling off a cliff in the movie's thrilling finale, but here he opted to stay in the studio.

Taking a cheap shot at the flirting between near senior citizens Roger Moore and Lois Maxwell, considering their incalculable contributions to the series, would be wrong and too easy, but watching Moore and Patrick Macnee back on assignment one can't help believing they would be more at home in a British version of *Tough Guys* (1986). Grace Jones as the aptly named assassin May Day brings some freshness to the formula and easily overshadows the laconic Walken. It's not enough.

It was time for another change if the series was to continue. There was speculation about the possible casting of Pierce Brosnan as Bond, but instead Broccoli went with Timothy Dalton, the actor almost selected to replace Connery fourteen years earlier. The choice would prove inspired, and *The Living Daylights* (1987), Dalton's debut, was a potent return to hard-boiled, Fleming-style espionage.

Dalton accomplishes what should have been almost impossible--he claims the role and ends up owning it not just after one film, but before the opening credits! After a furious car chase, he plummets over a cliff, but opens a parachute and lands safely on a nearby yacht. A woman emerges and asks who he is. Dalton delivers the expected reply--"Bond. James Bond," and darned if we don't already believe it.

The new interpretation of Bond was lauded for its seriousness and intensity, which impressed a lot of critics who thought the series was history. There were some lighter moments as well, such as when Bond and main squeeze Kara (Maryam d'Abo) slide down a mountain on a cello case, and his use of a gas pellet that goes off when "Rule Britannia" is whistled. But Dalton is primarily a no-nonsense hero, with a somber ferocity that even Sean Connery never matched.

The plot involves the defection of a KGB agent, who may or may not be linked to an American arms dealer with nefarious plans. Joe Don Baker as the dealer is not the best of villains, but Maryam d'Abo is the best Bond girl in five films. At the time 007's one-woman behavior was seen as an AIDS statement, but d'Abo is beautiful and charismatic enough to make Bond's fidelity understandable in less political terms.

As befits a new era, other updates were made as well; Caroline Bliss plays Miss Moneypenny, and Bond gets a new Aston Martin Volante. Desmond Llewelyn returns as Q to provide a link to the past. The song by Dutch group a-ha is even worse that "A View to a Kill." Clearly, the days of Bond themes automatically landing in the top 40 were over.

Dalton's second adventure, *License to Kill* (1989), is not a bad film, but it seemed inferior coming off the near-perfect *Living Daylights*. The usual location changes are limited to Florida and Mexico, which look pretty much alike here, and those weaned on Roger Moore will miss the gadgets and the humor. Dalton's incarnation, still flawless, is the right one to carry the series through the next decade, but too much change too quickly is not healthy either.

The villains are corrupt government agents and Colombian drug dealers, a necessary move away from superpower hostility in the era of *glasnost.* Bond is in the United States to attend the wedding of old friend Felix Leiter, but when the bride is killed and Leiter is thrown into a shark tank, 007 becomes consumed by anger and a thirst for vengeance. M tries to talk him out of action, and when Bond remains defiant he is stripped of his license to kill. Now a vigilante, he takes out the villains and their financial backer, a sleazy evangelist played by Wayne Newton.

James Bond so often seems detached from the danger around him, and the lives of friends and foes that end in his midst. Here, his personal obsession with a case is refreshing--the unflappable agent wears his heart on his sleeve more than in any film since *On Her Majesty's Secret Service.* The idea was great, but it is executed without the larger-than-life quality that is also essential to the series. *License to Kill* is reminiscent of a "Miami Vice" episode stretched to 133 minutes, and without the stylish trappings.

Robert Davi is a genuinely frightening as the vicious Sanchez, who is not the type of opposition Bond usually faces. David Hedison becomes the only actor to play Felix Leiter twice (he inherited the role in *Live and Let Die*). Bond girl Carey Lowell is another model turned would-be actress who needs a few more lessons.

And that's where we stand. Bond fans waiting for the new adventures of their character should see something by 1995, and wouldn't it be fun if Sean Connery also returned, this time with the full blessings of the Bond braintrust, to play the older Agent 007 in a straightforward remake of *Casino Royale*? His "never"s have already proven impermanent.

THE FILMS

Dr. No (United Artists, 1962, 111 minutes)
Directed by Terence Young; Written by Richard Maibaum, Johanna Harwood and Berkley Mather; Produced by Albert R. Broccoli and Harry Saltzman; Music by Monty Norman
Cast
SEAN CONNERY (JAMES BOND), Ursula Andress (Honey Rider), Joseph Wiseman (Dr. No), Jack Lord (Felix Leiter), Lois Maxwell (Miss Moneypenny), Bernard Lee (M)
Rating: ****1/2
Available on Videocassette

From Russia With Love (United Artists, 1963, 118 minutes)
Directed by Terence Young; Written by Richard Maibaum and Johanna Harwood; Produced by Albert R. Broccoli and Harry Saltzman; Music by John Barry, title song by Lionel Bart
Cast
SEAN CONNERY (JAMES BOND), Daniela Bianchi (Tania), Pedro Armendariz (Kerim Bey), Lotte Lenya (Rosa Klebb), Robert Shaw (Red Grant), Desmond Llewelyn (Q)
Rating: ****
Available on Videocassette

Goldfinger (United Artists, 1964, 111 minutes)
Directed by Guy Hamilton; Written by Richard Maibaum and Paul Dehn; Produced

by Albert R. Broccoli and Harry Saltzman; Music by John Barry, title song by Leslie Bricusse and Anthony Newley
Cast
SEAN CONNERY (JAMES BOND), Honor Blackman (Pussy Galore), Gert Frobe (Goldfinger), Shirley Eaton (Jill Masterson), Harold Sakata (Oddjob)
Rating: *****
Available on Videocassette
Awards: Academy Award nomination for Best Sound

Thunderball (United Artists, 1965, 129 minutes)
Directed by Terence Young; Written by Richard Maibaum and John Hopkins; Produced by Albert R. Broccoli and Harry Saltzman; Music by John Barry, title song by Don Black
Cast
SEAN CONNERY (JAMES BOND), Claudine Auger (Domino), Adolfo Celi (Largo), Luciana Paluzzi (Fiona)
Rating: ***1/2
Available on Videocassette
Awards: Academy Award nomination for Best Visual Effects

You Only Live Twice (United Artists, 1967, 116 minutes)
Directed by Lewis Gilbert; Written by Roald Dahl; Produced by Albert R. Broccoli and Harry Saltzman; Music by John Barry, title song by Leslie Bricusse
Cast
SEAN CONNERY (JAMES BOND), Akiko Wakabayashi (Aki), Mie Hama (Kissy Suzuki), Donald Pleasence (Blofeld)
Rating: ****
Available on Videocassette

Casino Royale (Columbia, 1967, 131 minutes)
Directed by John Huston, Kenneth Hughes, Robert Parrish, Val Guest and Joseph McGrath; Written by Wolf Mankowitz, John Law, Michael Sayers, Billy Wilder, Val Guest, Joseph Heller, Ben Hecht and Terry Southern; Produced by Charles K. Feldman and Jerry Bresler; Music by Burt Bacharach
Cast
Peter Sellers (Evelyn Tremble), Ursula Andress (Vesper Lynd), DAVID NIVEN (JAMES BOND), Orson Welles (Le Chiffre), Woody Allen (Jimmy Bond), Deborah Kerr (Agent Mimi), William Holden (Ramsome), Charles Boyer (Le Grand)
Rating: **
Available on Videocassette

On Her Majesty's Secret Service (United Artists, 1969, 140 minutes)
Directed by Peter Hunt; Written by Richard Maibaum; Produced by Albert R. Broccoli and Harry Saltzman; Music by John Barry, title song by Hal David
Cast
GEORGE LAZENBY (JAMES BOND), Diana Rigg (Tracy), Telly Savales (Blofeld)
Rating: ***1/2
Available on Videocassette

Diamonds Are Forever (United Artists, 1971, 119 minutes)
Directed by Guy Hamilton; Written by Richard Maibaum and Tom Mankiewicz; Produced by Albert R. Broccoli and Harry Saltzman; Music by John Barry, title song by Don Black
Cast
SEAN CONNERY (JAMES BOND), Jill St. John (Tiffany Case), Charles Gray (Blofeld), Lana Wood (Plenty)
Rating: ****
Available on Videocassette
Awards: Academy Award nomination for Best Sound

Live and Let Die (United Artists, 1973, 121 minutes)
Directed by Guy Hamilton; Written by Tom Mankiewicz; Produced by Albert R. Broccoli and Harry Saltzman; Music by George Martin, title song by Paul and Linda McCartney
Cast
ROGER MOORE (SEAN CONNERY), Jane Seymour (Solitaire), Yaphet Kotto (Dr. Kananga/Mr. Big), Clifton James (Sheriff Pepper), Julius W. Harris (Tee Hee), Geoffrey Holder (Baron Samedi)
Rating: ***1/2
Available on Videocassette
Awards: Academy Award nomination for Best Song

The Man With the Golden Gun (United Artists, 1974, 125 minutes)
Directed by Guy Hamilton; Written by Richard Maibaum and Tom Mankiewicz; Produced by Albert R. Broccoli and Harry Saltzman; Music by John Barry, title song by Don Black
Cast
ROGER MOORE (JAMES BOND), Christopher Lee (Scaramanga), Britt Ekland (Mary Goodnight), Maud Adams (Andrea) Herve Villechaize (Nick Nack), Clifton James (Sheriff Pepper)
Rating: **
Available on Videocassette

The Spy Who Loved Me (United Artists, 1977, 125 minutes)
Directed by Lewis Gilbert; Written by Christopher Wood and Richard Maibaum; Produced by Albert R. Broccoli and Harry Saltzman; Music by Marvin Hamlisch and Carole Bayer Sager
Cast
ROGER MOORE (JAMES BOND), Barbara Bach (Anya), Curt Jurgens (Stromberg), Richard Kiel (Jaws), Caroline Munro (Naomi)
Rating: *****
Available on Videocassette
Awards: Academy Award nominations for Best Song, Score and Art Direction

Moonraker (United Artists, 1979, 126 minutes)
Directed by Lewis Gilbert; Written by Christopher Wood; Produced by Albert R. Broccoli; Music by John Barry, title song by Hal David
Cast
ROGER MOORE (JAMES BOND), Lois Chiles (Dr. Holly Goodhead), Michael

Lonsdale (Hugo Drax), Richard Kiel (Jaws)
Rating: ****
Available on Videocassette
Awards: Academy Award nominee for Best Visual Effects

For Your Eyes Only (United Artists, 1981, 127 minutes)
Directed by John Glen; Written by Richard Maibaum and Michael G. Wilson; Produced by Albert R. Broccoli; Music by Bill Conti, title song by Michael Leeson
Cast
ROGER MOORE (JAMES BOND), Carole Bouquet (Melina), Julian Glover (Kristatos), Topol (Colombo)
Rating: ****
Available on Videocassette
Awards: Academy Award nomination for Best Song

Octopussy (United Artists, 1983, 130 minutes)
Directed by John Glen; Written by George Macdonald Fraser, Richard Maibaum and Michael G. Wilson; Produced by Albert R. Broccoli; Music by John Barry, title song by Tim Rice
Cast
ROGER MOORE (JAMES BOND), Maud Adams (Octopussy), Louis Jourdan (Kamal Khan), Kristina Wayborn (Magda)
Rating: ****
Available on Videocassette

Never Say Never Again (Warner Bros., 1983, 137 minutes)
Directed by Irvin Kershner; Written by Lorenzo Semple, Jr., based on a story by Kevin McClory, Jack Whittingham and Ian Fleming; Produced by Jack Schwartzman; Music by Michel Legrand
Cast
SEAN CONNERY (JAMES BOND), Klaus Maria Brandauer (Largo), Max von Sydow (Blofeld), Barbara Carrera (Fatima Blush), Kim Basinger (Domino), Bernie Casey (Felix Leiter)
Rating: ***
Available on Videocassette

A View to A Kill (United Artists,1985, 131 minutes)
Directed by John Glen; Written by Richard Maibaum and Michael G. Wilson; Produced by Albert R. Broccoli and Michael G. Wilson; Music by John Barry, title song by Duran Duran
Cast
ROGER MOORE (JAMES BOND), Tanya Roberts (Stacey Sutton), Christopher Walken (Max Zorin), Grace Jones (May Day)
Rating: *1/2
Available on Videocassette

The Living Daylights (United Artists, 1987, 130 minutes)
Directed by John Glen; Written by Richard Maibaum and Michael G. Wilson; Produced by Albert R. Broccoli and Michael G. Wilson; Music by John Barry, title song by Pal Waaktaar

Cast
TIMOTHY DALTON (JAMES BOND), Maryam d'Abo (Kara), Jeroen Krabbe (Koskov), Joe Don Baker (Brad Whitaker)
Rating: ****1/2
Available on Videocassette

License to Kill (United Artists, 1989, 133 minutes)
Directed by John Glen; Written by Michael G. Wilson and Richard Maibaum; Produced by Albert R. Broccoli and Michael G. Wilson; Music by Michael Kamen
Cast
TIMOTHY DALTON (JAMES BOND), Carey Lowell (Pam Bouvier), Robert Davi (Sanchez), Talisa Soto (Lupe)
Rating: **1/2
Available on Videocassette

TELEVISION
"Casino Royale" (teleplay, "Climax Mystery Theater," CBS, 1954--1958)
Cast
BARRY NELSON (JAMES BOND)

BUCKAROO BANZAI

The movie's full title is *The Adventures of Buckaroo Banzai--Across the 8th Dimension*, and nobody knew what to make of it back in 1984. Some critics described the film as brilliant, others found it incoherent. *Starlog* magazine included *Banzai* on its list of the fifty science fiction/fantasy videos that are essential for a comprehensive library. Outside the SF community, however, the film's reputation is not as sterling.

Actually, *Banzai* is neither brilliant nor incoherent, though it contains traces of both these qualities. It's a challenging movie, a hybrid of science fiction and comedy that refuses to fully commit to either genre. The mixture works more often than it doesn't, but this mercurial nature has always made *Banzai* almost impossible to categorize, and such films always seem to have difficulty finding an audience.

The movie opened well but faded quickly, and then began to resurface as the object of a cult following. *Banzai*-inspired comic books and other merchandise appeared, and grass roots organizations of Hong Kong Cavaliers and Blue Blazers (Buckaroo's support teams in the film) formed across the country to await the further adventures of their hero. A sequel, *Buckaroo Banzai Against the World Crime League*, was promised but never materialized, and the absence of any new product for a decade has put the kibosh on the Banzai cult. But if the movie is no longer revered, it at least deserves to be remembered.

W.D. Richter's script defies a rational plot synopsis. It's been called a puzzle, but it really isn't. Personally, I've never liked movies that only provide half the story, or are composed entirely of symbolic images--the films of Luis Bunuel, for example. But *Banzai* does not demand interpretation, just close attention. Lapses occur that force the audience to make a fairly significant leap, but these too become manageable with the second or third viewing. The film is certainly entertaining enough to make such repeat viewings enjoyable.

Buckaroo Banzai, we learn on an introductory title card, was "born to an American mother and a Japanese father, and thus began life as he was destined to live it--going in several directions at once." Banzai is a modern-day Renaissance man: a neurosurgeon, adventurer and rock singer who is well versed in both particle physics and martial arts. He is joined in his exploits by the Hong Kong Cavaliers, his scientific support team and back-up band.

As the movie opens, Buckaroo successfully tests his latest invention, an "oscillation overthruster," that allows him to pass through solid matter into the eighth dimension. Dr. Emilio Lizardo, who invented a similar device and was driven insane by his eighth dimension experience, watches Banzai's triumph on television at a mental institution. He escapes to plot anew.

The ranks of the Cavaliers are swelled by the arrivals of New Jersey, a doctor, and Penny Priddy, whom Banzai spots in the audience at one of his concerts. Attempts are made to steal the overthruster, and it is New Jersey who uncovers the would-be thieves' identity. On Halloween 1938, Red Lectroids from Planet Ten invaded earth. Orson Welles reported the invasion on radio, but was later hypnotized into claiming his broadcast was a fictional play. The Lectroids, led by Lizardo, want to return to their planet, and need the overthruster to do so.

As the team ponders its next move, Banzai receives a holographic message from the Black Lectroids, warning that if Lizardo is not stopped a bomb will be dropped on the Soviet Union, which will almost inevitably lead to World War III. Banzai, assisted by the Cavaliers and another network of supporters known as the Blue Blazers, infiltrates the Red Lectroid stronghold and saves the world.

The movie closes with an end-title sequence in which Buckaroo Banzai and the Cavaliers march proudly through a Los Angeles wash, backed by whistling theme music that will haunt your mind for days. It's always struck me as an extremely cool scene, and a great signature for a film series, like the sight of James Bond in the gun barrel, accompanied by John Barry's classic Bond theme. But sadly, Banzai's first walk also turned out to be his last.

Today the movie is best remembered by Buckaroo Banzai's maxim, "No matter where you go, there you are," a line that has been borrowed by several other films and television shows, and by its outstanding cast of then up-and-coming talent. Peter Weller, perfectly cast as the enigmatic title hero, went on to play another offbeat crimefighter in the megahit *Robocop* (1987). Ellen Barkin's post-Banzai work includes several steamy characterizations in movies such as *The Big Easy* (1987) and *Sea of Love* (1989). Jeff Goldblum and Christopher Lloyd also appear.

The film's best performance, however, belongs to John Lithgow. As Dr. Lizardo, Lithgow steals every scene he's in, and that Italian accent ("Laugh-a while you can-a, monkey-boy!") is a scream. It would be easy to classify Banzai as a comedy based on Lithgow's contribution, but action sequences such as the assault on Yoyodyne Labs are effectively shot, and there's nothing funny about the death of Cavalier Rawhide.

Buckaroo Banzai remains an unsung hero, but sometimes it takes the world a little while to catch up to a character, and a movie, that is this eccentric. It would be a crime worse than the Red Lectroid invasion if *Banzai* is not eventually discovered and given its due.

THE FILM

The Adventures of Buckaroo Banzai--Across the 8th Dimension (20th Century Fox, 1984, 103 minutes)

Directed by W. D. Richter; Written by Earl Mac Rauch; Produced by W.D. Richter and Neil Canton; Music by Michael Boddicker

Cast

PETER WELLER (BUCKAROO BANZAI), John Lithgow (Dr. Emilio Lizardo/Lord John Whorfin), Ellen Barkin (Penny Priddy), Jeff Goldblum (New

Jersey), Christopher Lloyd (John Bigboote), Lewis Smith (Perfect Tommy), Clancy Brown (Rawhide), Carl Lumbly (John Parker)
Rating: ****
Available on Videocassette

Fess Parker as Davy Crockett, king of the wild frontier.

DAVY CROCKETT

He's been called the King of the Wild Frontier, and he's been called a coward and a wife-deserter. Davy Crockett was in his own time a symbol of America's pioneer spirit, and the veracity of his reputation has been under attack from historians and other professional killjoys since his election to Congress in 1827. But the Crockett legend managed to stay just ahead of the facts, and when it was teamed up with Walt Disney in 1954 reality never had a chance.

David Crockett was born in Tennessee, but not on a mountaintop, on August 17, 1786. He received no formal schooling, but possessed an instinctive ability for storytelling and public speaking that was invaluable in his political career. He held a variety of odd jobs even in his preteen years, often disappearing from home for years at a time. He married Mary (Polly) Finley in 1806, and she bore him two sons, John and William, and a daughter named Margaret, before succumbing to illness in 1815. He married Elizabeth Patton in 1816.

Crockett's first taste of fame resulted from his exploits in the Creek War. The Creek Indians' alliance with the British in the war of 1812 led to the cession of twenty-three million acres of their land to Alabama and Georgia. With arms supplied by the Shawnee tribal leader Tecumseh, the Creeks killed 553 frontiersmen at the Fort Mims Massacre. Andrew Jackson led the American response, and Crockett distinguished himself in the war-ending battle of Horseshoe Bend.

His reputation as an Indian fighter and his talent for homespun speechmaking won Crockett two terms in the Tennessee legislature and, after losing in his first attempt, he was elected to the U.S. Congress in 1827. His stand against the Indian Removal Bill in 1830 caused a rift between Crockett and President Andrew Jackson, who is mainly responsible for the lingering negative assessment of Crockett's congressional career. He was not a particularly effective legislator, but he served with dignity and twice won re-election.

After losing another election bid in 1835, Crockett rejected a job offer as land agent in the Red River Valley and went to Texas, where he was killed along with fellow Colonels Jim Bowie and William Travis at the Alamo on March 6, 1836. He was one of fewer than two hundred men fighting a Mexican army four thousand strong, commanded by General Santa Anna. It was a conflict without heroes or villains--the Texans simply could not get along with their Mexican rulers, whom they outnumbered four-to-one, and Santa Anna made no attempt to bridge the cultural gap. The Texans believed they were fighting a second war for independence from a distant tyrannical ruler; the Mexicans attempted to hold on to their legally owned territory. The Alamo battle was an attempt by Texans to delay Santa Anna while Sam Houston assembled an effective army. The delay worked--Houston routed the Mexicans at San Jacinto, and Texas joined the United States.

Every film version of the story depicts Crockett fighting to the last, but that is actually not the case. He was one of a half-dozen men to survive the battle, and was executed after being captured by force. The most reliable account of Crockett's last days, a diary kept by a Mexican army lieutenant, reports that many of the Mexican soldiers recognized Crockett and asked Santa Anna to spare his life, but to no avail. The diary states that Crockett and the other prisoners died "without complaining and without humiliating themselves before their torturers."

Most accounts of Davy Crockett's life mix fact and fiction, including the four autobiographies Crockett wrote between 1833 and 1836. He was running for office at the time, and not above getting mileage out of his renown for frontier taming and "b'ar wrestlin'." However, the books were much closer to the truth than the *Crockett Almanacs* that were published throughout the 1900s, which grouped their subject with such tall-tale figures as Paul Bunyan. Crockett is depicted wringing the tail of Halley's Comet and lighting his pipe on the sun.

No mortal could live up to such fantasies and in fact, the final balance sheet shows very little justification for turning Davy Crockett into a world figure. It is true that he was a hard-working backwoodsman, a humorous downhome orator, a bear hunter and an Indian fighter, but so were a thousand other men at the time. Historically his life was noteworthy but would not have inspired such fervor had it not been for Crockett himself.

The source of the legend was indeed the source of the legend, but even Crockett had to wonder at how quickly his name grew to represent the best qualities of America's frontier expansion. In 1833, a play entitled *The Lion of The West* was based on his adventures, and was attended by Congressman Crockett when it arrived in Washington. Davy appeared on the stage opposite his portrayer James Hackett--they bowed to each other and the audience went wild. Such a meeting between fact and fiction is rare in history, and one of the best true Crockett stories that exists.

Almost every film in which Davy Crockett is portrayed deals primarily with the Alamo, either as a historical drama or a biography of one of its principal figures, such as Jim Bowie (*The Last Command*) or Sam Houston (*Man of Conquest* and *The First Texan*). His reign as a movie hero arguably peaked in the silent era, but sadly most if not all of those films have disappeared.

There were seven films about Crockett before the coming of sound--he was played by Charles K. French in *Davy Crockett--In Hearts United* (1909), Hobart Bosworth in *Davy Crockett* (1910), an uncredited actor in *The Immortal Alamo* (1911), W. E. Browning in *Davy Crockett Up-To-Date* (1915), A. D. Sears in *The Martyrs of the Alamo* (1916) and Cullen Landis in *Davy Crockett at the Fall of the Alamo* (1926).

He first spoke on screen in the person of Lane Chandler in *Heroes of the Alamo* (1937), an abysmal film that would be laughable if it weren't so dull. Explanations and introductions are forced into the script with the subtlety of a crowbar, and the stiff performances do an injustice to the historical personages portrayed.

Though second-billed, Chandler makes his entrance late and is only in a few brief scenes. It's all for the best, because he plays the most offensive Crockett in motion pictures. Upon arriving at the Alamo he chastises the "numbskull voters" in Tennessee for not returning him to Congress, and says he's not in Texas to defend freedom, but because "one fight is as good as another." Even if Crockett was not a legendary hero he was by all accounts an honorable man, and such statements do not do him justice.

Man of Conquest (1939) is a biopic of Sam Houston, whom we are told ranks only behind Washington and Jackson as the greatest warrior-statesman the United States produced. Perhaps he was, but Richard Dix's somewhat unflattering portrayal does not make the point strongly enough. The film hits all the major points, from Houston's early life with the Indians to his role in bringing Texas into the Union, but it doesn't delve into details and emerges as an unsatisfying, Cliff's Notes treatment. It also looks cheap, as did all Republic pictures in the thirties.

Joan Fontaine plays Houston's first wife Eliza, and while it's nice to have her in a Western, I wish it wasn't this one. Edward Ellis has the film's best moments as Andrew Jackson. Robert Barrat plays Crockett, who appears, gets killed at the Alamo, and disappears without comment.

The First Texan (1956) offered a better look at Houston's life, covering most of the same ground with more zest and a lot more insight. Joel McCrea is a convincing Houston, the San Jacinto Battle provides a stirring climax, but once again Crockett (James Griffith) is seen in little more than a cameo.

Two pretender Crockett films opened in the 1940s; *Son of Davy Crockett* (1941) has the frontier king's son helping out General Ulysses S. Grant after the Civil War in a forgettable one-hour programmer that starred Bill Elliot as "Dave" Crockett, Jr. And George Montgomery played Crockett's nephew and namesake in *Davy Crockett, Indian Scout* (1949), one of a thousand movies in which a defenseless wagon train is besieged by hostile redskins.

The next genuine, albeit brief, Crockett appearance was in Budd Boetticher's 1953 film *The Man from the Alamo*. Along with director Anthony Mann, Boetticher defined the Western in the fifties with films that were often somber in tone, and dealt with the kind of moral dilemmas not previously tackled in the genre. *The Man from the Alamo*, explored themes of alienation and obsession for revenge that Boetticher used in numerous Randolph Scott vehicles, notably *Decision at Sundown* (1957).

The title does not refer to Crockett but to the fictional Johnny Stroud, who is chosen among five men from the same settlement to leave the Alamo and take care of the women and children back home. Stroud reaches the settlement only to find it burned down, and all its inhabitants murdered by a guerrilla force led by Jess Wade, a Texan who sold his loyalty to Santa Anna. He rides to the nearby town of Franklin, but is branded a coward and ostracized by the residents for deserting the Alamo. Stroud later proves his heroism by rescuing the residents from an attack by Wade's men, and then riding off to join Sam Houston's army.

Veteran character actor Trevor Bardette plays Colonel Crockett, who is unceremoniously knocked off in the film's first twenty minutes. Glenn Ford stars as Johnny Stroud, and he is always worth watching in a Western, as are most of Boetticher's contributions to the genre. Victor Jory as Jess Wade is an effective villain.

Crockett finally received his due in 1954 as the subject of three episodes of the "Disneyland" TV series. This is the only Crockett project to date that depicts the frontiersman's adventures in the Creek War and in the federal government, as well as his demise at the Alamo. And if you were a young'un at the time, this is the only Davy Crockett that matters.

The story begins with Davy as a volunteer in the service of Andrew Jackson, using his tracking and fighting skills in the Creek War. After briefly visiting with his wife Polly, Davy and his sidekick Georgie Russell return to the conflict, which ends after Davy fights the Creek chief Red Stick in single combat. Crockett promises the tribe's members that they can keep their land if they remain peaceful.

Crockett removes a bully from a once-quiet town, and is urged to run for magistrate. This leads to a stint in the Tennessee State Legislature and then to Congress. President Jackson plots to get Crockett out of Washington while a bill seizing Indian land is passed. Georgie brings the news to Davy, who returns in time to deliver a stirring speech that reiterates his promise to Red Stick, and ends his political career. A few days later he reads about the trouble in Texas, and heads for the Alamo.

The series was an overnight sensation, spawning a one hundred million dollar merchandising industry and revitalizing Davy Crockett as a hero to a new generation. The demand for coonskin caps became so overwhelming that the raccoon was lucky to avoid extinction. The craze vanished as rapidly as it hit, in part because only five episodes of the series were produced, but they remain the most influential Crockett lore of the twentieth century. New biographies were written to meet the public demand, and coverage of Crockett in grade-school history books rose dramatically after 1955.

Disney cleaned up harsher aspects of the legend, but Davy did not become one of the studio's cartoon characters. As played by Fess Parker, Crockett was brave, noble and honest, a fearsome fighter and an eloquent representative of Tennessee. It's an uncomplicated, idealized portrayal, clearly aimed at children. There was some controversy at the time about its accuracy, but it died out with the fad. The famous last scene didn't happen but it should have--Davy is perched over the wall of the Alamo, knocking back soldiers with the butt of his rifle. The picture fades out before he is overwhelmed.

The character of Georgie Russell is mentioned in one of Crockett's autobiographies, but he was never the Tonto to Davy's Lone Ranger and was largely manufactured here. Buddy Ebsen played Georgie, and those who see it for the first time now will notice a lot of Jed Clampett sneaking in. Ebsen also sang the familiar theme song, which was recorded sixteen times in 1955. The Bill Hayes version reached number one, and thirty-six years later a new recording by the Kentucky Headhunters topped the country music chart.

Although Davy Crockett is killed in the third program, he was brought back nine months later in a prequel of sorts, in which he and Georgie beat the aptly-named Mike Fink at a river race and overcome battle pirates who harass innocent citizens. Both series were repackaged as feature films under the titles *Davy Crockett, King of the Wild Frontier* and *Davy Crockett and the River Pirates.*

Fess Parker would reprise the character once more, for a cameo appearance in the Bob Hope comedy *Alias Jesse James* (see WYATT EARP chapter). Five years later Parker would play Daniel Boone, the *other* famous frontiersman, in another successful series.

In 1955, at the height of Crockett-mania, Arthur Hunnicutt contributed another interesting variation on the character in *The Last Command*, a film about the last days of Colonel Jim Bowie. Bowie, whose close ties to Mexico included a wife and hundreds of acres of land, still sides with the Texans against Santa Anna's aggression. Bowie advises caution to both sides, but events soon spiral out of control, and he realizes war is inevitable. Inside the Alamo, a bedridden Bowie is killed in the siege.

Sterling Hayden is a commanding presence as Bowie, and bears a striking resemblance to the genuine article. There is good support from Ernest Borgnine and by Anna Maria Alberghetti, in her career-best role as a Mexican maiden with a crush on Bowie. Hunnicutt, a familiar face in countless Westerns, makes a memorable entrance as Crockett halfway into the film. His interpretation is similar to Fess Parker's but a little more authentically rustic. The corn-pone dialogue rings true and the scruffy, bearded look was probably closer to the truth than Parker's neatly trimmed stubble.

There's great action at the Alamo, with Crockett taking a dozen of the enemy with him in a powerful last moment. J. Carol Naish almost appears sympathetic as Santa Anna, especially in a conversation with Bowie on the eve of battle. The theme song, performed by Gordon McRae, is almost as catchy as "The Ballad of Davy Crockett."

Obviously, Santa Anna's victory over a small band of sturdy Texans has been a popular subject at the movies. But that didn't stop John Wayne from realizing a longtime dream of bringing his own version to the screen. In 1960, Wayne directed, produced and starred as Davy Crockett in *The Alamo*, a lavish three-hour epic that represents the best take on the story yet.

The events are played out as in previous versions, but the principal figures seem more three-dimensional this time. The running time allowed for more in-depth character development, only some of which is based on fact; Crockett tells Colonel William Travis that his Tennessee volunteers think they rode to Texas for some "huntin' and drinkin'." He then tries to trick them into staying, though almost immediately he retracts the ploy.

The depiction of Jim Bowie, played wonderfully by Richard Widmark, is less flattering than in *The Last Command*. He is usually drunk and threatens to leave the mission several times, after growing fed up with Travis's spit-and-polish command and the general hopelessness of the situation. According to the most reliable historical sources, the two men actually assumed joint command without animosity.

The Alamo gives Travis equal screen time with Crockett and Bowie, a welcome revision of past treatments. Laurence Harvey is superb as Travis, who must establish his authority knowing that the volunteers are all loyal to Bowie or Crockett. He also realizes early on that no one will be leaving the Alamo, but that he must keep morale high at any cost.

John Wayne, like Davy Crockett, was an archetype in his lifetime, and watching one legend play another is certainly part of the film's appeal. Crockett was the most famous nonfictional character Wayne ever played (we won't even count Ghengis Khan in *The Conqueror* [1956], and just by being and playing himself he captures the essence of the hero.

The Alamo is the first film to separate the Crockett image from reality. The character makes his first appearance in buckskin clothing and coonskin cap, but wears more appropriate garb for the locale and climate thereafter. The whole identification with the cap can be traced back to a famous portrait of Crockett painted in 1834 by John Gadsby Chapman; Crockett may have actually wore one but not every day of his adult life! Later, Travis actually accuses him of playing the yokel to win votes in his campaigns and to boost his reputation, which was certainly probable. Crockett neither confirms nor denies, but the twinkle in Wayne's eye tells the story.

The climactic siege is recreated on a scale undreamed of by previous attempts. John Ford may have helped his buddy John Wayne helm the battle scenes, but either way the result was an outstanding execution of a massive movement of men and horses--the widescreen format is a must if you rent the videocassette. Wayne made the job even more difficult by swelling Santa Anna's forces by three thousand more soldiers than history records.

There is also a healthy dose of patriotism, beyond what is inherent in the situation--no real surprise with the Duke in charge. Crockett's speech early on extolling the virtues of the Republic was trashed by critics in 1960, but sounds pretty good now. And lines such as "Being in Congress has ruined many a good man," are timeless. The scene in which Travis draws a line in the sand, and asks every man who plans to stay for the fight to cross over is a staple in Alamo movies, but has never been more movingly staged or underscored (by Dmitri Tiomkin).

A 1992 rerelease of *The Alamo* generated overdue praise of the film, but also added 30 minutes of additional footage that derail its pace. Stick to the 160-minute version, which is also still available.

The most recent Crockett/Alamo project was a two-part television miniseries broadcast in 1987. "The Alamo--13 Days to Glory" is very similar to the John Wayne film, though it often seems like a community-theater adaptation.

Performances are lacking. Alec Baldwin is not very authoritative as Travis, especially playing opposite James Arness as Jim Bowie and Brian Keith as Crockett. It's true that Travis was only twenty-five at the Alamo and his fellow colonels were twice his age, but it doesn't play out well with this trio of actors. Crockett must have had more charisma than he is given by Keith, or he wouldn't be so popular. Raul Julia emerges best as a proud, evil and slightly insane Santa Anna. David Ogden Stiers is also excellent as Santa Anna's aide Colonel Black, an important character ignored by previous versions.

As is surmisable from the title, there is more emphasis on actual time and place, with on-screen titles labeling the principal locations and events leading up to the siege. For instance, we now know that the Alamo is located one-half mile from San Antonio. Its main selling point is historical accuracy, including background information on the lesser-known men who died that day and details about the weaponry used. And for the first time on film, the attack begins in darkness, as it actually did. On that level it's a worthwhile addition to the canon, but for sheer entertainment stick with the Duke's film.

Sooner or later a "revisionist" film bio of Davy Crockett will completely set the record straight, but I'll bet audiences will still prefer Fess Parker and John Wayne.

THE FILMS

Davy Crockett--In Hearts United (New York Motion Pictures, 1909)
Cast
CHARLES K. FRENCH (DAVY CROCKETT)

Davy Crockett (Selig Polyscope, 1910)
Cast
HOBART BOSWORTH (DAVY CROCKETT)

The Immortal Alamo (Melies, 1911)

Davy Crockett Up-to-Date (United Film Service, 1915)
Cast

W.E. BROWNING (DAVY CROCKETT)

The Martyrs of the Alamo (Fine Arts-Triangle, 1915)
Cast
A.D. SEARS (DAVY CROCKETT)

Davy Crockett (Paramount, 1916)
Cast
DUSTIN FARNUM (DAVY CROCKETT)

Davy Crockett at the Fall of the Alamo (Sunset, 1926)
Cast
CULLEN LANDIS (DAVY CROCKETT)

Heroes of the Alamo (Columbia, 1938, 74 minutes)
Directed by Harry Fraser; Written by Roby Wentz; Produced by Anthony J. Xydias
Cast
Earle Hodgins (Stephen Austin), LANE CHANDLER (DAVY CROCKETT), Ruth Findlay (Anne Dickinson), Rodger Williams (James), Rex Lease William Travis), Julian Rivero (Gen. Santa Anna)
Rating: *

Man of Conquest (Republic, 1939, 105 minutes)
Directed by George Nichols, Jr.; Written by Wells Root and E.E. Paramore, Jr., based on a story by Root and Harold Shumate; Produced by Sol C. Siegel; Music by Victor Young
Cast
Richard Dix (Sam Houston), Gail Patrick (Margaret Lea), Edward Ellis (Andrew Jackson), Joan Fontaine (Eliza Allen), Victor Jory (William Travis), ROBERT BARRAT (DAVY CROCKETT), Robert Armstrong (Jim Bowie)
Rating: **

The Man from the Alamo (Universal, 1953, 79 minutes)
Directed by Budd Boetticher; Written by Steve Fisher and D. D. Beauchamp, based on a story by Niven Busch and Oliver Crawford; Produced by Aaron Rosenberg; Music by Frank Skinner
Cast
Glenn Ford (John Stroud), Julia Adams (Beth Anders), Chill Wills (John Gage), Victor Jory (Jess Wade), TREVOR BARDETTE (DAVY CROCKETT)
Rating: ***1/2
Available on Videocassette

The Last Command (Republic, 1955, 110 minutes)
Directed and produced by Frank Lloyd; Written by Warren Duff, based on a story by Sy Bartlett; Music by Max Steiner, song "Jim Bowie" by Steiner and Sidney Clare
Cast
Sterling Hayden (Jim Bowie), Anna Maria Alberghetti (Consuela), Richard Carlson (William Travis), ARTHUR HUNNICUTT (DAVY CROCKETT), Ernest Borgnine (Mike Radin), J. Carol Naish (Santa Anna)

Rating: ***
Available on Videocassette

The First Texan (Allied Artists, 1956, 82 minutes)
Directed by Byron Haskin; Written by Daniel B. Ullman; Produced by Walter Mirisch; Music by Roy Webb
Cast
Joel McCrea (Sam Houston), Felicia Farr (Katherine), Jeff Morrow (Jim Bowie), William Hopper (Travis), JAMES GRIFFITH (DAVY CROCKETT)
Rating: ***

The Alamo (Batjac/United Artists, 1960, 192 minutes)
Directed and produced by John Wayne; Written by James Edward Grant; Music by Dmitri Tiomkin
Cast
JOHN WAYNE (DAVID CROCKETT), Richard Widmark (Jim Bowie), Laurence Harvey (William Travis), Frankie Avalon (Smitty), Ruben Padilla (Santa Anna), Chill Wills (Beekeeper)
Rating: ****1/2
Available on Videocassette
Awards: Academy Award for Best Sound; nominations for Best Picture, Supporting Actor (Chill Wills), Cinematography, Editing and Score

TELEVISION
"Davy Crockett" (ABC miniseries,1954-55)
Cast
FESS PARKER (DAVY CROCKETT), Buddy Ebsen (Georgie Russell)
Rating: ***1/2
Available on Videocassette
Awards: 1955 Emmy nomination for Best Single Program

"The Alamo: 13 Days to Glory" (CBS miniseries,1987,180 minutes)
Directed by Burt Kennedy; Written by Clyde Ware and Norman McLeod Morrill, based on the book *Thirteen Days To Glory; The Siege of the Alamo* by Lou Tinkle; Produced by Briggle, Hennessy and Carrothers Productions and the Finnegan Company; Music by Peter Bernstein
Cast
BRIAN KEITH (DAVY CROCKETT), James Arness (Jim Bowie), Alec Baldwin (William Travis), Raul Julia (Santa Anna), Lorne Greene (Sam Houston), David Ogden Stiers (Col. Black)
Rating: ***1/2

DIRTY HARRY

It's easy to understand the popularity of the Dirty Harry movies, especially if you've ever been mugged or had your car stolen. In the moments right after your rights have been violated by some low-life thug, even the most liberal among us would love to see the bastard fry. That same feeling of outrage surfaces when we read about a confessed killer who avoids punishment with a slick legal maneuver. The bloodlust subsides in most of us given time, but what fun it still is to go to the movies and watch San Francisco Police Inspector Harry Callahan serve up fitting punishments on the spot.

Harry's system of justice offers no appeals, no loopholes, no insanity pleas. He respects the law as it exists, but has no problem superseding it under certain circumstances. Harry blows away bank robbers by the dozen, for instance, but covers for multiple murderer Jennifer Spencer in *Sudden Impact* because her targets, by Harry's law, deserved their fate.

It was actually *Dirty Harry* and not *Death Wish* that gave birth to the urban vigilante film genre. Technically, anyone who carries a badge is not a vigilante, but since Harry spends most of his time on suspension the badge doesn't make much difference. Trace the genre's lineage back another step and you'll find the Western, in which every dispute was settled with a gun. Harry Callahan's great-grandfather could have been the "Man With No Name" also played by Clint Eastwood in a series of Sergio Leone Westerns. The vigilante film blossomed more fully in the Reagan-Bush years, and turned martial arts masters such as Jean Claude Van Damme and Steven Seagal into bankable stars.

Harry Callahan first appeared on the nation's screens back in 1971, which in retrospect makes perfect sense. Vietnam had already slammed the lid on the peace-love-flower-power feeling of the sixties, giving way to a wave of cynicism that extended to all aspects of society. Harry was a product of this cynicism. He saw the ugliness of the world and tried to eliminate as much as he could on his own. Ironically, at a time when the police were still considered the enemy by a significant number of people, *Dirty Harry* (a huge hit) helped reverse the negative image of law enforcement. Although Harry was exactly the kind of cop that liberals most maligned, he was embraced by such left-wing publications as *Rolling Stone*. I guess there's something to be said for a man with integrity, no matter what his politics.

Like *Star Wars*, *Rocky* and other film series with widespread appeal, it is often easy to overlook the talent and skill that went into the Dirty Harry films, and that separates them from their many imitators. Let's face it, if killing bad guys were the only prerequisite for success, Wings Hauser would be a household name. Two differences quickly emerge--Clint Eastwood, of course, and director Don Siegel, who launched the series with a textbook course on how to shoot an action-suspense film.

Harry Callahan was Clint Eastwood's breakthrough role. Both Frank Sinatra and John Wayne turned it down, though Wayne may have thought twice after the film's blockbuster success. He made the Harry-esque *McQ* in 1974, which fizzled without the benefits of Siegel's direction. Sinatra, I think, might have pulled it off superbly, but at age fifty-six his sequel-making days would have been numbered. Eastwood, after distinguishing himself as a spaghetti cowboy, rode the film to mainstream superstardom, and would return to the Dirty Harry well periodically to maintain that status while working on projects that were closer to his heart.

Which should not suggest that he regards Harry as a throwaway. What Eastwood can get out of screen presence alone is formidable, but he has yet to compromise the character with a less-than-polished performance. Indeed, when the series slips with efforts like *The Enforcer*, Eastwood makes all the difference.

Dirty Harry borrows from actual events with its story of a killer called Scorpio, who demands $100,000 from the city of San Francisco to put down his rifle. Inspector Callahan and his new partner Chico Gonzales are assigned the case but turn up few leads. The mayor agrees to the ransom, and Harry is chosen to make the payment. He manages to apprehend the obviously deranged killer, but because he uses excessive force in the arrest Scorpio is released. Later, Scorpio has himself beaten up on purpose, and frames Harry for the assault.

Renewing his crime spree, Scorpio hijacks a school bus full of children and raises his price for their safe return. This time Harry decides to waive the killer's Miranda rights and end Scorpio's threat permanently. That accomplished, he tosses his badge into the San Francisco Bay.

Having already attained the rank of Inspector, Harry Callahan was hardly a rookie cop in his first film appearance, but his character in *Dirty Harry* does undergo a transformation from begrudged respect to a total disregard for the system. The series's most famous, oft-misquoted scene is here, the "Feel lucky?" speech, and by itself it tells you quite a bit about Harry. But other scenes provide even better insight.

When Harry confronts a potential suicide, he feigns indifference to the troubled man's plight, but it's just a tactic. He really does care about helping the man and others like him--this as much as courage and marksmanship make him a good cop, and a hero. But other demons drive Harry Callahan, and they are hinted at when Harry reveals that his wife was killed by a drunk driver. This plot thread is never further explored, but clearly he has never recovered from the loss.

Like the cop in 1990's *Short Time*, who repeatedly hurls himself into dangerous situations, believing that a terminal illness will soon take his life anyway, Harry Callahan walks boldly into one shooting gallery after another. After surviving each one, he walks out and never looks back. Does he have a death wish? Part of him certainly died with his wife. Harry sleeps with three women in the five films, but none of the relationships have any real emotional depth. Dead inside already, Harry may just be waiting for someone else to finish the job. Problem is, he's too good at his work for that to happen.

Harry cares about being a cop only because it gives him license to do legally what he would be compelled to do anyway--take criminals off the streets. But after Scorpio is let go, Harry is disgusted. When his partner's wife asks why he stays on the force, Harry says "I don't know... I really don't know." His repugnance culminates when he chucks his badge both literally and figuratively.

Had the story ended here, it would not be surprising to imagine Harry becoming another Paul Kersey, the vigilante in *Death Wish*. But such departures are not fit for sequels, so it is once again Inspector Callahan who returns with badge in *Magnum Force* (1973)

Criminals, from top-echelon mobsters to street pimps, are turning up dead. Harry suspects a traffic cop is pulling the trigger, because of the weapon type and the point-blank range of the shootings. It turns out to be three rookie cops who follow their own system of justice. Harry reports his findings to his superior, Lieutenant Briggs, only to find out that Briggs has sanctioned the officers' actions from the start. They turn on Harry when he learns their secret, but Harry knocks them off, one at a time.

Magnum Force is a step back for both Harry and the series. Its awkward attempt to backpedal away from the position of the first film is unconvincing, and undermines what Eastwood and Siegel accomplished two years earlier. Criticism of *Dirty Harry* as "fascist" was acknowledged, leading Harry to explain his position on the law more clearly; "I hate the system," he tells the three rookie cops who are killing every crook in sight, "but until [something better comes along], I'll stick with it." Harry telling these cops to tow the line is like Hannibal Lecter advocating the benefits of the four basic food groups.

There are other problems. The film is too long and the violence, turned up a notch over the first film, lacks the style and intensity injected by Don Siegel. Harry's partner Early Smith is not a fully fleshed-out character, so his death is not as meaningful as it should be. It's also no surprise--when Harry tells Early to "take care of yourself," you know he's a goner.

But there are compensations. The cast is packed with familiar faces (David Soul, Robert Urich, Tim Matheson, Hal Holbrook, Mitchell Ryan and a topless Suzanne Somers), and Clint Eastwood's star power is almost blinding. The opening credits sequence, a long close-up of the .44 magnum, "the most powerful handgun in the world," certainly sets the right mood, and San Francisco, the most beautiful city in the United States, is an unbeatable backdrop.

The Enforcer (1976) continued Harry's slide, but the series's low point is still watchable for its stars and scenery. The film opens with Callahan single-handedly foiling a hostage situation at a liquor store, and then being transferred to Personnel for using "excessive force." A terrorist group called the People's Revolutionary Strike Force steals a cache of explosives and murders Harry's partner. The police arrest the wrong group, and when Harry protests he is put on suspension. The cops realize their mistake when the mayor is kidnapped. Harry and his new partner, rookie inspector Kate Moore, trace the Strike Force to their Alcatraz hideout and rescue the mayor, but Moore is killed by one of the terrorists.

It's interesting to see a pre-"Cagney and Lacey" Tyne Daly play a less-than-seasoned officer, and it's the relationship between Harry and Kate that keeps the film afloat. Unlike Early's murder in *Magnum Force*, Kate's death is shocking and sad. It stands out even more because everyone else in the movie is less a character than a type--the mayor and police officials, for instance, are portrayed en masse as dimwits.

Sudden Impact (1983) is a strong return to form after a seven-year layoff, and the best written and directed (by Eastwood) entry since *Dirty Harry*. Still dirty, Inspector Callahan intimidates a mob boss into a heart attack and becomes a marked man. While avoiding hit men he begins investigating a new case of a man found murdered in his car. As he will later discover, the killer is Jennifer Spencer, a woman who was gang-raped ten years ago. She is now on a mission of revenge.

Jennifer continues to stalk and murder her attackers. Eventually Harry begins to suspect Jennifer, but sleeps with her anyway. Mick, the last of the rapists to remain alive, turns the tables on Jennifer, but Harry intervenes. He kills Mick and frames him for all the previous murders, allowing Jennifer to escape.

Where the previous two films offered only basic stories that were buoyed by Eastwood, the script for *Sudden Impact* was able to reprise the best elements of earlier entries, further develop the character of Harry Callahan in a substantial way, and raise questions about the shades of gray in crime and punishment that had never been confronted this effectively in the series.

The opening is vintage Dirty Harry, with another great tag line ("Go ahead. Make my day.") and Harry besting a gunman with an icy stare. Next, a bleeding-heart liberal judge (and a woman--even worse!) lets a slimy criminal walk because Harry didn't have probable cause to search his car, and of course the Inspector can't believe it. Also unchanged from earlier films is Harry's inability to drive ten blocks in any direction without encountering a crime in progress. What's different is the increased use of humor, as in Harry's commandeering a retirement bus to pursue a robber, and the ongoing problems with his dog, Meathead. In between lighter moments this is an extremely vicious movie with a high body count and the most repugnant villain (Paul Drake) in the series.

Usually a man of few words, Harry is a regular chatterbox this time. Eastwood had more lines to memorize in the first half-hour of *Sudden Impact* than for the previous two films combined. Another departure is Harry's becoming the pursued instead of the pursuer, a simple dynamic change that is explored well by Eastwood the director. The film's only drawbacks are its running time and a comatose performance from Sondra Locke. The blank expression that rarely leaves her face hardly communicates the hunger for vengeance that drives her character.

The Dead Pool (1988), the most recent Dirty Harry film, was widely perceived as the bargaining chip that allowed Eastwood to make *Bird*, the film biography of jazz great Charlie Parker. In fact, from *The Enforcer* on it is possible that Eastwood revives Harry only to keep the studio bean counters happy while he explores other subjects as both star and director. *Bronco Billy* (1980), *Bird* (1988), and *White Hunter, Black Heart* (1990) all received excellent reviews but flopped at the box office. Conversely, films such as *The Gauntlet* (1977), *Tightrope* (1984) and *The Rookie* (1990) were more successful, but Eastwood played a tough cop in each one. Clearly, a certain segment of the public is only interested in Eastwood when he carries a gun.

Once again Harry is paired with a new partner. A rock star is killed, and his murder is tied to a twisted game called The Dead Pool, in which the names of prominent people are placed on lists, and wagers taken on which ones will be first to die. Harry, now a celebrity himself after busting a mob kingpin, learns that his name is on the list. The director of the horror film from which the game first emerged is the chief suspect, but the killer turns out to be a psychotic fan of the director, whom Harry dispatches with a harpoon. And you thought the .44 Magnum was powerful.

By this time, knock-offs and parodies of Dirty Harry were everywhere, and Eastwood himself had even satirized his persona in the 1984 comedy *City Heat.* Unfortunately, *The Dead Pool* seems more like one of the imitators than the real thing. After the improvement of *Sudden Impact*, it's back to the old formula; the plot is simple, with an obvious red herring suspect and a real killer whom we never get to know and despise, as we do in previous films. There are jokes about the lifespan of Harry's partners (though this one survives), an unconvincing romantic subplot and some rather tired debates about freedom of the press.

Eastwood remains credible, but we gain no new insights into Harry except that he does not like being asked for an autograph. Watching Harry's discomfort in the limelight, we may actually be learning more about the actor than the character. There's a clever *Bullitt* parody using a remote-control car, Liam Neeson has some nice moments as the framed director, and watching Harry waste a few more felons is invariably a pleasure. Somehow, it's enough. Interesting that a Guns & Roses song is used in the film, when Janis Joplin was topping the charts when *Dirty Harry* opened. How time does fly.

It's been more than five years since *The Dead Pool* and hopefully about time for another case from the files of Inspector Callahan. It will no doubt be an audience-pleaser, but whether Eastwood will settle for just that or also add another dimension to the role remains to be seen.

THE FILMS

Dirty Harry (Warner Bros., 1971, 102 minutes)
Directed and produced by Don Siegel; Written by Harry Julian Fink, Rita M. Fink and Dean Riesner, based on a story by Fink and Fink; Music by Lalo Schifrin
Cast
CLINT EASTWOOD (HARRY CALLAHAN), Reni Santoni (Chico), Harry Guardino (Bressler), Andy Robinson (Scorpio)
Rating: *****
Available on Videocassette

Magnum Force (Warner Bros., 1973, 122 minutes)
Directed by Ted Post; Written by John Milius and Michael Cimino, based on a story by Cimino; Produced by Robert Daley; Music by Lalo Schifrin
Cast
CLINT EASTWOOD (HARRY CALLAHAN), Hal Holbrook (Lt. Briggs), Felton Perry (Early Smith), Mitchell Ryan (Charlie McCoy), David Soul (Davis), Tim Matheson (Sweet), Robert Urich (Grimes)
Rating: ***
Available on Videocassette

The Enforcer (Warner Bros., 1976, 96 minutes)
Directed by James Fargo; Written by Stirling Silliphant and Dean Reisner; Produced by Robert Daley; Music by Jerry Fielding
Cast
CLINT EASTWOOD (HARRY CALLAHAN), Tyne Daly (Kate Moore), Bradford Dillman (Captain McKay), Harry Guardino (Lt. Bressler)
Rating: **1/2
Available on Videocassette

Sudden Impact (Warner Bros., 1983, 117 minutes)
Directed and produced by Clint Eastwood; Written by Joseph C. Stinson, based on a story by Earl E. Smith and Charles B. Pierce; Music by Lalo Schifrin
Cast

CLINT EASTWOOD (HARRY CALLAHAN), Sondra Locke (Jennifer Spencer), Pat Hingle (Chief Jannings), Bradford Dillman (Captain Briggs)
Rating: ***1/2
Available on Videocassette

The Dead Pool (Warner Bros., 1988, 91 minutes)
Directed by Buddy Van Horn; Written by Steve Sharon, based on a story by Sharon, Durk Pearson and Sandy Shaw; Produced by David Valdes; Music by Lalo Schifrin
Cast
CLINT EASTWOOD (HARRY CALLAHAN), Patricia Clarkson (Samantha Walker), Evan C. Kim (Al Quan), Liam Neeson (Peter Swan)
Rating: ***
Available on Videocassette

WYATT EARP

"When legend becomes fact, print the legend," said director John Ford, who made a career out of following his own advice in dozens of classic Western films. Ford's words have been the unofficial credo of Western writers, filmmakers and even so-called historians, who unapologetically resorted to printing the legend when the facts turned out to be rather dull. There has perhaps been no other era in the history of the planet in which so much has been made of so little.

Case in point: Wyatt Earp. He was a lawman in the legendary towns of Tombstone and Dodge City, but he was a lot of other things as well. The gunfight at the O.K. Corral was a historical event, but no two versions of the event are the same. Unlike Doc Holliday, Wild Bill Hickok, Billy the Kid and so many others, Earp did not die with the Old West. He lived long enough to make a major contribution to his own myth, embellishing his experiences in dozens of newspaper articles and, with the advent of motion pictures, in interviews with such media pioneers as William S. Hart and the aforementioned John Ford.

Ford's own Wyatt Earp movie, *My Darling Clementine*, supposedly depicted events exactly as they were related from Earp to Ford. So why is Wyatt's brother Virgil killed before the gunfight at the O.K. Corral began, when in reality he was only wounded during the actual shootout? Doc Holliday is killed during the fight in *Clementine*, but he actually lived another six years, finally succumbing to tuberculosis in a Colorado sanitarium. Old Man Clanton, who orchestrates the confrontation in the film, was not at the real O.K. Corral. The McLowery Brothers, who were principal players in the event, do not appear in the movie.

Stuart Lake's book *Wyatt Earp, Frontier Marshal* was also based on conversations between subject and author, but is now considered to be one of the most inaccurate biographies ever published. It's a great read, though, and not surprisingly is also the source material most frequently used by Hollywood. Lake's book is listed as such in the credits for both *My Darling Clementine* and *Frontier Marshal* with Randolph Scott. Another Lake story was used for *Winchester '73*, in which Wyatt Earp plays a supporting role.

More than a dozen other books exist but there is a question as to whether any of them tell the full, factual story. Many follow Lake's example and depict Earp as a courageous force for justice in a lawless era. Others seem determined to overcompensate by painting Earp as a pimp, horse thief and con artist who used his badge to further his criminal ambitions. Frank Waters's book *The Earp Brothers of Tombstone* is a perfect example; you can almost see the chip on the shoulders of its author and his sources as they delightfully dismantle the Earp family's character with venomous prose.

To understand why such feelings existed, one must examine the animosity between the Western ranchers, who provided Waters with some of his information, and those who arrived in town from the East and Midwest, as did the Earps. The situation is analyzed in the introduction of one of the best Earp books, *The Earps Talk* by Alford E. Turner. Turner, possibly the foremost authority on the family, reconstructs principal events in Earp's life through original newspaper accounts, hundreds of documents still on file at the Chochise County Courthouse, and interviews with Earp conducted before his imagination kicked into overdrive. Cognizant of all the discrepancies and inconsistencies, Turner filters out as much bogus information as possible. What is left is a portrait of a man that was neither superhero nor scoundrel, undeserving of the reputation he has but worth remembering on his own merits.

Wyatt Earp was born in Monmouth, Illinois, on March 19, 1848. He had four brothers, Jim, Warren, Morgan and Virgil, all of whom wore the blue uniform in the Civil War. The family moved four times while Wyatt grew up, eventually settling on a farm in Missouri. When he was twenty-one, he married a woman who died months later from typhoid. The following year he took his first law- enforcement position as constable of Lamar County. In 1875 he joined the Wichita, Kansas police force and one year later he was hired as deputy city marshal of Dodge City. Here he met Doc Holliday and Bat Masterson and began to build a reputation as a tough and tempestuous lawman.

Between these episodes and during his time in Dodge there are numerous reports that Earp collected protection money from local businesses, stole horses from Indians, gambled excessively and spent many a night in the local brothel. If they are true, as they almost certainly are, one must make allowances for the prevailing of the time toward such activities.

Earp resigned his Dodge City post in 1879 and traveled through Texas and New Mexico. News of mining strikes in Tombstone, Arizona, prompted Earp's move to the city that he would later make famous. Brothers Jim, Morgan and Virgil joined Wyatt in Arizona, and together they organized the "Law and Order League." The roots of the legendary gunfight are in the League's confrontations with a band of cowboys, first led by Old Man Clanton and after his death by Curly Bill Brocius.

Brocius's forces included the McLowery Brothers, Frank and Tom, Old Man Clanton's sons and gunslinger John Ringo. Tensions between the cowboys and the Earps escalated for two years, until finally a showdown was inevitable. It happened on October 26, 1881. Wyatt, Virgil and Morgan Earp, accompanied by Doc Holliday, squared off against Billy and Joseph Isaac Clanton, the McLowery Brothers, William Claiborne and Wesley Fuller. When the fight was over, in less than a minute, Billy Clanton and the McLowerys were dead. Morgan and Virgil Earp were wounded. Exactly what happened is impossible to recount, since every survivor has offered a different version of the particulars.

The *Tombstone Epitaph* newspaper hailed the Earps as heroes, while the Tucson newspaper called them murderers. They stood trial but were acquitted (the trial transcript, reprinted in Alford Turner's book, may be the most accurate account of the gunfight available). However, the feud between the Earps and the cowboys did not end at the O.K. Corral. An attempt on Virgil Earp's life was made on December 28 of that year, and on March 18, 1882, Morgan Earp was killed by a gunshot in the back. One week later, Wyatt exacted his revenge by killing Curly Bill Brocius and his cohort Johnny Barnes.

Wyatt Earp's life after Tombstone was not very happy. His second wife Celia committed suicide in 1888, and his third wife Josephine was by all accounts a difficult woman. After Tombstone he drifted throughout the Southwest, taking various jobs both legitimate (saloon owner, fight referee) and otherwise (gambling, confidence games). He spent his final days in a Los Angeles bungalow near the intersection of Venice and Crenshaw boulevards, trying to interest writers and filmmakers in his story. He actually appeared in a few early silent films, most notably *The Half-Breed* (1915) with Douglas Fairbanks. He was a technical adviser on several William S. Hart Westerns, but could not convince Hart to play in his life story.

Finally, Earp met Stuart Lake, who agreed to write the Earp story as dictated by its source. Lake's book did everything Earp had hoped for, but sadly he did not live to experience the renewed fame and glory that followed. He died a year before its publication, on January 13, 1929, of prostate cancer.

Many books mistakenly list *Law and Order* (1932) as the first Wyatt Earp film, but star Walter Huston actually plays an Earp-like character in this Tombstone-based Western. *Frontier Marshal* (1939) was the genuine article, with Randolph Scott as Marshal Earp. The story has Earp taking the marshal's job in Tombstone after being roughed up by Curly Bill Brocius and his cowboys.

Frontier Marshal was first filmed in 1934, with the lead character called Michael Wyatt to avoid lawsuits with the estate of Earp or his biographers. This time Hollywood got permission and paid $5,000 for the rights, but were later sued anyway because of falsehoods in the story. There are lots of them--Doc Holliday (called Halliday here, and transformed from a dentist to an obstetrician!) is killed before the O.K. Corral shootout. Wyatt squares off alone against Curly Bill and his gang at the Corral, and no mention is made of the Clantons.

Because it also lists Stuart Lake's book as a source material, *My Darling Clementine* is considered a remake of *Frontier Marshal*, and certain scenes appear in both films. Among these are Wyatt's being offered the marshal's job after he subdues a drunk Indian, and his dumping of a saloon singer in a horse trough after she cheats in a card game. The Clementine character is called Sarah here, a nice girl from back East who loves Doc Holliday despite his faults.

It is interesting to compare to the two versions, for rarely has the difference between capable and transcendent filmmaking been so clearly defined. In *Clementine* John Ford improved upon everything achieved here by director Allan Dwan, who had directed the real Earp in *The Half-Breed*. Dwan does his best, but the result has nothing to distinguish itself from other formula Westerns of the period, and certainly none of the groundbreaking style and depth of its remake.

Randolph Scott, tall in the saddle as ever, gives his usual laconic performance, and is the first of many screen Earps to not wear his trademark moustache. Cesar Romero is equally laid-back and emotionless as Doc. The fine cast includes Binnie Barnes, John Carradine; Lon Chaney, Jr.; Ward Bond; who appears in both versions but in different roles; and Eddie Foy, Jr., who plays his own father.

Tombstone, the Town Too Tough to Die (1942) was based on a book by Walter Noble Burns, and is the very definition of an average "B" movie. Those partial to Westerns will like it a little more, others a little less. The title town is under siege by Curly Bill as the movie opens, and his activities go unchallenged by the ineffective sheriff and a corrupt judge. Wyatt Earp, the man who cleaned up Wichita, Abilene and Dodge City, now sets his sights on Tombstone. Curly Bill plants a spy in the Earp camp, but the guy soon comes to respect the lawman and changes sides. Bill then finds other allies in the Clantons and the McLowerys, and the gunfight at the O.K. Corral again closes the show.

Richard Dix, in his first role since the Oscar-winning *Cimarron* (1931) is a credible Wyatt Earp, but William Kent Taylor as Doc Halliday (sic) is disappointing. Edgar Buchanan plays Curly Bill, and he would also play the villain who opposes Earp in Wichita. Having the city itself serve as opening narrator is a cornball approach. The Burns book that inspired the movie is no more accurate than the Stuart Lake bio.

My Darling Clementine (1946) is lousy history as all Earp movies are, but by every other measurement it is beyond criticism. It's a classic Western, one of the best ever made certainly, and my choice for the best-looking black and white Western bar none. The film is even worth watching once with the sound off to better appreciate the chiaroscuro created by director John Ford and cinematographer Joseph P. MacDonald. Viewing the result, it makes it hard to complain about the inaccuracy of shooting in Monument Valley, which in no way resembles Tombstone.

The title provides the first clue to Ford's approach; he chose to stress the romance of Clementine and Wyatt, and the romantic triangle of Doc, Clementine and Chihauahua over the O.K. Corral confrontation. It is fitting then that the gunfight, though exciting, doesn't come close to being the most memorable scene. This is a kinder, gentler Old West than in most Ford films, and its the quieter moments that are most indelible--Doc Holliday reciting Shakespeare in the tavern; Wyatt leaning back in his chair, balancing himself against a post; the reactions to Wyatt's perfumed hair tonic; the dance at the church--all are etched in the memory.

The Earp brothers are driving cattle to California as the film opens, and stop in Tombstone for a rest. Wyatt's reputation as ex-marshal of Dodge City precedes him, and he is offered the same position in Tombstone, which he turns down. Until his cattle are stolen and his brother James is murdered. He suspects the Clanton family in both crimes. Clementine Carter, an old flame of Doc Holliday's, arrives in Tombstone, but Doc encourages her to head back East. Wyatt, who is attracted to Clementine, hopes she decides to stay. The Earps get the evidence they need against the Clantons, though Morgan Earp pays for it with his life. All scores are settled at the O.K. Corral.

As played by Henry Fonda, Wyatt Earp is a blissfully simple, honest, straightforward man who approaches law enforcement the same way he approaches cattle driving--as a job that deserves to be done right if it's to be done at all. He is soft-spoken and insecure with women, but possessed of the quiet courage that commands respect, as seen in his first meeting with Doc Holliday. Victor Mature is surprisingly restrained and eloquent as Holliday, and Walter Brennan is perfect as the evil incarnate Old Man Clanton. Linda Darnell is a vast improvement over *Frontier Marshal*'s Nancy Kelly as the dance-hall girl in love with Doc.

Wyatt Earp is a minor character in *Winchester '73* (1950), an early Anthony Mann Western also taken from a Stuart Lake story. The title firearm, "the gun that won the west," is offered to the winner of an open shooting contest in Dodge City. Lin McAdam wins the rifle, which is promptly stolen from him by old enemy Dutch Henry Brown. The film then follows the rifle through various owners and encounters, until at last it is returned to Lin's rightful possession.

James Stewart plays Lin McAdam, and this episodic film stalls when he's not around. This was the first of several Westerns Stewart made with Anthony Mann, who is credited with reviving the genre in the fifties. *Winchester '73* doesn't hold up as a landmark today, but its relaxed, introspective tone was influential at the time, and the stellar cast is fun to watch. Shelley Winters is here, and Dan Duryea, and in tiny roles Tony Curtis and Rock Hudson (almost unrecognizable as an Indian). Will Geer, now best remembered as Grandpa Walton, plays a middle-aged, pot-bellied, Will Rogers–like Wyatt Earp, who checks everybody's guns as they enter Dodge City. This same episode provides much of the plot for the later Earp film *Wichita.*

Gun Belt (1953) is a very minor fifties Western in which James Milican appears as Wyatt Earp in a few nondescript scenes. The story centers on Billy Ringo, who goes straight and becomes a rancher. But when his brother Chip robs a bank and frames Billy, he must strap on the guns again to prove his innocence. You could kill seventy-seven minutes in worse ways, but not for nothing did *The New York Times* review save its highest praise for the horses, noting that they "move with sure, easy confidence." The implication is that the actors don't, which is mostly accurate. Stars George Montgomery and John Dehner are in so many of these routine oaters that they become interchangeable. Tab Hunter plays the bad guy with the memorable name of Chip Ringo.

The first of several unrelated all-star Western team-ups involving Wyatt Earp was 1954's *Masterson of Kansas.* As the title suggests the focus is on Bat Masterson, played here by the above-mentioned George Montgomery, but Earp is here along with Doc Holliday. Together they uncover a plot to renew hostilities by negating a deal that would turn over large amounts of land to the Indians. Chief Yellow Hawk falls for the subterfuge and is ready for war, but Masterson and company set things right. Producer Sam Katzman and director William Castle were masters of the low-budget quickie, and could make a bland but O.K. movie like this every month. James Griffith nicely essays Doc Holliday, but Bruce Cowling's Earp could be any Western lawman.

Wyatt Earp is the featured character in *Wichita* (1955). Once again he hits town with plans that have nothing to do with law enforcement, but ends up taking the badge after witnessing some grievous injustice. This time it's a gang of cowboys who periodically shoot up the city for fun. After a small boy is killed during one of their visits, Wyatt and deputy Bat Masterson outlaw the wearing of guns in Wichita. The townspeople are uncertain about such a drastic step, but come around after more innocent blood is spilled.

The killing of a child, oddly enough named Michael Jackson, is a sobering moment not often seen in movies like this. It is one of many more realistic touches, including Earp getting flak for outlawing guns. The town would rather have the cowboys and the money they spend than safe streets. Jacques Tourneur's always-strong direction is helped here by a better script than he usually saw. Writer Daniel Ullman has a good ear for prairie dialogue, and throws in a few interesting twists that play with the expected formula. For what it's worth, Stuart Lake served as technical adviser.

Joel McCrea as Wyatt Earp leads a cast experienced in delivering the goods. McCrea's portrayal of a brave, honest marshal who is formidable in a showdown but awkward in romance is very similar to Henry Fonda's in *My Darling Clementine.* Like Tourneur, McCrea was often the victim of bad material, and when he got a good part he could act Randolph Scott under the table. Peter Graves has a memorable supporting turn as Morgan Earp, and Edgar Buchanan, long before he started movin' kinda slow at the Junction, plays nasty Doc Black, who led the opposition to Earp's hiring.

Gunfight at the O.K. Corral (1957) is the second outright classic based on the Earp legends. The ratio of fact to fiction is about the same as in *Clementine*, and the film is nearly as much fun. Most of the action takes place in Dodge City, where Marshal Earp falls for lovely lady gambler Laura Denbow and begins his uneasy alliancc with Doc Holliday. Hc plans to turn in his badge and marry Laura, but a distress call from brother Virgil in Tombstone breaks the engagement and sets the stage for the familiar finale.

Burt Lancaster plays Wyatt Earp and Kirk Douglas plays Doc Holliday, and that's almost all you need to know. This is the best of their many collaborations, though I can't help thinking that the film would have been even better had they exchanged roles; Douglas bears a stronger physical resemblance to the lean and wiry Earp, and Lancaster might have brilliantly essayed the cultured but cold-blooded Holliday. Rhonda Fleming, one of the best Western actresses, is terrific as Laura Denbow. Among the many familiar faces in the cast are Earl Holliman, Jack Elam, Lee Van Cleef and DeForrest Kelley, who plays a marshal, not a doctor.

Whereas *Clementine* painted the legend with the beauty and grace of epic poetry, director John Sturges gives *Gunfight at the O.K. Corral* a more down-to-earth treatment. His handling of the climactic gunfight is sensational. He also gives us (with writer Leon Uris) the best and most accurate depiction of the tempestuous, destructive relationship between Doc and Katie Elder, here called Kate Fisher. Jo Van Fleet plays Kate with a lot less whitewash than the script gave to Holliday.

Badman's Country (1958) is another team-up picture like *Masterson of Kansas*, but this time Wyatt is given much more screen time. The plot revolves around a plan by Butch Cassidy to rob a train outside of Abilene. Lawman Pat Garrett wants to lure Cassidy and his gang into town and ambush them there. Wyatt, Bat Masterson and Buffalo Bill are all in on the trap. Doc Holliday is also around, as is the Sundance Kid, played believe it or not by "Gilligan's Island"'s Russell Johnson. Perennial good guy Buster Crabbe plays Wyatt Earp, and his resemblance to the real Earp is closer than any actor who attempted the role. *Badman's Country* has everything a "B" western should--a fast pace, a not-too-deep storyline and lots of gunfights. As he did playing Flash Gordon and Buck Rogers, Crabbe's enthusiasm compensates for a lack of technique.

The actor who may be most identified with Wyatt Earp is Hugh O'Brien, as a result of his playing the character for six years on the television series "The Life and Legend of Wyatt Earp." The series is in many ways not unlike the hundred other Western shows that were on at the same time, except that the story continued throughout the run. Wyatt became a marshal in Kansas in the premiere, and in the ensuing years moved on to Dodge City. In the final year, Earp arrived in Tombstone and fought at the O.K. Corral, in a five-episode saga that concluded the series.

If we eliminate the usual criticisms regarding physical resemblance and historical accuracy, O'Brien is very good as the marshal, and the rotating supporting cast kept the series fresh throughout its run. Wyatt's brothers turned up occasionally, as did Doc Holliday, Bat Masterson, and in the Tombstone years all of the principals at the O.K. Corral.

O'Brien reprised the role in *Alias Jesse James* (1959), a Western spoof starring Bob Hope. Hope struck gold in this genre earlier with *Son of Paleface* (1952), but doesn't hit the mark this time. He plays Milford Farnsworth, an insurance agent who takes out a policy on Jesse James. The famous outlaw then lures Milford west and convinces the citizenry that he is actually Jesse James, so that when he is killed the real Jesse can collect on his own insurance policy.

The film is nothing to get excited about until the finale, when O'Brien, Roy

Rogers, Gene Autry, Gary Cooper, James Arness (as Matt Dillon), Fess Parker (as Davy Crockett), James Garner (as Maverick) and Jay Silverheels (as Tonto) all ride in to rescue Milford. It's a once-in-a-lifetime alliance that becomes more precious as time goes by.

In 1964 John Ford made his last business trip to Monument Valley for *Cheyenne Autumn*. The film almost qualifies as a landmark simply for being the final Western from the director who dominated the genre, but its pro-Indian stance is equally memorable. Ford is doing his penance here for *Stagecoach* (1939) and others, but this apology to Native Americans is too long and often falls into heavy-handed sentiment and self-righteousness. Still, even when he tries too hard, Ford makes you care.

The Cheyenne Tribe, relegated to a barren reservation in Oklahoma, travels to the nearest cavalry fort for a meeting with a team of U.S. senators to discuss improving their living conditions. When the senators are a no-show, it is one broken promise too many for the proud Cheyenne, and they elect to leave without permission for a fifteen-hundred-mile trek back to their original settlement in Wyoming. The cavalry give chase, but Captain Thomas Archer is not enthusiastic about the assignment. The tribe overcomes several hardships along the way, including a severe winter that decimates its population. Washington is called in and, led by Interior Secretary Carl Schurz, they confront the Indians just as they reach their destination. Despite the objections of some constituents, Schurz reopens negotiations with the Cheyenne and allows them to remain in Wyoming.

The performances range from excellent (Richard Widmark as Captain Archer and Karl Malden as a sadistic fort commander) to awful (Caroll Baker as a schoolteacher who travels with the tribe, and the very hard sell of Ricardo Montalban as an Indian). Wyatt Earp, played by James Stewart, appears in a Dodge City episode that was originally cut from the film, but has been restored in most video versions. It's a wonderful scene that provides the only comic relief in the film's 150-minute running time, and is all the more welcome for it.

Stewart, dressed in a white-striped suit and panama hat (the only Earp besides Hugh O'Brien to dress Eastern, which was actually the case), gives us a marshal who is more interested in his poker game with Doc Holliday than the news of an impending Cheyenne attack. If he had two pair or better, the depiction is probably accurate. When the local cavalry and most of the menfolk ride out to kill Indians, Wyatt and Doc head off in the other direction. We are not told if their motivation is fear or altruism. Underneath the uproarious tone of the sequence is the realization that the men of Dodge approach an Indian hunt the same way they would a turkey shoot. But it was nice of Ford to remember his old buddy Wyatt in a relatively positive light eighteen years after *My Darling Clementine*.

Gunmen of the Rio Grande (1965) has Wyatt Earp disguising himself as a drifter named Laramie to aid saloonkeeper Madeline LeBeau, whose friend's silver mine is being threatened by the usual ne'er-do-wells. The film is a French-Spanish-Italian production, with Spain standing in for the southwest. *Gunmen* is not as moody and introspective as most European Westerns are given to be, nor is it as arresting. Veteran cowboy actor Guy Madison plays Earp, but his part-within-a-part masquerade as Laramie makes it tough to gauge his interpretation of the marshal.

Big change of tone now to *The Outlaws is Coming*, released the same year. The Three Stooges, in their last film appearance, play agents for the Society for the Preservation of Wildlife. They are sent to Wyoming to protect the buffalo herds, but run afoul of a gang that wants to wipe the buffalo out and blame it on the Indians, which gives them an excuse to start a war. And that's more plot synopsis than you want or need with a Stooges film. Bill Camfield makes a brief appearance as Wyatt Earp, one of many Western legends that turn up as straight men.

Ten years after *Gunfight at the O.K. Corral*, director John Sturges returned to Tombstone for *Hour of the Gun* (1967), an excellent, underrated and underseen film. Based on Douglas Martin's book *Tombstone Epitaphs*, this is the only movie to deal Wyatt Earp's life after the O.K. Corral. "This picture is based on fact. This is how it happened," we are told at the beginning, and for the first half-hour at least this is true. The famed gunfight opens the film, and lasts about as long as the real thing. The trial of the Earps follows, and then the movie takes a left turn into fiction. Some actual events are mixed in, such as the murder of Morgan Earp and Wyatt's killing of Curly Bill, but the second half plot of Wyatt and Doc setting out on a mission of personal revenge is all Hollywood.

"Maverick" gave James Garner solid Western credentials, but his Wyatt Earp is far removed from the charming con man he played on television. In fact, his interpretation of the marshal as a stoic, complex, intimidating hero is quite a departure from his affable persona. There's good camaraderie between Garner and Jason Robards as Doc Holliday, and Robert Ryan is the most memorable Earp adversary since Walter Brennan in *My Darling Clementine*. The cynical script, Sturges's direction and Lucien Ballard's cinematography envision an Old West without romance. Most late sixties Westerns follow the same approach--the films of Sergio Leone, for example, or *The Wild Bunch* (1969). *Hour of the Gun* is not quite that good, but it's close.

It is also a darn sight better than the other "revisionist" treatment, 1971's *Doc*. Once again the movie's pretense was the facts behind the legends, but as good as the idea is to demythologize the Earps, that's how bad the film turned out. It's confused, ponderous storyline substitutes one set of false truths for another, including the suggestion of a sexual relationship between Wyatt and Doc Holliday. The climax has our heroes murdering the Clantons despite their willingness to end the feud amicably.

Doc aspires to the intellectual Western approach that Anthony Mann achieved with ease, but its repellent characters and hypocritical claims of setting the record straight do not wash. Harris Yulin plays Wyatt Earp, Stacy Keach plays Holliday. Only Faye Dunaway as Katie Elder brings some humanity to her role. The film appropriately lost the battle for the anti-establishment box office dollar to *Billy Jack*, which was released at the same time. For all its flaws *Billy Jack* was at least sincere in its vision; *Doc* seems to corrupt history only for fun and profit.

James Garner would play Earp again in *Sunset* (1988), but the less said the better. Though its the only film to depict Earp accurately in the Hollywood of the 1920s, its fanciful story of the real Wild West hero teaming with cowboy star Tom Mix (Bruce Willis) to solve a seedy Tinseltown murder is poorly executed by writer-director Blake Edwards.

Two Wyatt Earp TV movies restored the marshal's heroic image, if not always his dignity. "I Married Wyatt Earp" was made in 1981 but not broadcast until 1983, which is never a good sign. The film was based on a book by Earp's third wife Josephine, which is only slightly more reliable than the Stuart Lake bio, and was designed as a vehicle for Marie Osmond, who stars as Josephine. Bruce Boxleitner plays Wyatt Earp. And from 1992, "Four Eyes and Six Guns" is an engaging comedy starring Judge Reinhold as Eastern optometrist Ernest Albright, who dreams of moving to Tombstone and meeting his hero Wyatt Earp. Eventually he does so, but finds the famous Western town and its legendary lawman to be less then he expected.

The Doom Brothers, ten red-headed troublemakers, have not been confronted by Earp because the marshal's vision has deteriorated since the O.K. Corral. Optometrist Albright diagnoses the problem, but Earp refuses to wear a "sissy" pair of glasses. Though the movie does degenerate into silliness at times, it does make the point about how the reality of the Old West was never what East Coasters read about in sagebrush novels. Reinhold is very good as the doctor who can shoot with deadly accuracy but cannot draw to save his life, and as Wyatt Earp, who has the opposite problem, Fred Ward comes very close to the historical marshal by playing down the middle. Ward's Earp is an admirable lawman but is not perfect; his pride outstrips his ability, he drinks too much and gambles too much and cares more about his reputation than his life. That's pretty heavy stuff for a family-hour Western in which the hero would rather embarrass the villain by shooting his hat off than shooting to kill.

After the success of Clint Eastwood's *Unforgiven* (1992), the Western revival fallout has returned Marshal Earp to the screen in *Tombstone* (1993), starring Kurt Russell as Earp and Val Kilmer as Doc Holliday. In the summer of 1994, Kevin Costner portrays the marshal in another retelling of the legend.

THE FILMS

Frontier Marshal (20th Century Fox, 1939, 71 minutes)
Directed by Allan Dwan; Written by Sam Hellman, based on the book by Stuart Lake; Produced by Sol M. Wurtzel; Music by Samuel Kaylin
Cast
RANDOLPH SCOTT (WYATT EARP), Nancy Kelly (Sarah Allen), Cesar Romero (Doc Holliday), Binnie Barnes (Jerry), John Carradine (Ben Carter), Eddie Foy, Jr. (Eddie Foy), Ward Bond (Town Marshal), Lon Chaney, Jr. (Pringle)
Rating: **

Tombstone, the Town Too Tough to Die (Paramount, 1942, 79 minutes)
Directed by William McGann; Written by Albert Shelby LeVino and Edward E. Paramore, based on the book by Walter Noble Burns; Produced by Harry Sherman;
Cast
RICHARD DIX (WYATT EARP), Kent Taylor (Doc Holliday), Edgar Buchanan (Cury Bill Brocius)
Rating: **1/2
Available on Videocassette

My Darling Clementine (20th Century Fox, 1946, 97 minutes)
Directed by John Ford; Written by Samuel G. Engel and Winston Miller, based on a story by Sam Hellman from the novel by Stuart Lake; Produced by Samuel G. Engel; Music by Cyril J. Mockridge
Cast
HENRY FONDA (WYATT EARP), Linda Darnell (Chihauahua), Victor Mature (Doc Holliday), Walter Brennan (Old Man Clanton), Tim Holt (Virgil Earp), Cathy Downs (Clementine), Ward Bond (Morgan Earp)
Rating: *****
Available on Videocassette

Winchester '73 (Universal, 1950, 92 minutes)
Directed by Anthony Mann; Written by Robert L. Richards and Borden Chase, based on the story by Stuart Lake; Produced by Aaron Rosenberg; Music by Joseph Gershenson
Cast
James Stewart (Lin McAdam), Shelley Winters (Lola Manners), Dan Duryea (Waco Johnny Dean), Stephen McNally (Dutch Henry Brown), WILL GEER (WYATT EARP), Rock Hudson (Young Bull), Tony Curtis (Doan)
Rating: ***1/2
Available on Videocassette

Gun Belt (Global/United Artists, 1953, 77 minutes)
Directed by Ray Nazarro; Written by Richard Schayer and Jack DeWitt, based on a story by Arthur Orloff; Produced by Edward Small; Music by Irving Gertz
Cast
George Montgomery (Billy Ringo), Tab Hunter (Chip Ringo), John Dehner (Matt Ringo), William Bishop (Ike Clanton), JAMES MILLICAN (WYATT EARP)
Rating: **

Masterson of Kansas (Columbia, 1954, 72 minutes)
Directed by William Castle; Written by Douglas Heyes; Produced by Sam Katzman
Cast
George Montgomery (Bat Masterson), Nancy Gates (Amy Merrick), James Griffith (Doc Holliday), BRUCE COWLING (WYATT EARP)
Rating: **1/2

Wichita (Allied Artists, 1955, 81 minutes)
Directed by Jacques Tourneur; Written by Daniel Ullman; Produced by Walter Mirisch and Richard Heermance; Music by Hans Salter and Ned Washington
Cast
JOEL MCCREA (WYATT EARP), Vera Miles (Laurie), Lloyd Bridges (Gyp), Edgar Buchanan (Doc Black), Peter Graves (Morgan Earp)
Rating: ***
Available on Videocassette

Gunfight at the O.K. Corral (Paramount, 1957, 122 minutes)
Directed by John Sturges; Written by Leon Uris, based on a magazine article by George Scullin; Produced by Hal B. Wallis; Music by Dmitri Tiomkin and Ned Washington
Cast
BURT LANCASTER (WYATT EARP), Kirk Douglas (Doc Holliday), Rhonda Fleming (Laura Denbow), Jo Van Fleet (Kate Fisher), John Ireland (Johnny Ringo), Earl Holliman (Charles Bassett), Dennis Hopper (Billy Clanton), DeForrest Kelley (Morgan Earp)
Rating: ****
Available on Videocassette
Awards: Academy Award nominations for Best Sound and Film Editing

Badman's Country (Peerless/Warner Bros., 1958, 85 minutes)
Directed by Fred F. Sears; Written by Orville H. Hampton; Produced by Robert E.

Kent; Music by Irving Gertz and Robert Kent
Cast
George Montgomery (Pat Garrett), Neville Brand (Butch Cassidy), BUSTER CRABBE (WYATT EARP), Gregory Wolcott (Bat Masterson), Russell Johnson (Sundance)
Rating: ***

Alias Jesse James (Hope Enterprises/United Artists, 1959, 92 minutes)
Directed by Norman McLeod; Written by William Bowers and Daniel D. Beauchamp, based on a story by Robert St. Aubrey and Bert Lawrence; Produced by Jack Hope; Music by Joseph J. Lilley
Cast
Bob Hope (Milford Farnsworth), Rhonda Fleming (The Duchess), Wendell Corey (Jesse James), HUGH O'BRIEN (WYATT EARP)
Rating: ***1/2

Cheyenne Autumn (Warner Bros., 1964, 159 minutes)
Directed by John Ford; Written by James R. Webb, based on the novel by Mari Sandoz; Produced by Bernard Smith; Music by Alex North
Cast
Richard Widmark (Capt. Thomas Archer), Carroll Baker (Deborah Wright), Karl Malden (Capt. Oscar Wessels), JAMES STEWART (WYATT EARP), Edward G. Robinson (Carl Schurz), Ricardo Montalban (Little Wolf), Arthur Kennedy (Doc Holliday)
Rating: ***1/2
Available on Videocassette
Awards: Academy Award nomination for Best Cinematography

Gunmen of the Rio Grande (Llama-West-Flora-Pathe/Allied Artists, 1965, 86 minutes
Directed by Tulio Demicheli; Written by Gene Luotto, Giovanni Simonelli, Italo Zingarelli, Natividad Azro, Guy Lionel and Tulio Demicheli, based on a story by Chen Morrison; Produced by Italo Zingarelli; Music by Angelo Francesco Lavagnino
Cast
GUY MADISON (WYATT EARP), Madeline LeBeau (Jennie Lee)
Rating: *1/2

The Outlaws Is Coming (Columbia, 1965, 88 minutes)
Directed and produced by Norman Maurer; Written by Elwood Ullman, based on a story by Maurer; Music by Paul Dunlap
Cast
The Three Stooges (Themselves), Adam West (Kenneth Cabot), Nancy Kovack (Annie Oakley), BILL CAMFIELD (WYATT EARP)
Rating: **

Hour of the Gun (Mirisch-Kappa/United Artists, 1967, 101 minutes)
Directed and produced by John Sturges; Written by Edward Anhalt; Music by Jerry Goldsmith
Cast

JAMES GARNER (WYATT EARP), Jason Robards (Doc Holliday), Robert Ryan (Ike Clanton)
Rating: ***1/2

Doc (United Artists, 1971, 95 minutes)
Directed and produced by Frank Perry; Written by Pete Hamill; Music by Jimmy Webb
Cast
Stacy Keach (Doc Holliday), Faye Dunaway (Kate Elder), HARRIS YULIN (WYATT EARP), Mike Witney (Ike Clanton)
Rating: *

Sunset (Tri-Star, 1988, 107 minutes)
Directed and written by Blake Edwards; Produced by Tony Adams; Music by Henry Mancini and Duke Ellington
Cast
Bruce Willis (Tom Mix), JAMES GARNER (WYATT EARP), Malcolm McDowell (Alfie Alperin), Mariel Hemmingway (Cheryl King)
Rating: *
Available on Videocassette

TELEVISION

"The Life and Legend of Wyatt Earp" (series, ABC, 1955-1961)
Cast
HUGH O'BRIEN (WYATT EARP)
Rating: ***1/2
Awards: 1956 Emmy nomination for Best Actor (Hugh O'Brien)

"I Married Wyatt Earp" (movie, NBC, 1983, 100 minutes)
Directed by Michael O'Herlihy
Cast
BRUCE BOXLEITNER (WYATT EARP), Marie Osmond (Josephine Earp)

"Four Eyes and Six Guns" (movie, TNT, 1992, 92 minutes)
Directed by Piers Haggard; Written by Leon Prochnik; Produced by Salli Newman; Music by David Shire
Cast
Judge Reinhold (Ernest Albright), Patricia Clarkson (Lucy), FRED WARD (WYATT EARP)
Rating: ***1/2
Available on Videocassette

HENRY V

One has to wonder why the English feel a need to inflate the reputations of such shadowy figures as Robin Hood and King Arthur, when their national history is rich in genuine heroes whose exploits are well documented. It is possible, even probable, that both Robin and Arthur actually existed and may have accomplished some of the deeds attributed to them, but even their most devoted followers would have to acknowledge that many of the folk tales that they inspired have been, to say the least, exaggerated.

HISTORY

The facts concerning King Henry V are more accessible. By the time Henry acceded to the throne in 1413, the English monarchy had already been firmly established for nearly three hundred years. As a result, records from a variety of sources exist that identify the date of his birth (September 16, 1387), his succession, his three campaigns in France and his death from dysentery on August 31, 1422. Though he reigned only nine years, Henry is unrivaled among late medieval kings of England for both success and sheer ability.

Stories about Henry's reckless youth and his sudden maturity upon wearing the crown have been immortalized by William Shakespeare and substantiated by period historians. As king, Henry began to devote his boundless energy to renewing the Hundred Years War and reasserting claims to territory in France that he inherited from the Plantagenets. At Agincourt on October 25, 1415, Henry and thirty thousand English troops squared off against a French army sixty thousand strong. Thus began one of the most extraordinary and significant battles in the annals of military conflict.

The French numerical superiority was diminished by a scarcity of open ground, which Henry capitalized upon with guerrilla-style tactics. Eight thousand English archers rained arrows on the less mobile French, and after three hours of bloody fighting the French lost 6000 men and surrendered. English losses numbered less than six hundred.

This stunning victory restored England's continental empire, and Henry became the most powerful ruler in Europe. A second expedition in 1417--18 subdued Normandy and in 1420 the Treaty of Troyes assured the reversion of the French throne to England after the death of French King Charles VI. Henry also took Charles's daughter, Catherine of Valois, as his wife. However, Henry died before Charles after the siege of Meaux, and his heirs proved incapable of preserving the contract.

Stern, ruthless and intolerant of opposition, Henry's character flaws were overshadowed by his reputation as a chivalrous knight and a pious, well-educated monarch. Even French writers of the day hailed him as a brave, loyal and honorable fighter. Only a handful of leaders have ever been able to get that kind of press from a conquered people.

LITERATURE

Henry V is best remembered now from Shakespeare's plays *Henry IV, Pts. I and 2*, and *Henry V*. The Bard's primary sources, for these and all of his historical plays, were Edward Hall's *The Union of the Two Noble and Illustre Famelies of Lancastre and Yorke* (1542) and Raphael Holinshed's two-volume *Chronicles of England, Scotlande and Irelande* (1577). However, since Henry's accomplishments had already become the stuff of legend in Shakespeare's time, the playwright undoubtedly had a variety of chronicles, plays and juicy stories at his disposal. In fact, it was Tito Livio's biography *Vita Henrici Quinti* that first described Henry's wild youth. This account was later expanded and embellished until it became the Elizabethan version of the "prodigal son" story.

In *Henry IV*, the antics of Henry, then known as Prince Hal, are used as counterpoint to the serious dangers facing his father. While the prince cavorts with the errant knight Falstaff, King Henry IV prepares to do battle at Shrewsbury to consolidate his throne. When the king dies, Prince Hal vows to "pay the debt I never promised" by putting an end to his "loose behavior." He rejects the lifestyle of Falstaff and begins to emerge as the beloved warrior-king. Shakespeare made some adjustments in the ages and motives of his characters to heighten the drama, an accepted rite in historical fiction. Henry IV is depicted as old and fragile, when in reality he was only thirty-six when he emerged victorious at Shrewsbury and ten years older when he died. Prince Hal is portrayed as coeval of Hotspur, the son of the Earl of Northumberland. But Prince Hal was only sixteen at the time of Shrewsbury, and Hotspur was more than twice his age.

Henry V is not regarded by Shakespeare connoisseurs as one of his better works, which may explain why it's so popular among us common folk. Critics complain that watching Henry win all the time is not exactly suspenseful, and that Shakespeare did not puncture enough holes in the legend, which could easily have been accomplished by bringing back Falstaff.

These criticisms are, for the most part, justified. Henry's faults are not accentuated, though his ruthlessness is evident in Act II, scene ii in his diatribe against a band of conspirators. But when Henry is portrayed in his best light, as a leader and a motivator (his speech before Agincourt is one of the most rousing passages in the Shakespeare canon) we are willing to forgive him anything. The author, I guess, was content to celebrate with the rest of England the memory of a monarch who was able to unite his kingdom like no other ruler before.

As in *Henry IV*, Shakespeare again took liberties with certain facts and figures. In the play the Treaty of Troyes is negotiated immediately after Agincourt, and the casualty numbers from the battle are further exaggerated in favor of the English. In Shakespeare's version Henry loses only twenty-nine troops; the French lose ten thousand nobles and knights.

THE FILMS

The three most important film appearances of Henry V are all adaptations of Shakespeare, and thus share the play's strengths and inaccuracies. In each case the original text is followed with only minor variations: Shakespeare's play opens with

Henry being told by his advisers that he has a claim, albeit a flimsy one, to the French throne. As the decision to invade is debated a messenger is admitted bearing a gift from the brash Dauphin of France--a box of tennis balls. Henry's royal wrath is aroused, and preparations for war begin.

Henry and his troops lay siege to France, almost uncontested, for months, until finally the French assemble their best and brightest to turn back the exhausted and much smaller English force at Agincourt. It is Henry, however, who wins the day, and the country, and the French king's lovely daughter.

The first--and some still say definitive--film version came to life in England during the height of the German blitz. In 1944 Britain released Laurence Olivier from military service to portray Henry, the perfect historical figure to rally and inspire a country under siege. At a time of strife and shortages, mounting a lavish costume drama was an extremely difficult undertaking. But the project had a higher purpose, and somehow the sets and props were assembled. Looking at the film now you would never know that they were working on a shoestring.

The movie is framed with a play-within-a-play sequence set in the Globe Theater of the 1500s, where many of Shakespeare's works were debuted. To me the opening is awkward and undermines the necessary tension of the first scene, but I am clearly in the minority in this opinion.

There is a grandiose, theatrical air to the production; the cast members gesture and project as if they were actually in the Globe, and the colorful sets and costumes seem designed to be seen clearly in the third balcony. Considering the story behind the film, it's easier to understand why Olivier, who also directed (first choice William Wyler was unavailable) axed certain scenes from the play, such as Henry's discovery of traitors among his trusted aides. The depiction of threats from within did not send the right message.

Olivier does his best to put a *Mrs. Miniver* spin on the material, but there is still a certain world-weariness to his Henry, as if the king's crown wore as heavily as the director's cap must have felt at the time. Such insights only make the finished product more fascinating, and further justify the special Academy Award Olivier received for his achievement. Only regret: Olivier was unable to cast his wife, Vivien Leigh, as Catherine because she was still under contract to *Gone With the Wind* producer David O. Selznick. Although Renee Asherson was an able substitute, what a treat that would have been.

Comparisons were inevitable in 1989 when Kenneth Branagh directed and starred in his own *Henry V* at age twenty-eight, the same age as Olivier in 1944. Branagh cut down the original text of the play, hoping to make the material more accessible to a modern audience. However, this is hardly a Cliff's Notes version; not only does it contain the scenes that Olivier excised, there are also flashback scenes lifted from *Henry IV* depicting Prince Hal's rejection of Falstaff (Robbie Coltrane in a memorable cameo). As a result, Branagh's *Henry V* ends up being the most complete film adaptation yet, while still being streamlined enough to introduce Shakespeare to new generations.

For sheer bravado, Branagh's attempt to launch such a project merits comparison with Orson Welles's production of *Citizen Kane*. However, it is obvious from the opening scene that like Welles, Branagh had a clear vision of what he hoped to accomplish, and the ability to bring it to life in grand fashion, even with a minuscule $7.5 million budget. As an actor, Branagh commands the screen--his palpable outrage in the tennis ball scene immediately establishes his Henry as one not to be trifled with. The intensity of his wrath is apparent when the conspirators are discovered, and during the siege of Harfleur. The execution of Bardolph is far more emotional because of the *Henry IV* flashbacks, and the St. Crispin's Day speech, now a classic piece of cinema as well as theater, will give you chills.

War is dirtier here than in Olivier's version; the carnage and casualties depicted seem to support an antiwar stance, as opposed to the "fight the good fight" message needed in 1944. One could draw a parallel between Errol Flynn's Robin Hood and that of Kevin Costner. The Flynn-Olivier films are almost fairy tale like; the castle of Charles VI in the 1944 *Henry V* seems to sit upon the clouds. The battles are exciting but bloodless, like those staged in Elizabethan pageants--a lot of clanging and clashing, but no one gets hurt.

In the Branagh-Costner films, people get mud on their uniforms. Director Branagh uses more close-ups and mid-shots to capture the expressions of horror when the English troops return to find their camp servants slaughtered by the French. The victory is no less impressive, but the price seems higher. The film's more intimate direction also works toward a different purpose during Henry's wooing of Catherine, a lovely scene that contains the only laughs in the movie. Life reflected art when Branagh married his costar, Emma Thompson.

My only problem with the film is the use of Derek Jacobi as Chorus. At first he is helpful in easing transitions, but his appearances during Harfleur's fall and at Agincourt make his appear like a reporter covering the fight for the network news. Try not to be reminded of Howard Cosell doing play-by-play of the San Marcos revolution in Woody Allen's *Bananas* (1971), or you'll have to suppress a giggle.

A third video version of *Henry V* was produced by the BBC a part of its magnificent complete series of Shakespeare plays. These are straightforward renderings that prove how the material works just fine as it was originally intended, without panoramic battle scenes and authentic location shooting. David Gwillim's Henry is the one you'd most like to take to lunch. His greeting to the Dauphin's messenger is genuinely cordial, and he even manages a smile after seeing the tennis balls. But when he slowly and calmly speaks of retribution, it is as dramatically effective as Branagh's tirade. Likewise, whereas Branagh rails at the knowledge of conspirators in his service, Gwillim seems more hurt than angry at their betrayal. I don't know if he married his Catherine (gorgeous Jocelyne Boisseau) off-stage as well, but the thought must have crossed. Gwillim also plays Prince Hal in the BBC's production of *Henry IV 1 & 2* with the same affable quality, though inevitably he is somewhat overshadowed by Anthony Quayle's brilliant turn as the beloved Falstaff.

I admit being partial to the 1989 treatment, but there is no "better or worse" in comparing these three interpretations. Each one is superbly cast, exciting and entertaining in its own right, and the experience of watching all three is as rewarding for their similarities as well as for their differences.

Prior to launching its "Shakespeare Plays" series, the BBC produced adaptations of *Henry V* in 1951, 1953, 1957 and 1960. Since the BBC wiped much of its programming before 1970, chances are they no longer exist. A television adaptation of the Stratford Festival of Canada's production was broadcast on CBC in Canada in 1967. French Canadians played the French roles, which merits points for creativity but was not well received by reviewers, who found their accents incomprehensible.

The character of Prince Hal appears in two BBC adaptations of *Henry IV, Pts. 1 & 2*, and in the Orson Welles film *Chimes at Midnight* (1967). Welles had already filmed *Macbeth* and *Othello*, but with *Chimes* he spliced together excerpts from five Shakespeare plays into a character study of Falstaff, a role he inhabits with gusto. Keith Baxter plays Hal, and while he looks too old for the role his classical training is obvious, and he holds his own against two Shakespeare veterans, Welles and Sir John Gielgud as Henry IV.

The editing is choppy, the synthesis of different plays does not always work and the sound is very poor, but Orson Welles could not make a boring film or a bad looking one. His eye for composition of shadow and light is in the Rembrandt class; there are beautifully framed images here that are as memorable as anything the director ever conceived. The sight of Falstaff walking sheepishly into battle while the king's army charges into the fray on horseback is both pitiful and hilarious.

The Black Shield of Falworth (1954) is a long way from Shakespeare, but Prince Hal is one of the supporting players in this comic book swashbuckler starring Tony Curtis and Janet Leigh. The plot deals with a conspiracy against Henry IV, which is put down by a band of heroes including Hal and Myles Falworth, the knight-in-training played by Curtis. It's heavy on gloss but light on everything else. Daniel O'Herlihy as Hal and other supporting performances (Torin Thatcher, Barbara Rush) are spirited, but Curtis's Brooklyn delivery does not lend itself well to British nobility.

THE FILMS

Henry V (Two Cities/United Artists, 1946, 127 minutes)
Directed and produced by Laurence Olivier; Written by Olivier and Alan Dent, based upon the play by William Shakespeare; Music by William Walton
Cast
LAURENCE OLIVIER (HENRY V), Leslie Banks (Chorus), Renee Asherson (Princess Catherine), Harcourt Williams (King Charles VI), Max Adrian (The Dauphin)
Rating: *****
Available on Videocassette
Awards: Special Academy Award to Laurence Olivier, for "outstanding achievement as actor, producer and director in bringing *Henry V* to the screen." Nominations for Best Picture, Actor (Olivier), Interior Decoration and Score.

The Black Shield of Falworth (Universal, 1954, 98 minutes)
Directed by Rudolph Mate; Written by Oscar Brodney, based on the novel *Men of Iron* by Howard Pyle; Produced by Robert Arthur and Melville Tucker; Music by Joseph Gershenson
Cast
Tony Curtis (Myles Falworth), Janet Leigh (Lady Anne), David Farrar (Earl of Alban), Barbara Rush (Meg Falworth), DANIEL O'HERLIHY (PRINCE HAL), Torin Thatcher (Sir James)
Rating: **1/2

Chimes at Midnight (Internacional Films, 1967, 115 minutes)
AKA Campandas A Medianoche, Falstaff
Directed and written by Orson Welles, based on plays by Shakespeare and *The Chronicles of England* by Raphael Holinshed; Produced by Emiliando Piedra; Music by Angelo Francesco Lavagnino

Cast
Orson Welles (Falstaff), Jeanne Moreau (Doll Tearsheet), John Gielgud (King Henry IV), KEITH BAXTER (PRINCE HAL)
Rating: ***1/2

Henry V (BBC-Curzon-Renaissance/Goldwyn, 1989, 138 minutes)
Directed and written by Kenneth Branagh; Produced by Bruce Sharman; Music by Pat Doyle
Cast
KENNETH BRANAGH (KING HENRY V), Derek Jacobi (Chorus), Emma Thompson (Princess Catherine), Paul Scofield (King Charles VI), Michael Maloney (The Dauphin), Brian Blessed (Duke of Exeter), Robbie Coltrane (Falstaff)
Rating: *****
Awards: Academy Award for Best Costume Design; nominations for Best Actor (Branagh) and Director

TELEVISION

"Henry V" (BBC teleplay, 1951, 135 minutes)
Produced by Royston Morley and Leonard Brett
Cast
CLEMENT MCCALLIN (HENRY V), Varvana Piteoff (Catherine), Marius Goring (Chorus)

"Henry V" (BBC teleplay, 1953, 90 minutes)
Produced by Michael MacOwan and John Barton
Cast
COLIN GEORGE (HENRY V), Bernadette Sorel (Katherine)

"Henry V" (BBC teleplay, 1957, 120 minutes)
Directed and produced by Peter Dews
Cast
JOHN NEVILLE (HENRY V), Bernard Hepton (Chorus), Patricia Creb (Katherine)

"Henry V" (BBC teleplay, 1960, 120 minutes)
Directed by Michael Hayes; Produced by Peter Dews
Cast
ROBERT HARDY (HENRY V), William Squire (Chorus), Judi Dench (Katherine)

"Henry V" (CBC teleplay, 1967, 120 minutes)
Directed by Lorne Freed
Cast
DOUGLAS RAIN (HENRY V), William Hutt (Chorus), Diana LeBlanc (Katherine)

"Henry IV, Parts 1 & 2" (BBC teleplay, 1979, 280 minutes)
Directed by David Giles; Produced by Cedric Messina
Cast
Jon Finch (King Henry IV), DAVID GWILLIM (HENRY, PRINCE OF WALES),

Tim Piggot-Smith (Henry Percy), Anthony Quayle (Falstaff)

"Henry V" (BBC teleplay, 1979, 160 minutes)
Directed by David Giles; Produced by Cedric Messina
Cast
DAVID GWILLIM (KING HENRY V), Alec McCowen (Chorus), Jocelyne Boisseau (Princess Catherine), Thorley Walters (Charles VI), Keith Drinkel (The Dauphin)
Rating for "Henry IV, Parts 1 & 2" and "Henry V": ****

Steve Reeves in the prototypical sword and sandal epic, *Hercules* (1959)

HERCULES

The heroes that have emerged from Greek and Roman mythology have had a profound impact upon our language and culture. From the constellations in the nighttime sky to the poetic allusions of Byron and Spenser, their names are as familiar today as they were in the ancient world. The best-known of these heroes is Hercules, whose name is synonymous with superhuman strength and courage, more so than any other figure of history or fiction.

He is most commonly referred to by his Latin name; the Greeks called him "Heracles," literally "Hera's glory." The name is odd when one considers that Hera caused Hercules nothing but grief for most of his life, as she did with all the illegitimate children of her husband Zeus.

The first significant mentions of Hercules are found in the epic poetry of Pindar and Theocritus, who wrote in the fourth and third centuries B.C., respectively. Four hundred years later Apollodorus wrote down many of the folk tales about the Prince of Power that had already been around for centuries. Inconclusive evidence indicates that the character is based on a real chieftain of the Greek kingdom of Argos but, according to the venerable *Bullfinch's Mythology* Hercules had a higher birth. Variations on all the legends exist ad infinitum, but most have Hercules as the son of Zeus and the mortal woman Alcmena, who was the wife of Amphitryon. She became pregnant after Zeus visited her in the form of her husband, and became pregnant again when Amphitryon returned from battle. Twin boys were born, Hercules and Iphicles, each the product of their respective fathers. And that's not even close to being the strangest birth in the annals of mythology.

Hera sent two serpents to kill the infant Hercules, but the mighty tot strangled the serpents in his crib. When he grew to manhood, Hercules again found himself on the receiving end of Hera's wrath, after marrying a princess named Megara. Hera rendered Hercules temporarily insane, in which time he killed his wife and children and fell under the servitude of Eurystheus, the king of Greece. The king, jealous of Hercules's might, sent his nemesis on twelve "labors" which became the most renowned of Hercules's adventures:

1. Hercules strangles the Nemean lion, and brings the skin of the beast to Eurystheus.

2. Hercules battles the nine-headed Hydra, which had terrorized the country of Argos and blocked access to a fountain that would relieve a severe drought. Herc

learns quickly that two new heads grow where one is chopped, and that the center head is immortal. He defeats the creature by burning the heads and burying the immortal one under a rock.

3. Hercules captures the stag of Arcadia.

4. Another animal hunt--this time the wild boar of Mt. Erymanthus.

5. Possibly the most famous--Hercules is ordered to clean the Augean stables, which haven't seen a broom in thirty years. Once the three thousand oxen are removed, Hercules changes the course of the rivers Alpheus and Peneus so that they sweep through the stables and finish the job in one day.

6. Hercules aims his bow and arrow and grounds the man-eating birds of the Stymphalian marshes.

7. Herc sails to Crete to corral a mad bull.

8. The man-eating mares of King Diomedes have been eating too many men lately, so Hercules is sent to capture them.

9. Another well-known tale--Hercules is ordered to steal the girdle of Hippolyta, queen of the Amazons, for Eurystheus's daughter Admeta. Hippolyta turns out to be a sweetheart and agrees to surrender her girdle, but Hera interferes and convinces the Amazons that Hercules plans to kidnap their queen. When he spies their army charging toward him Herc believes that Hippolyta had planned the attack all along, and kills her before returning with the girdle.

10. Back in the saddle again to round up the cattle of the three-bodied giant Geryon. During this labor Hercules formed the Straits of Gibraltar to mark his path.

11. Hercules must retrieve the golden apples that were given to Hera at her wedding and entrusted to the daughters of Hesperus. Their location was a well-kept secret, so Hercules went to the titan Atlas, who had fathered the daughters of Hesperus. Atlas had been condemned to support the world on his shoulders after warring against the gods, but he agrees to find the apples if Hercules will hold up the earth for awhile.

12. Hercules descends into Pluto's netherworld to put a leash on Cerberus, the three-headed canine guardian of the Stygian gates.

Other adventure Bullfinch recorded include Hercules's battle with the giant wrestler Antaeus, who was invincible as long as he remained in contact with the earth. Hercules discovered his secret and strangled Antaeus while holding him aloft. He would later sail with Jason on the *Argo*, and rescue Theseus (of Minotaur fame) from Hades, while carrying Cerberus to the surface. After Hercules fell in love with the princess Iole, he was poisoned by a jealous rival and died. His mortal self was consumed by fire, while his divine part ascended to Mt. Olympus in a chariot. Hera, finally past her anger, accepted Hercules and gave her daughter Hebe, the cup-bearer of the gods, to be his wife.

Hercules has been the subject of countless paintings, poems and stories dating back to antiquity. He is usually described as a powerfully built man of medium height, with dark hair and a trim beard, whose appetite for food, wine and women is as voluminous as his strength. Though he often used a bow and arrow in the original stories, he is most often drawn wielding a mace or club.

The world's museums are home to ancient Greek black-figure pottery that depict his exploits, and sculpture and friezes from the same period still survive in Greece and Rome. The Temple of Zeus at Olympia, considered one of the finest examples of Classical architectural sculpture, contains meotopes of Hercules's labors. Sophocles and Euripides devoted plays to Hercules, and the Roman poet Ovid's writings were the source for Bullfinch. Antonio Pollaiuolo's painting and sculpture of Hercules and Antaeus are masterpieces of Renaissance art, and John Milton makes reference to the son of Zeus in both his *Comus* and *Paradise Lost*.

THE FILMS

At the movies, Hercules has not received the same respect. From Milton and Pollaiuolo to Steve Reeves and Lou Ferrigno--this is a class drop of Olympian proportions. Researching all of Hercules's film appearances presents a slew of problems, since the majority of them are Italian imports from the the late 1950s and 1960s. These "sword-and-sandal" films, as they have come to be known, were churned out with astonishing frequency after the freak success caused by the distribution of Joseph E. Levene's *Hercules* in 1957. Suddenly, there was a new toga-clad strong man movie every few months, featuring either Hercules, Samson, Ulysses, Goliath, Maciste (aka Atlas) or a combination thereof.

The fact that no attempt was made to connect the character with any already-established background or historical base should not disqualify them from consideration--evidence of this can be found in every chapter of this book. However, the fact that these films often turn up under different names indicates that in many cases there was not even an attempt to build a good story around one specific character. *The Fury of Hercules* (1961) is also known as *The Fury of Samson.* When *Maciste e la Regina de Samar* was dubbed into English, it became *Hercules Against the Moonmen* (1964). *Hercules Against the Barbarians* (1964) also started life as a Maciste film, and *Hercules vs. Ulysses* (1961) was also released under the title *Ulysses vs. the Son of Hercules*.

The generic action scenes and required dubbing of these films for foreign markets helped render such transitions almost imperceptible. There are examples of name-changes in other genres (see *Sadko* in the Sinbad chapter), but the sword and sandal films have clearly abused the privilege. Their indiscriminatory use of hero-rotation disqualifies many of the Hercules films as legitimate entries in any retrospective on the character. Every film that carries (or at one time carried) the Hercules name has been listed in this volume, but only those entries with some interesting or unique aspect will be described in detail--the rest are interchangeable.

A 1910 silent French short, *Hercules and the Big Stick*, depicts the god's battle with the Hydra. There is a 1909 silent called *Hercules and the Regiment*, but it has no connection to the mythological character, so the French effort ranks first. Surprisingly the serials never took a shot at the stories, so the next adaptation did not appear until 1957. Joseph E. Levene's *Hercules* is the movie that deserves the credit--or the blame--for launching the sword-and-sandal genre, for unleashing a plague of imitators, and in Austria for convincing a young Arnold Schwarzenegger that a career in movies was not beyond his grasp.

The film opens with Hercules rescuing the lovely Princess Iole from a runaway chariot. Iole tells Hercules of the troubles in her kingdom--her brother Jason and the Golden Fleece, the town's symbol of power, have both disappeared. Iole's father is among the chief suspects. Hercules rides back with her and is soon embroiled in the palace intrigue caused by the wanna-be ruler Pelias. Hercules eventually finds Jason and accompanies him on a voyage to retrieve the Golden Fleece.

Levene made *Hercules* a huge international hit by distributing the film in as many theaters as would take it, and then flooding the airwaves with superlative-laden advertising. Thus, the undeniable impact that *Hercules* had on the motion picture industry is due entirely to marketing, not artistic merit.

A convoluted mix of Jason mythology and original material forms the plot, which advances with all the speed of a snail-driven chariot. As befitting a prototype, Hercules contains all the scenes that would be repeated in most subsequent entries: lovely Italian women cavort in very short togas, Hercules bends a steel bar to demonstrate his strength, and wrestles a lion or some such beast--always an extra in a furry suit that's so phony you can almost spot the zipper. There is also the incongruous musical number, which makes about as much sense here as it did in the Marx Brothers movies, where at least it was capably performed.

Steve Reeves, a former Mr. Universe, played Hercules and is still the best-known inhabitant of the role, even though he bowed out of the series after one more film. Reeves looks the part but is not a convincing warrior in the fight scenes. His movements are so stiff that someone should have told the cleaners to lighten up on the toga starch. His performance is further hampered by poor dubbing and looping. The lighting and special effects were by horror director Mario Bava, which explains why Hercules is one of the better-looking entries.

A sequel, *Hercules Unchained*, was made the following year and, unlike future entries, someone paid attention to continuity. Besides Reeves, Sylva Koscina also returns as Iole, as does Gabriele Antonini as a young Ulysses and Andrea Fantasia as Laertes. Also back for an encore are the clumsy fight scenes and a lame mid-film musical interlude.

The plot has Hercules getting involved in a power struggle over the throne of Thebes. After losing his memory to an enchanted fountain, Herc becomes engaged to the evil Queen of Lydia, whose hobby is having her lovers killed and preserved as wax figures. Hercules regains his memory in time to avoid this fate and returns to the fight for Thebes. The usual man-eating tigers and armored battalions stand in his way.

Like most of the Hercules films, *Unchained* is not entirely lacking in production quality. It's just dull. There's not enough action to keep the kids interested, and not enough Sylva Koscina to keep their fathers around. But you gotta love the way they mix and match mythology. Jason turned up in Hercules, and this time Oedipus makes a guest appearance.

Reeves's retirement did not sidetrack the series very long. In 1960, *The Loves of Hercules* starred Mickey Hargitay as the strongman and his off-screen wife Jayne Mansfield in a dual role as both good Queen Deianira and evil Queen Hippolyta. It's the most inept attempt at creating two characters since Barbara Eden played her own sister on "I Dream of Jeanie."

Hercules's wife (not Iole--this and all subsequent films are unrelated) is killed by the king's counselor Lico, who then frames the king for the deed and kills him as well. Princess Deianira, now queen, convinces an angry Hercules that her father was innocent. Lico notices sparks between Herc and Deianira, so he kills the queen's betrothed, Acolos, and points the finger toward Hercules, who had already left town. During his journey Hercules battles the legendary Hydra and wins, but the fight knocks him out. He is found by Amazons and taken to their queen, Hippolyta. By magic she transforms herself into the image of Deianira, and tends to Herc's recovery while planning his execution. Though he is rather dim in this version, Hercules eventually escapes Hippolyta's clutches and returns to deal with Lico.

There is less FX action than in the Reeves films, and what's there is awful, often hysterically so. Herc's fight with a three-headed Hydra seems untoppable, but then the Amazons who rescue Hercules ride through a forest of talking trees! Everyone who played a tree in a grammar school play was more convincing. These two scenes alone nearly qualify the film for "so bad it's good" status, but *The Loves of Hercules* is a bit too self-aware of its own stupidity.

The dubbing of Mickey Hargitay makes him sound like Ronald Colman, which hardly seems synchronous with the open-mouthed stare that comprises the sum of his acting technique. Jayne Mansfield in a bad brunette wig purses her lips and puffs her chest and pouts her way through her pair of roles. Only Massimo Serato as Lico brings any conviction to his role.

Ulysses Against Hercules (1961) was actually a "Son of Hercules" film, so the next entry is *Fury of Hercules*, also from 1961. The film is also known as *Fury of Samson*, but this time Hercules came first. It's a run-of-the-mill entry dropped a notch by the lackluster performance of Brad Harris as Hercules.

In the city of Arpad, Hercules must prove his loyalty to the new queen through a series of trials. The evil captain of the queen's guard is played by Alan Steel, who would soon have his turn as the hero. There are more dancing girls than usual, a reminder that one of the series' strongest selling points in the repressed 1950s and early 1960s was the abundance of women in minitogas. But my favorite scene has Hercules stopping an elephant stampede by politely asking the beasts to leave. "Animals can always tell the difference between good and bad," he counsels. So can the audience, pal.

Hercules in the Valley of Woe (1962) is notable for Kirk Morris's debut in the role and for its time-travel storyline. When two con men use a time machine to escape the law, they wind up in ancient Thebes. Hercules makes them wish they'd never left. Morris's films are the toughest to find today, which is convenient because they're also the easiest to skip. The same basic concept was also used in another 1962 release, *The Three Stooges Meet Hercules*. The Stooges play Ithaca, New York pharmacists, who end up in the original Ithaca via the most unlikely looking time machine this side of Dr. Who's Tardis.

Hercules, as played by Samson Burke, is as dumb as they come, but that's to be expected for a foil of Moe, Larry and Curly Joe. The standard Italian muscleman epics are so close to self-parody that a full-tilt spoof is almost superfluous; still, this is as good as the post-Curly and Shemp Stooges got, and it's not every film that can segue from a chariot race to a pie fight.

The big guy had four more appearances in 1963, including one in a borderline classic; *Jason and the Argonauts* provided a dandy showcase for Ray Harryhausen's stop motion effects and offered up the best cast of any Harryhausen film. The "JASON" chapter has all the details, but special mention should be made here of Nigel Green's performance as Hercules. In a severe departure from all previous and future versions, Green plays Hercules as a mortal who has not yet been given the gift of godhood. He is an older man but one who still has much to learn, as evidenced by the trouble he causes Jason and his fellow Argonauts. The character is gone before the film is half over, but Green's robust portrayal is not soon forgotten.

Back to Italy now for *Hercules and the Captive Women*, which doesn't actually have any captive women but does have Reg Park, who rates the edge over all his sword-and-sandal predecessors. Park is more adept in the fight scenes, and shows signs of both a sense of humor and an occasional change of expression. Hercules and pal Androcles become shipwrecked in Atlantis, where they defeat a shape-shifting monster named Proteus and rescue Queen Antinea's daughter in the process. Far from being grateful, however, Antinea is outraged, for it is written that if the queen is survived by a daughter, Atlantis will be destroyed.

Hercules finally learns not to accept spiked wine from seductive foreign queens in this occasionally better-than-average entry. The destruction of Atlantis, interspersed with stock volcano footage, is impressively handled, but the dragon Proteus becomes is sixth-grade art class paper mache`.

Dan Vadis, a familiar face in several Clint Eastwood films including *The Gauntlet* (1977) and *Bronco Billy* (1980), got his start playing Hercules in *Hercules the Invincible*. As usual, dragons and tyrannical rulers provide the opposition, in a corrupt underground city that Hercules flushes out with lava. Vadis deserves credit for having a career after this start, but he adds nothing interesting to this very typical programmer.

The undisputed best of the sword-and-sandal Herculeses (Herculi?) was Gordon Scott, who made his debut in *Hercules Vs. Moloch*. However, here he actually plays a man named Glauco who adopts the name of Hercules before taking on the evil Queen Neri and her awful son. Also known as *Conquest of Mycene*, this is another of the many pretender Hercules films. Scott would get a real shot two years later, and the result was the best film the series has to offer.

The mighty son of Zeus really hit his stride in 1964, appearing in no less than ten spaghetti epics. Of these, three are contenders in name only: *Hercules of the Desert* with Kirk Morris was originally a Maciste film called *The Valley of the Thundering Echo*. *Hercules Against the Moon Men* started life as *Maciste Vs. the Moon Men*, and starred Alan Steel, who started life as Sergio Ciani. *Hercules Against the Barbarians* with Mark Forest originally released under the intriguing title *Maciste in Gengis Khan's Hell.*

Hell was a popular sword and sandal topic in '64. Dan Vadis returned for *Hercules Vs. the Giant Warriors*, in which the hero squared off against. . .well, a bunch of giant warriors, who are conjured up in Hades by an evil sorceress. Zeus saps his son's strength to make the fight more interesting. Vadis shows no signs of progress in his second and final outing.

Hercules in the Haunted World sent Hercules to Pluto's realm once more, in one of the few series entries that can be found in better video stores. This is due to the directorial effort of Mario Bava, best known for his work on such horror films as *Baron Blood* and the unforgettable *Black Sunday* (1961) with Barbara Steele. Bava photographed both of the Reeves films, but in his first and only shot as director his style is far more evident. From the opening shot, we are clearly looking at filmmaking on another level.

Lichas, a servant of Pluto, puts Princess Deianira under a curse. Herc risks his immortality to enter Hades and find a mystical stone that will cure the princess and others who have fallen under Lichas's power. Bava pulls an almost alert performance from Reg Park as Hercules, and Giorgio Ardisson provides good support as Theseus, the hero's teen sidekick. Christopher Lee, a veteran B-movie nasty, plays Lichas. The first capably choreographed fight in the series takes place when Herc and Theseus knock off Lichas's legions.

The same producer and writer worked on the earlier film *Hercules and the Captive Women*, but without Bava's flair it didn't gel. No one could get more atmosphere out of a dry ice machine. His decision to shoot many of the underworld scenes in semidarkness increases the mood of foreboding while hiding flaws, but it can be frustrating with a murky print.

Park also starred in *Hercules, Prisoner of Evil*, which represents a return to business as usual. The title "Evil" is a sorceress who turns men into werewolves. Alan Steel starred in the simply awful *Hercules Against Rome*, and reprised his role in a supporting turn for *Samson and His Mighty Challenge* (see "SAMSON" chapter). A new contender, Rock Stevens, inherits the role for *Hercules and the Tyrants of Babylon.* Nothing new storywise--Hercules defeats another demented sorcerer, but Stevens brings some fresh enthusiasm to the mix. Two years later, under his real name of Peter Lupus, he would achieve great success as Willie Armitage in the classic TV series "Mission: Impossible."

Rounding out the class of 1964, *Hercules Against the Sons of the Sun* is set in the Empire of the Incas, where Hercules becomes shipwrecked on his way back to Thebes. He teams up with a band of outlaw warriors who seek to overthrow the usurper king who has a fondness for human sacrifice. After introducing the warriors to such advanced military hardware as the wheel, he builds the fighting machines that lead them to victory and, as usual, takes time out to dazzle the local princess. The busy Mark Forest, in between jobs playing the son of Hercules and the son of Samson in two other endless series, returns as Hercules. He's a bit more graceful than the average bodybuilder and handles himself well in the fights. The setting change is a novelty for about ten minutes, but director Osvaldo Civirani loads up on the action and keeps things moving right up to the surprisingly exciting siege on the Inca fortress.

The following year, Kirk Morris played Hercules in the all-star team-up *Hercules, Samson and Ulysses.* Hercules and Ulysses are shipwrecked after battling a sea monster. The duo then joins forces with Samson to defeat a heartless king. As in *Samson and His Mighty Challenge*, it's fun for fans of this stuff to see all the ersatz legends together, but the alliance won't light any fires under nonconverts.

Hercules and the Princess of Troy, also from 1965, was as good as this series got. Joseph E. Levene returned as executive producer, lured perhaps by talk of a "Hercules" TV series. This was the pilot, and when the network passed on future adventures Levene released *Princess of Troy* theatrically. Audiences expecting the usual fare were in for a treat--the story was shot in English, not Italian, so for once the dialogue actually matched the lip movements of the actors.

The good ship *Olympia*, carrying Hercules, Diogenes and Ulysses, lands in Troy just in time for the annual maiden sacrifice. The king says it's necessary to appease a nasty sea monster, so Hercules offers to take care of the creature. It is eventually learned that the king is using the threat of the monster to hold onto his throne. After defeating the monster, Herc reveals the king's duplicity.

It is no coincidence that Gordon Scott, who plays Hercules, is also the star of the best Samson film, *Samson and the Seven Miracles of the World*, and several o.k. Tarzan movies. He is among the handful of B-movie players, along with Guy

Williams, Gene Nelson and Faith Domergue, who kept their dignity amidst what were often the most embarrassing of circumstances. Scott brings more than biceps to his portrayal of Hercules--he looks appropriately Greek myth-like, but there is also confidence, intelligence and nobility in his bearing. He shows genuine athletic prowess in the action scenes, and holds his own reading lines opposite a talented supporting cast.

Diana Hyland is the first "name" costar since Jayne Mansfield and by any criteria but cup size she's in another league. The distinguished actor Everett Sloane provides extensive narration which replaces the dull exposition scenes that weighed down previous entries. The film also benefits from a higher budget and its one-hour running time, which was really enough time for any of these films if you think about it. Those who remember enjoying the Hercules movies as children probably remember them all looking as good as *Princess of Troy*. They didn't. The 1957 Steve Reeves film may have built the franchise, but *Hercules and the Princess of Troy* is the only film that the uninitiated need to see. It was also fittingly the last entry in the series. Planned or not, they went out with their best effort.

Hercules, however, would return to the screen in 1970 in *Hercules in New York*, an ultracheap, ultralame comedy adventure that starred Arnold Schwarzenegger in his first film appearance. It's the worst debut for a major star since Paul Newman in *The Silver Chalice*. The film was later retitled *Hercules Goes Bananas* and returned to theaters to capitalize on Schwarzenegger's subsequent stardom. How he must have cringed.

Defying Zeus's orders, Hercules visits earth and winds up in the Big Apple, where he is befriended by a nebbishy opportunist named Pretzy. Juno, who never liked her mighty stepson, sends the evil Nemesis to earth to teach Hercules a lesson in humility. Just before a weightlifting contest, Nemesis steals Hercules's strength. Zeus takes pity on the kid and restores his power, which Herc uses to mop the floor with the crooked contest promoters. After a tearful farewell to Pretzy, he returns to Olympus.

Schwarzenegger has said in interviews that he was inspired by Steve Reeves in both bodybuilding and acting, so at the time he was probably thrilled to play the role that had established his hero in movies. He was billed as "Arnold Strong," since no one would ever expect Schwarzenegger to become a household name. Who could blame them? If Arnold had remained at this level, it never would have. Here he looks confused most of the time, and the dubbed voice kills any chance of his natural charisma coming through.

Incompetence reigned on both sides of the camera, from the grating non-stop Greek music to the Mt. Olympus set that resembles the pool area at a Holiday Inn. Arnold Stang's Pretzy is a geek with a tremendously irritating voice--think Daffy Duck with a chest cold. Schwarzenegger deserves credit not for making this film, but for surviving it.

A 1974 film entitled *Hercules vs. Kung Fu* had no relation to the mythical Hercules, so we jump ahead, regrettably, to 1983 and the first of two films starring Lou Ferrigno. It is no coincidence that the film was made soon after Schwarzenegger turned *Conan the Barbarian* into a hit. Producers Menahem Golan and Yoram Globus, who have never had an original idea in their lives, borrow elements from numerous other successful films, and still come up empty.

The film opens ambitiously enough with a discourse on the history of life in the universe and the creation of the planets, which is just an excuse for some *Star Wars*--like special effects that are as unconvincing as they are derivative. The shot of Hercules standing before an outer-space backdrop looks very silly. Hercules, who is not even the son of Zeus in this version, is born into the first family of Thebes, which is murdered soon after by agents of King Minos, who also steal the city's sacred sword. The infant Hercules is placed in a rowboat by a maidservant, and grows to manhood in a foreign land. His strength and skills are tested by various gods, who help or hinder his progress according to whim.

There are some nods to Bullfinch--the serpents in the crib and a stable-cleaning sequence, but other tales are equally prominent. Hercules's birth is similar to that of Moses, and there's a "sword-in-the-stone" episode that's a blatant rip-off of Arthurian legend. Mechanical laser-breathing dragons replace the monsters of myth in the film's most inexplicable refrain. Lou Ferrigno had his lines dubbed, but his inability as an actor still shines through. Whereas Steve Reeves and company were just stiff in the performance department, Ferrigno is completely clueless. And when he pulls a tree out of the ground it is no more lifelike than when Reeves did it twenty-six years earlier. The only entertainment value in the movie, which isn't much, is seeing former Hercules Brad Harris as King Augeias, and watching Sybil Danning's outfits stretch the 'G' rating. Zeus, Hera and Athena, meanwhile, are dressed like "Dance Fever" contestants.

The Adventures of Hercules (1985) offers the same odd mix of sci-fi with sword and sandal, and once again makes the Italian programmers of old look magnificent by comparison. The cast is the same except for Sybil Danning, whose bustier is ably filled by Milly Carlucci. Another crazy cosmic beginning intercuts scenes from the first film with futuristic opening credits, *exactly* like *Superman II*.

The story has Zeus ordering Hercules to retrieve seven stolen lightning bolts. Various creatures are dispatched along the way, before the climactic rematch with King Minos, who plans to use the lightning to crash the moon into the earth (don't ask). Amidst the incredible heights of idiocy there's a good performance by Maria Rosaria Omaggio as Hera, but that's no reason to go anywhere near the film.

After wading through the Reeve/Vadis/Steel etc. efforts, try to see the hilarious "Saturday Night Live" parody with Bill Murray as a pot-bellied Hercules. The off-kilter dubbing is perfectly captured, and Murray is even funnier than Lou Ferrigno.

THE FILMS

Hercules and the Big Stick (Gaum, 1910, 15 minutes)

Hercules (OSCAR/Galatea, 1957, 107 minutes)
Directed by Pietro Francisci; Written by Pietro Francisci, Ennio De Concini and Galo Frattini, based on a story by Francisci; Produced by Federico Teti; Music by Enzo Masetti
Cast
STEVE REEVES (HERCULES), Sylva Koscina (Iole), Fabrizio Mioni (Jason), Ivo Garrani (Pelias)
Rating: **
Available on Videocassette

Hercules Unchained (Lux-Galatea, 1959, 101 minutes)
Directed by Pietro Francisci; Written by Francisci and Ennio de Concini; Produced by Bruno Vailati: Music by Enzo Masetti, song "Evening Star" by Mitchell Parish
Cast

STEVE REEVES (HERCULES), Sylva Koscina (Iole), Primo Carnera (Antaeus), Sylvia Lopez (Omphale), Cesare Fantoni (Oedipus), Gabriele Antonini (Ulysses)
Rating: *
Available on Videocassette

The Loves of Hercules (Rome-Contact Organization, 1960, 94 minutes)
AKA Hercules and the Hydra
Directed by Carlo Ludovico Bragaglia; Written by Luciano Doria and Alessandro Continenza; Produced by Alberto Manca; Music by Carlo Innocenzi
Cast
Jayne Mansfield (Deianira/Hippolyte), MICKEY HARGITAY (HERCULES), Massimo Serato (Lico)
Rating: *

Fury of Hercules (Cineproduzioni Associates, 1961, 97 minutes)
AKA Fury of Samson
Directed by Gianfranco Parolini; Written by Gianfranco Parolini, Giovanni Simonelli, Arpad De Riso, Sergio Sollima and M. D'Amien; Produced by Mario Maggi; Music by Carlo Innocenzi
Cast
BRAD HARRIS (HERCULES)
Rating; 1/2 *

The Three Stooges Meet Hercules (Columbia, 1962, 89 minutes)
Directed by Edward Bernds; Written by Elwood Ullman; Produced by Norman Maurer; Music by Paul Dunlap
Cast
The Three Stooges (Themselves), SAMSON BURKE (HERCULES), Quinn Redeker (Schyler Davis), Vicki Trickett (Diane), George N. Neise (Mr. Dismal/King Odius)
Rating: **

Jason and the Argonauts (Columbia, 1963)
SEE JASON CHAPTER FOR CREDITS

Hercules and the Captive Women (SPA Cinematografica-Comptori Francasi/Woolner Bros., 1961, 93 minutes)
AKA Hercules and the Conquest of Atlantis
Directed by Vittorio Cottafavi; Written by Alessandro Continenza; Produced by Achille Piazzi; Music by Gino Marinuzzi and Armando Trovajoli
Cast
REG PARK (HERCULES), Fay Spain (Queen Antinea), Ettore Manni (Androcles), Laura Altan (Ismene)
Rating: * 1/2

Hercules, the Invincible (Metheus, 1963, 85 minutes)
Directed and produced by Alfredo Mancori; Written by Kirk Mayor, Pat Klein and Alfredo Mancori
Cast
DAN VADIS (HERCULES)

Rating: *

Hercules Vs. the Giant Warriors (Produzione Cinematografica, 1964, 90 minutes)
AKA The Triumph of Hercules, Hercules and the Ten Avengers
Directed by Alberto De Martino; Written by Roberto Gianviti and Alessandro Ferrau; Produced by Alberto Chimenz; Music by Francesco De Masi
Cast
DAN VADIS (HERCULES), Pierre Cressoy (Myles), Moira Orfei (Pasiphae), Marilu Tolo (Ate), Piero Lulli (Gordius)
Rating: 1/2 *

Hercules in the Haunted World (SPA Cinematografica, 1964, 83 minutes)
Directed by Mario Bava; Written by Mario Bava, Duccio Tessari, Alessandro Continenza and Franco Prosperi; Produced by Achille Piazzi; Music by Armando Trovjoli
Cast
REG PARK (HERCULES), Christopher Lee (Lico), Leonara Ruffo (Deianira) Giorgio Ardisson (Theseus)
Rating: ** 1/2
Available on Videocassette

Hercules, Prisoner of Evil (Royale Sodifilm, 1964, 90 minutes)
AKA Terror of the Kirghiz
Directed by Antonio Margheriti; Produced by Adelpho Ambrosiand
Cast
REG PARK (HERCULES), Mireille Granelli, Ettore Manni
Rating: *

Hercules Against Rome (1964, 90 minutes)
Directed by Piero Pierotti; Written by Arpad De Riso and Nino Scolaro; Music by Francisco Lavagnino
Cast
ALAN STEEL (HERCULES), Wandisa Guida, Domenico Palmara
Rating: * 1/2

Samson and His Mighty Challenge (1964)
SEE SAMSON CHAPTER FOR CREDITS

Hercules and the Tyrants of Babylon (Romania Films, 1964, 87 minutes)
Directed by Domenico Paolella; Written by Luciano Martino and Domenico Paolella; Music by Francisco Lavagnino
Cast
ROCK STEVENS (HERCULES), Helga Line (Tanit), Mario Petri (Phaleg), Anna Maria Polani (Esperia)
Rating: * 1/2

Hercules Against the Sons of the Sun (Wonder Films, 1964, 89 minutes)
Directed and produced by Osvaldo Civirani; Written by Franco Tannozzini and Osvaldo Civirani; Music by Lallo Gori

Cast
MARK FOREST (HERCULES), Giuliano Gemma (Mytha)
Rating: **

Hercules, Samson and Ulysses (MGM, 1965, 86 minutes)
Directed and written by Pietro Francisci; Produced by Joseph Fryd; Music by Angelo Francesco Lavagnino
Cast
KIRK MORRIS (HERCULES), Richard Lloyd (Samson), Liana Orfei (Delilah), Enzo Cerusico (Ulysses)
Rating: * 1/2

Hercules and the Princess of Troy (Embassy, 1965, 50 minutes)
Directed by Albert Band; Written by Larry Forester and Ugo Liberatore; Produced by Albert Band and Joseph E. Levene; Music by Fred Steiner
Cast
GORDON SCOTT (HERCULES), Diana Hyland (Princess Diana), Paul Stevens (Diogenes), Mart Hulswit (Ulysses), Steve Garrett (Petra)
Rating: ** 1/2

Hercules in New York (RAF, 1970, 90 minutes)
Directed by Arthur A Seidelman; Written and produced by Aubrey Wisberg; Music by John Balamos
Cast
Arnold Stang (Pretzy), ARNOLD SCHWARZENEGGER (HERCULES), Deborah Loomis (Helen), Ernest Graves (Zeus), Tanny McDonald (Juno), Tania Elg (Nemesis)
Rating: 1/2 *
Available on Videocassette

Hercules (Cannon/MGM/United Artists, 1983, 98 minutes)
Directed and written by Lewis Coates; Produced by Menahem Golan and Yoram Globus; Music by Pino Donaggio
Cast
LOU FERRIGNO (HERCULES), Sybil Danning (Andriana), Brad Harris (King Augeias), Ingrid Anderson (Cassiopea), Rossana Podesta (Hera), Mirella D'Angelo (Circe), William Berger (King Minos)
Rating: 1/2 *
Available on Videocassette

The Adventures of Hercules (Cannon/United Artists, 1984, 89 minutes)
AKA Hercules II
Directed and written by Lewis Coates; Produced by Alfredo Pecoriello; Music by Pino Donaggio
Cast
LOU FERRIGNO (HERCULES), Sonia Viviani (Glaucia), Milly Carlucci (Urania), Claudio Cassinelli (Zeus), Maria Rosaria Omaggio (Hera), William Berger (King Minos)
Rating: 1/2 *
Available on Videocassette

JASON

The story of Jason and the Argonauts is one of the archetypes of the quest adventure, which has formed the basis for classic literature from the Holy Grail stories of Arthurian lore to *The Lord of the Rings*. It's debatable as to whether Jason was the first to bring together all the requisite elements of the model, but after its publication it certainly influenced everything that followed.

Apollonius of Rhodes deserves credit for the first definitive version of the tale--a four-book epic entitled *Argonautica*, or *Quest For the Golden Fleece*, which topped the bestseller list in 295 B.C. However, the story itself dates back at least to Homer's time, which places its beginnings as far back as the ninth century B.C.. Its mythological roots are apparent in the presence of the dragons and monsters that threaten Jason's success, but the voyage of the *Argo* was regarded as historical fact at one time, and Jason himself was credited with establishing new areas for Greek colonization and commerce. It seems likely that an actual expedition provided the foundation for the story, but the line between history and mythology blurs considerably after that.

THE LEGEND

Jason was the son of Aeson, King of Thessaly. When the kingdom was seized by Aeson's brother Pelias, the young Jason was sent to live with a centaur (half-horse, half-man) named Chiron. He grew to manhood and returned to Thessaly to claim his father's throne. Pelias complied, but first suggested to Jason that he retrieve the Golden Fleece, which was the rightful property of his family and would become the symbol of his claim to rule.

The Fleece was a gift from the cloud goddess Nephele to her children Phrixus and Helle, two of Jason's cousins. Their father Athamus was convinced through sorcery that only the sacrifice of Phrixus would prevent a devastating famine, but before the knife fell the kids escaped on a ram with a golden fleece, sent by Nephele. When the ram flew over the strait that divides Europe and Asia, Helle slipped off and drowned in a spot that is still called Hellespont. Phrixus reached the island of Colchis, sacrificed the ram and hung the fleece in the Grove of Ares, where it was protected by a dragon.

Pelias believed that the quest was impossible, so he was elated when Jason agreed to attempt it. He wished the young man well, confident that he would never see him again. Jason assembled a crew of heroes and warriors that included Hercules, Theseus, Orpheus and Nestor. They set sail on a huge ship called the *Argo*, named after its builder, and found adventure on every island where they stopped to rest.

The most formidable obstacle were the Cyanean Rocks, which guarded the passage to Colchis. The huge rocks were known to crash together, destroying any ship that happened to be sailing in between. Through the strait Jason sent a dove, which was nicked by the converging rocks, and while they receded the *Argo* sailed through.

At last the crew reached Colchis, where they encountered a new set of problems. Aeetes, the king, agreed to give up the Fleece if Jason could plow the Field of Ares with two fire-snorting bulls. When Jason finished, the king took the teeth of the dragon that guarded the Fleece and planted them in the field, where they grew into armed warriors. With the help of Aeetes's daughter Medea, Jason escaped with the prize. Medea accompanied Jason back to Thessaly, where she used her powers of sorcery to kill Pelias when he refused to give up the throne. The great quest still turned out to be for naught, however, since the warriors were run out of Thessaly by Pelias's son and forced to flee to Corinth, where they were given asylum by King Creon.

Bullfinch's Mythology tells one of the many different versions of the events. But once Jason and Medea reach Corinth the story takes a dark turn that is recorded by Euripides in his tragedy *Medea*. Jason, once heroic, is now an ungrateful philanderer who leaves Medea for Creon's daughter. The sorceress murders Creon, his daughter, and her two sons by Jason, before leaving for Athens. Medea's life is further chronicled by Roman authors Ovid and Seneca, and much later in the plays of Franz Grillparzer and Jean Anouilh.

As with other heroes of antiquity, Jason has been a favorite subject of classical art and literature for centuries. A painting of the Argonauts by Lorenzo Costa (1460–1535), now hanging in Padua, Italy, is one of the best-known. Bullfinch quotes poetry from Alexander Pope and John Dyer describing the expedition.

THE FILMS

Film treatments of the character fall into two clearly distinct camps--Jason's voyage to retrieve the Fleece, and adaptations of *Medea*. Only one film, Pier Paolo Pasolini's *Medea* (1971) attempted to merge incidents from both episodes, and the blend proves awkward. Likewise, the convoluted, unsavory events that follow Jason's time with the Argonauts in Apollonius's history are wisely avoided in the movies, which conclude with Jason overthrowing the usurper Pelias and ruling Thessaly with Medea by his side.

The first of these was the Italian-made *Giants of Thessaly* (1961), which borrows liberally from other Greek myths to paint a story of Jason's voyage that bears little resemblance to any of the well-known variations. The performances and production values are above-average for the sword and sandal genre, but if they wanted to film *The Odyssey*, they just should have done so.

In 1250 B.C., Zeus gives the Golden Fleece to the people of Thessaly as a gift. When the Fleece is stolen, an angry Zeus curses the people for their carelessness, promising a weather forecast full of volcanic fire until his gift is returned. King Jason assembles a crew and sails for Colchis, where he believes the Fleece is being held. A storm at sea forces the ship to stop on an island ruled by the sorceress Gaea, who turns Jason's crew into sheep. Back in Thessaly, meanwhile, Jason's wife Creusa must fight off the advances of a challenger to the throne. Once free of Gaea, the Argonauts battle a Cyclops on another island, before at last reaching Colchis and obtaining the Fleece. Jason returns home in time to save his wife, his throne and the city.

The Cyclops fight is straight out of *The Odyssey*, and while the adventure on Gaea is reminiscent of Jason's experiences on the island of Lemnos in the *Argonautica*, it has far more in common with Odysseus's encounter with Circe. The Italian muscleman films were notorious for such myth-mixing, and are best enjoyed by less discriminate tastes.

At first glance *Jason and the Argonauts* appeared to be another sword-and-sandal programmer, which may explain why it was totally ignored by audiences back in 1964. Today it is recognized as the best example of Ray Harryhausen's special-effects wizardry, and one of the best adventure movies ever made.

The story begins with Pelias usurping the throne of Thessaly, but being warned by a soothsayer that the child of the rightful king will return one day to defeat him. For twenty years Pelias looks over his shoulder, until he meets Jason by chance and learns of his plan to attack. Without revealing his identity, Pelias advises Jason first to sail in search of the fabled Golden Fleece, which will make his army invincible. With help from the goddess Hera, Jason builds the *Argo* and assembles a crew. Pelias believes the danger passed, but places his son among the crew as insurance. After battling living statues, monsters and sword-wielding skeletons, Jason manages to steal the Fleece by slaying the seven-headed Hydra that guards it, expose the traitor among the Argonauts and, with the help of Medea, he manages to make his way back to Thessaly.

The recurring weakness in most Harryhausen films is a weak lead performance, as anyone who's watched the *Sinbad* trilogy can attest. *Jason and the Argonauts* is the exception, boasting a cast that is every bit the equal of its special effects. Todd Armstrong is a splendid, heroic Jason, and Nancy Kovack is just right as Medea--beautiful and strong willed enough to suggest that she could become the vengeful character described by Euripides. The fine supporting cast is led by Patrick Troughton, Nigel Green (outstanding as Hercules) and "The Avengers"'s Honor Blackman, a truly regal queen of the gods.

The story is surprisingly faithful to Bullfinch, right down to Hercules's early departure and the battle with the winged harpies. The emergence of Triton from the waters between the clashing rocks is superbly staged by Harryhausen, and the temple on Colchis is an extraordinary combination of special effects and art direction. But it is the now-legendary swordfight with seven skeleton warriors that ranks as Harryhausen's greatest achievement and the film's unqualified highlight. There aren't many technical feats from the 1950s that can still drop the average jaw in amazement today--this is one of them.

One more film version of the Golden Fleece story exists, but good luck finding it. From Germany, *Das Goldene Ding* (1971) retold the familiar story with a cast of children, a` la *Bugsy Malone* (1976). A cast of preteen Argonauts certainly has novelty value, but is probably best enjoyed by preteen audiences.

Also from 1971, the aforementioned *Medea* by Pier Paolo Pasolini blends the Argonaut story with the Euripides tragedy, with the tone of the latter clearly pervasive. Pasolini's films are not for all tastes--at his worst he combines the unpleasant excesses of Fellini, Bunuel and Peckinpah without any of their respective artistry. *Medea* is the most watchable of his later films because it is his most constrained, a by-product possibly of having the ghastly violence already built into the story.

Beginning with the infant Jason being told of his heritage by the centaur, Pasolini skips rapidly ahead to the adult Jason's return to Thessaly, Pelias's proposition of the voyage, and his arrival at Colchis. where he first meets Medea.

Another disjointed jump spans the ten years between the Fleece's recovery, Jason's second marriage and Medea's revenge.

The chief point of interest about this *Medea* today is the casting of opera legend Maria Callas as Medea in her only film role. She had played the character many times on stage in the Luigi Cherubini opera of the same name, and had they just filmed the opera the result would be far more satisfying. The only music in Pasolini's version consists of ear-splitting dissonance "composed" by the director. There are endless profile shots of Callas staring motionless into the horizon, which cut down on subtitles but do not have the dramatic effect that Pasolini intended. The great diva is too old here to be the Medea who steals Jason's heart on Colchis, and though more convincing as the scorned older woman, she cannot recreate here the formidable presence that was hers on the world's concert stages.

Jason, stiffly rendered by Giuseppe Gentili, is not an important figure in what is clearly meant to be Callas's dominion. The fabled *Argo* is just a big raft, and his recovery of the Fleece is practically a nonevent. The whole thing is too esoteric for mainstream audiences, who will be frustrated by the apparently mismatched scenes and an abrupt ending that seems to occur in the middle of a key development.

A more comprehensible and much better *Medea* was filmed on stage at the Kennedy Center in 1982. The play was adapted by Robinson Jeffers, who first brought the material to Broadway with Judith Anderson in the title role. Anderson returned to play the nurse in the Kennedy Center production opposite Zoe Caldwell as Medea and Mitchell Ryan as Jason. The play was broadcast on PBS, and most universities have a copy on tape. It's worth seeking out--more than two thousand years after its composition, the horrific events depicted in *Medea* have still not lost their power to shock.

THE FILMS

Giants of Thessaly (Alexandra P.C./Medallion, 1961, 86 minutes)
AKA The Argonauts, Jason and the Golden Fleece
Directed by Riccardo Freda; Written by Giuseppe Masini, Mario Rossetti and Riccardo Freda; Music by Carlo Rustichelli
Cast
ROLAND CAREY (JASON), Ziva Rodann (Creusa), Massimo Girotti (Orpheus)
Rating: * 1/2

Jason and the Argonauts (Columbia, 1963, 104 minutes)
Directed by Don Chaffrey; Written by Jan Reed and Beverly Cross; Produced by Charles H. Schneer; Music by Bernard Herrmann
Cast
TODD ARMSTRONG (JASON), Nancy Kovack (Medea), Gary Raymond (Acastus), Laurence Naismith (Argus), Niall MacGinnis (Zeus), Douglas Wilmer (Pelias), Honor Blackman (Hera), Patrick Troughton (Phineas), Nigel Green (Hercules)
Rating: ****
Available on Videocassette

Das Goldene Ding (Reitz-Film, 1971, 118 minutes)
AKA The Golden Thing
Directed, written and produced by Edgar Reitz, Ulla Stoeckl, Alf Brustellin and

Nicos Perakis; Music by Nikos Mamangates
Cast
CHRISTIAN REITZ (JASON), Oliver Jovine, Colombe Smith, Ulla Stoeckl, Alf Brustellin, Angela Elsner, Katrin Seybold, Erich Beth

Medea (San Marco-Rosima Anstaldt-Les Films Number One-Janus Fernsehen/ New Line Cinema, 1971, 100 minutes)
Directed and written by Pier Paolo Pasolini, based on the play by Euripides; Produced by Franco Rossellini; Music by Pasolini
Cast
Maria Callas (Medea), Massimo Girotti (Creon), GIUSEPPE GENTILI (JASON)
Rating; **

TELEVISION

"Medea" (broadcast of play, PBS, 90 minutes)
Directed by Robert Whitehead; Written by Robinson Jeffers, after Euripides; Produced by the Kennedy Center
Cast
Zoe Caldwell (Medea), MITCHELL RYAN (JASON), Paul Sparer (Creon)
Rating: ****

Ingrid Bergman as the Maid of Orleans in *Joan of Arc* (1948)

JOAN OF ARC

Some may be troubled by the inclusion of only one woman in a book on Hollywood's greatest heroes. There were, after all, excellent film biographies of Madame Curie, Florence Nightingale, Queen Elizabeth I, Helen Keller and Babe Didrickson Zaharias. To those who would cry, "sexism!" I can only request that they refer once again to the preface, and the admittedly limited definition of "hero" used in the selection process. Restricting the search to action heroes and warriors severely reduces the roster of women that qualify. There is Wonder Woman, of course, but three comic book creations are already included here, and besides there hasn't yet been a first-rate film adaptation of the famous Amazon princess. So we are left only with Joan of Arc, or Jeanne d'Arc in her native French. And since her momentous effect on history is worth any five of the males here, perhaps that helps to balance the scale.

HISTORY

So unique were her life and her exploits that no fiction writer would dare concoct such a story. France was not yet a country as we know it when Joan first heard her voices, but it was primarily through Joan that the various villages, towns and regions united under a cause and formed a national consciousness. She was born in 1412, the daughter of Jacques d'Arc, in the village of Domremy. At the age of thirteen she began to hear voices, which she believed belonged to St. Michael, St. Catherine and St. Margaret. They continued to counsel her until she was sixteen, at which time they told her to seek out Charles, the Dauphin, who was heir to the throne but unable to claim it. It took some convincing for the captain of the guard to admit her, but she was finally granted an audience in February 1429.

The Dauphin stood among his courtiers and did not reveal his identity, but when Joan entered the room she singled him out immediately, and announced her intention to aid him in defeating the English, who occupied most of the kingdom, and in crowing him at Reims, the traditional place for the investiture of Frenchkings that was presently held by the forces of Henry VI. In desperation, the Dauphin agreed to follow her advice. It was on her order that the French attacked at Orleans on May 4, and after this victory she led them in cleaning the English out of other towns throughout the Loire Valley. The particulars of the battles are fascinating reading, and recommended to anyone who could dare claim that history is dry and dull.

So thorough were the victories achieved by the Dauphin's forces that many areas gave up when they saw Joan, believing her to be invincible. True to her promise, the Dauphin was crowned King in Reims on July 17. Now a national symbol of what had just begun to be a nation, Joan urged continued attacks on other cities on the way to Paris. But the King began to back away from more fighting and, although she would spearhead many more victories, it was no longer with the full support of the court. In 1430 she was captured by the Duke of Burgundy's forces, and on January 9, 1431 she was put on trial at Rouen.

Joan was accused of heresy allied with witchcraft, but remained steadfast in her claims of divine guidance. She was interrogated more than a dozen times during the next three months, but the verdict was a foregone conclusion. Her request for an appeal to the pope was denied, but ultimately after being threatened repeatedly with sentencing by a secular authority she agreed to sign a form of abjuration. But a few days later she told the authorities that her voices expressed anger at her compliance, which they called an act of treason. Once more she was defiant, and would never again be convinced to disavow her mission. Although some English clerics and theologians were impressed with Joan's deportment and may have believed "The Maid of Orleans" to be everything she claimed to be, the authorities had no recourse but to find her guilty.

On May 30, 1431, Joan the Maid was burned at the stake and buried in Rouen. She had been granted permission to receive Communion first, which for a convicted heretic was inconceivable, but apparently the English wanted to cover their backsides just in case. The executioner was scared to death to light the flame, according to several accounts, and later declared that Joan's heart was found in the ashes, not even singed.

Twenty years later Charles VII of France called for an investigation into the trial, and Joan's reputation, which the people had never doubted, was restored. In 1803 Napoleon constructed a monument to her at Orleans. In 1894 she was declared venerable by Pope Leo XIII. In 1920 Joan was canonized as a saint, making her the only person in history to be both condemned and canonized by the Catholic church.

"Johannic Studies" is the name that has been given to the enormous body of literature, of varying quality and accuracy, devoted to the Maid. The field has become so voluminous that now books are devoted to compiling and reviewing the material available. The best of these, *Joan of Arc in History, Literature and Film* by Nadia Margolis, lists more then fifteen hundred sources of information, from the original trial records published in 1431 to biographies written in the 1980s. Among the most important is the five-volume edition on Joan's trials compiled by Jules Quicherat and published between 1841 and 1849. Quicherat also included excerpts from chronicles and literary works of the period, and continued to revise and update his research until his death in 1882.

No other medieval figure is as well documented as Joan of Arc, but few of these accounts are reliable as history. The trial transcripts are closest to the truth, but even here alteration and deletion no doubt occurred (as depicted in several versions of Joan's life). Of her early life little can be confirmed, and there is no record of her physical appearance outside of a crude sketch in the margin of a government document, drawn by a clerk in 1429. Certain features have been ascribed to her in paintings (Peter Paul Rubens in 1620 and many others), on stage (Sarah Bernhardt in 1890 in a play by Jules Barbier) and later on film--men's clothes, a cropped haircut, a petite frame and a comely face, with vivid eyes that seem to look inward as well as out--that are now a permanent part of the legend.

THE FILMS

Joan was a popular subject in the early days of motion pictures, her story having been told in silent treatments dating back to 1900. Most of these films were less than fifteen minutes long and are now believed lost: *Jeanne d'Arc* by Georges Melies, starring Louise d'Alcy (1900--one copy does exist at the Centre Jeanne d'Arc at Orleans), *La Beatification de Jeanne d'Arc* (Italian, 1901), directed by Albert Capellani, *Jeanne d'Arc*, also by Capellani (French, 1908), *Vie de Jeanne d'Arc* starring Tina Balli (Italian, 1908--09), *Giovanna d'Arco* (Italian, 1913) directed by Nino Oxilia and starring Maria Jacobini as Joan, and *Joan of Arc* (French, 1914).

In 1916, Cecil B. DeMille tried to outdo D. W. Griffith's epic film *Intolerance* with his first grand religious drama, *Joan the Woman*. The story is told in the dream sequence of a French soldier during World War I, who finds a sword in a trench and wonders whether it belonged to the legendary Maid. He falls asleep and in his dream becomes one of Joan's followers. He accompanies her from Orleans to her execution. He awakes, inspired by her example, and attacks a German unit, sacrificing his life for his country as well.

The *Intolerance* influence is apparent in its use of Joan's story as an allegory for a then present-day conflict, its massive scale of the battle sequences, and its negative portrayal of the religious establishment when confronted with the embodiment of their faith. A complete version of the film does not exist, but there are fragments that are clear precursors to DeMille's later classics. Among the sequences that survive is one shot in color. Geraldine Farrar, a well-known opera singer, played Joan with zest, though her age and borderline robust physical appearance are atypical in Joan's filmography.

One would not expect the DeMille version to be surpassed very quickly, but in 1927 Carl-Theodore Dreyer directed *La Passion de Jeanne d'Arc*, one of the greatest silent films ever made. Concentrating exclusively on the trial and subsequent execution, Dreyer shows us Joan being questioned and probed, and later teased and tormented by her captors, and then burned at the stake in one of the most excruciating moments in cinema.

It is easier for most viewers to notice and judge the work of the director in a silent film. Without the distraction of dialogue one is more cognizant of the composition of a frame, how shots are placed together and the movement of the camera. In the hands of lesser talent the film's continual use of close-ups would be laborious viewing, but Dreyer's cross-cutting between Joan's sincerity, expressed flawlessly in the moving performance of Maria Falconetti, and the smugness of her accusers is riveting. Though she remains defiant, Falconetti's Joan can also revert to being a confused and frightened teenager. This was her only film appearance, and is still often cited on lists of the ten best film performances of all time. The organ, as the instrument of choice of both the church and the silent movie, is effectively used to convey a variety of moods.

La Merveilleuse Vie de Jeanne d'Arc, [*Saint Joan the Maid*] {1929}, was the last of the silent treatments. Simone Genevois played Joan in this French production directed by Marc Gastyne. Its reputation is nowhere near that of DeMille's or Dreyer's version, but it does make use of such authentic locations as Rheims in telling Joan's story from her early life in Domremy to her death.

The 1935 German film *Das Maedchen Johanna* received the most limited of releases in the United States and, to my knowledge, hasn't surfaced over here since. One contemporary review lauded the performance of Angela Salloker as Joan and Gustav Ucicky's direction, but questioned its historical accuracy; in this version King Charles is both wiser and craftier than history records. He uses Joan for all she's worth as a national symbol, and then allows her to be executed, knowing that her martyrdom is the most effective weapon France could possess in the war against England.

The golden-age Hollywood biography starred Ingrid Bergman, and was a huge hit with critics in 1948 but turned out to be a huge financial failure. Bergman realized her lifelong dream to play the Maid of Orleans, but it took years before her performance and the film found a receptive audience.

History as we know can be followed with comparative precision; the problem is to make such fantastic history credible. It becomes apparent in this chapter that the success of each film hinges almost solely on the casting of Joan. At this time in Hollywood, Bergman was the ideal choice--no other actress, with the possible exception of the as-yet-undiscovered Audrey Hepburn, could have played the role so well. It was said that whenever Bergman visited Paris she would hear "Welcome home, Jeanne d'Arc," high praise indeed considering the many French film and television treatments. Her quiet intensity and passion compare favorably with the legendary Falconetti.

The script, based on the play *Joan of Lorraine*, begins at the trial and covers all the major events in Joan's life through flashbacks. Though many of the battle scenes are clearly studio-bound, the cinematography is excellent and director Victor Fleming effectively creates the illusion of a French countryside. With credits such as *The Wizard of Oz* (1939) and *Gone With the Wind* (1939), Fleming can certainly handle any subject, and the bigger the better. He unfolds the Maid's story in a leisurely 145 minutes (shorter versions also exist), but every time the action threatens to drag, Bergman pours on the acting accelerator and ignites the screen. Jose Ferrer is equally outstanding as the duplicitous Dauphin. *Joan of Arc* gives us the best insight into the complex relationship between Charles and the Maid.

The French are heard from again in 1953's *Destinees`*, also known as *Daughters of Destiny*. The film consists of three sketches, each concerning famous women whose destinies were shaped by war. Joan, featured in the middle sketch, is depicted at the moment that she is deserted by her king and her soldiers in 1430. In her moment of need she calls upon her "voices" for assistance. Michele Morgan plays Joan.

All of these films are consistent in their portrayal of Joan, but Otto Preminger's innovative *Saint Joan* (1957) is something of a departure. Based on George Bernard Shaw's play, the film was dismissed when first released but seems to get better every year.

Though it is not a comedy or a revisionist treatment, there is a more modern feel to the story. The dialogue in previous films was psuedo-classical, heavy in aristocratic accent and finishing school diction. Here Shaw's words are filtered through Graham Greene's wonderful script and now we have Joan calling theDauphin "Charlie." One of the film's best devices, borrowed from the play, is a prologue and epilogue in which Joan appears to the Dauphin after her death and discusses the events of her life. They are joined by many of Joan's supporters and accusers, now all deceased and gone to their just rewards.

Preminger launched a massive nationwide talent search to find his Maid of Orleans, and settled on newcomer Jean Seberg. Her performance was much-maligned by critics at first, but the qualities of sweetness, naivete` and almost Shirley Temple--like pluck she displays have aged well. Today they might actually be preferable to an audience to the more traditionally theatrical work of Bergman and Falconetti, who played Joan as if she had one foot in heaven already. Seberg essays several moving moments, such as her Joan's inability to understand why she is not believed right away by the court, and later her shock and dismay at how quickly they forget her role in their victory.

Richard Widmark plays the Dauphin as a whining ninny, who plays hopscotch in his royal robes while Joan advises marching on Paris. His performance provokes anger but also pity, for a simpleton unfit to play a part on the world stage. Sir John Gielgud is brilliant as the Earl of Warwick, who buys Joan for the British, and Anton Walbrook plays the haughty archbishop who wouldn't know a miracle if he tripped over it.

Preminger doesn't open up the play very much, except for a large crowd scene at Joan's execution. There are no big battles; instead he cleverly segues' from the eve of the Orleans conflict to Charles's coronation at Rheims. He saved a lot of money on extras and didn't damage the impact of the film, by far the director's best, in the least. *Saint Joan* is long overdue for reassessment.

Also from 1957, *The Story of Mankind* was a disastrous recounting of global history from prehistoric times to the present. Any movie that would bring together Ronald Colman and the Marx Brothers is worth seeing, but the wild shifts in tone are enough to give the viewer whiplash. As the Spirit of Man, played by Colman, debates with the Devil (Vincent Price) over whether the human race should be picked up for another few centuries, various historical figures are called upon as evidence on each side. Joan of Arc is played by a blond Hedy Lamarr, second-billed even though she is not around very long. William Schallert, Patty Duke's dad on TV, plays the Earl of Warwick. It is a bizarre movie, definitely a failure, but hard to resist.

The Trial of Joan of Arc (1962) has much in common with the Dreyer silent film, with its almost exclusive concentration on the trial and attention to actual testimony, but it does not inspire the same passion. Writer-director Robert Bresson brings the same stark austerity to medieval France as he would later bring to Camelot in *Lancelot du Lac* (1974) The "look" of Bresson's films is unique, but he tends to cast amateurs who manage the near-impossible feat of blending into unadorned scenery. There is little drama and less action, in fact at times it's difficult to determine if the film is moving at all. Florence Carrez plays Joan in the spirit of the piece, which is to say dull and lifeless.

One other variation on Joan of Arc's contribution to history is provided by William Shakespeare in his play *Henry VI, Part One*. As an Englishman in the sixteenth century, Shakespeare's outlook on Joan's victories in battle is understandably less enthusiastic. The play itself is one of the Bard's least admired works, and some scholars are even reluctant to believe that he actually wrote it. The prevailing view is that the play we have now is an incomplete and/or incorrectly transcribed version of an earlier work, that presumably is more polished.

As with all of Shakespeare's histories the dates and facts are telescoped and distorted to fit the drama. The play primarily concerns the political division between the Houses of Lancaster and York, which sparked the War of the Roses. Joan, referred to as Joan de Pucelle, is the witch who leads the French forces of the Dauphin to victory after victory, while the ineffective English monarch is forced to deal with the power struggle at home.

The BBC's "Shakespeare Plays" series presented *Henry VI, Part One* in 1983 with Peter Benson as the King. The role of Joan went to Brenda Blethyn, whose fiery performance was dictated by Shakespeare's coarse depiction of the lady who sent his ancestors packing from the continent.

THE FILMS

Jeanne d'Arc (Star Films, 1900, 15 minutes)
Directed by Georges Melies
Cast
LOUISE D'ALCY (JOAN OF ARC)

La Beatification de Jeanne d'Arc (1901)
Directed by Mario Caserini
Cast
MARIA GASPERINI (JOAN OF ARC)

Jeanne d'Arc (Pathe'-France, 1908)
Directed by Albert Capellani

Vie de Jeanne d'Arc (Cines-Italia, 1908-9)
Written by Guido Gozzano
Cast
TINA BALLI (JOAN OF ARC)

Giovanna d'Arco (Pasquali, 1913)
Directed by Nino Oxilla
Cast
MARIA JACOBINI (JOAN OF ARC)

Joan the Woman (LAS/Cardinal, 1917, 80 minutes)
Directed by Cecil B. DeMille; Written by Jeanie Macpherson
Cast
GERALDINE FARRAR (JOAN OF ARC), Raymond Hatton (Charles VII), Hobart Bosworth (Gen. La Hire), Theodore Roberts (Cauchon)

The Passion of Joan of Arc (Societe Generale Des Films, 1928, 77 minutes)
Directed and written by Carl Theodore Dreyer; Music by Victor Alix and Leo Pouget
Cast
MARIE FALCONETTI (JOAN OF ARC), Eugene Silvain (Bishop Pierre Cauchon), Maurice Schultz (Nicholas Loyseleur), Michel Simon (Jean Lemaitre)
Rating: *****

La Merveilleuse Vie de Jeanne d'Arc (Aubert-Natan, 1929)
AKA Saint Joan the Maid
Directed by Marco de Gastyne
Cast
SIMONE GENEVOIS (JOAN OF ARC), Philippe Heriat (Charles VII)
Rating: ***

Das Madchen Johanna (UFA, 1935)

Directed by Gustav Ucicky
Cast
ANGELA SALLOKER (JOAN OF ARC)

Joan of Arc (RKO, 1948, 145 minutes)
Directed by Victor Fleming; Written by Andrew Solt and Maxwell Anderson, based on the play *Joan of Lorraine* by Anderson; Produced by Walter Wanger; Music by Hugo Friedhofer
Cast
INGRID BERGMAN (JOAN OF ARC), Jose Ferrer (The Dauphin), Francis L. Sullivan (Pierre Cauchon), J. Carroll Naish (Count John of Luxembourg) Ward Bond (La Hire)
Rating: ****1/2
Available on Videocassette
Awards: Academy Award for Best Cinematography and Best Costume Design; nominations for Best Actress (Ingrid Bergman), Supporting Actor (Jose Ferrer), Art Direction-Set Direction, Editing and Musical Score

Destinees`(Cinedis/Franco-London, 1954, 105 minutes)
AKA Daughters of Destiny
Directed by Marcel Pagliero, Jean Delannoy and Christian Jaque; Written by Jean Aurenche, Vladimir Pozner, Sergio Amidei, Pierre Bost, Jean Ferry, Henri Jeanson, Carlo Rim and Andre Tabot; Produced by Marcel Pagliero;
Cast
Claudette Colbert (Elizabeth), Eleanora Rossi-Drago (Angela), MICHELE MORGAN (JEANNE), Martine Carol (Lysistrata)

Saint Joan (Wheel/United Artists, 1957, 110 minutes)
Directed and produced by Otto Preminger; Written by Graham Greene, based on the play by George Bernard Shaw; Music by Mischa Spoliansky
Cast
JEAN SEBERG (JOAN OF ARC), Richard Widmark (Charles the Dauphin), Richard Todd (Dunois), Anton Walbrook (Cauchon), John Gielgud (The Earl of Warwick), Felix Aylmer (The Inquisitor)
Rating: ****1/2
Available on Videocassette

The Story of Mankind (Warner Bros., 1957, 100 minutes)
Directed and produced by Irwin Allen; Written by Irwin Allen and Charles Bennett, based on the book by Hendrik Willem van Loon; Music by Paul Sawtell
Cast
Ronald Colman (Spirit of Man), HEDY LAMARR (JOAN OF ARC), GrouchoMarx (Peter Minuit), Harpo Marx (Isaac Newton), Chico Marx (Monk), Virginia Mayo (Cleopatra), Vincent Price (Devil), Agnes Moorehead (Queen Elizabeth), Peter Lorre (Nero), Charles Coburn (Hippocrates), Sir Cedric Hardwicke, Cesar Romero, John Carradine, Dennis Hopper
Rating: **

The Trial of Joan of Arc (Pathe Contemporary, 1965, 65 minutes)
Directed and written by Robert Bresson, based on "Proces De Condemnation Et De

Rehabilitation De Jeanne d'Arc"; Produced by Agnes Delahaie; Music by Francis Seyrig
Cast
FLORENCE CARREZ (JOAN OF ARC), Jean-Claude Fourneau (Bishop Cauchon), Marc Jacquier (Jean Lemaitre), E.R. Pratt (Warwick)
Rating: **

TELEVISION
"Henry VI, Pt. 1" (BBC teleplay, 1982, 120 minutes)
Directed by Jane Howell; Adapted by David Snodin; Produced by Jonathan Miller; Music by Dudley Simpson
Cast
Peter Benson (Henry VI), David Burke (Gloucester), BRENDA BLETHYN (JOAN)
Rating: ***1/2

INDIANA JONES

The *Indiana Jones* films are a fond remembrance of a cinematic age gone by, updated with the kind of talent and technology that their predecessors could only dream about. Indiana Jones himself is an amalgam of several characters with equally silly names, such as Red Ryder and Brick Bradford.

ORIGINS

From the opening moments of *Raiders of the Lost Ark*, Indy tips his fedora affectionately to his fellow adventurers, who performed their heroics in the serials that ran in theaters from the 1930s to the early 1950s. Each serial offered at least ten chapters of thrills, in which the hero must appear to be killed at the end of each installment. So even if the main feature was lousy, the kiddies would still have to come back to the theater next week.

The stories usually involved stolen idols, exotic locations, and chases that would lead to desperate cliffhangers. *Raiders* borrowed liberally from dozens of these potboilers, improving on their execution without sacrificing their sense of innocent, goofy fun. The series would then develop its own running gags, from the stomach-churning encounters with various vermin to Indy's hilarious standoffs with cocky swordsmen.

The gun vs. sword scenes in particular are a perfect microcosm of the entire series. The idea and its unexpected climax are not original, but still work. And when the act is replayed in the sequel, it's a safe bet that the same scene would have worked again, but that was too easy. So they added something new to the something old, and made something even better.

It's a rare film series indeed that suffers no drop in quality over three chapters, but you can add that to Dr. Jones's list of achievements as well. *Raiders* will always be the sentimental favorite, for introducing the world to a new hero, but *Indiana Jones and the Temple of Doom* and *Indiana Jones and the Last Crusade* easily equal and in some ways surpass *Raiders* in rollercoaster thrills.

The vigilance of Indiana Jones creators George Lucas and Steven Spielberg had much to do with the series's artistic consistency. Lucas and Spielberg practically own the list of all-time top grossing movies; as of 1991, one of their names appears in the credits of eight of the top ten entries, with *Raiders* at number 8, *Last Crusade* at number 9 and *Temple of Doom* at number 10.

THE FILMS

Lucas and Spielberg were also smart enough to end the series when they did, going out on top instead of slowly fading into mediocrity (like the *Superman* series and countless others). Because of its relatively simple premise, there are only so many ways that Indy could reinvent himself, and the action sequences could not be improved upon, so why risk redundancy? Smart move.

It was 1981 when we first met Indiana Jones, though on screen the year is 1936, the place South America. Indy avoids a series of booby traps to retrieve a golden idol, only to have it stolen at gunpoint by Belloq, a rival archaeologist. He returns empty-handed to his regular job--professor of archaeology at a California university.

U.S. Army intelligence uncovers evidence that the Nazis are in Egypt searching for the Ark of the Covenant, which, according to the *Bible* , contains the stone tablets on which God inscribed the Ten Commandments. If the legends are true the Ark will make Hitler invincible, so Uncle Sam wants Dr. Jones to find it first. Along the way Indy stops in Nepal to see Marion Ravenwood, a former paramour and the daughter of the world's foremost authority on the Ark. After fighting off a band of goosestepping Sherpas, Indy and Marion head for Cairo with a medallion that reveals the Ark's location.

Dr. Jones wins the race, but Belloq, now allied with the Nazis, once again steals the prize. Indy chases the caravan containing the Ark across land and sea, until he and Marion are also abducted. Before they are killed, Belloq allows them to witness the opening of the Ark. When the Nazis pop the lid, they are destroyed by angry spirits. Having witnessed the Ark's power, Indy decides not to risk its falling into the wrong hands again. The Ark is buried where no one will ever find it--a U.S. government storage warehouse.

You can see traces of Zorro and Superman in the concept of a bespectacled, mild-mannered professor who can transform into a roguish adventurer. The difference lies in Dr. Jones's dry sense of humor, which demonstrates his lack of the effortless confidence most heroes possess. "I'm making this up as I go," he answers when someone asks how he plans to retrieve the Ark. Of course, he finds a way.

Indy's motivation is also unique. He fights not only for justice but for archaeology, and it is his love and respect for the past that saves his life when the Ark is opened. Jones wants to give the Ark to the world, while the Nazis want only to take its power. Indy's triumph is one for both science and religion, against those who have no use for either other than how they can line their pockets. Belloq tells Indy at one point that archaeology *is* his religion, but if that's true at the beginning it certainly isn't at the end.

Raiders won four Oscars for technical achievement, and its ring-around-the-truck chase scene is indeed a legend-making set piece, but don't overlook the contribution of Harrison Ford. He still *re*acts more than acts, but nobody does it better. Tom Selleck had a shot at the role, and while he demonstrated an Indy-like self-effacing quality in the "Magnum, P.I." series, I don't think he'd have worked out as well. It's tough to speculate, but I think his imposing height and physique would have made Indy appear less of the underdog than he usually was (as in the fistfight with the bald muscleman). Selleck flopped in the *Raiders*-type action-comedy *High Road to China* (1983) but to be fair he didn't have Lucas and Spielberg behind the cameras.

Raiders also gave Ford his best leading lady in Karen Allen, a tomboyish beauty who more than holds her own. Her spirit is missed in the later installments. The one problem I've always had with *Raiders* is its relatively weak climax. After fighting the good fight for one hundred minutes, our hero ends up passively tied to a post when the villains finally get theirs. To me that has never seemed right, and it's a problem that was corrected in Dr. Jones's next adventure.

Indiana Jones and the Temple of Doom is set one year before *Raiders*. This time we find Indy in a Shanghai nightclub, where he is poisoned in a diamond exchange gone sour. After retrieving the antidote, he makes his escape accompanied by club chanteuse Willie Scott and his young companion Short Round. After a desperate leap from a pilotless plane, Indy and friends land in a small village in India, where all the children have been abducted to work as slave labor in a maharajah's palace. Indy heads for the palace and Willie, knowing he's her only chance to get back to civilization, tags along. Following a suspiciously gracious reception, and an elegant but unusual dinner, Indy discovers a secret passage in the palace that leads to a hidden temple, where children are used as human sacrifices to the demon god Kalid. While attempting a rescue Indy falls under the spell of mind-altering drugs and temporarily changes sides. Short Round breaks the spell with a torch to the gut, and Indy revives and cleans house. The temple is destroyed, and the children are returned to their village.

Temple of Doom was actually criticized in some circles for having *too* much action, and not allowing the audience to catch its collective breath between thrills. Are they kidding? If I want tranquility I'll rent *Autumn Sonata*. There's no such thing as too much action, especially if it's as well shot and choreographed as it is here by Spielberg and veteran cinematographer Douglas Slocombe. The film can also get away with it because it's a sequel; we already know Indy and like him, so there's no need to waste time with introductions. *Temple of Doom* opens with guns blazing and never slows down. Indy's recovery from the cult's drugs begins one of the best extended action sequences in movie history.

Kate Capshaw is no Karen Allen, but once she stops whining (sometime after the elephant ride), she becomes an engaging foil, especially during the gross-out dinner scene. The movie's real find is Ke Huy Quan as Indy's pint-sized sidekick. Short Round has none of the saccharine precocious qualities of most screen kiddies. He has the gumption of a street survivor and a resourcefulness to rival Dr. Jones himself. Look quickly for Dan Aykroyd at the Shanghai airport, and Indy's emergence from the Club Obi Wan, Lucas's inside joke.

Indiana Jones and the Last Crusade opens with a teenage Indy trekking through Utah with his boy scout troupe, in a prologue that inspired the "Young Indiana Jones" television series. This "origin" story, in which Indy tries to steal the "Cross of Coronado" from an archaeologist who plans to sell it for personal gain, uncovers the story behind his trademark hat, jacket, whip and his fear of snakes.

Flash forward twenty-six years, when the action picks up on the Portuguese coast, where Indy finally recovers the Cross and donates it to his university museum. But after just one day in the classroom he is forced into another field assignment; philanthropist Walter Donovan informs Indy that his father, Professor Henry Jones, has disappeared while searching for the legendary Holy Grail. The trail begins in Venice, where Indy makes contact with Dr. Elsa Schneider, a colleague of his father's. Together they find more information on the Grail, and learn that the senior Dr. Jones is being held captive by the Nazis in an Austrian castle.

When they reach the castle Indy is captured as well, after Dr. Schneider shows her true colors. Resourceful as ever, Indiana rescues his father and, with the help of some old friends, they recover the professor's diary, which provides crucial information on obtaining the Grail. With the German army in pursuit, father and son find the cavern where the Grail is kept, and the ancient knight who guards it. Donovan, a German sympathizer, and a squad of Nazis crash the party, but Donovan fails the knight's test and is killed, along with the other goosesteppers. Indy passes the test, but turns down the job as new Grail guard.

Last Crusade might have become repetitive had it stuck to the same formula, but once again the folks in charge were too smart to let that happen. The innovative prologue with River Phoenix gets things rolling, and the introduction of Sean Connery as Professor Henry Jones adds yet another dimension to the Indiana Jones character. The motorcycle chase scene is particularly revealing; Indy sends two Nazis flying and then looks to his dad for approval, which he doesn't get. No wonder the guy's such an overachiever.

There's a bit of the old in with the new as well, with the return of *Raiders* supporting cast members Denholm Elliot and John Rhys-Davies, and another story based on Christian symbolism. And even though it's not how the series is best remembered, when was the last time you saw such an affirmation of religion in movies this across-the-board popular without complaints from offended atheists or Bible-thumpers? "The search for the cup of Christ is the search for the divine in us all," says Brody (Elliot) early on, as Indy once again scoffs at what he calls "mythology" early on, but becomes a believer.

The action is still there, of course, along with a higher quotient of comedy than ever before. Most of it works, especially Indy's phony Scottish brogue, his celebrated gift for understatement ("Nazis. I hate these guys.") and the scene with the librarian in Venice. *Last Crusade* also contains the best Hitler-induced laugh since *The Producers* (1968).

Sunday school lessons aside, the Indiana Jones series has no aspirations of enlightening, educating or moralizing. The idea here is to just fasten your seatbelt and enjoy the ride. There will always be a place for movies like this, though rarely are they created with this much love and care. Education is definitely an objective, however, of "The Young Indiana Jones Chronicles," a pseudo-spinoff of the prologue in *Last Crusade*. Executive producer George Lucas attempts to teach a history lesson with every episode, as either ten-year-old Indy (Corey Carrier) or sixteen-year-old Indy (Sean Patrick Flannery) find themselves in the company of such luminaries as Teddy Roosevelt and Lawrence of Arabia. The lavish production values are far beyond most weekly TV series, but death-defying action is not on the menu.

Neither Carrier nor Flannery are interesting enough variations on the theme to tune in, so the series depended on the strength of its guest historical figures. It was a workable but limited hook, that could have lasted until everyone from the designated eras had been met. But the network had other ideas, and Indy was cancelled after a sporadic two-season run.

THE FILMS

Raiders of the Lost Ark (Paramount, 1981, 115 minutes)
Directed by Steven Spielberg; Written by Lawrence Kasdan, based on a story by Philip Kaufman; Produced by Frank Marshall; Music by John Williams
Cast
HARRISON FORD (INDIANA JONES), Karen Allen (Marion Ravenwood), Paul Freeman (Belloq), Ronald Lacey (Toht), John Rhys-Davies (Sallah), Denholm Elliot (Brody)

Rating: *****
Available on Videocassette
Awards: Academy Awards for Best Art Direction, Best Sound, Best Editing and Best Visual Effects; nominations for Best Picture, Best Director, Best Cinematography and Best Score

Indiana Jones and the Temple of Doom (Paramount, 1984, 118 minutes)
Directed by Steven Spielberg; Written by Willard Huyck and Gloria Katz, based on a story by George Lucas; Produced by Robert Watts; Music by John Williams
Cast
HARRISON FORD (INDIANA JONES), Kate Capshaw (Willie Scott), Ke Huy Quan (Short Round), Amrish Puri (Mola Ram)
Rating: *****
Available on Videocassette
Awards: Academy Award for Best Visual Effects; nomination for Best Score

Indiana Jones and the Last Crusade (Paramount, 1989, 127 minutes)
Directed by Steven Spielberg; Written by Jeffrey Boam, based on a story by George Lucas; Produced by Robert Watts; Music by John Williams
Cast
HARRISON FORD (INDIANA JONES), Sean Connery (Dr. Henry Jones), Denholm Elliot (Dr. Brody), Alison Doody (Dr. Elsa Schneider), John Rhys-Davies (Sallah), Julian Glover (Walter Donovan), River Phoenix (Young Indy)
Rating: *****
Available on Videocassette
Awards: Academy Award for Best Sound Effects Editing; nomination for Best Score and Sound

TELEVISION
"The Young Indiana Jones Chronicles" (ABC series 1992- 1993)
Cast
COREY CARRIER (INDIANA JONES, age 10), SEAN PATRICK FLANNERY (INDIANA JONES, age 14)
Rating: ***

William Shatner as Captain James T. Kirk from the television series *Star Trek*.

CAPTAIN JAMES T. KIRK

From 1966 to 1969, "Star Trek" brought sophisticated science fiction to television. . .and languished in obscurity. But after being canceled by NBC, the series that broke its share of rules the first time around rendered the rulebook obsolete. When it jumped almost immediately to syndication, an unprecedented surge in popularity transformed "Trek" into the first true cult TV show, and more than twenty-five years later its following still outstrips every other network attempt to create such a phenomenon, with the possible exception of "Star Trek: The Next Generation."

THE PHENOMENON

Dozens of television series have created characters that have become part of our popular culture, but the *Enterprise* crew members are now beyond even that status. They have been a near constant presence via reruns and movies and novels. They have added words and expressions to our language, and created technology that has been debated in scientific journals. They have inspired the name of a U.S. space shuttle, and been honored by NASA.

The series's most significant contribution is a twenty-third century as envisioned by "Star Trek" creator Gene Roddenberry that gives our species a goal to work toward, and illustrates what the human race can become if we don't screw up. There are challenges on both the humanistic and scientific fronts, with the emphasis placed strongly on the former. Maybe we'll never get the hang of transporters, but if we can eliminate racism and learn to greet the unknown with kindness instead of fear, "Star Trek" will have taught its lessons well.

Our principal tour guide in this brave new world is *Enterprise* Captain James Tiberius Kirk. For awhile he was Admiral Kirk, but when Starfleet orders stood in the way of rescuing Mr. Spock he placed friendship above regulations and was busted back to captain for insubordination. He lost his rank, but tells Spock's father in *Star Trek III* that if he hadn't tried, "I'd have lost my soul." That's the kinda guy he is.

Kirk and his fellow crew members have been dissected and studied and psychoanalyzed in scores of fan publications for the past twenty years. The trekkers do overdo it sometimes, but they tend to get a bad rap. Attend their conventions and you'll find a diverse assortment of creative, imaginative people and a higher overall I.Q. level than at most public gatherings. The payback for their support has been a mutual respect from "Trek"'s creators, who pay strict attention to the history and continuity of their fictional world. Note the opening scenes in *Star Trek IV*, which are included only to wrap up loose ends from the previous film.

So those seeking further information on Kirk will find no shortage of material, but almost everyone agrees on the basics: he's a seasoned commander who still loves to play the space cowboy. He enjoys being in charge and, like the warriors of our own age, he is disturbed when the human factor is replaced in conflict by technology. Kirk's distrust of computers provided the plot for two series episodes, "The Return of the Archons" and "The Ultimate Computer." And in "A Taste of Armageddon" he is outraged when the Enterprise lands in the war zone of two planets that fight entirely through their computers to reduce property damage.

There is a parallel here with the relationship between Kirk and Mr. Spock and their series staple debates on logic vs. emotion. The ideal commander, as Kirk himself admits in *Star Trek IV*, would use both in equal measure, but where Spock will always favor the logical, at times appearing to have as much in common with the ship's computer as his crewmates, Kirk leans heavily toward shooting from the hip. His emotions have frequently led to trouble (movies III and VI, and several series episodes), but in the end he always saves the ship and even lands the babe in the aluminum foil swimsuit.

Kirk could live long and prosper without machines, but he'd be lost without his crew. Though his individualism often stands out, he remains a team player, realizing that his officers provide the skills and personality traits that complement his own--Spock, to balance his outbursts with rational argument, Dr. Leonard "Bones" McCoy to ground the sometimes grandiose captain with common sense, and Scotty to keep the ship running no matter what situation Kirk leads them into. And this of course has been the message of "Star Trek" from the beginning--we need each other.

"Trek Classic", as it has been rechristened by fans, took but seventy-nine voyages, as opposed to a hundred episodes and counting for "New Trek." Originally envisioned by Gene Roddenberry as an outer space western, the series quickly put that simplistic premise to shame with stories that grasped with religion, philosophy and ethics. The messages were ultimately hopeful, though they were often presented as warnings to the wise.

When we first meet Kirk in the series second pilot attempt, "Where No Man Has Gone Before," he is already firmly in command, and thus we are denied his first encounters with Spock, Bones, etc. and the chance to watch him grow into the job. We gain our insights into Kirk in the best episodes--his brilliance at starship warfare in "Balance of Terror," his self-confidence in several gut check situations in "The Corbomite Maneuver," and his vulnerability to true love after playing the Casanova of the galaxy in "The City on the Edge of Forever."

There were some poor shows along the way, and it is in these that actor William Shatner acquired his reputation for overtheatrics. Episodes such as "The Omega Glory," in which Kirk recites the preamble to the U. S. Constitution in exactly the way he has been parodied ever since are indefensible, but not as abundant as Shatner's detractors would believe. When the material was there, as it usually was with Trek Classic, Shatner was superb. It was mostly later, when he signed on to dross like "T. J. Hooker" that his scenery-chewing became a trademark.

After its cancellation, an animated version of "Star Trek" appeared on Saturday mornings, and ran from 1973 to 1975. Several episodes were written by "Trek"'s best writers (D. C. Fontana, David Gerrold), and all the cast members save Walter Koenig (Chekhov) returned to voice their characters.

THE FILMS

However, not until 1979 did the fans' unwavering support finally pay off. *Star Trek--The Motion Picture* brought everybody back and gave them $40 million worth of hardware to cavort in, but most fans would have gladly substituted the tin can effects of the original series for the presence of a worthwhile story.

The film begins with three Klingon vessels being sucked up by a huge glowing cloud that is on a collision course with earth. Admiral Kirk is given back command of the *Enterprise*, replacing the envious Captain Will Decker. The lifeform within the cloud takes possession of Ilia, the ship's navigator, and communicates through her its intention to join with its creator. Turns out the lifeform is a three-hundred year-old NASA *Voyager* probe that merged with a higher form of machine life, and has been gathering information on the universe ever since. Now it wants to complete its mission by transferring the information to "the creator." Since Voyager was created by man, Decker volunteers to join with the machine, and the result is a new lifeform that may represent man's next evolutionary step. Say what?

This isn't quite the total failure that it's remembered as, but not for nothing did audiences rename it "Star Trek--The Motionless Picture." Blame George Lucas--after *Star Wars* revolutionized science fiction filmmaking two years earlier, the Trek folks felt compelled to keep up technologically. So they hired FX wizard Douglas Trumbull and poured a mint into some undeniably pretty pictures. Then they made sure to get their money's worth by lingering over these scenes ad nauseum. Kirk and Scotty's shuttle transfer to the *Enterprise* is twice as long as it need be, and the *Enterprise*'s approach to the cloud center goes on forever. That said, were it not for *Star Wars*'s success the Trek reunion may well have been a made-for-TV venture, so a thank you is also in order.

After a decade without new material, the Trek-starved faithful were primed, but once past the "Oooh! Klingons! Ooooh! There's Spock! Ooooh! There's Kirk!" stage, they waited for something to actually happen. And waited, and waited. Director Robert Wise expected the crowd to be awestruck at routine movement--note the fanfare that accompanies such incidentals as the docking of Kirk's shuttlecraft with the *Enterprise*, and the ship's departure from the space station. The audience was easy, but not that easy.

Other bad ideas abound. Giving Spock an attitude problem after he flunked a Vulcan SAT ruins the joyful reunion that fans dreamed about. A battle against a cloud is not that exciting, and the resolution is a mess. And who designed those drab earth-tone pajama-like uniforms? And why would new crewmember Persis Khambatta, an appalling actress, get more screen time than the old familiars?

But if you're even a casual fan, you gotta see it once. Shatner, Leonard Nimoy and DeForest Kelley back together is reason enough. Video-seekers may be shocked to find another 12 minutes of footage added to the already 134 minute opus, which is highly illogical.

Fortunately, *Star Trek* was by this time a force too powerful to be sidetracked by one bad movie. As soon as someone remembered what made the series so popular in the first place, improvement was inevitable. It happened with *Star Trek II--The Wrath of Khan* (1982), which drew the inspiration for its story from the 1966 series episode "The Space Seed." It's a testament to the Trek following that writer Jack B. Sowards and Director Nicholas Meyer would allow several specific references to the twenty-year-old episode, knowing that most of the audience would pick up on each one.

The film opens with Kirk and most of the *Enterprise* crew training new Starfleet cadets in the workings of a starship. Kirk suggests a field trip, but the routine voyage takes a serious turn when the ship receives a garbled distress call. Forced to investigate, the *Enterprise* is attacked by Khan, whom Kirk remembers as the megalomaniacal leader of a superhuman race. Kirk had banished Khan to a barren planet, and now Khan is ready to have his revenge. After crippling the *Enterprise*, Khan demands information on Genesis, a scientific project that can create life by shifting subatomic particles. The ever-resourceful Kirk stalls his nemesis until he can lead his crew to safety.

At the space station that first sent the SOS to the *Enterprise*, Kirk is reunited with his old flame Carol Marcus and his estranged son, David. Father and son have much to work through, but circumstances force the discussion to be tabled. Kirk works on Khan's ego, and manages to lure him into a compromising position. Victory is achieved, but the cost is devastating when Spock sacrifices his life to save the ship (yeah, right).

This is *Trek* at its very best, with the cast firing on all cylinders plus Kirstie Alley in her breakthrough role as the Vulcan cadet Saavik and Ricardo Montalban hamming up to the heavens as Khan. The only drawback is Merritt Butrick as Kirk's whiny, morose son David, though his existence does bring to light another side of Kirk's character. The admiral is confronted with the life he could have led, raising his boy with Dr. Marcus, and for a time perhaps he has regrets about his military career. Watching his impatience in the film's early moments, however, makes it clear that Kirk was born to search the skies. The "death" of Spock is an obvious sequel-inducer but still packs a punch. Note how Kirk quotes Dickens at the end, a passion he shares with New Trek's Captain Picard.

Star Trek III was predictably subtitled *The Search for Spock*, though it is still best remembered as "the one between II and IV." It's much better than that, and is probably perceived as a disappointment only because it is sandwiched between the two best series entries.

Spock's tomb is launched toward the Genesis planet. Almost immediately, signs of life are detected within his casket, and are first noticed by David Marcus and Saavik. Kirk is refused permission to take the *Enterprise* back to the planet, so he steals the ship and returns anyway, accompanied by his loyal crew. David and Saavik beam down to the planet and find a Vulcan child, whom they believe to be a regenerated Spock. While they search for answers, their ship is destroyed by the Klingons, who want the secret of Genesis to use as a weapon. Genesis, however, proves to be a failure when both Spock and the planet begin to age rapidly. The Klingons still want it, and kill David to demonstrate their resolve. Kirk is devastated by his son's murder and exacts his revenge on the Klingons, though it costs him the *Enterprise*. Spock is returned to Vulcan via the Klingon's ship, where his recovery is completed.

The film begins by repeating the final scene from *Trek II*, and indeed *The Search for Spock* is a continuation of the story arc that began there, resolving not only Spock's fate but the results of the Genesis Project and the tragic end to Kirk's reunion with his son. Other story threads would be wrapped up in the next film. *Trek III* is very similar in tone to the TV series, and is buoyed (as many episodes were) by the camaraderie of the leads. It's especially nice to see the *Enterprise* crew out of uniform at an informal gathering, a rarity in any Trek incarnation. Other delights are the appearances of James B. Sikking as the smug starship commander ordered to chase the *Enterprise*, Christopher Lloyd as the dumbest Klingon in the

Empire, and Dame Judith Anderson, in her eighty-fifth year, as a high priestess (or whatever--as the nearest Trekker) of Vulcan. Robin Curtis replaces Kirstie Alley as Saavik.

So three films produced one hit, one miss and one in the middle for the *Enterprise* crew--translated to a batting average, that would probably put them on the bench. If the next film bombed, it might have ended the series. But *Star Trek IV--The Voyage Home* was a grand slam critically and commercially, and remains arguably Trek's finest moment ever.

After wrapping up loose ends from the last movie, Kirk and company head back to earth to face the consequences of stealing the *Enterprise*. But the earth has bigger problems--a mysterious probe has created severe weather disturbances that may lead to the planet's destruction. Spock recognizes the probe's signal as the song of a humpback whale; theoretically if a whale answered the signal the probe might depart, but the humpback did not survive into the twenty-third century. A plan is hatched--time travel back three hundred years, beam up a pair of whales, and bring them back. After surviving a variety of adventures among the "primitive and paranoid" culture of late twentieth century San Francisco, our heroes accomplish their mission with help from marine biologist Gillian Taylor. Back in the twenty-third century, the probe is satisfied by the whales' answers and departs. A grateful government drops all charges against the *Enterprise* crew save one--disobeying a superior officer. Kirk is busted back to the rank of captain as punishment, and is returned to active duty on a new ship, christened the *Enterprise*.

This was as tongue-in-cheek as *Trek* ever got, but we should not have been surprised that this cast could shift into comedy gear with flawless timing and chemistry--anybody remember such episodes as "The Trouble with Tribbles" and "Shore Leave"? By now their reactions with each other are instinctive, and the wordplay if anything has only become more polished. The comedy seems effortless, because of the seasoned cast and the chosen targets (the way our chaotic lifestyle must look to an advanced future race). But the delicate balancing of broad humor (Spock using profanity) with a serious environmental message (save the whales) is actually quite an achievement. The film also managed to expand upon its built-in audience without alienating the "Trek is my life" people.

Unlike the last two films, where a background in *Trek* lore is almost a prerequisite, *The Voyage Home* can be enjoyed by those who have never seen these characters before. Having said that, however, it is also true that only a fan could fully relish Spock responding to Kirk with "One damn minute, Admiral."

Perhaps the funniest scene in the film is when Kirk is introduced to the twentieth century by getting the bird from a cussing cab driver. The confused and embarrassed deflation of this heroic leader registers perfectly on Shatner, and his desperate attempt to retaliate provides the first of many classic moments. All crewmembers get their share of screen time, most having more than in previous films, though sadly a scene with Sulu meeting his ancestors in Chinatown was cut. Gillian Taylor was played by Catherine Hicks, who spent her whole career as the saving grace in lousy projects. It's nice to see her working with material this good for a change.

Star Trek V--The Final Frontier (1989) was a step back but, like the third film it is better than its rep and improves on a small screen with repeat viewings. Script has Sybok, a renegade Vulcan and half-brother to Spock, kidnapping three ambassadors on the planet Nimbus III, in hopes of luring a starship to their rescue. He gets the *Enterprise*, and tells Kirk his intention to take the ship through the Great

Barrier, where he expects to find the deity that is worshiped in different ways by every known culture.

The barrier is crossed by the *Enterprise* and a pursuing Klingon vessel, but the only "God" they meet is a shape-shifting huckster who tries to convince Sybok to take him back across the barrier. Sybok now regrets his foolhardy quest, and sacrifices his life to save the *Enterprise*. The Klingon threat is neutralized and the crew returns home to resume their vacations.

Too many inconsistencies and unlikely coincidences fire the story. I can forgive the big one--Sybok's being Spock's brother, and even the possibility that Kirk is the only experienced commander at the helm near the hostage situation on Nimbus III. But notice how various systems on the *Enterprise* are either operable or inoperable depending on plot requirements. Early on the transporters are down, forcing Kirk and company to attempt a rescue "Bonanza"-style (and where did they get the horses?). Minutes later though their shuttle's manual landing is executed without a hitch, and later the ship survives the Great Barrier crossing, something no vessel ever achieved.

The premise is irresistible--this time the *Enterprise* really is going where no man has gone before. But David Loughery's script doesn't follow through. The finale is watered-down *Wizard of Oz*, damaged further by poor special effects that director William Shatner cannot conceal. We should have gained some insight into Kirk's spiritual side, but the movie tiptoes around such revelations. Even the comedy that flowed so naturally in the previous film seems forced this time, though the occasional line hits the mark.

Lawrence Luckinbill's Sybok is a charismatic opponent, and all the regulars, thanks to the quarter-century of familiarity on their side, prove that no behind-the-scenes flaw can keep them down. Poor Nichelle Nichols fares the worst; her gray hair makes her look ten years older than in the last film, there are hints of a romance with Scotty for which there is no precedent after twenty-five years of space travel, and on Nimbus III she performs a fan dance to lure security forces away from the hostages. The series couldn't end like that.

Star Trek VI--The Undiscovered Country may be the last *Enterprise* voyage, and it would be hard to complain if it were. Any lost dignity from *Trek V* is restored, the film was a critical, popular and financial success, and the inclusion of Michael Dorn as an ancestor of New Trek's Worf can be construed as a symbolic passing of the torch.

When the Klingon Empire is threatened with extinction, Kirk is assigned to escort its ambassadors to a peace conference with the Federation. Personally Kirk would rather see the whole race wiped out, but orders is orders. The Klingon ship is destroyed by torpedos that appear to have been fired by the *Enterprise*, and when Kirk and Dr. McCoy beam over to assist the wounded they are taken into custody. While Spock tries to determine what happened, Kirk and McCoy are found guilty in Klingon court and sent to a prison colony.

Spock discovers that the torpedos were actually fired by a cloaked Klingon vessel, in an attempt to halt the peace talks. Kirk and McCoy mount a jailbreak and are beamed up by the Enterprise. They race back to earth to prevent more assassinations by the same conspirators. The traitors are exposed, and among them are several members of the Federation, who could not tolerate a peaceful universe any more than the Klingons.

Star Trek VI contains some disturbing messages--has mankind become so accustomed to conflict that we are unable to live without it? Now that the Cold War is over, it's a question that has never been more relevant. We also see Captain Kirk, a man of the future to us, wonder if time has passed him by. It's a perfect way to address the senior citizen status of certain twenty-third century officers, while again holding a mirror to a twentieth century problem like racial intolerance.

Have we seen the last of the original *Star Trek* cast? Since recasting the roles is inconceivable, the day they hang it up will be the end of an era. *Trek VI* proved that advancing age cannot hold them back; the issue is only raised in reviews of the lesser films. I think they have more to say--somebody put together a good script, and I bet they fly again.

TELEVISION

"Star Trek" (NBC series, 1966--69)

Cast

WILLIAM SHATNER (CAPTAIN JAMES T. KIRK), Leonard Nimoy (Mr. Spock), DeForest Kelley (Dr. Leonard "Bones" McCoy), James Doohan (Engineer Montgomery Scott), Nichelle Nichols (Uhura), Walter Koenig (Chekhov--1967-1969), George Takei (Sulu), Majel Barrett (Nurse Christine Chapel)

Rating: *****

All episodes available on videocassette

Awards: Emmy nominations, 1966 and 1967, for Outstanding Dramatic Series, nominations, 1966, 1967 and 1968 for Best Supporting Actor (Leonard Nimoy)

THE FILMS

Star Trek: The Motion Picture (Paramount, 1979, 132 minutes)

Directed by Robert Wise; Written by Harold Livingston and Gene Roddenberry, based on a story by Alan Dean Foster; Produced by Gene Roddenberry; Music by Jerry Goldsmith

Cast (series regulars plus:)

Persis Khambatta (Ilia), Stephen Collins (Cmdr. William Decker), Mark Lenard (Sarek), Grace Lee Whitney (Janice Rand)

Rating: **1/2

Available on Videocassette

Awards: Oscar nominations for Art Direction, Original Score and Visual Effects

Star Trek II: The Wrath of Khan (Paramount, 1982, 113 minutes)

Directed by Nicholas Meyer; Written by Jack B. Sowards, based on a story by Sowards and Harve Bennett; Produced by Robert Sallin; Music by James Horner

Cast (series regulars plus:)

Ricardo Montalban (Khan), Bibi Besch (Dr. Carol Marcus), Merritt Butrick (David), Kirstie Alley (Saavik), Paul Winfield (Captain Terrell)

Rating: *****

Available on Videocassette

Star Trek III: The Search For Spock (Paramount, 1984, 105 minutes)

Directed by Leonard Nimoy; Written and produced by Harve Bennett; Music by James Horner

Cast (series regulars plus:)

Robin Curtis (Saavik), Merritt Butrick (David), Christopher Lloyd (Kruge), John Larroquette (Maltz), James B. Sikking (Captain Styles), Mark Lenard (Sarek), Dame Judith Anderson (High Priestess)

Rating: ****
Available on Videocassette

Star Trek IV: The Voyage Home (Paramount, 1986, 119 minutes)
Directed by Leonard Nimoy; Written by Harve Bennett, Steve Meerson, Peter Krikes and Nicholas Meyer, based on a story by Bennett and Leonard Nimoy; Produced by Harve Bennett; Music by Leonard Rosenman
Cast (series regulars plus:)
Catherine Hicks (Dr. Gillian Taylor), Jane Wyatt (Amanda), Mark Lenard (Sarek), Robin Curtis (Saavik)
Rating: *****
Available on Videocassette
Awards: Oscar nominations for Original Screenplay, Original Score, Sound Effects and Cinematography

Star Trek V: The Final Frontier (Paramount, 1989, 108 minutes)
Directed by William Shatner; Written by David Loughery, based on a story by Loughery, William Shatner and Harve Bennett; Produced by Harve Bennett; Music by Jerry Goldsmith
Cast (series regulars plus:)
Lawrence Luckinbill (Sybok)
Rating: ***1/2
Available on Videocassette

Star Trek VI: The Undiscovered Country (Paramount, 1991, 109 minutes)
Directed by Nicholas Meyer; Written by Nicholas Meyer and Denny Martin Flinn, based on a story by Leonard Nimoy, Lawrence Konner and Mark Rosenthal; Produced by Ralph Winter; Music by Cliff Eidelman
Cast (series regulars plus:)
Kim Cattrall (Lt. Valeris), David Warner (Chancellor Gorkon), Christopher Plummer (Chang), Mark Lenard (Sarek)
Rating: ****
Available on Videocassette

BRUCE LEE

In any field of activity there is an inherent pleasure, regardless of one's personal interest in the activity, in watching it performed by its master. You don't have to love basketball to applaud a reverse lay-up by Michael Jordan; you don't have to love opera to appreciate Luciano Pavarotti's singing "Nessun Dorma." And you don't have to be a fan of martial arts movies to admire the artistry of Bruce Lee.

Through his charisma as an actor Bruce Lee elevated the chop-socky genre to a level it had never reached before, and has yet to achieve since. Still more impressive was Lee's elevation of the centuries-old discipline of martial arts through his astonishing innovation, speed and power. Dan Inosanto, a black belt and Lee protege`, estimated in a Lee biography that his teacher was one hundred years ahead of his time. It has been two decades since his untimely death at the age of thirty-two, and in that time several kung fu actors have tried to claim his throne--Chuck Norris, Jackie Chan, Sho Kosugi and even Lee's son Brandon before he, like his father, left us too soon--but compared to the master they all move in slow motion.

Bruce Lee is listed under his name in this book and not under one of his movie roles because his characters were always thinly disguised versions of himself. Audiences flocked to his movies the same way Western fans supported the work of John Wayne. As long as the Duke rode a horse and fired a six-shooter, it was reason enough to see the movie. Likewise, the chance to watch Bruce Lee square off against a dozen bad guys at once made sitting through the often derivative storylines of his films worthwhile. Usually, the wait between fights wasn't very long.

Bruce Lee also deserves the hero label because he was revered away from the movies as well. Long before Elvis became the dead guy most likely to be spotted at Burger King, the Lee cult had circulated stories of its idol's survival, believing he was simply too tough to die. The irregular cause of his death and the surrounding circumstances further stoked the coals, and allegations of a cover-up have never been fully dismissed.

Elvis has his impersonators and so does Lee; lookalikes under the names Bruce Li and Bruce Le starred in dozens of films, including *Bruce Lee Fights Back From the Grave*, a definite low point on the good-taste meter. They had some of the moves but none of the style, and only confirmed the inimitable skill of the one and only.

THE MAN

Jun Fan Lee was born in San Francisco on November 27, 1940, and moved to Hong Kong with his family before his first birthday. The name Bruce was given to the baby by the doctor who delivered him. He was a fighter from birth and, as a child, quickly gained the reputation of a bully, which inevitably led to more fights and later membership in a gang.

Bruce's father, a well-known singer in Hong Kong, tried to steer his son away from show business, but Bruce started taking bit parts in movies, and his screen presence was immediately discovered. Lee had a prolific film career long before American audiences ever saw him, including several starring roles (1958's *The Orphan* and others). At about the same time, he had discovered martial arts at a local school, and became the Chinese boxing champion of his high school (he won the trophy for cha-cha as well).

After graduation Lee left for the United States and attended the University of Washington, where he met and married his wife Linda. His ability at kung fu had progressed to the point where he began developing his own unique style. It was called "*jeet kune do*", loosely translated as the "way of intercepting fists," but Lee also incorporated moves and elements from other martial arts. He was a great fan of Muhammad Ali, and borrowed some of the heavyweight champ's technique as well.

Lee opened a martial arts school in Seattle, and would later open two more in Oakland and Los Angeles. At the time, before *Five Fingers of Death* ignited the kung fu movie craze in 1973, and before Carl Douglas recorded the memorably awful song "Kung Fu Fighting" the following year, karate was an art form practiced and studied in private, and almost exclusively by men of Chinese heritage.

Lee wanted to get back into acting, and was able to do so because of his martial arts. He won the role of Kato in the 1966 television series "The Green Hornet," and appeared briefly in the 1969 movie *Marlowe*. But it wasn't until he suffered a serious back injury while training that he committed to show business full time. Hospital bills wiped out his savings, and with a wife and two children he needed a more lucrative income. After his appearance as a kung fu instructor on four episodes of the James Franciscus series "Longstreet," Lee was offered a longterm contract from both MGM and Warner Bros. Instead, he returned to Hong Kong and began a two-year collaboration with producer Raymond Chow. The series of films that resulted broke all box office records in Asia and the Far East, and made Bruce Lee the number one star in the world.

The fight scenes, the unequivocal highlight of any Bruce Lee movie, may have been choreographed and edited for maximum effect, but no special effects were used or needed. In fact, where most martial arts films accelerate the projection speed to make the action seem faster, Lee's moves were already too quick for most cameras to capture at regular speed. He didn't use trampolines to make the jumps seem higher or break balsa wood boards, because he didn't need to. During personal appearances, Lee would give demonstrations of his ability by knocking a man off his feet with a punch delivered from a distance of one inch. How could the movies improve on that?

When *Enter the Dragon* grossed more than twenty times its production cost, Lee seemed on the verge of a long and prosperous career. On July 20, 1973, he was dead. The autopsy listed the cause of death as a cerebral edema, in layman's terms a congestion of fluid in the brain, but rumors of foul play were rampant. Lee was found in the apartment of a woman named Betty Ting Pei, who has been assigned the Yoko Ono role by many fans. If Bruce was murdered by a lethal injection, as the conspiracy buffs believe, Betty played an instrumental role. She has since written a book that raises some provocative questions but provides little in the way of facts. The official story has now been accepted by all but the most rabid Lee fanatics.

THE FILMS

A look back at Bruce Lee's film career always begins with "The Green Hornet," since the films he made as a teenager in Hong Kong were not martial arts-related and have never been released in the United States. Lee played Kato, the chauffeur and manservant to newspaper editor Britt Reid (Van Williams), who is secretly the Green Hornet. The series debuted in 1966 and lasted thirty weeks.

A spinoff of the camp classic "Batman" (the Hornet and Kato guest-starred in a memorable episode), "The Green Hornet" borrowed the Caped Crusader's narrator and penchant for gadgets, but could not adapt the hilarious tongue-in-cheek writing style that made its progenitor a hit. It is now best remembered for launching Bruce Lee and for its catchy theme music, an upbeat variation of Rimsky-Korsakov's "Flight of the Bumble Bee." But the passage of time has lent a nostalgic charm that many shows from the 1960s now enjoy, thanks to the baby boomers' all-consuming interest in the period.

Lee was not required to act much as Kato; he uttered three or four lines per episode and executed the same number of kung fu moves. For many Americans it was their first look at martial arts, which Lee insisted be performed with a high degree of authenticity. Business went up at his training schools after the series debuted, and he was offered a chance to go national with a chain of schools under the Kato name. Believing it would trivialize the self-defense discipline, he refused.

Marlowe (1969) starred James Garner as Raymond Chandler's fictional sleuth Phillip Marlowe. Hired by a Kansas farm girl to find her missing brother, the detective follows a winding trail through assassins, strippers, famous actresses and crooked doctors. Almost everyone ends up dead when it's over, except for Marlowe and his client, who is not as innocent as she first appeared. It's the type of labyrinthian plot one expects from material based on Chandler--much ado about very little but diverting while it's on.

James Garner brings a laid-back approach to the role that he would later use to better advantage on "The Rockford Files." Bruce Lee has two brief scenes, one of which may be the film's most memorable; as Winslow Wong, hired muscle for a mobster, he offers Marlowe a bribe to forget his current case. When Marlowe refuses Wong assumes his kung fu stance, but instead of beating up the detective he beats up his office, chopping through shelves and kicking in walls and leaving the place in a pile of rubble. When he does attack Marlowe in his final scene, it would be the only time Lee would lose a fight on screen. Although he appears for less than ten minutes, Lee clearly demonstrates his ability as an actor, and his smile is already the most disarming in movies.

Fists of Fury (1971) began Lee's collaboration with Raymond Chow. The plot has kung fu student Cheng (Lee) returning to his family in Bangkok, after promising his teacher never to fight again (for reasons unexplained). He begins working with his cousins at an ice factory, which unbeknownst to them is a cover for a drug smuggling operation. Two of Cheng's cousins learn the factory's secret and are murdered. Cheng breaks his vow to put the druglords out of business, though he is too late to prevent the slaughter of his family.

Lee doesn't start fighting until halfway into the film, but when he does it's magic. His first big screen confrontation, though shorter than most of those that would follow, is one of his best. Violence is a given in Lee's movies, but *Fists of*

Fury approaches slasher film levels of blood-letting. There isn't much honor in Cheng's vengeance-driven fighting style--he resorts to groin punches, slices up attackers with knives and pounds on foes who are already unconscious.

All of Lee's Hong Kong films were released in the United States. after his death, so audiences who got to know the man in "The Green Hornet" and *Enter the Dragon* were in for a couple of surprises. First, the Hong Kong films are not as technically proficient. The direction uses gimmicky, "Wayne's World" type rapid zooms to build suspense, the dubbing is terrible and the editing ragged. But in his first outing as a leading man, Lee proved once and for all that in between jump kicks he was a talented actor. His expressions of shock and anguish after discovering his slain family, and after using his kung fu to kill, are riveting.

Only Lee's presence elevates *The Chinese Connection* (1972) from routine chop-socky fare. Another good Lee performance is undercut by poor dubbing that makes the star sound like an American disc jockey. Since Lee's death has made every frame of him that exists more valuable, someone should start treating these movies like the important documents that they are. Subtitles are now used on most foreign films, and would better serve the material here.

Lee plays the student of a legendary Chinese hero whose sudden death is attributed to pneumonia. Lee doesn't buy it, and suspects the jealous students of a rival Japanese school. He tracks down the killers of his mentor and hangs them from lampposts in the city. Rather than surrender to the police for his crimes of retribution, he leaps ferociously into a cadre of armed officers in the film's final shot.

Lee's famous fight against an entire martial arts school is here, but it's shot too close up to fully appreciate the balletic movements of the combatants. The film has a welcome dose of humor, first when Lee encounters a "No Dogs and Chinese Allowed" sign at a private club. His reaction when a dog walks through the gates unmolested is priceless, as is his shattering of the sign with an amazing jump kick. Later, he masquerades as a nebbishy telephone repairman to infiltrate the enemy school. There is also an interesting insight into the long-standing racial tension between the Chinese and Japanese.

Return of the Dragon (1973) represents a giant step forward, and remains one of Lee's best. The title made it sound like a sequel to *Enter the Dragon*, but there was no connection between the films or the character Lee portrayed. Actually, the plot is more similar to *Fists of Fury*, in which a somewhat naive country boy is forced into fighting big city bad guys to save his loved ones. The story is set in Rome, a pleasant change from previous films. Tang (Lee) arrives in the Eternal City at the request of friends who own a small restaurant. The location is coveted by a criminal syndicate, so they try to shut the place down. Tang wins the first few rounds, but then the mob boss hires his own kung fu champion to even the score. After a fierce battle in the Coliseum, Tang kills his rival and puts the syndicate out of business.

Bruce Lee not only stars but writes and directs this time, and proves that he knew more about how to present himself and his abilities than any other filmmaker. His script is a good basic set-up with a crackling pace and room for beaucoup brawls. His direction eschews frequent cuts in the fight scenes, and lets the action speak for itself. Like Fred Astaire, who insisted that his dancing be shot with his full body in view, Lee backs up the camera so that his deadly dance could be appreciated in similar fashion. When the camera does move in, it's to capture Lee's expression of supreme confidence going into battle, and his mocking smile prior to demonstrating his virtuosity with a non chaku.

This is the best-dubbed of the Hong Kong films, at least on Lee's character. The voice seems to fit, and thankfully they've lowered the volume on his "kiah"--the banshee-like shriek he uses in battle that is very irritating to Western ears. Other characters do not fare as well--two black villains are given voices from the Antonio Fargas school of diction, and a homosexual character swoons and lisps like a bad Liberace impersonator.

Chuck Norris, in his first featured role, plays the syndicate's hired gun, and his climactic showdown with Bruce Lee is a touchstone for the genre. Appropriately set in the Roman Coliseum, their battle is a dazzling display of spin kicks and punches thrown faster than the eye can follow. And just as Lee was defeated in his first film role, Norris comes up short here. As in *The Chinese Connection*, Lee again stresses the superiority of Chinese boxing over Japanese karate, something he believed in completely. Although he understood the spiritual side of martial arts, he was not controlled by it.

Enter the Dragon, Lee's last film and his first as a star for an American studio, is the best martial arts movie ever made. There is almost wall-to-wall action, and for the first time the fight scenes that do not include Lee are equally absorbing, thanks to a cast of kung fu all-stars. Lee's allies include Jim Kelly (*Black Belt Jones* [1974]) and John Saxon; among the bad guys are veteran Lee adversary Bob Wall and Yang Sze, the "Chinese Hercules." Angela Mao Ying, the genre's most famous lady martial artist (1973's *Deadly China Doll* is an underappreciated gem) appears in flashback as Lee's sister. Though she's gone after one scene, Mao Ying puts on an incredible exhibition as she is pursued by would-be rapists, and is the only memorable female character in any of Lee's films.

The story has Lee being hired by the British government to infiltrate the island stronghold of a suspected drug trader and white slaver named Han. Twice a year, a martial-arts tournament is held on the island, from which Han is able to recruit assassins. Lee uses the tournament as a cover, and he is able to bring down Han's empire, avenge the killers of his sister, and win the tourney as well.

No need for in-depth analysis here--the plot is necessary only to put Lee and company in a position of defending themselves from a hundred attackers. What happens next is every action scene in his previous films multiplied by ten. *Enter the Dragon* should have been the starting point of a career in which Lee carried the martial arts film to greater and greater heights. Instead, it serves only as an elegy of the genre's brightest star.

At the time of his death, Lee had filmed about fifteen minutes of what was to be his next film, *Game of Death*. The film was completed six years later with the use of a lookalike and some obvious patchwork editing. Outtakes of Lee and Chuck Norris from *Return of the Dragon* were used, along with clips from almost every other film Lee made. The result is what you might expect from such an assemblage of unrelated material.

Billy Lo, the character Lee would have played, is an action movie star who is pursued by a management agency that is in league with the Chinese mob. The agency plans to fix a martial arts tournament and clean up on the betting, but Lo must be controlled for that to happen. After several attempts on his life, Lo fakes his death to take the pressure off, and then goes after the crooks. There's a great opening titles sequence that recalls Maurice Binder's work on the James Bond films, but it's all downhill from there until the final half-hour, in which the real Bruce Lee emerges and takes on a series of foes with twice the speed and grace of his doppelganger. The highlight is a battle with Kareem Abdul-Jabbar, who like James Coburn and Steve McQueen was a former student at Lee's school. Jabbar's kung fu was average at best, but Lee makes him look good, and the visual of them squaring off is worth the whole movie.

It is sadly ironic that the best martial arts movie to be released since Lee's death is *Dragon*, the Bruce Lee biopic that leans more toward fiction than fact. With the exception of its depiction of racial intolerance, which is fairly distributed among both the Chinese and Americans, the film either downplays or avoids altogether most of the controversies of Lee's life, and the circumstaces surrounding his unusual death are completely glossed over. It is also somewhat disappointing that 70 percent of *Dragon* takes place before Lee's first martial arts movie; there is one brief scene involving "The Green Hornet," and only one scene from one Lee film is recreated. But the action scenes blaze with the same intensity as the master's work, and the script possesses a sense of humor that seems surprising for a story overshadowed by tragedy. Jason Scott Lee (no relation) has the same wiry but powerful physique as the man he portrays, and though the physical resemblance is not ideal Lee does tap into the inner fire that was most palpable in Bruce Lee's eyes during a fight, and the effect is stunning.

We can only speculate on what might have been, on the films that good friends Bruce Lee and Chuck Norris might have made together, on the comedies Lee could have made on the strength of his personality, on how he would have reinvented himself for new genres and new challenges. Only James Dean left the film world with more unfinished business.

THE FILMS

Marlowe (MGM, 1969, 95 minutes)
Directed by Paul Bogart; Written by Stirling Silliphant, based on the novel *The Little Sister* by Raymond Chandler; Produced by Gabriel Katzka and Sidney Beckerman; Music by Peter Matz
Cast
James Garner (Philip Marlowe), Gayle Hunnicutt (Mavis Wald), Carroll O'Connor (Lt. Christy French), Rita Moreno (Dolores Gonzales), William Daniels (Mr. Crowell), Jackie Coogan (Grant W. Hicks), BRUCE LEE (WINSLOW WONG)
Rating: ***
Available on Videocassette

Fists of Fury (Golden Harvest, 1971, 103 minutes)
AKA: The Big Boss
Directed and written by Lo Wei; Produced by Raymond Chow; Music by Ku Chih-hui
Cast
BRUCE LEE (CHENG), Maria Yi (Mei), Han Ying Chieh (Mi), Malalene (Prostitute)
Rating: ***1/2
Available on Videocassette

The Chinese Connection (Golden Harvest, 1972, 107 minutes)
Directed and written by Lo Wei; Produced by Raymond Chow; Music by C.H. Ku
Cast
BRUCE LEE (CHEN)

Rating: ***
Available on Videocassette

Return of the Dragon (Golden Harvest, 1973, 90 minutes)
Directed and written by Bruce Lee; Produced by Raymond Chow; Music by KuChia Hui
Cast
BRUCE LEE (TANG LUNG), Chuck Norris (Kuda), Nora Miao (Chen Ching Hua), Robert Wall (Robert), Jon T. Benn (Boss)
Rating: ****
Available on Videocassette

Enter the Dragon (Warner Bros., 1973, 98 minutes)
Directed by Robert Clouse; Written by Michael Allin; Produced by Fred Weintraub and Paul Heller, in association with Raymond Chow; Music by Lalo Schifrin
Cast
BRUCE LEE (LEE), John Saxon (Roper), Jim Kelly (Williams), Shih Kien (Han), Bob Wall (Oharra), Angela Mao Ying (Su-Lin), Yang Sze (Bolo)
Rating: ****1/2
Available on Videocassette

Game of Death (Golden Harvest, 1978, 102 minutes)
Directed by Robert Clouse; Written by Jan Spears; Produced by Raymond Chow; Music by John Barry
Cast
BRUCE LEE (BILLY LO), Gig Young (Jim Marshall), Dean Jagger (Dr. Land), Hugh O'Brien (Steiner), Colleen Camp (Ann Morris), Robert Wall (Carl Miller), Kareem Abdul-Jabbar (Hakim)
Rating: **
Available on Videocassette

Dragon: The Bruce Lee Story (Universal, 1993, 105 minutes)
Directed by Rob Cohen; Written by Edward Khmara, John Raffo and Rob Cohen, based on the book by Linda Lee Cadwell; Produced by Raffaella De Laurentiis; Music by Randy Edelman
Cast
JASON SCOTT LEE (BRUCE LEE), Lauren Holly (Linda Lee Cadwell)
Rating: ****
Available on Videocassette

TELEVISION
"The Green Hornet" (ABC series, 1966-67)
Cast
Van Williams (The Green Hornet/Britt Reid), BRUCE LEE (KATO), Lenore Case (Wende Wagner), Mike Axford (Lloyd Gough)
Rating: ***

Clayton Moore (left) and Jay Silverheels were not the first actors--or the last--to portray the Lone Ranger and Tonto, but they are certainly the most popular.

THE LONE RANGER

A fiery horse with the speed of light, a cloud of dust and a hearty hi-yo Silver! The Lone Ranger! With his faithful Indian companion, Tonto, the daring and resourceful masked rider of the plains led the fight for law and order in the early West. Return with us to those thrilling days of yesteryear--the Lone Ranger rides again!

He wore a black mask and a white hat, an unlikely combination that confused friend and foe alike. But his fans weren't thrown--the Lone Ranger became such a success on radio, television and film that the stories of his exploits were as celebrated as those surrounding Wyatt Earp and other historical figures. Indeed, the Lone Ranger was created at a time when the actual Old West was still a memory for folks older than fifty.

The difference between the Lone Ranger and other Western heroes, real and fictional, is his squeaky-clean lifestyle. We still associate the cowboy with saloons and showdowns and poker games that often end in gunfire, but such pursuits were not for the Lone Ranger; he never shot to kill, never touched booze or the barmaids, and didn't even play Crazy Eights. This was a gunslinger with the Good Housekeeping Seal of Approval, and that's why most of us first discovered the Lone Ranger before we hit puberty. Our affection for him survives into adulthood primarily through nostalgia. We forgive the simplistic, moralistic stories for the warm feeling that is derived from reliving pleasant childhood memories. It's the same reason I still tape "The Brady Bunch."

You can't think of the Lone Ranger and Tonto without thinking of Clayton Moore and Jay Silverheels, in spite of the fact that they were neither the first actors to inhabit the roles, nor the most recent. They were the best, however, and today it is only their interpretation, still widely syndicated on television, that keeps the characters alive.

THE STORY

The saga of the Lone Ranger began in the early 1930s at radio station WXYZ in Detroit. An attorney turned theater executive named George W. Trendle came up with the concept, and hired writer Fran Striker to develop the idea. Striker added Tonto and the silver bullets, and wrote the origin story that most of us remember even if we don't know how.

It is Texas in the late 1800s, and six Texas Rangers led by Captain Dan Reid are on the trail of outlaw Butch Cavendish and his Hole in the Wall Gang. The outlaws lure the Rangers into an ambush at a canyon passage near Bryant's Gap, and gun them down. One of the Rangers, Dan's brother John Reid, survives the attack, and is found by Tonto, a Potawatomie Indian. Tonto recognizes Reid as the man who had saved his life after renegade Indians raided his village. He nurses Reid back to health and plants six crosses in Bryant's Gap, including one for John Reid, to hide his survival from Cavendish. Reid assumes the identity of the Lone Ranger after fashioning a mask made from his brother's vest. He then exacts his revenge on the Cavendish gang and cuts a trail of law and order across seven states. He would never accept money for his help, but was comfortably staked by the profits from the family silver mine, which also was the source for his trademark silver bullets.

Two of Trendle's and Striker's were inspired: first, the teaming of a cowboy and Indian, perennial enemies in the Old West, as allies and friends. What better way to teach kids about racial harmony? The second was the use of Gioacchino Rossini's "William Tell Overture" as theme music. It has been a fixture in every adaptation of the story, and is now more associated with the Lone Ranger than William Tell (and a guaranteed way to get classical music haters into symphony halls). I also like the idea of the Green Hornet, another Trendle and Striker creation, being John Reid's great-nephew.

TELEVISION AND FILM

"The Lone Ranger" was first broadcast on radio in 1933, with WXYZ staffer Earle Graser providing the hero's voice. Graser played the role for eight years, until he was killed in a car accident. World War I veteran Brace Beemer then voiced the Ranger until the series ended in 1955. The first film adaptation was a 1938 Republic serial starring Lee Powell as the Lone Ranger and Chief Thunder Cloud as Tonto. It's one of the worst serials ever produced by the usually reliable Republic, and bears little resemblance to the character as he is best known now.

The story opens with bad guy Marcus Jeffries impersonating a federal tax agent and lining his own pockets with the townfolk's money. Five Texas Rangers set out to stop Jeffries, but are gunned down by his hired militia. One of the Rangers is found barely alive by Tonto. He recovers and creates the Lone Ranger identity. After his scam becomes threatened, Jeffries has five Rangers jailed on suspicion of being the Lone Ranger. The real Ranger reveals his identity to his cellmates, and they all agree to keep the secret. The five Rangers and Tonto form an alliance to stop Jeffries. Four of them fall, the last in a struggle with Jeffries that sends them both tumbling off a cliff. Once again, the Lone Ranger stands alone.

The serial's hook was its altering the story to have five Rangers, one of whom was our hero. The audience is invited to guess, but since we never get to know each of the choices very well the ploy is wasted. After two hours of episodes I still couldn't tell them apart. The black scarf that covers the Lone Ranger's entire face makes the game even more difficult. Chief Thunder Cloud bears a close resemblance to Jay Silverheels, but with four other Rangers around he is often lost in a crowd. Even worse, there's not a "*kemo sabe*" in the whole thing (and let's end that rumor while we're here--the phrase "*kemo sabe*" was made up by Striker, and does not mean "faithful friend" in the language of the Iroquois or any other Indian tribe).

What we're left with are endless shots of the Lone Ranger (Lee Powell) riding furiously across the plains and an unending supply of barrels with "EXPLOSIVES" written on them, which are rolled around the desert like bowling balls. It's never really inept--Republic was at least too good for that. But it's completely uninvolving, with hollow performances and little excitement.

The Lone Ranger Rides Again, made by Republic in 1939, is a vast improvement in every way and still holds up as one of the better Western serials ever made. What a difference a year makes! The action this time revolves around a group of homesteaders led by Jed Scott, who move West and butt heads with cattle baron Craig Dolan, who is determined to prevent the "nesters" from moving in. A group called the Black Riders begin terrorizing the homesteaders, and Jed Scott suspects that Dolan is behind the raids.

The Lone Ranger and Tonto help the nesters file claims to land and get their claims registered in Washington. They are assisted by Juan Vasquez, a man who originally planned to kill the Lone Ranger, believing the masked man responsible for the death of his brother. The Lone Ranger exposes the real killer, and Juan becomes an ally. Dolan learns that his nephew Bart is behind the Black Riders and orders him to disband the group. When Uncle Craig insists on only using legal means to fight the nesters, Bart shoots him and redoubles his campaign of terror. The Lone Ranger and Tonto manage to put a stop to the Raiders, and Bart is killed in the final battle. By this time everyone is tired of fighting, and Jed Scott and Craig Dolan agree to settle their differences peaceably.

In the first serial, the Lone Ranger's face was covered entirely throughout. This time, we see the Ranger unmasked in the first episode, and at regular intervals throughout. Robert Livingston is thus able to create a more substantial character, having been given the opportunity to use such basic acting tools as facial expression that were denied Lee Powell. Livingston, with his Dudley Do-Right voice and the experience of a career spent almost entirely on horseback, gives a robust performance.

The Lone Ranger and Tonto have more scene together, though the two would not become a true crimefighting team until the Moore-Silverheels era. Here, Tonto spends too much time watching the horses while *kemo sabe* goes after the Raiders. A good supporting cast is led by Duncan Renaldo, who would later play The Cisco Kid. As Craig Dolan, Ralph Dunn delivers with relish such lines as, "I believe in giving every man fair warning before stepping on him." And the redoubtable Jinx Falkenburg (billed as Jinx Falken), best known for her work with Rita Hayworth in *Cover Girl* (1944), plays Dolan's niece Sue.

The story packs more excitement into its first chapter than the last serial managed in its full run, plus a solid cliffhanger with a resolution that doesn't cheat. There's another good one between chapters five and six. Directors William Witney and John English keep things moving and even manage to work a quicksand cliffhanger into the mix, which is no small feat for a story set in the desert. The "William Tell Overture" is joined by Franz von Suppe's "Light Cavalry Overture" in some chase scenes, and works just as well.

Despite this much-improved effort, the Lone Ranger's serial days were over. It would be ten years before the character would reappear, this time on the small screen. George Trendle hand-picked Moore and Silverheels, who had worked together previously in the 1949 film *The Cowboy and the Indians*, to play the leads. The "Lone Ranger" series premiered later that same year and ran until 1957. It was television's first Western series and was the biggest hit the burgeoning ABC network had in its preadolescence. It even received an Emmy nomination in 1950 as "Best Children's Show." Moore and Silverheels earned their enduring identification with the Lone Ranger and Tonto with consistently earnest performances. Most people don't know that Moore sat out two years (1951--53) in a salary dispute, while John Hart played the Lone Ranger, because these episodes are never rebroadcast.

Moore and Silverheels also starred in the 1956 film *The Lone Ranger*, which represents their best work in the roles and is a first-class Western by any standard. The story, which sounds pretty typical on the surface, has a bit more substance than the television tales and is not aimed solely at children; rancher-Indian relations are strained for the usual reasons, and the governor asks the Lone Ranger to intervene. Turns out the problems are being caused by Reece Kilgore, who covets a silver mine in Indian territory. He orders his ranchhands to impersonate troublemaking injuns, to provide a phony excuse to start a war. Angered by the frame-up, the real Indians kidnap Kilgore's daughter. Conflict seems inevitable, but the Lone Ranger unravels Kilgore's scheme and keeps the peace.

Why is Moore the definitive Lone Ranger? Start with his ability to turn the ultimate straight arrow into a three-dimensional character, and his chemistry with Silverheels, who like Moore is underrated as an actor because of the perceived frivolity of the role. But they wouldn't have left such indelible marks if the job weren't well done. The Lone Ranger's use of disguises, a series staple, is also here, as Moore does his "old prospector" bit. It's another chance for Moore to show his versatility, though I still prefer his Don Pedro O'Sullivan.

Veteran director Stuart Heisler opens up the action from the somewhat confined setting of the series, making the most of some gorgeous Utah scenery. All this plus Bonita Granville, the one-time Nancy Drew, in her last film appearance as Kilgore's wife. Grand entertainment.

A second film, *The Lone Ranger and the Lost City of Gold*, was released in conjunction with the character's twenty-fifth anniversary. It's not bad, but unlike the first film there is no discernible increase in budget or scope from the TV series. The brisk pace and direction are missing as well.

After a recap of the Lone Ranger's origin, the story begins with the local Indian tribe under siege (as usual) by a pack of hooded raiders. Town matriarch Francis Henderson is the guilty party this time--she wants the medallions worn by some of the Indians, because together they form a map that leads to a legendary city of gold. The Lone Ranger assumes the guise of Southern gentleman Brett Reagan and charms his way into Francis's confidence. Just as the Indians prepare to fight back, the Lone Ranger and Tonto expose Francis and her raiders. The golden city is found on Indian land, and is melted down to finance a hospital.

Reruns aside, the Lone Ranger bowed out of sight for awhile after this disappointing sequel. An animated series premiered on CBS in 1966, with William Conrad (billed as J. Darnoc--spell it backwards) and Ivan Naranjo lending voice to the Lone Ranger and Tonto. The drawing is stiff, and Conrad did a better job narrating the animated events in Frostbite Falls. Somehow, it ran three years.

There is a Lone Ranger--like character in three films produced in Turkey. *Five Masked Men*, *The Return of Five Masked Men* and *Landless Wolves* were all made in 1968, but good luck finding any of them outside of Istanbul. Judging from most Turkish film industry product, it probably isn't worth the effort.

When the Lone Ranger finally did return to the movie screen, most people wished that he hadn't. In 1981, *The Legend of the Lone Ranger* was a flop on the *Ishtar* scale, and may have ruined any chance the character might have for a quality comeback anytime soon. Once again the origin story is retold, but here John Reid becomes an attorney before heading West to join his brother Dan and the Texas

Rangers. After the Bryant's Gap massacre, Reid creates the Lone Ranger to have his revenge on Butch Cavendish. Meanwhile, the Cavendish gang hijacks a train carrying President Ulysses S. Grant, General George Custer, Buffalo Bill Cody and Wild Bill Hickok. Cavendish wants Grant to declare him the governor of a newly independent American territory. Grant prepares to cave in, but the Lone Ranger, joined by Custer and the other Western heroes, shoots several holes in the "Hole in the Wall" gang, and rescue the president.

What a mess. With its stilted dialogue, terrible direction and lifeless acting, *The Legend of the Lone Ranger* looks like a first-time effort by everyone involved. Five writers on one screenplay is always a sign of trouble. These guys should wear masks themselves--you can't draft a story by committee. The script is slow, light on action, as full of holes as Cavendish in the last reel and shows no sign of a sense of humor. Give them a modicum of credit for telling the origin accurately, but attempts to make the story more adult-oriented fall flat. The Lone Ranger is given a love interest (Juanin Clay) for the first time, but after being introduced the poor girl is completely forgotten.

Every plot advance is telegraphed to the point where you could turn the volume down and supply the dialogue yourself--and probably do a better job. When the talking stops the singing begins--oh, my. Merle Haggard performs "The Man in the Mask," written by Dean (*Fame*) Pitchford, and it's the most godawful musical narration in motion picture history.

Director William Fraker made his first film, *Monte Walsh*, in 1968, and then took thirteen years off before landing this assignment. To see how little progress he made in that time, watch the scene where the Lone Ranger rescues Tonto from the gallows; the townspeople stand almost motionless throughout. *Monte Walsh* was partially salvaged by Jack Palance's charismatic performance, but *Legend* has no such savior. As the Lone Ranger, Klinton Spilsbury (whatever happened to Hollywood name changes?) doesn't don the mask until an hour into the movie. When that happens, it should be an inspiring moment. It's not. Spilsbury, whose voice was dubbed, managed to be an adequate John Reid, but he's a miserable Lone Ranger.

There is hardly any dialogue between *kemo sabe* and Tonto (Michael Horse, who learned to act between this and "Twin Peaks"), so they are not allowed a chance to establish any camaraderie. Jason Robards is miscast as a sober, not very boisterous President Grant (who rolls over far too quickly to Cavendish's demands). Christopher Lloyd emerges best, playing Cavendish as a soft-spoken psychopath with ice water in his veins.

For all its delusions of grandeur, *The Legend of the Lone Ranger* pales next to its 1956 counterpart. Only the littlest buckaroos might overlook its flaws, but they'd probably prefer Clayton Moore as well. To this day, fans still head for Topanga Canyon, California, to visit the "Lone Ranger rocks" that were seen over and over in the TV series. Someone ought to put a plaque there to commemorate their contribution to the thrilling days of yesteryear. In silver, of course.

THE FILMS

The Lone Ranger (Republic serial, 1938, 250 minutes)
Directed by William Witney and John English; Written by Barry Shipman, Franklyn Adreon, Ronald Davidson, George Worthing Yates and Lois Eby, based on the Lone Ranger radio serial; Produced by Sol Shor; Music by Alberto Colombo
Cast

LEE POWELL (THE LONE RANGER), Chief Thunder Cloud (Tonto), Stanley Andrews (Marcus Jeffries), George Cleveland (Blanchard), Lynn Roberts (Joan)
Rating: *

The Lone Ranger Rides Again (Republic serial, 1939, 250 minutes)
Directed by William Witney and John English; Written by Franklyn Adreon, Ronald Davidson, Sol Shor and Barry Shipman; Produced by Robert Beche; Music by William Lava
Cast
ROBERT LIVINGSTON (THE LONE RANGER), Chief Thunder Cloud (Tonto), Duncan Renaldo (Juan Vasquez), J. Farrel MacDonald (Jed Scott), Ralph Dunn (Craig Dolan), Jinx Falken (Sue Dolan)
Rating: ***

The Lone Ranger (Warner Bros., 1956, 86 minutes)
Directed by Stuart Heisler; Written by Herb Meadow; Produced by Willis Goldbeck; Music by David Buttolph
Cast
CLAYTON MOORE (THE LONE RANGER), Jay Silverheels (Tonto), Lyle Bettger (Reece Kilgore), Bonita Granville (Welcome Kilgore)
Rating: ****
Available on Videocassette

The Lone Ranger and the Lost City of Gold (United Artists, 1958, 80 minutes)
Directed by Lesley Selander; Written by Robert Schaefer and Eric Freiwald; Produced by Sherman A. Harris; Music by Les Baxter
Cast
CLAYTON MOORE (THE LONE RANGER), Jay Silverheels (Tonto), Douglas Kennedy (Ross Brady), Noreen Nash (Francis Henderson)
Rating: **1/2
Available on Videocassette

The Legend of the Lone Ranger (Universal, 1981, 98 minutes)
Directed by William A. Fraker; Written by Ivan Goff, Ben Roberts, Michael Kane, William Roberts and Jerry Berloshan; Produced by Walter Coblenz; Music by John Barry and Dean Pitchford
Cast
KLINTON SPILSBURY (THE LONE RANGER), Michael Horse (Tonto), Christopher Lloyd (Butch Cavendish), Juanin Clay (Amy Striker), Jason Robards (President Grant), Richard Farnsworth (Wild Bill Hickok)
Rating: *
Available on Videocassette

TELEVISION
"The Lone Ranger" (ABC series, 1954-57)
Cast
CLAYTON MOORE (THE LONE RANGER), JOHN HART (THE LONE RANGER, 1952-1954), Jay Silverheels (Tonto)
Rating: ***1/2

Awards: 1949 Emmy nomination for Best Film Made-For-Television; 1950 nomination for Outstanding Children's Show

MAD MAX

Mad Max was never intended to be the first film in a series. Cocreator (with Byron Kennedy) George Miller has openly stated that he had no aspirations beyond putting together a tight little action-chase movie for the Australian drive-in crowd. But what began as a one-shot down-under *Death Wish* evolved into a tragedy examining one man's journey to recover his soul. In retrospect, the spiritual redemption of the title character is almost as memorable as the trials he must overcome to achieve it.

Max is the "reluctant hero" personified. The heroic deeds he accomplishes are born not of nobility but of necessity and circumstance. In *Mad Max*, Max is a police officer, but he displays little regard for protecting the innocent. Even after being told by a fellow officer that he should stay on the force, because the public needs its heroes, Max would rather stay home with his family. When his wife and son are killed, however, he is compelled (by vengeance, not altruism) to take action.

In *The Road Warrior*, Max only agrees to aid the compound dwellers after they agree to supply him with fuel and provisions. His motive is again self-contained, but a spark of humanity at last begins to surface. It is only in the last hour of the last movie, *Mad Max Beyond Thunderdome*, when Max returns to the hellish Bartertown to rescue a group of innocent children, that he at last embarks on an unselfish quest. Max the man is finally resurrected.

Max's redemption takes place in a world that has not yet earned the same privilege. Miller's post-apocalyptic society, in many ways as rich in detail as the make-believe worlds of J.R.R. Tolkien, illustrates the after-effects of mankind's failure to control its own greed and aggression. In *Mad Max* there seems to be little hope for man's future, and *The Road Warrior* follows through on its predecessor's dark foreshadowing. But in *Thunderdome*, Max's recovery is reflected in the mercy shown him by Auntie Entity, and the children he saves represent a next generation that will not repeat the mistakes of the past.

Mad Max returned more than $100 million on a $300,000 investment, and outgrossed *Star Wars* in its native Australia. In the United States, the film was dumped into third-rate theaters by an apathetic distributor who also decided to dub the voices, which made the film appear even more slipshod than it actually was. As a result, most Americans saw *The Road Warrior* first, and then sought out *Mad Max* on tape.

Viewed in this order, *Mad Max* is bound to disappoint. The film contains only traces of the post-apocalyptic (you use this word a lot when talking about Max) feel of *The Road Warrior* and *Thunderdome*, and actually bears a stronger resemblance to *A Clockwork Orange* (1971) than its own sequels. Miller's vision would blossom in later chapters, but happily without sacrificing the cheap thrills of the original.

The story is set "A few years from now," and opens with police officer Max pursuing an escaped cop killer known as the Night Rider. When the Rider is killed, his allies seek revenge. One of Max's friends and fellow officers is brutally murdered, and Max decides then that he's had enough of police work. However he is persuaded by another cop to take a vacation before turning in his resignation. When Max's wife and son are killed by the Rider's gang, Max abandons law and order and wipes out the gang, saving a particularly nasty fate for the ringleader.

It's a bare-bones plot, reminiscent of hundreds of other movies, and is padded out with gratuitous nudity in the grand tradition of quickie-master Roger Corman. The emphasis is clearly on the chase, and this is what separates Max from the usual "B" movie mix. Though the major stunt sequences would only qualify as throwaways in *The Road Warrior*, the opening chase does grab your attention, and the last stand of Max's family is superbly shot. When the action stops, however, the film reverts to cliche`, with stock footage of gathering storm clouds played over ominous creature feature music.

The worship of fuel and speed is the one consistent element Max shares with its sequels. Other aspects of the film do not seem to belong to the same series; there is still a functioning civilization at work, albeit one that is overrun with violence and corruption (from a distance it could be present day-Detroit). The movie ends rather suddenly, but the opening scene of *The Road Warrior* answers the question of what happened next.

It is the aftermath of a war that has destroyed the world's fuel supplies. Those who survive have reverted to an almost primitive state. Max, now a nomad, learns about an operating gasoline refinery from the Gyro Captain, whom he encounters in the desert. The refinery is controlled by a peaceful tribe which is under attack by a gang of ruthless marauders. Max agrees to help the compound dwellers in exchange for a share of the fuel. He brings a truck to transport a tanker full of gas to "the promised land," a place far away from the marauders' threats. However, he refuses their request that he drive the truck there for them. Later, Max is accosted by the gang, and his dog is killed. The Gyro Captain rescues him. Max then agrees to drive the truck, to decoy the marauders and allow the compound dwellers a chance to escape in another direction. After a furious chase in which all of his attackers are killed, Max discovers that the tanker is filled with sand. The Gyro Captain joins the tribe and becomes its leader. They never see Max again.

The Road Warrior is the series' undisputed high point. The character of Max is explored in greater depth, and when the gentlemen start their engines it's like nothing you've ever seen before. Miller's brilliant direction, the camerawork and the jaw-dropping stunts all punctuate the bizarre sight of dozens of patchwork vehicles roaring through a barren landscape. Because of its setting, the climactic chase in *Warrior* isn't usually categorized with acknowledged classic pursuits like those in *Bullitt* (1968) or *The French Connection* (1971), even though it blows them off the screen. It may be the most exciting chase sequence ever committed to film.

Mel Gibson is allowed to speak this time, but he doesn't say very much. Max buried his emotions with his family years earlier and he is content to avoid human contact. His *Shane*-like arrival and alliance with peaceful settlers begins Max's transformation into a figure of legend. Gibson deserves credit for communicating many emotions with few words.

The story is told in flashback by the Feral Kid, one of the settlers who idolized Max as a child. It is the settlers who remind Max that he is not the only person who has suffered and lost in the war, and it is the Kid who first causes Max to once again care about another human life. We can read much into Max helping the compound dwellers, who are clad in white, to a place they call the Promised Land. Max wears black, the same color as the marauders, suggesting that he may still have more in common with them than the people he rescues. Max is back on the right road, but he is not yet deserving of the Promised Land himself. It is not the only religious connotation in the series, but it may be the most pronounced.

The beginning of *Thunderdome* finds Max by his lonesome again, when his property is stolen by a man in a flying machine (the Gyro Captain?). He tracks his belongings to a place called Bartertown, run by the enigmatic Auntie Entity. Auntie offers to reequip Max if he will fight the champion of the town's underworld, Master Blaster, who has challenged her authority by cutting off the fuel supply. In the Thunderdome, the place where all disputes are settled, Max defeats Master Blaster, but refuses to kill him. His punishment for refusal is banishment back to the desert. Days later, near death, Max is found by a clan of children who mistake him for the man in their prophecies who will lead them to "Tomorrow-morrow Land."

Recovered, Max tries to shatter their illusions, but a smaller group leaves the pack to find Tomorrow-morrow Land on their own. They are captured in Bartertown. Max and the remaining children slip into the city and rescue them. Max fires up a vintage locomotive and creates a diversion while the children escape. Auntie and her warriors chase Max into the desert and derail the train, but Auntie spares his life.

The theater audience became restless during *Thundrdome*'s middle third, when they realized that this film would not be another ninety-minute desert drag race. However, the scenes featuring Max and the children seem to get better with every repeat viewing, and are imperative to illustrate his emotional progress. He rejects the clan at first, in one of the most agonizing moments in the series, but he cannot turn his back on the kids who are abducted in Bartertown. His recovery is now complete.

Of course, a Mad Max film without an all-out chase is as unimaginable as a Superman film without a flight sequence, and the audience can certainly be forgiven for breaking into applause when Max stops playing babysitter and blasts out of Bartertown in a runaway locomotive, with Auntie's warriors right behind. The climax is not as good as *The Road Warrior*'s--what could be?--but the use of a train allows for a myriad of interesting complications, all of which Miller exploits to the fullest.

Thunderdome also has the most impressive supporting cast of the three films; Bruce Spence returns from *The Road Warrior*, though there is some confusion as to whether he is playing the same character. Tina Turner, in her first film performance since playing the Acid Queen in *Tommy* (1975) brings the same commanding presence to Auntie Entity that she brings to her live performances--why is she not making more movies?! Helen Buday provides the film's most lyrical moments as idealist Savannah Nix, who refuses to abandon her belief in a better world despite Max's assertions. Her reading of the clan's history is a hauntingly poetic mix of Biblical phrasing and pop culture. As The Master, screen veteran Angelo Rossitto gives us one of the few series characters besides Max worth cheering for.

There is more comedy this time also; Spence's antics, Max removing his weapons when entering Bartertown, and the children's interpretation of the airline artifacts are all highlights. There is also a variation on the old "gun vs. knife" confrontation, used by Indiana Jones in *Raiders of the Lost Ark*.

Bartertown is an amazing creation, a triumph of both script and set design that simultaneously represents the first step forward of a new civilization, and the first step back for one that has lost everything. It also contains the Thunderdome arena (all together now--"Two men enter. One man leave."), which should have inspired less fatal versions for game shows and high-tech health clubs, but didn't.

Will Max race again? I'd put the odds at about 50-50. Mel Gibson is now a megastar who can pull money from a studio to film *Hamlet* (if that isn't clout I don't know what is), with another popular recurring role in the *Lethal Weapon* series. Mad Max cocreator Byron Kennedy was killed just before the release of *Thunderdome*, so even if Gibson was willing (and the jury's out on that one) it's very possible that George Miller might not wish to continue without his partner. Anything is possible, however, and it would be fascinating to see where Miller would take the character and his world next.

THE FILMS

Mad Max (Mad Max Pty/AIP Filmways, 1979, 90 minutes
Directed by George Miller; Written by George Miller and James McClausland, based on a story by Miller and Byron Kennedy; Produced by Byron Kennedy; Music by Brian May
Cast
MEL GIBSON (MAX), Joanne Samuel (Jessie), Hugh Keays-Byrne (The Toecutter), Roger Ward (Fifi Macaffee), Vince Gil (Nightrider)
Rating: ***
Available on Videocassette

The Road Warrior (Warner Bros., 1982, 94 minutes)
Directed by George Miller; Written by Terry Hayes, George Miller and Brian Hannat; Produced by Byron Kennedy; Music by Brian May
Cast
MEL GIBSON (MAX), Bruce Spence (Gyro Captain), Vernon Wells (Wez), Emil Minty (The Feral Kid), Kjell Nilsson (Humungus)
Rating: *****
Available on Videocassette

Mad Max Beyond Thunderdome (Kennedy-Miller/Warner Bros., 1985, 106 minutes)
Directed by George Miller and George Ogilvie; Written by Terry Hayes and George Miller; Produced by George Miller and Doug Mitchell; Music by Maurice Jarre
Cast
MEL GIBSON (MAD MAX), Bruce Spence (Jedediah), Adam Cockburn (Jedediah, Jr.), Tina Turner (Auntie Entity), Angelo Rossitto (The Master), Paul Larsson (The Blaster), Helen Buday (Savannah Nix)
Rating: ****
Available on Videocassette

AUDIE MURPHY

The character of John Rambo is this generation's personification of a super-soldier. Back in the 1940s, that title was held by Audie Murphy, who was as much a household name during World War II as MacArthur, Eisenhower and Patton. To look at them both now you'd think Rambo could have Murphy for lunch, but that would be confusing fiction with reality. Rambo fought actors and stuntmen on a Hollywood soundstage--Murphy fought the real-life foes of democracy throughout Europe, and the bullets were real.

Audie Murphy's road to motion picture stardom is unique in the annals of Hollywood. He achieved fame as a World War II hero, became a movie star after the war, and found his most memorable role playing himself in a film adaptation of his military exploits. For modern comparison, imagine General Norman Schwarzkopf starring in *Desert Storm--The Movie*.

THE MAN

Murphy was the most decorated soldier in U.S. military history, earning twenty-one medals including the nation's highest accolade, the Congressional Medal of Honor. He would battle his way through two years of continuous combat in Sicily, Anzio, France and Germany, and is credited with killing more 240 enemy soldiers, all before his twenty-first birthday.

When Murphy's picture appeared on the cover of *Life* Magazine on July 16, 1945, he became the symbol of America's fighting spirit. Details of his life before the war only reinforced his underdog image; he was born into poverty on June 20, 1924, the son of a Texas sharecropper. He was a good student but was forced to leave school after the fifth grade to work on the family farm. The movie *Sergeant York* (1941) was an early inspiration for him, and its story of a poor Southern farmer who became a World War I hero would prove prophetic.

"I had always wanted to be a soldier," recalls Murphy in his autobiography *To Hell and Back*, but he had to do plenty of fighting just to get to the war. On his eighteenth birthday he tried to join the Marines, but was turned down. After being rejected by the paratroops as well he joined the infantry, but his youth and baby-faced appearance induced his commanders to steer him toward a mess hall assignment or stateside service. They thought they were doing the kid a favor, but Murphy appealed for a trip to the front and finally got his wish.

Murphy recalled his experiences in *To Hell and Back*, a spirited account of a war from ground level in which he describes army life as "a bog of monotony marked by moments of excitement." The book contains vivid descriptions and sensual details of life from battle to battle, and the endless waiting in between. "This is the worst moment." he writes. "Just ahead the enemy waits silently. It will be far better when the guns open up. The nerves will relax; the heart, stop its thumping. The brain will turn to animal cunning. The job lies directly before us: Destroy and survive."

He assumes a matter-of-fact approach to his own achievements, preferring to shift the spotlight onto his fallen comrades, to whom the book is dedicated. He recalls numerous friends with great affection, and their sudden deaths, often just minutes after trading jokes and stories with Murphy, are among the book's most moving passages. But his modesty requires us to turn to other accounts, such as Don Graham's excellent Murphy biography *No Name on the Bullet*, for a more balanced chronicle. Graham depicts Audie as an aggressive soldier, an uncanny marksman and a natural leader. In Sicily, where Murphy saw his first major action, Graham recounts how Murphy disabled a German tank single-handedly and won a Bronze Star.

When he landed in France on the beach of St. Tropez, Audie fought like a man possessed. After watching another friend fall he flew into a berserker rage, becoming a one-man battalion both literally and figuratively. Murphy earned the Congressional Medal of Honor for his actions on January 26, 1945, which constitute one of the most extraordinary moments in the war. Murphy was almost alone against two hundred German soldiers and, with an unceasing barrage of Tank Destroyer and machine gun fire, he forced them to retreat.

THE FILMS

After returning from the war following Germany's surrender, Murphy was the uncomfortable recipient of ticker tape parades and public adulation. Then James Cagney saw the *Life* cover, and invited Murphy out to Hollywood. Though he could probably sell tickets on his name alone, Murphy took acting classes and studied with Cagney. As an actor his talents were only fair but, by wisely concentrating on action roles that traded on his persona, he carved out a consistent, though not necessarily distinguished body of work. Between 1948 and 1971, Audie Murphy appeared in forty-five films, more than thrity-five of which were forgettable "B" westerns. His still youthful appearance led to casting as Billy the Kid in *Kid From Texas* (1950), and later to more heroic kid roles (*The Cimarron Kid* in 1951 and others).

In 1951 Murphy starred in *The Red Badge of Courage*, one of the few occasions when he worked with superb material and a first-rate director (John Huston). The result was his best performance in his best film. His most famous role, however, was as Audie Murphy in the film version of *To Hell and Back*, released in 1955.

Murphy was never comfortable discussing his achievements or receiving the accolades he certainly deserved, so when the film was proposed he had to be talked into playing himself. "I don't believe in heroics," he said in his book. "The great man of the war to me was the little fellow who did what was asked of him and paid whatever price that action cost." With that in mind, once Murphy agreed to the film he took special interest in the casting, taking great pains to ensure that the friends he lost were given their due.

The movie is introduced by a real-life general who reads off cue cards the old spiel about ordinary men rising to face an extraordinary challenge--it's the first of countless cliches` that weaken the film every time the shooting stops. The rapport between soldiers that Murphy captured so well in his book seems forced and overwritten on screen. The action scenes work fine, however, with Murphy vigorously recreating his exploits and sharing the glory with his company. Director

Jesse Hibbs is no Sam Peckinpah, but he generates excitement with simple framing and a brisk pace.

Early scenes of young Audie on the farm, quitting school to support his family, quickly give way to his combat experiences. Audie distinguishes himself in seven different campaigns, earning both medals and promotions. A hip wound forces his return to the states, and the movie closes with Audie being awarded the Congressional Medal of Honor.

This was a difficult role for Murphy, though certainly not in the traditional sense. To relive so many unpleasant moments in a life marked by poverty, war and death must have been disquieting. The circumstances add resonance to his performance, which is quiet and understated and typical of his work in other, less personal movies. Other performances vary, but the casting works to the extent that thirty-year-old Murphy still looks ten years younger than the other soldiers in his company. But the friendships that develop under fire and then suddenly end are not adequately brought to life. There is an attempt here as in the book to give equal credit all around for the achievements of Murphy's unit, and even the scene of Murphy receiving the Medal of Honor is integrated with ghostly images of the men who didn't make it home.

The Red Badge of Courage and *To Hell and Back* are the only must-see films in Murphy's career, but Western fans might also enjoy *Duel at Silver Creek* (1952), one of Don Siegel's first films, *Walk the Proud Land* (1956) with Anne Bancroft as an Indian and Jay Silverheels as Geronimo, and *Night Passage* (1957), which costars James Stewart. Murphy also played the villain occasionally, including Jesse James twice (*Kansas Raiders* in 1950 and *A Time for Dying* in 1971).

Audie Murphy died in a plane crash in 1971. His later years were not exceptional and included forays into heavy gambling, womanizing, and loans financed by organized crime. Biographer Don Graham attributes this downfall to delayed stress from the war. It is appropriate that Murphy be best remembered for his amazing World War II accomplishments--what I find most regrettable is that today he is hardly remembered at all.

THE FILMS

To Hell and Back (Universal, 1955, 106 minutes)
Directed by Jesse Hibbs; Written by Gil Doud, based on the autobiography *To Hell and Back* by Audie Murphy; Produced by Aaron Rosenberg; Music by Joseph Gershenson
Cast
AUDIE MURPHY (HIMSELF), Marshall Thompson (Johnson), Jack Kelly (Kerrigan), Charles Drake (Brandon), David Janssen (Lt. Lee), Richard Castle (Kovak)
Rating: ***1/2
Available on Videocassette

Robert Stack as Treasury Agent Eliot Ness in television's *The Untouchables.*

ELIOT NESS

Chicago in the Roaring Twenties has become one of the most colorful and romanticized places in American history. The gangster film genre can trace its roots to Prohibition and the war between treasury agents and bootleggers. Hollywood churned out numerous fabricated accounts of their battles and turned James Cagney and Edward G. Robinson into major stars. But one of the era's greatest stories actually happened--the battle of wits, guts and firepower between mob chief Al Capone and Treasury Agent Eliot Ness.

Time and television have upped the ante on the actual events, but the basics that everybody knows are all factual. It was Ness's two-and-a-half year campaign against the Chicago bootleggers and the creation of a group called the Untouchables that brought about the downfall of Al Capone. Because the plotlines of the "Untouchables" TV series and the 1987 Brian De Palma film were fictional, some have concluded that Ness's actual role in Capone's arrest and conviction was likewise manufactured, but that is not the case. He may never have called the gang to arms with "Rico! Youngfellow!" or received guidance from an Irish cop with a Scottish brogue, but it was indeed his leadership and dedication that put history's most infamous mobster out of commission.

THE MAN

Eliot Ness was born (April 19, 1903) and raised on the south side of Chicago. As a boy he listened to the cops-and-robbers stories spun by his older sister's husband Jamie, an agent with the Justice Department. The origin of his passion for law enforcement can be traced to these tales, and his other interests were all perfect training for his future profession; Eliot often accompanied Jamie to the firing range, where he practiced his marksmanship. He also trained in jujitsu, and devoured the Sherlock Holmes stories of Arthur Conan Doyle. After graduating from the University of Chicago in 1925, Ness worked briefly as an investigator for a credit company and then joined the Treasury Department as a special agent.

Ness became one of three hundred agents in the Prohibition Bureau, whose formidable task was to corral the owners and operators of more than twenty thousand speakeasies in the Windy City, not to mention their suppliers and importers. Bullets flew in the streets between bootleggers and police and between rival crime gangs. Al Capone, who arrived in Chicago via New York in 1919, outstripped his competition by sheer ruthlessness and, by 1925, was the unchallenged leader of the city's criminal empire.

Capone's legend is probably more famous than that of Eliot Ness, and many of the more seemingly outlandish aspects of that legend were actually true. He did own an armor-plated, chauffeur-driven limousine specially built by General

Motors for $30,000. He dressed in expensive suits and diamond jewelry and filled his home with priceless artwork, easily afforded on his annual $120 million income. He was a respected figure among the city's elite, who always RSVPed for his lavish parties, but his reputation was equally sterling on the streets. Capone captured the public's imagination in much the way that John Gotti has in recent years. When Capone attended an opera or a Cubs game at Wrigley Field, his entrance brought applause from those assembled.

The cheering stopped after the Capone-orchestrated St. Valentine's Day Massacre in 1929. In the previous year, Eliot Ness's first as an agent, the mob in Chicago murdered seventy-two people, and the residents were getting fed up with the wholesale slaughter. The Massacre, in which seven mobsters were slain by rival thugs dressed as police officers, also put the first dent in the government's nudge and wink policy toward the bootleggers. Orders to deal with Capone came directly from President Herbert Hoover, prompting the formation of a special squad of agents to bring down the flamboyant kingpin. Eliot's brother-in-law Jamie was in on the ground floor, and it was his recommendation that put twenty-six-year-old Eliot in charge.

At least half of Chicago's treasury agents were taking bribes, and it was assumed that Ness would follow the established pattern. But Ness was an impeccably honest man with a profound belief in law and order. The main accuracy of the film portrayals was his single-minded dedication to justice and the zealousness of his crusade. Finding like-minded officers in a city where Capone could (and did) knock the mayor down the stairs of City Hall in broad daylight would not be easy. After extensive searching Ness personally selected nine men for the war that would follow.

The team had already caught a break upon its formation--Capone was stuck in a Philadelphia prison for ten months after being convicted of carrying a concealed weapon. His Chicago operation was being run by the much-dumber Frank "The Enforcer" Nitti, which allowed Ness and his agents to make several quick strikes and infiltrate the Capone organization. When Big Al returned he recognized this new team of agents as a threat to his security, and arranged for bribes to be offered to Ness and two of his agents, all of which were vehemently rejected. It was a reporter for the *Chicago Tribune* who coined the term "Untouchables" in an article about their honesty and success.

Months of raids and seizures and arrests followed and, by the summer of 1931, the Untouchables had cut the liquor production in the city by 80 percent, and had assembled a list of five thousand offenses Capone had committed against Prohibition laws. But the Justice Department had been working the income-tax angle at the same time, and beat the Untouchables to the courts by one week. The U.S. District Attorney chose to prosecute Capone on the tax charge and, on October 6, 1931, Al Capone went to trial. He was found guilty and sentenced to eleven years in a federal penitentiary. The Untouchables' last mission was to escort Capone from Cook County Jail to the train that would take him up the river.

Direct confrontations between Ness and Capone are frequent in the "Untouchables" TV series, but the two men actually spoke only once, after one of Ness's men was found brutally murdered. Ness called the mobster in his Lexington Hotel suite and told him to look out the window at eleven o'clock. Capone did so and witnessed forty-five trucks seized in Untouchable raids being driven single-file to the auction block (a moment recreated--with dramatic license--in the pilot for the "Untouchables" series). Three attempts on Ness's life soon followed. And Ness was a spectator at Capone's trial, as seen in the De Palma film.

In 1933, Eliot Ness was transferred to Cincinnati and became a "revenuer," tracking down hillbilly stills and seizing moonshine. As a city boy he was not thrilled with this kind of work and moved to Cleveland, where he became the city's director of public safety. There he continued his already legendary career, arresting bootleggers by the hundreds. But Prohibition had been repealed, and his exploits were no longer as celebrated. Although Ness would notch many more victories against organized crime, his failure to solve a lurid serial murder case (that remains unsolved today) was more widely reported and contributed to his defeat as a candidate for mayor of Cleveland in 1947.

Eliot Ness died of a massive heart attack on May 16, 1957. He was 54 years old. His last ten years were not happy ones. After losing the mayoral election he was forced to take any job he could to support his family. In 1955 Ness met journalist Oscar Fraley, who urged him to write a book about his career in Chicago. Together they wrote *The Untouchables*, which became an instant bestseller, but sadly Ness did not live to see its publication or to enjoy the folk hero status bestowed upon him.

TELEVISION AND FILMS

The book was optioned by Desi Arnaz in 1958 and turned over to the prolific television producer Quinn Martin, who wrote and directed the series pilot, which aired on ABC on April 15, 1959. The pilot began with the formation of the Untouchables and concluded with Al Capone's tax evasion conviction, and established the elements that made the ensuing series one of television's best crime dramas; Walter Winchell's rapid-fire narration, which was perfectly in sync with the rat-a-tat of the tommy guns on screen; Eliot Ness and his men breaking huge kegs of bootleg hooch with axes, blowing mobsters away by the carload, and shattering the limits for lurid sex and violence that restrained fifties television.

Crooks were gunned down on TV before, especially in Westerns, but on "The Untouchables" mobsters were dispatched in a hail of bullets and died ugly, screaming, bestial deaths. The camera also didn't blink during Barbara Nichols's burlesque striptease in the pilot, which might not get past some censors today. There were protests throughout the series' run, but the most irate viewers may have been surviving relatives of Al Capone, who filed a defamation lawsuit. The Untouchables beat Capone again when the case was thrown out.

The series was not a hit based solely on shock value. "The Untouchables" was one of the most technically proficient shows on television. Its black-and-white "newsreel" ambience was augmented by slick production values and a precise attention to period detail. Most of the action took place after dark, which drove up the budget but added to the film noir look, as did the Jacques Tourneur–like lighting and camera angles.

Robert Stack won an Emmy for his no-nonsense portrayal of Eliot Ness. He bore little resemblance to the almost baby-faced lawman and played the character as a veteran of the street wars, which Ness was not when the Untouchables were formed. Names were changed, but Stack's team included a wiretap expert, a driving expert and an undercover specialist, just like the real thing. In the pilot Ness married Elizabeth (Betty) Andersen, but the truth is that Ness met Andersen in Cleveland long after his Untouchables days, and she was actually his third wife. Ness was single in Chicago, and chose only single men for his special team. The TV Untouchables continued for four years after nabbing Capone, unlike their actual counterparts. Their nemesis returned as well, played by Neville Brand as a cigar-chomping psychotic with an exaggerated accent.

Before jumping ahead to 1987, there is one brief and usually overlooked film appearance of Eliot Ness circa 1979. *The Lady in Red* is a highly fictionalized biography of Polly Hamilton, the "lady in red" who was with John Dillinger when he was killed by FBI agents in front of Chicago's Biograph Theater. Robert Conrad is excellent as Dillinger, but "Dynasty"'s Pamela Sue Martin is merely adequate as the title character (called Polly Franklin). In one brief scene, Polly is interrogated by Ness after witnessing a mob shootout. Phillip R. Allen is nondescript as the lawman, but to be fair he's not around very long.

The film is pure exploitation, with heavy doses of gratuitous nudity and violence, and even an extended women's prison sequence complete with sadistic matron. Real drive-in stuff, but worth a look for the Conrad performance and the early-career contributions of writer John Sayles, music composer James Horner and Christopher Lloyd, chilling as a creepy enforcer.

It would also be remiss not to mention Dan Aykroyd's dead-on impression of Robert Stack in the "Saturday Night Live" parody of "The Untouchables," which as a comic take is matched only by Stack's self-mocking portrayal in a subsequent SNL appearance. The Aykroyd skit appears on the "Best of Saturday Night Live Classics, Vol. 5" videocassette.

And now we return to the main road and the most ballyhooed and fantastical Untouchables project to date. Brian De Palma's film opens in 1930 with Ness's appointment as head of a special unit within the treasury department, assigned to combat bootleggers. Ness's first attempted raid is a total failure, and he begins to doubt his ability. That night, he meets a beat cop named Malone who proves to be an invaluable ally. Malone tells Ness that the police department is rife with corruption, so Ness assembles his team elsewhere, recruiting crack marksman George Stone from the Police Academy and crack accountant Oscar Wallace from, well, the accounting department. It is Wallace who first discovers that Al Capone hasn't filed an income tax return in five years. The case takes them to the Canadian border for a Wild West shootout and then back to Chicago to capture Capone's bookkeeper. Wallace and Malone do not survive the war, and neither does Capone's top lieutenant Frank Nitti. Despite an attempt to buy the jury, Capone is convicted of tax evasion and goes directly to jail.

Brian De Palma is a good choice for directors-in-training to study, because he constantly calls attention to himself through the use of slow motion, shot selection and a whirling, swooping camera. He is often maligned for such indulgent technique, but in *The Untouchables* it works, resulting in several terrifically memorable scenes. Ness calling out Capone after Wallace is murdered, Capone's baseball monologue, the Canadian sequence in which gangsters fire tommy guns on horseback, and Ness throwing Nitti off the courthouse roof are all high points.

But the movie's undisputed star centerpiece is a train station shootout surrounding a runaway baby carriage. It's a direct steal of the Odessa Steps sequence in Sergei Eisenstein's *Battleship Potemkin* (1925), familiar to students in Film 101 courses everywhere. De Palma is one of the first students to do something with that knowledge, and he has crafted an amazing montage that can be studied on its own merits. The scene is also helped immensely by Ennio Morricone's music.

Ness's rejection of an alderman's bribe is the only moment of truth in the movie. Everything else came from writer David Mamet's fantasyland. In Mamet's version Ness not only has a wife but a daughter--in reality Ness raised only one adopted son, during his marriage to Betty Andersen. Kevin Costner's Ness is less than superheroic, unlike the stoic Robert Stack, and its the best thing about his uneven performance. Costner was not yet a star at this time and often seemed overshadowed by costars Sean Connery and Robert De Niro. His subsequent celebrity has helped make up the imbalance.

De Niro matches the general atmosphere of flamboyance with a performance that makes Neville Brand look subdued. Strong supporting work emerged from Andy Garcia in his first notable role and Charles Martin Smith as the accountant turned warrior. But even with the focus on Ness vs. Capone and De Niro's theatrics, the film was Sean Connery's to steal and he did so from his first entrance. The scene in which he explains "the Chicago way" to Ness won him the Oscar, and Malone's premature death is the film's only major flaw.

It was inevitable, after the movie's success and after the successful revival of countless 1960s TV series with special made-for-TV movies, that Robert Stack would be asked to dust off his badge. It happened in 1992 in "The Return of Eliot Ness," an anemic attempt at memory-jogging that only leaves one longing for the original series. We are introduced to Eliot Ness in 1947, at the funeral of a former Untouchable, whose reputation is tainted after he is found murdered in a compromising position. Ness teams up with Gil Labine, the son of his fallen friend, to restore that reputation. Ness spots white roses at the funeral, a calling card of former Capone lieutenant Art Malto. Malto and his hotheaded son Bobby become prime suspects in the senior Labine's murder, and the investigation is aided by nightclub singer Madeline Whitfield, Art's girlfriend.

Gil falls for Madeline, until Ness discovers that the twist is actually in cahoots with Bobby Malto, who is planning to hijack surplus wartime weapons from the army and use them to take over the Chicago underworld. Ness breaks up the weapons transfer and kills Bobby, while Gil recovers from a gunshot wound inflicted by Madeline. Art knows his son isn't smart enough to concoct the hijack, and blames Madeline for his death. He strangles the songbird just before Ness arrives to place him under arrest.

Once again the narrative is complete fantasy, but that is hardly the film's greatest sin. The story is dull, there is very little action, and the all-important period feel is absent. Stack is unflappable as ever, but a full Untouchables reunion would have been far more interesting. Instead of Rico, Youngfellow, Flaherty, Cam Allison and the rest, we're stuck with Jack Coleman as dopey cop Gil Labine, the most bland sidekick since Binzer on the old "VEGA$" series. As Madeline, Lisa Hartman sings some pretty songs, but this ain't no musical.

Just one year later The Untouchables surfaced again on television in a syndicated series starring Tom Amandes as Eliot Ness and William Forsythe as Al Capone. The sharp visuals and period detail are a testament to the sudden quality of shows in syndication after "Star Trek: The Next Generation" proved they could make money, but there is not much beneath the gloss but rehashed "T.J. Hooker" plots played in pinstripes. Amandes, to his credit, does not imitate the humorless spirit of vengeance interpretation of Robert Stack or the boy-scout naivete` of Kevin Costner, but he can substitute no defining traits to make his own interpretation memorable. The series's resounding success despite such flaws is an indication of the enduring interest in the battle between Ness and Capone, which shows every sign of evolving into a clash of titans that will be played out again and again by future generations of moviemakers.

THE FILMS

The Lady in Red (New World Pictures, 1979, 93 minutes)
Directed by Lewis Teague; Written by John Sayles; Produced by Julie Corman; Music by James Horner
Cast
Pamela Sue Martin (Polly Franklin), Robert Conrad (John Dillinger), Louise Fletcher (Anna Sage), PHILLIP R. ALLEN (ELIOT NESS)
Rating: **1/2
Available on Videocassette

The Untouchables (Paramount, 1987, 119 minutes)
Directed by Brian De Palma; Written by David Mamet; Produced by Art Linson; Music by Ennio Morricone
Cast
KEVIN COSTNER (ELIOT NESS), Sean Connery (James Malone), Charles Martin Smith (Oscar Wallace), Andy Garcia (George Stone), Robert De Niro (Al Capone)
Rating: ****1/2
Available on Videocassette
Awards: Academy Award for Best Supporting Actor (Connery); nominations for Best Score, Art Direction, Costume Design

TELEVISION

"The Untouchables" (ABC series, 1959-1963)
Cast
ROBERT STACK (ELIOT NESS), Jerry Paris (Martin Flaherty), Abel Fernandez (William Youngfellow), Nick Georgiade (Enrico Rossi), Anthony George (Cam Allison), Paul Picerni (Lee Hobson), Steve London (Jack Rossman), Bruce Gordon (Frank Nitti), Neville Brand (Al Capone)
Rating: ****
Pilot Available on Videocassette
Awards: 1959-60 Emmy Award for Best Actor (Stack), Cinematography, Editing, Art Direction; nomination for Best Drama Program. 1960-61 nominations for Best Drama Program, Best Actor (Stack), Best Single Performance by an Actress (Elizabeth Montgomery, "The Rusty Heller Story" episode)

"The Return of Eliot Ness" (NBC movie, 1992, 120 minutes)
Directed by James Costner; Written by Michael Petryni; Produced by Joseph B. Wallerstein; Music by Lee Holdridge
Cast
ROBERT STACK (ELIOT NESS), Jack Coleman (Gil Labine), Philip Bosco (Art Malto), Anthony DeSando (Bobby Malto), Lisa Hartman (Madeline Whitfield), Charles Durning (Roger Finn)
Rating: **

"The Untouchables" (syndicated series, 1993-)
Cast
TOM AMANDES (ELIOT NESS), William Forsythe (Al Capone)
Rating: **

GENERAL GEORGE S. PATTON

For most of us who were born after World War II, we learned everything we know about General George S. Patton from actor George C. Scott. Movies are history teachers, whether they do the job responsibly or not. Dramatic license being what it is, Hollywood's history of the world is filtered through editing and rewrites, which means it's more entertaining than a textbook but hardly as reliable. Once in a while, though, we get a film that so deftly treads the line between fact and fiction that there is almost no longer any divergence. *Patton* is such a film.

We remember Patton best for the most memorable scene in the movie, in which the general slaps a shell-shocked enlisted man. As a defining moment the incident is both flawed and appropriate; it is an ideal illustration of Patton's personal philosophy in his natural element, but it should not overshadow his extraordinary European campaigns and genius for military strategy.

THE MAN

George S. Patton, Jr., was born in 1885 and graduated from West Point in 1909. He served in the U.S. Tank Corps in World War I, and by World War II he had become a master practitioner of mobile tank warfare in both the European and Mediterranean theaters. The campaign that etched Patton's name in history began when he led the 3rd Army across France in the summer of 1944, and culminated in December with the defense of Bastogne in the Battle of the Bulge. Patton's army didn't stop there--in January they reached the German border and by March they had jumped the Moselle River, joined the 7th Army and swept through the Saar and the Palatinate, taking more than a hundred thousand prisoners.

Patton was a controversial figure throughout his career, alternately praised and lambasted by the press and a constant headache to his superiors. He thrust his personal code of discipline, toughness and self-sacrifice was thrust upon his troops, and those who couldn't get with the program would suffer the consequences. His victories, including a defeat of Rommel's forces in Africa, did much to deflect criticism, but when in 1943 he verbally abused and then struck a soldier in full view of doctors, nurses and other patients it could not be overlooked, and would haunt the remainder of his career.

When General Eisenhower demanded an apology Patton complied, with dignity but not much sincerity. In his diary, published under the title *War As I See It*, he called the apology an order to "soft-soap a skulker to placate the timidity of those above." According to many accounts, it was this incident that kept Patton out of the loop when planning began for the initial invasion of France later that year.

After a long delay he was relegated to backing up the forces of General Omar Bradley, who had been Patton's deputy during his African campaign. Thus, one slap in the face is repaid with another.

Patton's lack of compassion is easy to criticize, but his real fault was a failure to recognize that his genuine love for military conflict was not shared by those in his command, many of whom were no doubt drafted into service. Addressing the 45th Division in June 1943, Patton referred to battle as "the most magnificent competition in which a human being can indulge. It brings out all that is best, it removes all that is base." To the man pulled from his wife and children with a terse note from Uncle Sam, this outlook was assuredly alien.

This attitude, combined with a daunting ego, helped earn Patton his "Old Blood and Guts" moniker, though the actual blood and guts were spilled among his own forces as well as the opposition. He was confident to the point of arrogance, and wrote of his preeminence prior to the Normandy invasion: "When I think of the greatness of my job and that I am what I am, I am amazed, but on reflection who is as good as I am? I know of no one."

Americans admire rugged individualists, the brave few who fly in the face of authority and pursue their destiny with or without assistance or approval. From the pilgrims to the pioneers, our country was built from their drive and vision. George S. Patton, who always thought he was smarter than everyone else (and often was, with benefit of hindsight) is cut from this cloth, although the glorification of the individual has no place in the military. And yet, Patton enjoyed his reputation, he loved notoriety and hated when another commander stole his thunder. If it was his greatest flaw as a leader, it is also why his exploits are the subject of movies, while those of such equally heroic generals as Omar Bradley and Mark Clark are not.

THE FILMS

Two actors preceded George C. Scott in the role of Patton, but neither was around long enough in their respective films to make a significant impression. In 1963, Disney's *Miracle of the White Stallions* dramatized the true story of how Vienna's Royal Lippizaner Stallions were transported from the Spanish Riding School to safety during World War II. It's an interesting story rendered dull by long windy speeches and a meandering, often confusing script.

Colonel Podhajsky, the man in charge of the School, is given permission by the Germans to transport the Lippizaner Stallions to a distant village, where they will be safe from the war and from Austrian refugees who want to steal the horses and ride them to safety. The stallions and mares are separated, however, and when the danger is passed it becomes critical to bring them together, or the future of the three hundred-year-old breed could be threatened. General Patton and his troops reach Vienna, and Podhajsky arranges a show for the soldiers in the hope of convincing Patton to offer assistance. The general is so impressed with the stallions that he personally helps guide the mares back to Vienna safely.

Miracle of the White Stallions is one of those films that just kind of lies there. If it turns up on the late show you might keep it on, but you're likely to fall asleep before it's over. Performances are uniformly flat; Robert Taylor came out of retirement to play Podhajsky, who gets the gang together to put on a show, but Mickey Rooney he's not. Lilli Palmer adds some class as the missus, and Eddie Albert plays a singing Austrian soldier. Character actor John Larch plays Patton, but it's a brief appearance that does not allow Larch enough time to build a character. He does his best to compensate by barking out his handful of lines with gruff conviction.

Director Arthur Hiller cannot generate any suspense during the movement of the horses and also throws away the one scene you'd expect to be foolproof--the actual performance of the Lippizaner Stallions. But what should have been the film's centerpiece is spliced into poorly shot segments that only hint at the grandeur of what horse and rider can accomplish.

The movie makes much of Patton's love for horses, and mentions that he rode in the 1912 Olympics. The actual event was the military pentathlon, which was comprised of steeplechase, pistol shooting, swimming, fencing and a five thousand meter cross-country run. Patton finished fifth of forty-three competitors. In the film, Patton is amazed by Colonel Podhajsky's exhibition--for the actual story we must turn to Ladislas Farrago's book *The Last Days of Patton*, in which the general's reaction is less than enthusiastic; "it was rather peculiar to realize that in a world tearing itself apart in war, about twenty middle-aged men in perfect physical condition and about an equal number of grooms had spent their time teaching horses tricks," Patton writes. "As much as I like horses, it seems to me there is a place for everything."

The second film incarnation of Patton is too brief for critical appraisal; Kirk Douglas appears as the general in *Is Paris Burning* (1966), a good movie masquerading as an epic, complete with overture and all-star cast. Some serious trimming would have produced a better movie, in which the plot would not frequently take a back seat to a game of spot the celebrity cameo.

The story is set in Paris circa 1944, as the allies close in after four years of Nazi occupation. Hitler orders the city burned if it cannot be held. Members of the French resistance work feverishly to reach the American forces, while the Nazis plant explosives beneath every bridge, reservoir and monument in the City of Lights. But the German commander, General von Choltitz, is hesitant to destroy the city, knowing the war is already lost. The allies reach Paris, the explosives are deactivated, and von Choltitz is almost relieved to be taken prisoner.

The film was made in black and white, to allow for seamless fusion of actual footage of wartime Paris, which lends a newsreel look to the project. Gert Frobe is excellent as von Choltitz, as is Orson Welles as a Swedish diplomat. It's also nice to see so many familiar art-house faces blending with the American mainstream--Jean-Paul Belmondo, Yves Montand, Alain Delon and Simone Signoret all turn up, if only for a few moments. Leslie Caron, an underrated dramatic actress, also appears in her best postingenue role. If you blink you'll miss Douglas as Patton--in fact, by the time the audience finishes whispering "Kirk Douglas!" to each other, he's gone.

Patton finally received his due in 1970 with one of the best film biographies ever made. *Patton* begins with the general assuming command of U.S. troops in North Africa and defeating the vaunted German forces of Erwin Rommel. A brilliant Sicilian campaign is clouded by controversy when Patton slaps a frightened enlisted man and receives a reprimand from General Eisenhower. He is relieved of command and reduced to acting as a decoy to keep certain German forces from the Normandy invasion.

After humbling himself before General Omar Bradley, Patton is given command of the 3rd Army, which he leads through hundreds of miles of Germany and Czechoslovakia. Politics, however, force him to halt at the border and allow British General Montgomery to mop up the remaining German troops. When Patton expresses a desire to march on the Soviet Union, an ally, he is again relieved of command and forced into involuntary retirement.

To label George C. Scott's work as a performance is almost insufficient. Scott inhabits the role as completely as it is possible for an actor to do. Every biography of Patton, every personal remembrance from colleagues, even the general's own diary, further praises his effort. Start with the physical resemblance; Scott assumes Patton's round face, hard eyes, cropped white hair and bushy eyebrows, and the effect is amazing. The dichotomy in the general's personality is brilliantly explored--refined, well-versed in language, food, wine and classical poetry, but barbaric in a fight and intolerant of cowardice. Patton eschews individuality in the classic opening monologue, but strives for applause and adoration throughout his career. While the 3rd Army sweeps across Germany, Bradley quips "Give Patton a headline and he's good for another thirty miles."

His other faults are apparent as well: jealousy of Montgomery and other allied commanders, a dislike of Britain and a distrust of Arabs and Soviets. But Scott and writer Francis Ford Coppola compel us to admire the man, especially when framed by director Franklin Schaffner standing with stoic serenity in the midst of a raging battle.

Scott deserved his Oscar whether he wanted it or not, and Karl Malden as Bradley at least should have been nominated. Schaffner's straightforward direction befits his subject. The chaos of war is captured well in scenes depicting German infantrymen being run over by their own tanks. And Schaffner knows the value of silence, which is used to chilling effect in such unlikely situations as the battlefield.

Any subsequent film treatment of Patton runs the risk of being decimated by the fallout from this classic, but *Brass Target* (1978) would be a loser, had *Patton* never been made. It's pure fiction, one of those Len Deighton-type alternate-reality war stories, alleging that the auto accident that killed Patton in 1945 was not accidental. There were actually some allegations from some very unreliable sources at the time, and they were played to the hilt by MGM in its promotional campaign. But the supposed cover-up failed to capture the public's curiosity, and died away quietly along with the movie.

The story begins with Patton's 3rd Army discovering $250 million in gold, the entire German Reichsbank reserve, in an abandoned salt mine. Patton has the gold sent to Frankfurt by train, but it never reaches its destination. A cadre of corrupt U.S. officers led by Colonel Donald Rogers pulled the heist and, when they learn of Patton's plan to investigate the crime personally, they arrange to have the general assassinated. Their plan begins to unravel when Major Joe DeLuca takes over the case and uncovers most of their plan. Rogers and his men are killed by DeLuca in self-defense, but the hit man they hired remains at large and carries out his assignment. The gold is never found.

Brass Target has a provocative "what if?" premise, and it's fun to watch a cast of distinguished actors (John Cassavettes, Sophia Loren, Robert Vaughn, Max Von Sydow) try to elevate what is at heart a trashy adaptation of a dime-store novel, but the package is poorly presented by director John Hough. The crime itself is over in seconds, without *Rififi*-like intricacy in planning and execution. It's not a whodunit since we're told right away, and there are too many dead-end distractions, such as the romance between Cassavettes and Loren. Robert Vaughn emerges best as the ultimate cool criminal mastermind.

The role of Patton fell to George Kennedy, whose grouchy performance contained none of the warmth beneath the bluster conveyed by Scott. Kennedy's unsympathetic portrayal lacks any trace of humanity, and his death becomes a plot device that carries no meaning.

It seemed a cause for celebration when George C. Scott was convinced to reprise his greatest role in the made-for-TV movie, "The Last Days of Patton," but it turned out to be more of a mixed blessing. Although shorter than *Patton* by half an hour, the movie seems twice as long. The biggest problem is that Patton's "last days" weren't all that eventful, and were not deserving of such detailed scrutiny, even to get Scott back in uniform.

The story opens in 1945, with the war over and Patton serving as military governor in Bavaria. Still upset at not receiving a command in the Pacific, Patton refuses to obey Eisenhower's rule against hiring ex-Nazis to help rebuild their country. As a result, he is transferred to the 15th Army, the division responsible for writing the history of the war. He is appalled at being assigned to command a "paper army." Just before his retirement begins, Patton is killed in a car accident.

It's eerie to watch this back to back with *Patton*. "Last Days" picks up Patton's life immediately after the first film, but sixteen years have passed, and Scott looks it. He is still wonderful and has familiarity on his side, but there are moments, such as his roadside conversation with an overeager MP, in which he drifts dangerously close to caricature. There are good performances from Richard Dysart as Eisenhower, Eva-Marie Saint as Beatrice Patton and Kathryn Leigh-Scott (no relation to George) as Mrs. Patton's attractive niece and Mr. Patton's mistress, Jean Gordon. Karl Malden is missed as Omar Bradley.

Since almost all of *Patton* takes place on or near the battlefield, "Last Days" also makes an interesting companion piece, showing us Patton with his wife, Patton at parties, and Patton as diplomat and administrator, the type of work he despised. However, such scenes are not enough to sustain a 150-minute telefilm, which explains the inclusion of flashbacks to Patton's West Point days, which add nothing even though they should, and the addition of characters such as Jean that did not appear in the book on which the movie is based. There is irony, of course, in a veteran of two wars dying in a car accident, but the movie beats it to death.

Since "Last Days," no one has touched the role of Patton, and the fact that even George C. Scott couldn't match the standard he set the first time may discourage future attempts. His definitive performance in Oscar's Best Picture of 1970 probably won't be challenged for decades.

THE FILMS

Miracle of the White Stallions (Disney, 1963, 117 minutes)
Directed by Arthur Hiller; Written by A.J. Carothers, based on the book *The Dancing White Stallions of Vienna* by Col. Alois Podhajsky; Produced by Walt Disney and Peter V. Herald; Music by Paul Smith. Song "Just Say, Auf Wiedersehen" by Richard M. Sherman and Robert B. Sherman
Cast
Robert Taylor (Col. Podhajsky), Lilli Palmer (Verena Podhajsky), Curt Jergens (Gen. Tellheim), Eddie Albert (Rider Otto), James Franciscus (Maj. Hoffman), JOHN LARCH (GEN. PATTON)
Rating: **1/2
Available on Videocassette

Is Paris Burning? (Paramount, 1966, 173 minutes)
Directed by Rene Clement; Written by Gore Vidal, Francis Ford Coppola, Jean

Aurenche, Pierre Bost, Claude Brule, Marcel Moussy and Beate von Molo; Produced by Paul Graetz; Music by Maurice Jarre

Cast

Jean-Paul Belmondo (Morandat), Charles Boyer (Monod), Leslie Caron (Francoise Labe), Alain Delon (Jacques Chaban-Delmas), KIRK DOUGLAS (GEN. PATTON), Glenn Ford (Gen. Omar Bradley), Gert Frobe (Gen. Dietrich von Choltitz), Orson Welles (Raoul Nordling), George Chakiris, E.G. Marshall, Yves Montand, Anthony Perkins, Simone Signoret, Robert Stack, Jean-Louis Trintignant and Billy Frick (Cameos)

Rating: ***

Available on Videocassette

Awards: Oscar nominations for Best Cinematography, Art Direction-Set Direction

Patton (20th Century Fox, 1970, 170 minutes)

Directed by Franklin Schaffner; Written by Francis Ford Coppola and Edmund H. North, based on material in the books *Patton: Ordeal and Triumph* by Ladislas Farago and *A Soldier's Story* by Gen. Omar Bradley; Produced by Frank McCarthy; Music by Jerry Goldsmith

Cast

GEORGE C. SCOTT (GEN. PATTON), Karl Malden (Gen. Omar Bradley), Michael Bates (Field Marshal Montgomery)

Rating: *****

Available on Videocassette

Awards: Academy Awards for Best Picture, Best Actor (Scott), Best Director, Best Screenplay, Best Art Direction-Set Direction, Best Sound, Best Film Editing; nominations for Cinematography, Special Visual Effects, Original Score

Brass Target (United Artists, 1978, 111 minutes)

Directed by John Hough; Written by Alvin Boretz, based on the novel *The Algonquin Project* by Frederick Nolan; Produced by Arthur Lewis; Music by Laurence Rosenthal

Cast

Sophia Loren (Mara), John Cassavettes (Major DeLuca), GEORGE KENNEDY (GEN. PATTON), Robert Vaughn (Col. Rogers), Patrick McGoohan (Col. McCauley), Max Von Sydow (Shelley)

Rating: **

Available on Videocassette

TELEVISION

"The Last Days of Patton" (CBS movie, 1986, 150 minutes)

Directed by Delbert Mann; Written by William Luce, based on the book by Ladislas Farago; Produced by William F. Storke; Music by Allyn Ferguson

Cast

GEORGE C. SCOTT (GEN. PATTON), Richard Dysart (Gen. Eisenhower), Murray Hamilton (Gen. Hobart Gay), Ed Lauter (Lt. Col. Paul Hill), Kathryn Leigh-Scott (Jean Gordon), Eva-Marie Saint (Beatrice Patton)

Rating: **1/2

Available on Videocassette

ROBIN HOOD

The brave researcher who attempts to delve into the truth behind the legend of Robin Hood faces a dozen questions for every one answer. And even that one answer won't be that enlightening. Since 1977, when Oxford historian Maurice Keen's landmark study in his book *The Outlaws of Medieval Legend* was published, there has not been another comprehensive investigation into the facts. A second look seems overdue, but there may not be enough material to justify any expectations of surprising new results.

THE LEGEND

About all the researchers can agree on is that somebody lived at some point in the early history of England who stood up to some unscrupulous authority figures and inspired some stories and poems. But who he was, when he lived (and where--even Sherwood Forest is not universally accepted), and what he actually did seem lost to the ages. Tales place his exploits anywhere from the reign of William the Conqueror (1066–1087) to that of Edward II (1307–1327), a span of more than 250 years. Even more discouraging is that fact that most of the tales weren't written for yet another 400 years.

According to Maurice Keen, the earliest surviving versions of the Robin Hood legend date from the fifteenth century, the end of the English Middle Ages. Their authors were minstrels whose names are not recorded, which indicates that they were not employed by the royal court. The very first reference to Robin Hood occurs in the poem *Piers Plowman*, written around the year 1377, which alludes to "rymes of Robin Hood and Randolf Erle of Chester." Beyond that the poem says nothing, but it does seem to prove that Robin was already a legend in the fourteenth century.

The most popular legend, which some scholars have claimed to be at least partly factual, is set during the period when King Richard I left England to fight in the Crusades. Richard's no-account brother John is left in charge and steps up his enforcement of the onerous Forest Laws, which promised the death penalty to anyone caught killing the king's game. Robert Fitzooth, the Earl of Huntingdon (born 1160) objected to these laws and the exorbitant taxes levied on the poor serfs of England. Together with other like-minded men (including all the familiar names--Little John, Friar Tuck, Will Scarlett, Allan-a-Dale) he challenged the king's forces, which were led by the Sheriff of Nottingham, until Richard returned to reclaim his kingdom.

Several problems with this story exist, not the least of which is a complete lack of reliable documentation. Robin Hood's unwavering loyalty to Richard is also suspect, considering that the king known as "the Lion-Heart" was an apathetic ruler who was far more concerned with fighting the Crusades than governing England. Though he reigned for ten years, he actually spent only a total of five months in England. One of the most poignant moments in many Robin Hood movies is when the outlaw bows to Richard upon his return, now convinced that the country is once again in good hands and that the scourge of Prince John will soon be purged. The fact is that John, who succeeded his brother in 1199, was a far more capable king, who was left to clean up Richard's mess and did so admirably. History has judged him a failure primarily as a result of several military defeats which led to the loss of Normandy, and, just maybe, five hundred years of bad press in the Robin Hood legends.

Another theory has been advanced, in which Robin Hood is a follower of Simon de Montfort, the brother-in-law of King Henry III. Henry succeeded King John and levied a plethora of exorbitant taxes, which resulted in Simon's declaring war. His forces actually captured the king at one point, but the victory was only temporary--Henry regained the throne and executed Simon. Simon's followers, who became known as the "Disinherited" after their lands were seized by the court, took to the forests and continued the fight for another decade.

Still another theory attaches Robin Hood to the 1322 uprising against Edward II engineered by Thomas, Earl of Leicester. Here, Robin Hood was later pardoned by the king and even joined the royal court with his wife Matilda (Maid Marian was a post-medieval addition to the story).

The earliest tales locate Robin's heroics in Barnesdale Forest in Yorkshi e, not Sherwood Forest in Nottinghamshire. There is a grave in Yorkshire where Robin is supposedly buried (according to legend, on the spot where his last arrow landed), but the stone was carved in an age when he was already famous. Questions and more questions.

THE FILMS

There is no doubt, however, that Robin Hood has inspired more independent quality films (as opposed to a film series such as those devoted to Tarzan and James Bond) than any other hero in this book. A few losers were made as well, but the wealth of first-rate adaptations make them all the easier to ignore.

The first Robin Hood film was a 1912 silent short starring Robert Frazer. The following year, a film adaptation of *Ivanhoe* premiered, in which W. Thomas played Robin in a supporting role. A film entitled *Robin Hood* opened in 1914, but the character (played by W. Russell) was again only seen in support, with the main story devoted to one of the most popular medieval tales, the romance between Will Scarlett and Lady Christabel.

After his triumph in 1920's *The Mark of Zorro*, Douglas Fairbanks tried to top himself in swashbuckling elan' with an epic version of *Robin Hood*. The story wasn't as tight as *The Mark of Zorro*, but on sheer scale the film has few equals in silent cinema. Calling itself a "compound of legend and chronicle," *Robin Hood* (1922) quickly introduces us to brave King Richard, slimy Prince John, beautiful Maid Marian Fitzwalter and despicable Guy of Gisbourne, on the occasion of a royal tournament that precedes the Crusades. Gisbourne, the odds-on favorite, is upset by the Earl of Huntingdon, who finds himself tangling with Guy again for Marian's affections. Marian learns of John's plan to raise taxes, and tells Huntingdon. The Earl is tempted to go to Richard, but realizes that the king will turn back and cancel his trip to the Holy Land. So instead he takes up the people's cause himself. As Robin Hood, he is reunited a year later with Marian at the Priory of St. Catherine's, where she's been hiding since John's rule began. When she is later discovered and abducted by the prince, Robin storms the castle.

The use of automatic weapons by the action heroes of today seems such a shame after watching a movie like this. The sight of Fairbanks grinning from ear to ear as he runs and jumps and climbs through a huge castle is thrilling, with the actor's graceful acrobatics achieving an almost balletic beauty. Fairbanks doesn't appear in the familiar Robin Hood regalia until the halfway point, but once the Merry Men are assembled the film rarely slows down. His box-office power opened the studio coffers, giving the movies' first action hero plenty of soldiers, attendants and equipment to play with, plus a full-size castle complete with massive drawbridge that inspires the film's most memorable scene. Fairbanks put $1 million of his own money into the production, believing that the film should be done right or not at all.

Robin Hood set the standard for all subsequent films on the subject, and presented for the first time all the scenes that would become mandatory for future treatments--the tournament, the quarterstaff duel with Little John (or in this case Friar Tuck) over a raging river, the assault on Prince John's castle and, of course, the reunion with good King Richard (played here by Wallace Beery).

The 1922 version would seem difficult to surpass, but *The Adventures of Robin Hood* (1938) was as close to perfection as an imperfect world can achieve, and reveals the need in our language for a word that means more than "classic." It's that good.

Errol Flynn, the only actor who could equal Fairbanks in swashbuckling, is joined by Olivia de Havilland as Maid Marian, Claude Rains as Prince John, Alan Hale as Little John, Basil Rathbone as Sir Guy of Gisbourne, Eugene Pallette as Friar Tuck and Ian Hunter as King Richard. Everyone is just right, and from the first notes of Erich Wolfgang Korngold's dynamic score to Flynn's final tip of his green woodsman's cap as he dashes off with Marian, not a single element in its 102 minute running time is open to criticism. Certainly the film is highly stylized, presenting a premedieval age as only Hollywood could envision it, but with so few facts on which to base a historical treatment, there's no sense in complaining about the film's flawless fairy-tale appearance. Any more elaboration would be needless preaching to the converted; if you haven't seen *The Adventures of Robin Hood* yet, you're probably the only one.

No one in Hollywood went near the story after this definitive treatment for a decade, except 1946's *Bandit of Sherwood Forest.* But *Bandit* wimped out of comparisons by doing away with Robin Hood (Russell Hicks) early on and concentrating on Robin's son Robert of Nottingham, who returns to Sherwood Forest to save the king from a scheming Regent. Cornel Wilde plays Robert, not very memorably.

Prince of Thieves (1948) took its story from the Alexander Dumas novel in which Robin helps unite Lady Christabel with Sir Allan Claire and steer her away from the lascivious Gavin Muir. Alan Mowbray's cut-up performance as Friar Tuck tags the film as a kiddie matinee special, as does Jon Hall's half-comic, half-serious performance as Robin (or maybe he just appears comic when he's trying to be serious). Sam Katzman, whose name turns up in several chapters of this book alongside the cheapest versions of each story, delivers a respectable-looking production.

Rogues of Sherwood Forest (1950) is another son-of-Robin story, starring a before-Bo-was-even-born John Derek. Alan Hale again plays Little John with panache, but this time its in a lost cause. *Tales of Robin Hood* (1951) is a one-hour filmette that started life as an unsold TV series. The usual forest fights and familiar characters help the sixty minutes pass quickly, but that's not really the point, is it? Robert Clarke plays Robin, and Broadway veteran Mary Hatcher plays Marian. As in *Prince of Thieves* the Friar Tuck role (played by Ben Welden) is broadly written and is the principal source of comic relief.

Leave it to Disney to launch the first respectable challenge to the landmark 1938 model. *The Story of Robin Hood* (1952) hits all the right targets, telling a story that follows the Flynn version with only minor variations. Prince John starts acting up as soon as King Richard is gone, and Robin's father is killed for speaking out against John's harsh taxes. Robin and his men rob from the rich and give to the poor, of course, and then learn that King Richard in being held for ransom in Europe. Robin shames and then tricks John's court into raising money for his release and makes certain that the money is delivered. When the rightful king returns, he knights Robin Hood as the Earl of Locksley.

The Story of Robin Hood was Disney's second live-action feature and, like its predecessor *Treasure Island* (1950) and many others that followed, it was unfairly overshadowed by the studio's animated classics. Richard Todd, Disney's resident dashing hero in the 1950s, acquits himself well as the famous archer, and his scenes with Joan Rice as Marian merit comparison with those of Flynn and de Havilland. Peter Finch plays the Sheriff of Nottingham.

Also from 1952, MGM's lavish production of Sir Walter Scott's *Ivanhoe* starred Robert Taylor in the title role, Elizabeth Taylor as Rebecca, and Joan Fontaine as Rowena. The familiar story of the knight Sir Wilfred of Ivanhoe's attempt to raise the sum needed to free King Richard from an Austrian prison was transformed into one of the most beautiful films of the fifties. Harold Warrender makes a brief, incidental appearance as Robin Hood, referred to here as Locksley.

Robin Hood came to television in 1955 in "The Adventures of Robin Hood." Filmed in Britain, the pilot takes quite a few liberties with established traditions. Little John, for example, is introduced here as a serf who is promised freedom in exchange for Robin Hood's capture. He only changes sides after the Normans renege on the deal. The sets aren't very elaborate, and the swordplay not as deft as it might be. Slow motion is used at pivotal points in the action, an awkward effect considering that the rest of the story doesn't move much quicker. Richard Greene, though somewhat dashing as Robin Hood, is dressed like a cross between a court jester and a pimp. He would repeat the role, to only slightly better advantage, in the 1961 film *Sword of Sherwood Forest*. Bernadette O'Farrell is a most unappealing Maid Marian.

From 1959, *Son of Robin Hood* is the most interesting of the offspring films, primarily because the "son" in this case is actually a daughter named Deering Hood, played by June Laverick. The film has her exposing a pretender son of Robin Hood and leading her father's followers to another victory. Another film worth seeing that doesn't exactly fit the mold here is *Robin and the Seven Hoods* (1964), a parody of the old stories set in Prohibition-era Chicago. Frank Sinatra plays "Robbo," Dean Martin is Little John, Sammy Davis, Jr., is Will Scarlett, Bing Crosby plays Allan-a-Dale and Peter Falk plays Guy of Gisbourne. *Robin* is the best of the Rat Pack movies, with the cast's off-screen friendships clearly in evidence and a score that includes "My Kind of Town," performed by Sinatra.

The most forgettable and unnecessary film based on Robin Hood is 1967's *A Challenge for Robin Hood*, starring Barrie Ingham. We are introduced to Robin's evil cousin Roger de Courtenay in this Hammer production, which illustrates why the studio's nonhorror films were not as well received. Eliminating such can't-miss scenes as Robin's quarterstaff duel with Little John didn't help.

Robin Hood is played for laughs in *Up the Chastity Belt* (1971), which was later retitled *The Ribald Tales of Robin Hood*, even though Robin is just a supporting character. This very British comedy recalls a lesser entry in the famed "Carry On" series, but there's nothing here that Monty Python (or Daffy Duck, for that matter) didn't do better. Frankie Howerd and Graham Crowden star along with Hugh Paddick as Robin Hood. Eartha Kitt, inexplicably, also appears.

Disney returned to Sherwood in 1973, this time with an animated musical described as "the animal kingdom version" by its rooster narrator Allan-a-Dale. The film was made during the slump at Disney's animation department, which includes everything made after *The Aristocats* and before The *Little Mermaid*. That doesn't mean that *Robin Hood* is a bomb, but it cannot compare to the string of classics produced by the studio for more than four decades. Roger Miller contributes some catchy, lazy Sunday melodies, performed in his trademark easygoing style. Other standout voices include Brian Bedford as Robin Hood (drawn as a fox) and Phil Harris as Little John, a large gregarious bear that cannot help but recall Baloo in *The Jungle Book*. The biggest disappointment is the flat, motionless backgrounds; the characters seem to walk in front of, instead of through, these not-very-detailed drawings.

"Maid Marian and her Merry Men" (1974) is quite possibly the worst television comedy the BBC ever broadcast. This painfully unfunny spoof tells us that Marian was the real hero, while Robin's only contribution was designing the group's uniforms. A Rastafarian rapper introduces us to the cast, which includes a dwarf named "Little Ron." Wayne Morris plays the effeminate yuppie Robin of Kensington. A much, much, much better TV spoof premiered the following year in the United States, though it didn't last very long on the air. "When Things Were Rotten," created by Mel Brooks during his amazing 1970s streak of successes, fondly recalled the vintage silly slapstick comedy and wordplay of "Your Show of Shows" (also cowritten by Brooks), while predating stylistically similar movies such as *Airplane!* (1980) and *The Naked Gun* (1988).

One of the show's strengths was its guest stars, including Sid Caesar as a French ambassador and Dudley Moore as an Arabian sheik. The jokes are sophomoric, anachronistic (a character named the Duke of Earl, a magician whose magic words are Enos Slaughter), but undeniably funny. My favorite moment was in the second episode, in which Robin Hood disguised himself as Zorro to save the day. The cast was led by Dick Gautier as Robin Hood, Dick Van Patten as Friar Tuck and Misty Rowe as Maid Marian. Now that it's on videocassette, "When Things Were Rotten" deserves to be rediscovered.

In 1976 there were three Robin Hood projects, but I bet only one of them sounds familiar. A Russian film entitled *Robin Hood* was released that year starring Boris Khmielnitski in the title role, but I could find no other information about it.

From somewhere in Europe, a low-budget movie with the awful title *The Scalawag Bunch* alleges to tell a Robin Hood story, but its possible that the names of Tuck and Scarlett et.al. were only dropped in for the English version. The lead character, called Richard at one point and Henry later on, returns to England after fifteen years of Holy Crusading with the news that King Richard, long believed dead, is actually alive. Prince John, however, refuses to listen, and orders what's-his-name killed so the news will not reach the people. He flees and joins up with a group of Saxon revolutionaries led by Allan-a-Dale. He takes the name of Robin Hood only because he borrows a hooded jacked that used to be worn by someone named Robin. The dubbing is sloppy, the production is cheap, but the movie comes alive in its action scenes, which have the frantic high energy of a martial-arts movie. Performances are credible, and Mark Damon as Robin is infectiously enthusiastic.

The big 1976 Robin Hood release was *Robin and Marian*, which brought the exquisite Audrey Hepburn out of a decade-long retirement to play Maid Marian, and featured Sean Connery as a middle-aged bowman in the middle ages. It has been twenty years since Robin Hood and Little John left England to join King Richard at the Crusades. After the king loses his sanity and his life in short order, the legendary heroes head home to Sherwood Forest, where they are greeted by Will Scarlett and Friar Tuck. Robin is eager to be reunited with Maid Marian, but is surprised to learn that she is now running a nunnery! She is thrilled to see him again, but refuses to leave the other nuns. King John and the Sheriff of Nottingham are still in charge, and have ordered all those still loyal to Rome to be executed. Though she claims neither to want nor need his help, Robin releases the nuns already captured by the Court, and takes Marian back to Sherwood Forest.

It isn't long before Robin and the Sheriff are at odds again and, during the war between Merry Men and John's army that ensues, the Sheriff is killed and Robin is critically wounded. Marian helps him back to the nunnery and realizes that he is near death. She pours them both a glass of poisoned wine, knowing that she couldn't bear to lose him again.

Writer James Goldman used the same "history with a twist" approach he brought to *The Lion in Winter* (1968), maintaining the dignity of the characters but deflating their larger-then-life image. The scene in which Robin and Little John rescue the nuns, for instance, shows them both to be true heroes, but as they struggle to hurl their old bones over a castle wall, they are revealed as all too human as well. I'm still not sure I agree with the ending, but *Robin and Marian* certainly offers a departure from other treatments of the Robin Hood legend, and Connery and Hepburn are magic together.

Time Bandits (1981) is a movie that doesn't sink in until the second or third viewing--there's just too much to absorb the first time. Terry Gilliam's first triumph in fantasy filmmaking (in set design if not always in storyline) follows a young boy named Kevin on his travels through different historical periods, accompanied by six muddled dwarfs. It's basically Peabody and Sherman with a budget, but there are enough big-name guest stars, stunning visuals and jokes that work to make it worth seeing--twice. John Cleese appears in a brief but memorable curio as the tallest Robin Hood in the canon--and the dimmest.

The Zany Adventures of Robin Hood (1984) is the basic King Richard-held-for-ransom story played for laughs. The movie opens promisingly with an amusing scene in which Prince John (Roddy McDowall) is in psychoanalysis, but then settles down into the tame irreverence of a "Carol Burnett Show" sketch. George Segal plays Robin Hood, dropping modern references left and right and winking at the viewer all the way. If you think it's funny that Robin recalls meeting the king at summer camp, you'll like the movie.

After the pathetic "Maid Marian and her Merry Men," the BBC got its act together in 1984 and tried again. The dramatic series "Robin of Sherwood" has a mystical, ethereal quality that no other version shares; sophisticated and strange, its stories often pitted Robin and his men against the forces of the occult. Robin Hood himself is not the carefree forest sprite of other films, but a grim avenger who is anything but merry. Some action is sacrificed for atmosphere, but from the first strains of the new-age theme music the series has a way of drawing the viewer into its dreamlike world. Expertly done, but probably not for all tastes. The episodes with Michael Praed as Robin are better than those starring Jason Connery.

Two high-profile Robin Hood movies were scheduled for 1991, and approached their subject from entirely different angles. The first, starring Patrick Bergin and directed by John Irvin, was a historical action film in the classic tradition; the second, starring Kevin Costner and directed by Kevin Reynolds, may likewise be set in the twelfth century, but the characters have a definite 1990s sensibility. Bereft of stars on the level of Costner, Morgan Freeman and Christian Slater, the Bergin effort became the also-ran in the 1991 shootout. It started life as *Robin Hood*, but by summer audiences had retitled it "the other one." As a result, the film was only released theatrically overseas, and debuted in the United States on television.

As the movie opens, Robert Hode, the Saxon Earl of Huntington (Bergin) is arrested for aiding a poacher by the Norman Baron Daguerre. After mouthing off Hode and his friend Will Scarlett are stripped of title and lands and left to the mercy of the forest. They are taken in by Little John and his settlement of Saxons who were left destitute by Norman taxes. The usual skirmishes follow, along with a battle between Robin and Miles Falconer, the Baron's right-hand man, over the hand of Maid Marian.

Both this film and the Costner version offer something of an origin story for Robin Hood, though it is not the same one. This movie acknowledges history, setting the story partially in Barnesdale Forest, but Prince John and the Sheriff are replaced as the villains by Baron Daguere and Miles Falconer, the most German-sounding Englishmen you'll ever hear. Not surprising, then, that they are played by Jeroen Krabbe and Jurgen Prochnow, respectively. Bergin is a roguish adventurer in the Errol Flynn mode, but Uma Thurman is a vacuous Maid Marian. Although its runner-up status was appropriate, *Robin Hood* still deserved more attention than it received.

Robin Hood: Prince of Thieves became the blockbuster, despite concerns over the tone of the performances of the leads, which reflect its year of release as much as the year in which the story is set. Robin Hood and his men speak in a modern, slang-laden cadence, and Kevin Costner doesn't even attempt an English accent (good thing, too). Marian, marvelously played by Mary Elizabeth Mastrantonio, is an assertive, liberated maid who handles a sword as well as any man. They are opposed by the Sheriff of Nottingham (Alan Rickman), whose threats and epithets are delivered with the snap of a stand-up comic. The back-to-back action scenes that conclude the movie are edited MTV-style, complete with an amazing arrow-cam shot.

The film opens, like *Robin and Marian,* in the Holy Land, with Robin stuck in a Jerusalem jail. He escapes with a Moor named Azeem and arrives in England four months later, only to find his father murdered and his country being run into the ground in King Richard's absence. You know the rest. The main departure is Azeem, who is not just another Merry Man. Having an equal and a confidante among the band adds another dimension to the Robin Hood character.

It's a long movie--144 minutes--but all the requisite scenes are played well enough to seem new again, and the action sequences are as deftly executed as any in recent memory. The cast is superb; you can criticize Costner's flat American delivery all you want, but no other actor can convey inherent integrity without trying quite as easily. Bonus treats are Michael Kamen's haunting score and the unannounced cameo by Sean Connery as Richard. It's too soon to anoint it as a classic, but don't be surprised if *Robin Hood: Prince of Thieves* is one day remembered as the equal of the 1922 and 1938 models.

THE FILMS

Robin Hood (1912)
Cast
ROBERT FRAZER (ROBIN HOOD)

Ivanhoe (IMP, 1913, 45 minutes)
Directed and written by Herbert Brenon
Cast
King Baggot (Ivanhoe), W. THOMAS (ROBIN HOOD)

Robin Hood (1914)
Directed by Theodore Marston
Cast
WILLIAM RUSSELL (ROBIN HOOD), Gerda Holmes (Maid Marian), James Cruze, William Greenwood

Robin Hood (United Artists, 1922, 120 minutes)
Directed by Allan Dwan; Written by Lotta Woods, based on a story by Douglas Fairbanks; Produced by Douglas Fairbanks
Cast
DOUGLAS FAIRBANKS (ROBIN HOOD), Wallace Beery (Richard the Lion-Hearted), Sam De Grasse (Prince John), Enid Bennett (Lady Marian Fitzwalter), Paul Dickey (Sir Guy of Gisbourne), William Lowery (Sheriff of Nottingham)
Rating: ****1/2
Available on Videocassette

The Adventures of Robin Hood (Warner Bros., 1938, 102 minutes)
Directed by Michael Curtiz, William Keighley; Written by Norman Reilly Raine and Seton I. Miller; Produced by Hal B. Wallis and Henry Blanke; Music by Erich Wolfgang Korngold
Cast
ERROL FLYNN (ROBIN HOOD), Olivia de Haviland (Maid Marian), Basil Rathbone (Sir Guy of Gisbourne), Claude Rains (Prince John), Patric Knowles (Will Scarlet), Eugene Pallette (Friar Tuck), Alan Hale (Little John), Melville Cooper (Sheriff of Nottingham)
Rating: *****
Available on Videocassette
Awards: Academy Awards for Best Score, Best Art Direction and Best Film Editing; nomination for Best Picture.

Prince of Thieves (Columbia, 1942, 72 minutes)
Directed by Howard Bretherton; Written by Maurice Tombragel and Charles H.

Schneer, based on the novel by Alexander Dumas; Produced by Sam Katzman; Music by Mischa Bakaleinikoff
Cast
JON HALL (ROBIN HOOD), Patricia Morison (Lady Marian), Adele Jurgens (Lady Christabel), Alan Mowbray (The Friar), Michael Duane (Sir Allan Claire)
Rating: **

Tales of Robin Hood (Lippert, 1951, 61 minutes)
Directed by James Tinling; Written by Leroy H. Zehren; Produced by Hal Roach, Jr.; Music by Leon Klatzkin
Cast
ROBERT CLARKE (ROBIN HOOD), Mary Hatcher (Maid Marian), Paul Cavanagh (Sir Guy), Wade Crosby (Little John), Ben Welden (Friar Tuck), Robert Bice (Will Scarlett), Tiny Stowe (Sheriff of Nottingham)
Rating: **

Story of Robin Hood (Disney, 1952, 84 minutes)
Directed by Ken Annakin; Written by Lawrence E. Watkin; Produced by Perce Pearce; Music by Clifton Parker
Cast
RICHARD TODD (ROBIN HOOD), Joan Rice (Maid Marian), Peter Finch (Sheriff of Nottingham), James Hayter (Friar Tuck), James Robertson Justice (Little John), Hubert Gregg (Prince John)
Rating: ***1/2
Available on Videocassette

Ivanhoe (MGM, 1952, 106 minutes)
Directed by Richard Thorpe; Written by Noel Langley; Produced by Pandro S. Berman; Music by Miklos Rosza
Cast
Robert Taylor (Ivanhoe), Elizabeth Taylor (Rebecca), Joan Fontaine (Rowena), HAROLD WARRENDER (LOCKSLEY [ROBIN HOOD])
Rating: ****
Available on Videocassette
Awards: Academy Award nominations for Best Picture, Cinematography, Score

Men of Sherwood Forest (Hammer, 1957, 77 minutes)
Directed by Val Guest; Written by Allan MacKinnon; Produced by Michael Carreras
Cast
DON TAYLOR (ROBIN HOOD), Reginald Beckwith (Friar Tuck), Leslie Linder (Little John)
Rating: **

Sword of Sherwood Forest (Hammer, 1961, 80 minutes)
Directed by Terence Fisher; Written by Alan Hackney; Produced by Sidney Cole and Richard Greene; Music by Alun Hoddinott
Cast
RICHARD GREENE (ROBIN HOOD), Peter Cushing (Sheriff of Nottingham), Niall MacGinnis (Friar Tuck), Sarah Branch (Maid Marian), Nigel Green (Little John)

Rating: **

A Challenge for Robin Hood (20th Century Fox, 1967, 85 minutes)
Directed by C.M. Pennington-Richards; Written by Peter Bryan; Produced by Clifford Parkes; Music by Gary Hughes
Cast
BARRIE INGHAM (ROBIN HOOD), James Hayter (Friar Tuck), Leon Greene (Little John), Peter Blythe (Roger de Courtenay), Gay Hamilton (Maid Marian), John Arnatt (Sheriff of Nottingham)
Rating: *1/2

Up the Chastity Belt (EMI, 1971, 94 minutes)
Directed by Bob Kellett; Written by Sid Colin, Ray Galton and Alan Simpson; Produced by Ned Sherrin; Music by Carl Davis
Cast
HUGH PADDICK (ROBIN HOOD), Frankie Howerd, Graham Crowden, Bill Fraser
Rating: **

Robin Hood (Disney, 1973, 83 minutes)
Directed and produced by Wolfgang Reitherman; Written by Larry Clemons, based on a story by Ken Anderson); Music by George Bruns and Roger Miller
Cast (voices of)
BRIAN BEDFORD (ROBIN HOOD), Roger Miller (Allan-A-Dale), Monica Evans (Maid Marian), Phil Harris (Little John), Andy Devine (Friar Tuck), Peter Ustinov (Prince John)
Rating: ***
Available on Videocassette

Robin Hood (USSR, 1976)
Cast
BORIS KHMIELNITSKI (ROBIN HOOD)
No other information available

Robin and Marian (Columbia, 1976, 106 minutes)
Directed by Richard Lester; Written by James Goldman; Produced by Denis O'Dell; Music by John Barry
Cast
SEAN CONNERY (ROBIN HOOD), Audrey Hepburn (Maid Marian), Robert Shaw (Sheriff of Nottingham), Richard Harris (King Richard), Nicol Williamson (Little John), Denholm Elliot (Will Scarlett), Ronnie Barker (Friar Tuck), Ian Holm (King John)
Rating: ****
Available on Videocassette

The Scalawag Bunch (Universal Cinema Corporation, 1976, 103 minutes)
Directed by George Ferron; Produced by Ernest Boeton; Music by John Metal
Cast
MARK DAMON (ROBIN HOOD), Silvia Dionsio (Marian)
Rating: **1/2

Available on Videocassette

Time Bandits (Handmade Films, 1981, 110 minutes)
Directed and produced by Terry Gilliam; Written by Michael Palin and Terry Gilliam; Music by Mike Moran
Cast
JOHN CLEESE (ROBIN HOOD), Sean Connery (King Agamemnon), Shelley Duvall (Pansy), Katherine Helmond (Mrs. Ogre), Ian Holm (Napoleon), Michael Palin (Vincent), Ralph Richardson (Supreme Being), Craig Warnock (Kevin)
Rating: ***1/2
Available on Videocassette

The Zany Adventures of Robin Hood (1984, 97 minutes)
Directed by Ray Austin; Written by Robert Kaufman; Produced by Andrew Donally; Music by Stanley Myers
Cast
GEORGE SEGAL (ROBIN HOOD), Morgan Fairchild (Marian), Roddy McDowall (Prince John)
Rating: *
Available on Videocassette

Robin Hood (20th Century Fox, 1991, 104 minutes)
Directed by John Irvin; Written by Sam Resnick and John McGrath, from a story by Resnick; Produced by Sarah Radclyffe; Music by Geoffrey Burgon
Cast
PATRICK BERGIN (ROBIN HOOD), Uma Thurman (Maid Marian), Jurgen Prochnow (Miles Falconer), Jeroen Krabbe (Baron Daguerre)
Rating: ***1/2
Available on Videocassette

Robin Hood: Prince of Thieves (Warner Bros., 1991, 144 minutes)
Directed by Kevin Reynolds; Written by Pen Densham and John Watson, from a story by Densham; Produced by John Watson, Pen Densham and Richard B. Lewis; Music by Michael Kamen
Cast
KEVIN COSTNER (ROBIN HOOD), Morgan Freeman (Azeem), Christian Slater (Will Scarlett), Alan Rickman (Sheriff of Nottingham), Mary Elizabeth Mastrantonio (Maid Marian), Nick Brimble (Little John), Sean Connery (King Richard)
Rating: ****1/2
Available on Videocassette
Awards: Academy Award nomination for Best Song

TELEVISION

"The Adventures of Robin Hood" (series, CBS, 1955-1958)
Cast
RICHARD GREENE (ROBIN HOOD), Bernadette O'Farrell (Maid Marian), Ian Hunter (Sir Richard), Alexander Gauge (Friar Tuck), Archie Duncan (Little John), Alan Weatley (Sheriff of Nottingham), Donald Pleasence (Prince John)
Rating: **

"Maid Marian and Her Merry Men" (series, BBC, 1974)
Cast
Kate Lonergan (Marian), WAYNE MORRIS (ROBIN)
Rating: Zero
When Things Were Rotten (series, ABC, 1975)
Cast
DICK GAUTIER (ROBIN HOOD), Dick Van Patten (Friar Tuck), Bernie Kopell (Alan-a-Dale), Misty Rowe (Maid Marian)
Rating: ****
Available on Videocassette

"Robin of Sherwood" (series, BBC, 1984--86)
Cast
MICHAEL PRAED (ROBIN HOOD, 1984-1985), JASON CONNERY (ROBIN HOOD, 1986)
Rating: ***1/2
Available on Videocassette

ROCKY

Does anyone need to be reminded of how terrific a movie *Rocky* was? Maybe not, but the reputation of its sequels is definitely due for a reformation. The five *Rocky* movies are taking a worse beating now than their protagonist did in their collective final scenes. The tributes to creator and star Sylvester Stallone that began as sincere almost two decades ago have become more backhanded every year, as witty scribes "congratulate" Stallone for successfully making the same movie five times. Sequels have tarnished the reputations of their predecessors before, but the four *Rocky* sequels have almost scraped the gloss clean off of a film that won the Academy Award for Best Picture in 1976.

The irony is that as sequels go *Rocky II, III* and *V* are outstanding entertainment, and even *Rocky IV* has its moments. There is substantial character development throughout the series and Stallone's performance never wavers from perfection. He's so good as this dumb but likable palooka that a lot of people think that Stallone really is a dumb but likable palooka. This despite the fact that he wrote all five movies and directed the middle three.

The ceaseless quips about Stallone alternating Rambo and Rocky sequels until both characters are in rest homes have only increased with Stallone's failure to make an impact in any other role. But if he never makes another good movie, which these days seems entirely possible, he has already created from scratch two of the most popular movie heroes in history. And unlike, say, Roger Moore's James Bond and Simon Templar, they are two very different characters.

John Rambo is a machine--Rocky Balboa runs entirely on heart. Rocky is a shy and simple man, not a Rhodes Scholar but aware enough to know that he will probably live and die in the same rundown South Philly neighborhood. His greatest dream is to marry the plain, introverted girl who works in the pet shop, until a bigger dream presents itself--a million to one chance for glory in a profession he was sure had passed him by. But it's a hollow fantasy--play the sacrificial lamb to make a rich man richer, and then fade back into obscurity. Rocky just isn't smart enough to know that he's supposed to lose.

ORIGINS

The triumph of the poor but honest over the rich and cynical is a perennial movie formula, perfected by Frank Capra in *Mr. Smith Goes to Washington* (1939) and *Meet John Doe* (1941). *Rocky* tells the same story, substituting the world of boxing for the equally corrupt world of politics. *Rocky* has his roots in the characters of these films and, like Capra, Sylvester Stallone doesn't try to mask the simplicity of his story. We like to see good things happen to good people. Rocky

Balboa's courage and determination appeal to us on a basic, human level. To accomplish this is no less difficult than finding characters who touch our intellectual and spiritual selves. Obviously the five Rocky films follow a similar course, and it works every time, but that does not mean the formula is foolproof. Movies such as *Youngblood* (1986) try for the same audience identification and fail miserably. The simplest stories can be the most difficult to tell, because the tired must be made fresh. Except for the *Indiana Jones* trilogy, no one has managed this better than Sylvester Stallone.

Everything *Rocky* needed to earn its Oscar was on the screen, but the film received an extra boost from its well-documented backstage history. At the time Stallone wrote the script, his career consisted of bit parts in great movies such as *The Prisoner of Second Avenue* (1975) and leading roles in lousy movies such as *The Lords of Flatbush* (1974). After watching a boxing match on TV in which Muhammad Ali had more trouble than expected with an unknown fighter named Chuck Wepner, legend has it that Stallone sat down and wrote *Rocky* in three days. I'd believe he finished a treatment in that time, but the full screenplay is a stretch.

Regardless, Stallone began presenting himself and the script to producers as a package deal. He was offered more than $200,000 for the script, on condition that the title role be given to an established star. At the time he could barely afford bus fare, but still he refused to let anyone else play the character. Finally United Artists and producers Irwin Winkler and Robert Chartoff took a chance, and the rest is history. The film grossed sixty times its production costs, brought Oscars to Winkler and Chartoff, and made Stallone the highest-paid actor in Hollywood.

THE FILMS

Rocky is already too old for boxing when we first meet him, a beaten down club fighter who supplements his income by collecting payments for a loan shark. He goes to the gym now more out of habit than any burning desire for success, and is reminded by his trainer, Mickey, that at one time he might actually have been a good boxer. But that day is long gone, and Rocky is content with sparring a few rounds and then trying to romance the geeky girl at the pet shop, Adrian. He does better here, but unfortunately with Adrian he also inherits her churlish brother Pauly.

Rocky's life takes a sudden, thrilling turn when Apollo Creed, the heavyweight champion, decides to give an unknown fighter a shot at the title on July 4, to prove that America is still the land of opportunity. Rocky, because of his catchy "Italian Stallion" nickname, is offered the shot. Mickey agrees to train him, and it's time to cue the thrilling Bill Conti theme music. To fully appreciate its importance, watch the film's most memorable scene, Rocky's run through the streets of Philadelphia and up the steps of the Museum of Art, with the sound off.

The night of the match. Rocky meanders in, surprised at the turnout, while Creed struts down the aisle, supremely confident. The fight quickly escalates into a war, with Creed winning a split decision. Rocky also raises his fist in triumph, as he embraces Adrian and hears the cheers of the crowd for what should be the first and last time.

The final, oft-parodied shot, of Rocky bellowing "A-dree-ennnnne!" is one of the great choke-up scenes in movies, set up beautifully by the rest of the film and striking just when the audience has already been emotionally drained by the fight. It was the last perfect moment in a film that never takes a wrong turn.

Rocky was a low-priority production for its studio, thus the cast was composed of unknown and "B" movie veterans, all of whom came through with career-best work. Oscar nominations went to Stallone, Talia Shire (Adrian), Burt Young (Pauly) and Burgess Meredith (Mickey), but it was an uncommonly rich year in the acting categories, and Rocky would take home gold only for its producers, director (John G. Avildsen) and its editors.

Rocky II (1979) opened as future sequels would with a reprise of its predecessor, putting everyone in the right mood before the credits even start. The story begins immediately after the last fight, with both combatants taken directly from the arena to the hospital. After his release, Rocky proposes to Adrian in one of the many lovely quieter moments in the series that aren't as frequently recalled as the knockouts. He spends money from his title shot on new clothes and a sports car, but his revitalized career is threatened when doctors discover an eye disorder that could render Rocky blind if he fights again.

The fortune quickly won is quickly lost, and Rocky resorts to TV commercials to support his family. Apollo Creed, meanwhile, is tired of hearing about the Italian Stallion and tries to arrange a rematch. Against Adrian's wishes Rocky signs the contract, but his heart's not in it. Adrian collapses at the pet store and lapses into a coma after giving birth to Rocky, Jr. When she awakens, Adrian tells Rocky to go out and win the title. Well, that does it. Cue music again, as Rocky and Mick go back to work. This time, Rocky wins the championship after another brutal bout.

Rocky begins his belated maturity here, taking on the responsibility of a wife and child, but judging from how he first spends his money he still has some adolescence left to burn. The parts we've seen before we don't mind seeing again, because Stallone continues to push all the right buttons. *Rocky II* belongs in the ranks of the great American crowd-pleasers. You feel yourself being led through the story like a mouse in a laboratory maze, but you enjoy every step of the well-trodden passage. Only one complaint--the intrusive use of slow-motion in the boxing match.

When *Rocky III* (1982) opens, the Stallion has been champ for three years, and his family enjoys the tremendous wealth that comes with the heavyweight title. Mickey the trainer has his boy take on all comers except one--a loudmouth bruiser named Clubber Lang. Instead, Rocky fills his off hours by battling wrestlers for charity and trying to appease his still-hostile brother-in-law. When the press won't allow Rocky to duck Clubber any longer, a match is scheduled. Rocky, distracted by the frail health of his trainer, loses the bout. Mickey dies soon after. The loss of his friend plunges Rocky further into depression. Apollo Creed offers to train him for a rematch. Creed takes the millionaire champion back to the slums, where he hopefully will regain the fire in his gut. Rocky learns to box under Creed's tutelage, but come the rematch the brawler within emerges and pounds Clubber into the canvas.

Rocky III has the best opening of any film in the series--rapid-fire clips of Rocky's first few title defenses in which the champ knocks opponents into mid-air. I half-expect to see one challenger fly straight up through the roof of the stadium like in a Popeye cartoon. The movie gets docked half a star for cramming Survivor's "Eye of the Tiger" down our throats, but otherwise it's another bang-up outing. Mr. T was a real find as Clubber Lang, and Stallone's script allows all the regulars to continue moving forward; Adrian has become more self-assured, Pauly's inveterate sullenness proves that money can't buy class, and Rocky learns the price a fighter pays for a comfortable life.

The only partial justification for lambasting Stallone's continuation of the series can be found in *Rocky IV*. It's the shortest and the slowest entry, and shows signs of being a half-hearted effort throughout. The climactic fight proves Stallone can direct action as well as anyone in Hollywood, but for the first time it's a chore to get there.

Drago, the boxing champion of the Soviet Union, starts talking trash through Ludmilla (yes, Ludmilla), his wife and manager. Rocky's enjoying the good life and puts Drago on hold, but Apollo Creed becomes fed up with the Soviet's diatribes against America. Creed schedules an exhibition bout in Las Vegas, where Drago kills Creed in the ring. Rocky is then forced to avenge his friend. In the wilds of Siberia, Rocky begins his rigorous training regimen, and then he decks Drago in front of the Politburo to the cheers of the all-Soviet crowd (right, just before their bus for the gulag leaves).

As Drago and Ludmilla, Dolph Lundgren and Brigitte Nielsen (Mrs. Stallone at the time) are Robo-fighter and his Robo-wife, stereotypes instead of human beings, and they would be as out of place in any earlier Rocky film as Boris and Natasha. Even worse, the wonderful character of Apollo Creed is thrown away just to set up a climax that was inevitable anyway. The entire Las Vegas sequence rings very artificial, though it did give James Brown his first hit record in decades ("Livin' in America"). Together, these scenes mark the first time that Stallone the screenwriter takes the easy way out.

The painting of a U.S.-Soviet boxing match as a global conflict metaphor has been done before (like in every Olympic games since 1952), but Stallone's version could not have been timed any worse. Commie-bashing had just started to go out of style in 1986, so *Rocky IV*'s explicit jingoism was outdated upon its arrival. Stallone had the same problem with *Rambo III* (1988). From now on he ought to keep his superheroes out of politics. He should also leave the music to Bill Conti. The MTV influence that crept into *Rocky III* has now erupted into a rock soundtrack of disposable songs, and that includes the James Brown hit.

With this mishap coming four films into the series, Stallone was left with a difficult choice--a fifth outing would either allow Rocky to go back out on top, or dig a deeper hole for his reputation. Stallone took the gamble and, for added insurance, he brought back John Avildsen to direct. The result is a generally entertaining film that doesn't fit the mold of previous entries, but still belongs in the win column.

As usual, the story picks up immediately after the last movie, with Rocky returning from Moscow and being hailed as a great American hero. His good mood is short-lived, however, after learning that his fortune, thanks to Pauly, has been squandered by incompetent financial advisers. Rocky's ready to fight again, but doctors warn him that he has already suffered brain damage, and one more bout could be fatal. After selling their house and possessions, Rocky, Adrian and Rocky Jr., head back to Philadelphia, where they settle in a modest house in their old neighborhood. The class drop is tough on Junior, who is forced to defend himself constantly in his new school, and ends up falling in with a bad crowd. Flashy promoter George Washington Duke offers Rocky huge money for a comeback fight, but Adrian will not allow it.

A young boxer named Tommy Gunn approaches Rocky and asks the champ to become his trainer. Rocky is hesitant at first but then becomes grateful for this re-entry into the fight game. His son, however, becomes jealous of his father's protege` and takes another step toward juvenile delinquency. Tommy becomes impatient with his mentor and joins the Duke camp, where he tries to taunt Rocky into fighting him. After repairing his relationship with Rocky, Jr., the Italian Stallion challenges Tommy to a streetfight, and teaches the kid a few more lessons.

The Balboa family's move back to poverty and Philadelphia was a splendid idea that made perfect sense. Rocky had been used and exploited since he was first offered the title shot. First it was Creed, then the advertisers and promoters in films *II* and *III*, then his casting as champion of liberty in *Rocky IV*. Now the accountants take their piece, and then Rocky is used and distracted yet again by the Don King-like George Washington Duke and by Tommy Gunn, the Eve Harrington of boxing.

After the overblown spectacle of the last film the focus returned to the characters. Stallone, Talia Shire and Burt Young have their roles down to a science by this time, and Tommy Morrison is a much more intriguing adversary than the monolithic Drago. Too bad Rocky, Jr., grew up to be such a brat, but he's well-played by Stallone's pouty son Sage.

The decision to keep Rocky out of the ring may have been logical, but the fifth go-round is no time to start worrying about realism. The boxing matches in films *I* through *IV* bore about as much resemblance to real bouts as the skirmishes between Tom and Jerry. But even in *Rocky IV*, after the worst table-setting yet, the fight still provided a satisfying conclusion. I don't care how old Stallone was or how old Rocky was supposed to be, *Rocky V* needed to strap on the gloves for its climax. But it's a tribute to the film that it succeeds without the traditional Rocky ending.

Rocky V came and went without the fanfare that surrounded its predecessors, and barely made the talk show monologues with jokes about Rocky fighting Buddy Ebsen. Since disinterest is almost worse than well-publicized failure in Hollywood, the chance of a *Rocky VI* is about equal to that of a *Cobra II.*

THE FILMS

Rocky (United Artists, 1976, 119 minutes)
Directed by John G. Avildsen; Written by Sylvester Stallone; Produced by Irwin Winkler and Robert Chartoff; Music by Bill Conti, Carol Connors, Ayn Robbins and Frank Stallone, Jr.
Cast
SYLVESTER STALLONE (ROCKY BALBOA), Talia Shire (Adrian), Burt Young (Pauly), Carl Weathers (Apollo Creed), Burgess Meredith (Mickey), Thayer David (Miles Jergens)
Rating: *****
Available on Videocassette
Awards: Academy Awards for Best Picture, Best Director and Best Editing; nominations for Best Actor (Stallone), Actress (Shire), Supporting Actor (Young and Meredith), Screenplay and Song ("Gonna Fly Now")

Rocky II (United Artists, 1979, 119 minutes)
Directed and written by Sylvester Stallone; Produced by Irwin Winkler and Robert Chartoff; Music by Bill Conti
Cast
SYLVESTER STALLONE (ROCKY BALBOA), Talia Shire (Adrian), Burt Young (Pauly), Carl Weathers (Apollo Creed), Burgess Meredith (Mickey)
Rating: *****

Available on Videocassette

Rocky III (MGM-United Artists, 1982, 99 minutes)
Directed and written by Sylvester Stallone; Produced by Irwin Winkler and Robert Chartoff; Music by Bill Conti, song "Eye of the Tiger" by Jim Peterik and Frankie Sullivan III
Cast
SYLVESTER STALLONE (ROCKY BALBOA), Talia Shire (Adrian), Burt Young (Pauly), Carl Weathers (Apollo Creed), Burgess Meredith (Mickey), Mr. T (Clubber Lang), Hulk Hogan (Thunderlips)
Rating: ****
Available on Videocassette
Awards: Academy Award nomination for Best Song

Rocky IV (MGM-United Artists, 1985, 91 minutes)
Directed and written by Sylvester Stallone; Produced by Irwin Winkler and Robert Chartoff; Music by Vince DiCola and Bill Conti
Cast
SYLVESTER STALLONE (ROCKY BALBOA), Talia Shire (Adrian), Burt Young (Pauly), Carl Weathers (Apollo Creed), Brigitte Nielsen (Ludmilla), Dolph Lundgren (Drago)
Rating: **1/2
Available on Videocassette

Rocky V (MGM-United Artists, 1990, 104 minutes)
Directed by John G. Avildsen; Written by Sylvester Stallone; Produced by Irwin Winkler and Robert Chartoff; Music by Bill Conti
Cast
SYLVESTER STALLONE (ROCKY BALBOA), Talia Shire (Adrian), Burt Young (Pauly), Sage Stallone (Rocky, Jr.), Burgess Meredith (Mickey), Tommy Morrison (Tommy Gunn), Richard Gant (George Washington Duke)
Rating: ***1/2
Available on Videocassette

SAMSON

The Bible's Book of Judges is a collection of stories from the period of Israel's history between the invasion of Canaan and the establishment of the monarchy, first under Saul and then King David. The "judges" described were leaders of Israeli tribes who earned their rank in battle, not in court. The most famous judge was Samson, whose history was told in chapters 13 through 16. The entire tale comprises only five or six pages in most translations, but the exploits described therein have made Samson one of the best-known Old Testament figures.

THE STORY

According to *The Bible*, God had sentenced Israel to forty years of Philistine rule for screwing up once again. As the sentence neared its end an angel appeared in the town of Zorah to visit the wife of a man named Manoah. Though unable to bear children, Manoah's wife is told that she will give birth to a son. The boy, Samson, will be the instrument chosen by God to overthrow the Philistines.

Samson falls in love with a Philistine girl and, despite his parents' objections, becomes engaged. One day as he walks to meet her, he is attacked by a lion and kills the beast with his bare hands. Passing the carcass later and finding it infested with bees, Samson composes a riddle, which he recites as a challenge to the Philistines at his wedding feast:

> "Out of the eater came something to eat;
> Out of the strong came something sweet;"

Samson wagers a new garment for 30 Philistine men if the riddle is solved. The guests are unable to do so, but they coerce Samson's new wife into revealing the answer. A week later, when they tell Samson the solution--"What could be sweeter than honey? What could be stronger than a lion?"--he knows his wife has betrayed him. Samson kills 30 men, and gives their garments to the guests. While he is out, his wife is betrothed to another. Samson, understandably piqued about losing a bet and his wife in the same week, ties torches to the tails of three hundred foxes and points them toward the Philistine wheat fields.

When the Philistines attack the town of Lehi, Samson pretends to surrender, and when they draw close he attacks and kills a thousand men with the jawbone of an ass. More battles follow, and then Samson meets Delilah, another alluring Philistine babe. Her ruler offers a fortune to learn the secret of Samson's amazing strength. After deceiving her three times, Samson finally reveals that his hair, which has never been cut, is the source of his power. While Samson sleeps Delilah breaks out the scissors, and the strongman is taken into Philistine custody.

His captors blind Samson and lead him into a temple as an object of public ridicule. He positions himself between two columns and prays for the restoration of his strength one last time. God answers his prayer, and Samson brings down the temple, killing all five Philistine kings, the three thousand in attendance, and himself.

The story of Samson is more a celebration of God's mercy than God's strength. Samson repeatedly betrays the Lord by breaking the covenants that gave him his power, but each time he realizes his error and sincerely begs forgiveness, he is taken back. However, it was the more spectacular aspects of the tale that attracted Hollywood, and if there was a good moral at the end, all the better.

THE FILMS

Even when told in the formal language of the *King James Bible*, there is a pulp-novel quality to the Samson saga that filmmakers have found irresistable. It is the original *Fatal Attraction*, chronicling the downfall of an indestructible and virtuous man who failed to resist the temptation of a beautiful woman. The same scenario has fueled such classics as *The Blue Angel* (1930) and *Double Indemnity* (1944). But Samson, like Adam, was a forerunner to all the males who dropped the ball for the love of a woman. However, unlike similar stories both ancient and modern, Samson is forgiven and restored to glory, a good sign for the rest of us who have come up short in the battle of the sexes.

The overwhelming majority of Bible movies treat their subject with a certain degree of reverence--even such nontraditional treatments as *Jesus Christ, Superstar* (1973) remain true to the spirit and teachings of the source. On the rare occasion that something different is tried, such as *The Last Temptation of Christ* (1988), all hell tends to break loose. Which makes Samson an interesting case. To date he is the only Biblical figure to be used in a series of totally fictional, secular adventures. Granted, many of them started out as films about a character named Maciste and only became Samson movies when dubbed into English. Innocuous as these films were, however, the sight of a Biblical persona praying to Zeus for strength should have raised a few eyebrows.

The first Samson film is also arguably the first Biblical film of any kind--a 1903 French production titled *Samson and Delilah*, directed by Ferdinand Zecca. Zecca then remade the story five years later, doubling the fifteen-minute running time of his first effort and fading out on Samson ascending into Heaven. Following the two French featurettes, the first full-length version of Samson was released in 1914, and starred J. Walter Kerrigan as Samson and his sister Kathleen Kerrigan as Delilah. It was trashed by critics of the day, but audiences loved it. It is notable today for its casting of a brother and sister as lovers, and for the appearances of Hal Roach and Harold Lloyd, two silent screen legends, as extras. Yet another version appeared the following year starring William Farnum.

From Great Britain, a silent film short based on Camille Saint-Saens's opera *Samson and Delilah* was released in 1922, with W. D. Waxman as Samson and the one-named "Valia" as Delilah. Though a silent film version of an opera seems pretty strange, the same material was covered a second time in 1927, with William Anderson as Samson. An Austrian *Samson and Delilah*, directed by the great Alexander Korda, premiered in 1922 with Franz Herterich and Maria Corda in the title roles.

Not surprisingly, Cecil B. DeMille made the first high-budget high-profile film adaptation. Having already brought *Ben Hur* (1926), *The Ten Commandments* (1923) and *King of Kings* to the silent screen, DeMille produced and directed *Samson and Delilah* in 1949--an epic, faithful retelling of the tale. It is not the classic that his second *Ten Commandments* (1956) would become, but it clearly emerged from the same source. DeMille once said "To transfer *The Bible* to the screen you cannot cheat. You have to believe." This too accounts for the film's ability to captivate an audience despite obvious shortcomings--DeMille knew how to tell a story, and he certainly believed.

The pertinent chapters in Judges are adhered to with a few departures; Delilah is introduced as the sister of Samson's Philistine wife and first meets Samson well before his marriage. A tryst between Samson and a prostitute is deleted, and the incident with the fire-toting foxes is mentioned but not played out (a shame--if anyone could do it DeMille could). Also, there is no mention of Delilah in *The Bible* after she learns Samson's secret, but it is assumed she died in the temple, as is the case here.

Since *The Bible* contains no physical descriptions, and paintings by Anthony Van Dyck, Rembrandt, Peter Paul Rubens and Eugene Delacroix show no clear consensus, Victor Mature and Hedy Lamarr are the mental pictures most of us conjure of the tragic lovers. At first they seemed unlikely choices for the title roles, but what seems like a classical piece on the surface is at heart a soap opera, and in that spirit the performances are perfect. Lamarr's first appearance is a Technicolor stunner--watch the movie on laserdisc and freeze-frame it for about a week. Her still-pronounced German accent actually works in her favor, by emphasizing a cultural difference between the Philistine ruling class and the plain-talking Dannites, personified by Samson. Victor Mature is just right as the long-haired strongman and, like Lamarr, he achieves a career peak here.

George Sanders, an expert at soft-spoken malevolence, plays the Philistine leader Saran. Though his army comes off as schoolyard bullies good only for Israeli lunch-money collection, Sanders brings class to his role. The climax is perfect--Samson destroys the Philistine temple, and Saran's only reaction before hitting the rubble is an urbane tip of the wine glass. It was also such lines as "Delilah, what a dimpled dragon you can be!" spoken by Sanders, that have made *Samson and Delilah* a perennial top-ten choice on any list of guilty pleasures.

There is no shortage of spectacle--Samson's battle with a lion, the kind of scene that almost always looks phony and unintentionally funny, comes pretty close to working here. The temple-crumbling finale is justifiably famous. When the crowd falls silent after the first creaks of the stone pillars, it's a moment to be savored. Gorgeous cinematography accentuates the costumes and art direction, both of which deservedly won Oscars.

Hold on to the safety bar now because it's a rollercoaster drop from here. *Samson* (1960) was the first sword-and-sandal treatment of the character and one of the few films in the genre that began as a Samson film. Most of the Italian Samsons started life under the name Maciste or Atlas. As explained in the Hercules chapter, rampant title-switching is a given in the genre, and the generic nature of the heroes makes such adjustments simple. As played here by Brad Harris, Samson frequently exclaims "By Zeus!" and "By the lame foot of Vulcan!"--grounds for holy retribution if this were the Biblical Samson.

The film is a thinly disguised revision of an equally undistinguished film, *The Fury of Hercules*. The same cast and crew play out a very similar story on the same sets. In the city of Sulim, Queen Romilda is manipulated by a corrupt adviser to persecute her people and keep her sister, the rightful queen, in prison. Samson joins forces with another strongman named Millstone to restore order. As in *Fury*, the only interesting element is the appearance of both Brad Harris and Alan Steel, who often played Hercules, as Millstone. They were foes in the last film, but this time they're allies. A long, drawn-out brawl between them offers more fisticuffs than in most films of this ilk, but the World Wrestling Federation has better choreography. Harris, as one of the least charismatic sword-and-sandal actors, is another drawback.

Samson and the Sheik, also from 1960, is even worse. Ed Fury, who starred in the Italian "Ursus" series and was immortalized in the unforgettable *Wild Women of Wongo* (1959), plays a character named Samson who lives in the Middle Ages. Although this was also a Samson film in its original incarnation, its tie to the character is tenuous, at best.

Two more pretenders followed--*Samson and the Seven Miracles of the World* and *Samson vs. the Giant King*, both originally Maciste films. The former, however, is notable as Gordon Scott's first sword-and-sandal film. Just off a stint as Tarzan, Scott kept the same loincloth for this role, as he saves a prince and princess from Tartars in thirteenth century China. He can make a film watchable if given half a chance, but it doesn't happen here.

Samson and the Sea Beasts (1963) is a film listed in some sourcebooks, but good luck tracking it down. Kirk Morris plays Samson and, judging by his work in several Hercules films, there is no reason to expect any exciting revelations here. Another Maciste film, which later became *Samson and the Slave Queen* (1963) must be discussed because of its bizarre superhero team-up. This time the setting is fifteenth century Spain, and Samson (Alan Steel) joins forces with the swashbuckling Zorro to help good sister Spina win the throne of Navarre over bad sister Orfei. The novel backdrop inspires Steel to another level, and Pierre Brice is quite impressive as Zorro.

Of all the Italian Samson films, the most watchable is *Samson and His Mighty Challenge* (1964). A spaghetti epic all-star team are united in this conscious parody of their previous efforts and, while the comedy doesn't always work, they do display a refreshing sense of humor. The story has Hercules (Alan Steel) falling in love with the Princess Omphale. She agrees to marry him if he can defeat the strongest man in the world, Samson (Nadir Baltimore).

The queen's guards track down Samson and he agrees to the grudge match. However, his wife Delilah is angered at the prospect of being left alone and cuts Samson's hair, sapping his strength. On the return trip they are joined by two more heroes, Maciste (Howard Ross) and Ursus (Yann Larvor). Omphale then tells Hercules that she had no intention of marrying him, and the four musclemen ride off into the sunset together. Fans of the genre will find the concept irresistable, so if the term "best" carries any weight in this context it applies here--though considering the competition it's rather like choosing a favorite member of the Bay City Rollers.

Samson in King Solomon's Mines, also from 1964, is another Maciste movie. The following year, *Hercules, Samson and Ulysses* attempted to recapture whatever crumbs of quality that were generated by *Samson and His Mighty Challenge*, without the satiric overtones. Richard Lloyd plays Samson to Kirk Morris's Hercules and Enzo Cerusico's Ulysses. Liana Orfei is a fetching Delilah, and there's even an appearance by the Philistines, led by Saran (Aldo Guiffre`). This one actually comes closest to connecting with the Biblical scenario, though with Hercules around it can hardly be taken devoutly. Production values are above average.

After the Italians had their way with the character, the Mexican film industry chimed in with *Samson Vs. the Vampire Women* (1961) and *Samson in the Wax Museum* (1963). Before the dubbing into English, both films were entries in the endless series of films featuring a wrestling superhero named Santo, who first appeared in 1952 and body-slammed across south-of-the-border screens for more than twenty years. Santo always wore a silver mask to hide his identity, which also made it easy for different actors to play the role with the public none the wiser.

Samson makes a very brief appearance as part of an Olympian rescue party in the absolutely awful *Hercules in New York* (1970--see Hercules chapter). Mark Tendler executes the walk-on, which lasts less than a minute.

The 1984 model of "Samson and Delilah" was a made-for-TV movie that cast newcomers Antony Hamilton and Belinda Bauer in the leads. Their continuing unknown status provides the first clue regarding the success of this capable but unnecessary remake. The storyline parallels DeMille's version, except that Delilah survives the destruction of the temple to realize the error of her ways. Some of the Hollywood gloss is removed, but nothing emerges to fill the void. If the film had better performances or better special effects or even a stronger sense of time and place, it could justify its existence, but the 1949 original still wins on all counts.

Antony Hamilton's overmannered performance and Crocodile Dundee accent are not conducive to the material and Belinda Bauer, supposedly playing one of the most alluring temptresses in recorded history, just isn't all that tempting. Max Von Sydow as Philistine captain Sidka is not as gleefully smarmy as George Sanders, and Daniel Stern seems completely out of place in period costume. The movie's big novelty was casting Victor Mature as Samson's father, but the role isn't that great and he's gone in ten minutes. There is, of course, the cheap thrill of watching a big building fall on people near the end, but even here DeMille did it better. His version remains definitive.

THE FILMS

Samson and Delilah (Pathe, 1903, 15 minutes)
Directed by Ferdinand Zecca

Samson and Delilah (Pathe, 1908, 40 minutes)
Directed by Ferdinand Zecca

Samson (Universal, 1914, 70 minutes)
Directed and written by Lorimer Johnston; Produced by J. Farrell MacDonald
Cast
J. WARREN KERRIGAN (SAMSON), Kathleen Kerrigan (Delilah)

Samson (Box Office Attractions, 1915, 60 minutes)
Directed by Ben Lewis; Written by Garfield Thompson, from the play by Henri Bernstein; Produced by William Fox
Cast
WILLIAM FARNUM (SAMSON), Maud Gilbert (Delilah)

Samson and Delilah (Master Films, 1922, 15 minutes)
Directed by Edwin J. Collins; Written by Frank Miller, based on the opera by

Camille Saint-Saens; Produced by H.B. Parkinson.
Cast
W.D. WAXMAN (SAMSON) Valia (Delilah)

Samson and Delilah (Corda-Film/Vita-Film, 1922, 60 minutes)
Directed by Alexander Korda; Written by Sidney Garrick, Alexander Korda and Ernest Vajda
Cast
FRANZ HERTERICH (SAMSON), Maria Korda (Delilah)

Samson and Delilah (Song Films, 1927, 20 minutes)
Directed by H.B. Parkinson; Produced by John F. Blakeley, based on the opera by Camille Saint-Saens
Cast
WILLIAM ANDERSON (SAMSON)

Samson and Delilah (Paramount, 1949, 127 minutes)
Directed and produced by Cecil B. DeMille; Written by Jesse Lasky, Frederick M. Frank, Harold Lamb and Vladimir Jabofinsky, based on *The Bible* and the novel *Judge and Fool* by Jabofinsky; Music by Victor Young
Cast
VICTOR MATURE (SAMSON), Hedy Lamarr (Delilah), George Sanders (Saran), Angela Lansbury (Semadar), Henry Wilcoxson (Ahtur), Olive Deering (Miriam), Russ Tamblyn (Saul), William Farnum (Tubal), George Reeves (Messenger)
Rating: ****
Available on Videocassette

Samson (Cineproduzione Associates, 1960, 95 minutes)
Directed by Gianfranco Parolini; Written by Giovanni Simonelli and Gianfranco Parolini; Produced by Mario Maggi; Music by Carlo Innocenzi
Cast
BRAD HARRIS (SAMSON), Brigitte Corey (Jasmine), Alan Steel (Millstone)
Rating: *

Samson and the Sheik (1960, 90 minutes)
Cast
SAMSON (ED FURY)
Other credits unavailable
Rating: 1/2 star

Samson and the Sea Beasts (1963)
SAMSON (KIRK MORRIS)
Other credits unavailable

Samson and His Mighty Challenge (Senior Cinematografica, 1964, 95 minutes)
AKA Hercules, Samson, Maciste and Ursus: The Invincibles
Directed by Giorgio Capitani; Written by Sandro Coninenza and Roberto Gianviti, based on a story by Giorgio Cristalini; Produced by Giorgio Cristalini; Music by Piero Umiliani

Cast
Alan Steel (Hercules), Howard Ross (Maciste), NADIR BALTIMORE (SAMSON), Yann Larvor (Ursus)
Rating: *1/2

Hercules, Samson and Ulysses (1965)
See Hercules chapter for credits

Hercules in New York (1970)
See Hercules chapter for credits

TELEVISION
"Samson and Delilah" (ABC movie, 1987, 100 minutes)
Directed by Lee Philips; Written by John Gay; Produced by Frank Levy; Music by Maurice Jarre
Cast
ANTONY HAMILTON (SAMSON), Belinda Bauer (Delilah), Max Von Sydow (Sidka), Stephen Machi (Maluck), Daniel Stern (Micah), Jose Ferrer (High Priest), Maria Schell (Deborah), Victor Mature (Manoah)
Rating: **

Douglas Fairbanks Jr. in a rare somber moment from *Sinbad the Sailor* (1947)

SINBAD

The Thousand And One Nights is the most renowned literary work to emerge from the Arab nations since *The Koran*. Its cast of characters--Scheherazade, Aladdin, Ali Baba and the Forty Thieves and Sinbad the Sailor--are known to children the world over as part of the core curriculum of Bedtime Stories 101.

We are familiar with the fairy tales, which are usually collected in colorful picture books in simple language and large, friendly type, but the original *Arabian Nights* (as they also are known) were racy little tales that were written as a response to the deeply theological Oriental literature of the day, and were certainly not meant for children. What you won't find in the picture books are machete-slinging sultans who hack their slaves to pieces, sexual escapades on a Harold Robbins level, and lesser-known stories such as *The Historic Fart*. Ironically, these adult themes are the reason that the *Tales* are not embraced in their geographic area of origin today.

The first written translation of the *Tales* appeared somewhere around 850 A.D. (first English translation: 1706), but the stories themselves date back even further, as folk tales told in India, Persia and Arabia. To bind them together another tale was created, of a king named Shahriyar who had the nasty habit of marrying virgins and having them killed the next day. New bride Scheherazade tries to beat the system by telling the king a story, which so entertains Shahriyar that he lets her live another night. The stories and reprieves continue for 1001 nights, by which time Scheherazade has given the king three children, and Shahriyar has reconsidered his marriage policy.

THE STORY

Aladdin may be the most popular *Arabian Nights* figure, especially after his Disney makeover, but for derring-do and heroics the highlight of the collection are the seven voyages of Sinbad. The reader will find some parallels with Homer's *Odyssey*, in which another valiant hero sails for twenty years encountering monsters, sorcerers and more bad luck than the crew of the S.S. *Minnow*. The difference is that Odysseus endures his trials through one continuous voyage; Sinbad keeps returning voluntarily to the sailor's life after each miraculous escape.

The story begins with a wealthy and finally retired Sinbad inviting a weary porter into his home for food and rest. He is delighted to learn that the porter is also named Sinbad, and tells his namesake about his adventures at sea:

Voyage 1: After squandering a large inheritance, Sinbad joins a ship's crew. The ship is wrecked, and he floats to an island where he finds favor with the king. He stays there until the other survivors return.

Voyage 2: Sinbad encounters the roc, a giant bird that feeds elephants to its young. Sinbad unfurls his turban and ties one end to the roc's talon, and is flown home.

Voyage 3: Sinbad is shipwrecked on the island of the Zughb, a race of ape-like dwarfs. He blinds a man-eating Cyclops-like monster and escapes.

Voyage 4: Sinbad is tossed into the Cavern of the Dead on an island inhabited by cannibals.

Voyage 5: The Old Man of the Sea attaches himself to Sinbad.

Voyage 6: Another shipwreck, another escape, this time through dangerous rapids on a raft.

Voyage 7: On an island of devil-worshippers, Sinbad meets his wife and helps defeat the evil tribe. He remains for twenty-seven years before returning home.

The stories depict a man who is pious, brave and resourceful in difficult situations, but not very bright. On each voyage he is shipwrecked and almost killed, and he berates himself for leaving his comfy home. When he gets back to Bagdad he quickly forgets the misfortune of the last excursion and sets out again. After three voyages it's amazing he was able to assemble a crew. What you won't see in the fairy tales is how Sinbad will not hesitate to kill others to save his own life, as he does repeatedly in the Cavern of the Dead. The movies also have sanitized this side of his character.

The story of Sinbad is continued in 1844 by Edgar Allen Poe, in *The Thousand and Second Tale of Scheherazade*. Poe relates how the lovely storyteller spins one more adventure of Sinbad, in which he sails around the world, and describes actual places that were well known in the nineteenth century. But the king, who had earlier swallowed stories about rocs and giants, can't believe Scheherazade's descriptions of Kentucky's Mammoth Cave and a petrified forest in Texas, and has her killed after all. It's a very clever short story with a typically cynical Poe denouement.

THE FILMS

Several attempts were made to bring Sinbad to the screen, but there has yet to be a superior, definitive treatment. *The Seventh Voyage of Sinbad* (1958) is usually categorized as a classic at the video store, but only for its Ray Harryhausen special effects. The movie lacks a strong narrative and a commanding lead performance, and it doesn't do much for me except outdistance some even lamer competition.

Sinbad has been jinxed on the screen since 1942, when he was first brought to life in the unlikely person of. . .Shemp Howard. Yep, everybody's least favorite Stooge played the dashing sailor for laughs in *Arabian Nights*. In this version Sinbad, Aladdin and Scheherazade are part of a traveling theater troupe who help the rightful Caliph regain his throne after he is almost killed by his evil brother. Scheherazade marries the Caliph after he is back in power.

The film has nothing to do with the original stories, a trait shared by all subsequent Sinbad movies. It's still not bad--Maria Montez is a fetching Scheherazade, Sabu is energetic as ever as the troupe acrobat, and there's a healthy dose of action. Shemp, unrecognizable behind a beard and turban, plays a past-his-prime Sinbad as a boorish braggart, which Sinbad often was. The movie was praised upon its release for its sumptuous Technicolor look, but today it's hard to find a print that is not almost completely washed out.

Another movie entitled *Arabian Nights* was released in 1980, but feel free to ignore it. None of the characters are familiar, and the film is just a string of soft-porn vignettes conceived by the most demented auteur in cinema, Pier Paolo Pasolini.

Sinbad the Sailor (1947) is the only major Hollywood take on the character. Despite obvious flaws the film is bright, colorful, cheery, and by default still the best version to date. Douglas Fairbanks, Jr., stars, and he is the only actor to bring Sinbad to life with the appropriate exuberance. The performance may be a heartfelt tribute to his father, or graceful acrobatics and roguish charm may simply run in the Fairbanks genes. Either way, Doug Jr.'s resemblance to Doug Sr. in 1924's *The Thief of Bagdad* is amazing, right down to the exaggerated arm movements and gestures that are standard in silent cinema.

The film begins with Sinbad recounting the tales of his seven voyages for the seven hundredth time to an obviously bored audience. Sensing their disinterest, he tells the story of an eighth voyage, from which he has just returned. In it, Sinbad discovers clues to his forgotten heritage as Prince of Deryabar, an island where Alexander the Great was rumored to have hidden a vast treasure. Along the way Sinbad woos Princess Shireen, raising the ire of her betrothed, the Emir of Daibul, who wants the Princess and the treasure for himself. A Mongolian sailor named Melik concocts a scheme to find the treasure, with help from Sinbad and the emir. They reach Deryabar together, where Melik is poisoned after double-crossing his partners and the emir is killed while trying to prevent Sinbad and Shireen from fleeing together. His tale concluded, Sinbad shows his doubtful audience the jewels from the island.

The movie is too long and the story too convoluted, and that should matter a great deal. But most of the time you're too busy being dazzled by the sets and costumes and the beauty of Fairbanks and Maureen O'Hara falling in love in the kind of movie Technicolor was invented for. *Sinbad the Sailor* could have been a minor classic, but it settles for just being great, great fun.

Doug Jr.'s best film work was done in supporting roles (*Gunga Din*, *The Prisoner of Zenda*), but of the films he was expected to carry this is the most successful. Maureen O'Hara was never lovelier on screen, not even in *Bagdad* (1949) or *The Quiet Man* (1952). The cast also includes Anthony Quinn as the emir, Walter Slezak as the shifty Melik, George Tobias as Sinbad's sidekick and comic foil, Jane Greer just before *Out of the Past* and Alan Napier, who was even playing old codgers back in 1947.

Two less distinguished "B" movie treatments followed, both in 1952. *Babes in Bagdad* was an adaptation of the Greek satire *Lysistrata*. The ladies of the harem go on strike, much to the frustration of the "Arabian Knights." Good source material with a lot lost in the translation. There's curiosity value in the casting of Paulette Goddard and Gypsy Rose Lee as veiled vamps, but both were over forty and should have known better. The supporting role of Sinbad belonged to Sebastian Cabot, and Mr. French is no better or worse than anyone else in this misfire. Edgar G. Ulmer directed, on the tail end of a career downslide that began after *Detour* (1945).

Thief of Damascus starred Paul Henreid as General Abu Andar, who must protect the city of Damascus from the usual hordes of invaders. He is assisted by the Scheherazade all-star team of Aladdin, Sinbad and Ali Baba. Another interesting cast--Henreid, Lon Chaney, Jr., as Sinbad, Elena Verdugo and Robert Clary, but again the talent is wasted. The film was cranked out by assembly-line producer Sam Katzman, who lifted several scenes directly from *Joan of Arc* (1948).

In *Son of Sinbad* (1955), Dale Robertson plays the sailor's first-born as the James Bond of the Middle East, in a film that works best when it tries for Bond-style tongue-in-cheek action: compare the attack by the daughters of the Forty Thieves to the female tactical squad raid in *Octopussy* (1983). It's a Howard Hughes production, which means it's high on babes and low on plot. There are dozens of harem girls doing dance numbers in costumes that might have seemed pretty racy thirty-five years ago, but would barely qualify as "PG" today. Now bereft of its scandalous reputation, the film offers little else that is noteworthy.

The story has Sinbad, Jr., captured during one of his frequent visits to the Caliph's harem, and sentenced to death. But Tamerlane and the Mongol hordes come a'callin', and Sinbad offers to save the city in exchange for his life. He allies himself with the daughters of the original Forty Thieves, and together they make Tartar sauce out of Tamerlane's army. This is the third intriguing cast in a row given nothing to do. Vincent Price, in one of his too-infrequent departures from the horror genre, provides adequate comic relief as Sinbad sidekick Omar Khayam, and Dale Robertson seems to be having fun as well. Lili St. Cyr, the most famous burlesque dancer since Gypsy Rose Lee, plays one of the dancers, and if your eye is sharp you'll catch Kim Novak behind a veil as well. But other than a good "Open Sesame" joke, there's not much here.

Gene Kelly played a character named Sinbad in the last and best section of his all-dancing no-talking cinematic experiment, *Invitation to the Dance* (1957). The sequence, entitled "The Magic Lamp," opens with Kelly once again in sailor whites a` la *On the Town* (1949), this time on furlough in Bagdad. He rubs a lamp, finds a genie, and together they dance through a Hanna-Barbera animated world to the music of Rimsky-Korsakov's "Scheherazade." You can't argue with the soundtrack, but the animation is barely above Scooby-Doo level, though Kelly's interaction with the characters is masterful.

Next up is the first of Ray Harryhausen's "Sinbad" trilogy, *The Seventh Voyage of Sinbad*. The real star of all three films is the special effects, but as Hollywood continues to break new ground in this area the sense of wonder at Harryhausen's creations will probably diminish for future generations. For their time they were astonishing, but after the *Star Wars* films and *Terminator 2*, stop-motion animation is starting to look more quaint than incredible. The dueling skeleton is still impressive, but the same effect was used better in *Jason and the Argonauts* (see JASON chapter).

The story has Sinbad and crew members landing on the island of Colossa, where they are run back to the ship by a Cyclops. A magician named Sokurah tags along, but demands to return to Colossa for his magic lamp. When Sinbad refuses, Sokurah casts a spell on his fiancee`, Princess Parisa, causing her to shrink to Thumbelina size, and tells Sinbad that the only cure for her condition is back on the island. Another voyage to Colossa ensues, where Sinbad recruits the genie in Sokurah's lamp to his side and overcomes various monsters and the sorcerer's machinations. A defeated Sokurah restores the princess.

This has been called Harryhausen's masterpiece, but for me he never topped the destruction of Washington, D. C. in *Earth Vs. the Flying Saucers* (1956) Clean-cut Kerwin Mathews gives an uninspired performance as Sinbad, but he capably handles the physical demands of the role. Much better is Kathryn Grant (later Mrs. Bing Crosby), who brings class, grace, maturity and a refreshing sense of humor to her role as Parisa. The casting of a child as the genie is a novel approach (also used by Gene Kelly in *Invitation to the Dance*). Young Richard Eyer does a nice job.

Other assets include the Spanish locations, Bernard Herrmann's regal score and Harryhausen's rendition of the Cyclops and the roc. At last, someone actually read the book.

The Magic Voyage of Sinbad is the first of two foreign films that originally had nothing to do with the *Arabian Nights*, but were rechristened as Sinbad films to attract an American audience. In its original form, the 1952 Russian film *Sadko* told a story familiar to most children in its native land, about a man named Sadko from Novgorod who sets out to find the fabled Bird of Happiness. The film was released in the west as *Magic Voyage* in 1962. Sadko becomes Sinbad, who returns from his latest adventurous voyage to find his homeland of Covasan in turmoil. He vows to bring the Bird of Happiness home, but despite help from the sea god Neptune and his daughter, the trip is unsuccessful. However, Sinbad tells the people of Covasan to "Follow your heart to happiness, [because] it's already there."

Considering the required dubbing and other Westernizations, it's surprising the film works as well as it does. It probably helped that the man in charge of writing the American version was none other than Francis Ford Coppola. But the film cannot hide its heritage, especially when Sinbad's crew breaks into a cossack sabre dance. As a theme, the search for happiness has a philosophic bent not uncommon in Soviet cinema, but not usually found in swashbucklers.

As Sadko/Sinbad, the blond and bearded Sergey Stolyarov gives a bland, mannered Jack Cassidy-like performance. No one else in the cast can be recalled an hour after watching the film. The technical quality varies widely; Neptune's undersea realm and the giant chess game are triumphs of set design, but battles with rubber octopi and guys in bad bear suits are unintentionally hilarious. In both its original and adapted form, *The Magic Voyage of Sinbad* was intended as a children's film, and its fairy tale elements may still hold the younger ones.

The Japanese jumped on the Sinbad bandwagon in 1965 with *The Lost World of Sinbad*, original title *Daitozoku*, or *Samurai Pirate*. From the folks at Toho Productions who brought you Godzilla, the film starred Toshiro Mifune, obviously in between phone calls from Kurosawa, as the hero who assembles a group of pirates to battle an evil premier and a witch who turns people into stone. A tough to find movie, and not worth the effort.

Captain Sinbad (1963) is capably mounted but dull, dull, dull, though Guy Williams is the most sprightly Sinbad since Douglas Fairbanks. The town of Baristan is under the ruthless control of El Kerim, who seemingly cannot be killed. Sinbad tries by stabbing him through the chest, but El Kerim just laughs and has him arrested. After overcoming an invisible monster in a Romanesque arena, Sinbad escapes his captors, and El Kerim puts a price on the sailor's head. Sinbad makes his way to the wizard Calgo, who reveals El Kerim's secret: the tyrant's living heart is kept away from his body, under heavy guard at an impenetrable tower. While El Kerim plans to wed Sinbad's beloved, Princess Jana, the captain and his crew storm the tower and break El Kerim's heart. . .literally.

Offsetting Williams's positive contribution is Abraham Sofaer as the whining, bumbling magician Calgo, one of the most annoying characters in this entire book. The movie will be best enjoyed by the under-ten crowd, who may not find his antics as grating, and will delight in Sinbad's ghoulish quest to destroy El Kerim's disembodied heart. Made in Germany, *Captain Sinbad* has some impressive sets and a wonderful score by Michel Michelet that I actually prefer to Bernard Herrmann's famous work on *The Seventh Voyage of Sinbad.*

Seventh Voyage was a huge success in 1958, but Harryhausen would not work on another Sinbad film for sixteen years. When it finally happened, the result was another mixed bag of animated monsters and wooden actors. *The Golden Voyage of Sinbad* begins with Sinbad coming into possession of an amulet that contains a clue to the location of three golden tablets that provide youth, wealth and power. The amulet is coveted by Prince Koura, who uses his magic powers to trail Sinbad to the island of Lemuria. Koura ages every time he casts a spell, but the tablets will enable him to reverse the process. He gets them for a minute but, of course, mystical forces of good never last long in the hands of bad guys.

The script was written by Brian Clemens, who wrote many of the better episodes of the "Avengers" TV series. He might have adapted his skill for witty banter and droll understatement here and it would have worked, but the dialogue in the film is lifeless, and the story lacks focus and direction. We're never sure why Sinbad is sailing to Lemuria, what he expects to find and what he'll do when he finds it.

John Phillip Law, probably best known as the blind angel Pygar in *Barbarella* (1968), is the only screen Sinbad to attempt an accent, and it works well but his voice lacks resonance. Law tried to be a more cerebral Sinbad, but he does not have the noble bearing necessary to carry off the role. Poor Caroline Munro is reduced to set decoration when she is capable of a more substantial contribution. The film's best performance belongs to Tom Baker as Koura, who appears here just before his legendary portrayal of Doctor Who. The character is not very well drawn, but Baker gives the villain shadings and a sense of authority not provided by the script.

The expected assortment of bug-eyed monsters turn up, and there's a rerun of the cyclops-dragon fight, this time with a centaur and a griffin. The difference is that this battle is not integrated at all into the story; the plot stops as the creatures emerge and fight, and then it continues. However, an earlier duel between Sinbad and a six-armed statue of Kalid is the FX high point of the Harryhausen trilogy.

The final film in the series sailed into theaters three years later. *Sinbad and the Eye of the Tiger* shares the strengths and weaknesses of its predecessors, and once again the lead performance is the worst in the cast. Patrick (son-of-Duke) Wayne looks right but can't read a line to save his life and doesn't react as well opposite the special effects as either Kerwin Matthews and John Phillip Law.

In this adventure, Sinbad returns home to find Kassim, the future caliph, transformed by witchcraft into a baboon. Before Sinbad can marry Princess Farah, Kassim's sister, he vows to restore the Caliph to normal. They sail to meet with Melanthius, rumored to be the wisest man in the world, who tells them that a cure exists on the icy island of Hyperboria. Hot on the trail of Sinbad and crew is Kassim's stepmother Zenobia, who made a monkey out of Kassim so her own son could become caliph. At the Shrine of the Four Elements on Hyperboria, Zenobia's magic is pitted against that of Melanthius and, with help from Sinbad, Prince Kassim is cured. Zenobia's worthless son is killed in the fight.

Patrick Wayne aside, the performances here are the best in the series. Patrick Troughton who, like Tom Baker, also played Doctor Who, is superb as a very Who-like character--a brilliant eccentric with a profound reverence for all forms of life, even the giant walrus that devours some of Sinbad's crew. Jane Seymour makes it easy to understand why Sinbad would give up the sea for Princess Farah. Taryn daughter-of-Tyrone Power plays the daughter of Melanthius and is good enough to make you wonder why she disappeared after one more movie. And Margaret Whiting is nasty enough as Zenobia but please, an evil stepmother?

The Harryhausen menagerie is getting old by this time, and he tries to compensate for lack of originality with sheer volume. There are lots of rerun moments in the action scenes, and the climax is very similar to that of *Golden Voyage*, but the bewitched baboon is a stand-out, one of his most intricate and subtle creations. Director Sam Wanamaker sets a more serious tone this time around. It's a great-looking movie--the scenes on frozen Hyperboria attain an almost Zhivago-esque beauty, but the film would have been improved further by losing twenty minutes. And though it still falls within the parameters of family entertainment, *Sinbad and the Eye of the Tiger* is quite violent for a "G" rated film, and contains more discreet nudity than the supposedly obscene *Son of Sinbad.*

The most recent attempt at filming Sinbad never achieved a theatrical release, and it's easy to see why. From 1989, *Sinbad of the Seven Seas* is jaw-droppingly bad, a cavalcade of incompetence that merits comparison to the works of schlockmeister Edward D. Wood, Jr., though Sinbad doesn't contain as many laughs. Lou Ferrigno plays Sinbad, who returns to Basra as the movie opens to find the city under the control of an evil wizard named Jaffar. Five sacred gems will take care of Jaffar, so Sinbad sails out to retrieve them. Along the way he encounters various monsters and an island of amorous Amazons, but Sinbad stays true to his mission and saves Basra.

An introduction states that the film was based on Poe's Sinbad story, which would have been a good idea. But the statement is a lie and Poe's estate should sue. The producers will get away with it because the audience for this trash does not get to the library much.

Ferrigno plays the role as Hercules in pointed shoes. His dialogue is wisely kept to a minimum (he had more lines as the Hulk). Sinbad's crew is straight from Central Casting--there's a handsome prince, a Chinese cook, a dwarf and a burly Viking--it looks like a Halloween party. The acting is atrocious across the board, and the writing is even worse. I cringed when a princess of ancient Arabia shouted "Hey, I'm talkin' to you!" Later, Sinbad is asked if he'll fight Jaffar and replies "I'll give it a shot!"

It's unfortunate to close on such a low note, but there hasn't been a decade since the 1940s without at least one Sinbad film, so it's a good bet that another attempt is coming soon.

THE FILMS

Arabian Nights (Universal, 1942, 86 minutes)
Directed by John Rawlins; Written by Michael Hogan and True Boardman; Produced by Walter Wanger; Music by Frank Skinner
Cast
Sabu (Ali Ben Ali), Jon Hall (Haroun al Raschid), Maria Montez (Sherazad), John Qualen (Aladdin), SHEMP HOWARD (SINBAD)
Rating: ***

Sinbad the Sailor (RKO, 1947, 117 minutes)
Directed by Richard Wallace; Written by John Twist, based on a story by Twist and George Worthing Yates; Produced by Stephen Ames; Music by Roy Webb
Cast
DOUGLAS FAIRBANKS, JR. (SINBAD), Maureen O'Hara (Shireen), Walter Slezak (Melik), Anthony Quinn (Emir), George Tobias (Abbu), Jane Greer (Pirouze), Sheldon Leonard (Auctioneer), Alan Napier (Aga)
Rating: ****
Available on Videocassette

Babes in Bagdad (United Artists, 1952, 79 minutes)
Directed by Edgar G. Ulmer; Written by Felix Feist and Joe Anson; Produced by Edward J. Danziger and Harry Lee Danziger; Music by J. Leoz
Cast
Paulette Goddard (Kyra), Gypsy Rose Lee (Zohara), SEBASTIAN CABOT (SINBAD)
Rating: *1/2

Thief of Damascus (Columbia, 1952, 78 minutes)
Directed by Will Jason; Written by Robert E. Kent; Produced by Sam Katzman; Music by Mischa Bakaleinikoff
Cast
Paul Henreid (Abu Andar), John Sutton (Khalid), Jeff Donnell (Sheherazade), LON CHANEY, JR. (SINBAD), Robert Clary (Aladdin), Phillip Van Zandt (Ali Baba)
Rating: *1/2

Invitation to the Dance (MGM, 1956, 93 minutes)
Directed and written by Gene Kelly; Produced by Arthur Freed; Music by Jacques Ibert, Andre Previn and Roger Edens
Cast
GENE KELLY (SINBAD), Carol Haney (Scheherazade), David Kasady (Genie)
Rating: **1/2
Available on Videocassette

The Seventh Voyage of Sinbad (Columbia, 1958, 87 minutes)
Directed by Nathan Juran; Written by Kenneth Kolb; Produced by Charles S. Schneer; Music by Bernard Herrmann
Cast
KERWIN MATHEWS (SINBAD), Kathryn Grant (Princess Parisa), Richard Eyer (Baronni), Toran Thatcher (Sokurah)
Rating: ***
Available on Videocassette

The Magic Voyage of Sinbad (Mosfilm/Filmgroup, 1962, 79 minutes)
Directed by James Landis (U.S.), Aleksandr Ptushko (USSR); Written by Francis Ford Coppola (U.S.), K. Isayev (USSR); Produced by Art Diamond; Music by V. Shebalin
Cast
SERGEY STOLYAROV (SINBAD), Alla Larionova (Luberia), Mark

Troyanovskiy (Trifon)
Rating: **

Captain Sinbad (MGM, 1963, 85 minutes)
Directed by Byron Haskin; Written by Samuel B. West and Harry Relis; Produced by Frank and Herman King; Music by Michel Michelet
Cast
GUY WILLIAMS (SINBAD), Heidi Bruhl (Princess Jana), Pedro Armendariz (El Kerim)
Rating: **

The Lost World of Sinbad (Toho Productions, 1965, 94 minutes)
Directed by Senkichi Tangiguchi; Written by Takeshi Kamura; Produced by Yuko Tanaka; Music by Masaru Satoh
Cast
TOSHIRO MIFUNE (SINBAD)
Rating: **

The Golden Voyage of Sinbad (Columbia, 1974, 105 minutes)
Directed by Gordon Hessler; Written by Brian Clemens; Produced by Charles H. Schneer; Music by Miklos Rozsa
Cast
JOHN PHILLIP LAW (SINBAD), Caroline Munro (Margiana), Tom Baker (Koura)
Rating: **
Available on Videocassette

Sinbad and the Eye of the Tiger (Columbia, 1977, 112 minutes)
Directed by Sam Wanamaker; Written by Beverley Cross, based on a story by Cross and Ray Harryhausen; Produced by Charles H. Schneer; Music by Roy Budd
Cast
PATRICK WAYNE (SINBAD), Taryn Power (Dione), Margaret Whiting (Zenobia), Jane Seymour (Princess Farah), Patrick Troughton (Melanthius), Damien Thomas (Prince Kassim)
Rating: **1/2
Available on Videocassette

Sinbad of the Seven Seas (Cannon Films, 1981, 90 minutes)
Directed by Enzo G. Castellari; Written by Tito Capri and Enzo Castellari. Story by Lewis Coates; Produced by Enzo Castellari; Music by Dov Seltzer
Cast
LOU FERRIGNO (SINBAD), John Steiner (Jaffar), Roland Wybenga (Ali), Alessandra Martines (Alina), Stefania Girolami (Kyra)
Rating: 1/2 *
Available on Videocassette

LUKE SKYWALKER

So much hoopla has accumulated around the *Star Wars* films that critiquing them objectively is difficult. Distance has lent some perspective, but putting the movies under a microscope only exposes their flaws, not the magic that has made them immortal.

It was more than fifteen years ago that George Lucas created a movie and a universe that rivaled the "Star Trek" following and filled toy stores with merchandise. The series sustained strong interest between installments, but now that we're a decade removed from the Rebels' ultimate triumph against the Empire, all the junior Jedis seem to have moved on to other heroes. Such is the ebb and flow of popular culture. "Beam me up, Scotty" still sounds cool, but, "May the Force be with you," makes you sound like a geek.

Its days as a national obsession may be long gone, but when it first opened *Star Wars* revolutionized science fiction filmmaking and gave the genre a new lifeforce that has only recently begun to decline. The film *2001: A Space Odyssey* (1968), laid the foundation for how space should look in a movie, but *Star Wars* filled that space with battling heroes and villains, magnificent starships and a dizzying array of oddball creatures.

But the movies are only science fiction on the surface--spaceships and robots and death rays. Deep down they're science fantasy, and if you strip away all the outer trappings they are fairy tales. The look may be futuristic, but the story is set in the past, a long time ago in a galaxy far, far away like all our cherished myths and legends.

These same myths and legends gave George Lucas a wealth of material as inspiration. He borrows from the best, and the parallels are obvious; King Arthur and Merlin, David and Goliath, dozens of Westerns and, like Lucas's *Indiana Jones* series, the serials--*Flash Gordon* (1936) in particular. It's been reported that Lucas originally wanted to remake Flash Gordon but couldn't secure rights to the characters. By creating his own mythos, he added more money to his bank account than most countries have in their treasuries.

Even the droids, perhaps the one genuine spark of originality in the trilogy, were modeled after characters in Akira Kurosawa's film *The Hidden Fortress* (1958). I think it's okay to point all this out but also okay not to really care all that much. I can pick apart the details all day, but I can also remember my excitement at age sixteen, waiting to see *The Empire Strikes Back* in a line that looped the theater building. And when I watched all three films back to back again on a rainy weekend, I had a wonderful time. Movies shouldn't have to do any more than that. I'll even forgive them for inspiring "Battlestar: Galactica."

Luke Skywalker, the character whose exploits are at the very center of the storyline, can best be described as everyhero. He's the boy who becomes a man after several trials by fire. He's the innocent who is tempted by darkness but chooses light. You can kill an afternoon counting the times it's been done before. Mark Hamill is a good actor who brings a genuine personality to the role, and it's needed; in a universe of simply drawn characters, Luke is the simplest of the lot.

Ostensibly he's the protagonist, but we emerge knowing more about Han Solo, Princess Leia, and even the droids--all of whom have as much screen time as Luke. When the center is weak the entire project is at risk, but since the *Star Wars* films are not character driven, the effect is not as damaging as it could be. Any sketch of Skywalker always ends up not answering who he is but what happens to him, and only his environment makes him memorable.

THE FILMS

There is civil war in the universe as *Star Wars* (1977) opens; the rule of the oppressive Empire is challenged by a rebel alliance. One of their leaders, Princess Leia, is held captive on the Deathstar, the Empire's planet-sized super weapon. Leia plants blueprints of the weapon in the droid R2D2, which finds its way to the barren planet of Tattooine. There, R2D2 is purchased by Luke Skywalker, who listens to Leia's holograph message and her request for help from Obi-Wan Kenobi, whom Luke knows as a hermit named Ben. While Luke visits Ben, his aunt and uncle are killed by imperial stormtroopers searching for the droid. Luke vows to join the rebels and follow in the footsteps of his father, a great pilot and warrior who attained the ultimate rank of Jedi Knight.

Ben and Luke hire a starship and pilot, a brash opportunist named Han Solo, and fly toward Alderaan, Leia's homeworld. But the Deathstar destroys Alderaan before they arrive and captures their ship. However, Han and Luke manage to escape and reach a rebel base. Ben is killed by one of the Empire's commanders, Darth Vader. A flaw is discovered in the Deathstar--one shot from one ship in the right place will blow it up. Luke, with help from Han Solo, gets the opening and fires the perfect shot.

The action moves at a breakneck pace and culminates in a thrilling climax that is unequaled by few movies in any genre. Performances are strong from a relatively untested cast who must fight to be noticed among the incredible special effects. This was Mark Hamill's film debut, and Carrie Fisher (Leia) had only one previous credit, a minor role in *Shampoo* (1975). Harrison Ford (Han Solo) had played only bit parts prior to *Star Wars* in movies like *Journey to Shiloh* (1968) and *American Graffiti* (1973). Peter Cushing is excellent as first mate to the asthmatic Darth Vader and Alec Guinness, the only other "name" actor in the company, does here what Marlon Brando would later do for *Superman*--adding depth to shallow waters.

In *The Empire Strikes Back* (1980), Luke sees Obi-Wan in a vision, telling him to go to the Dagobah system and study with the Jedi master Yoda. After a fierce battle with the Empire on the ice world of Hoth, Luke departs to begin his training. Han and Leia, after outrunning Empire Tai Fighters and navigating an asteroid field, end up in the cloud city of Bespin, home of Han's old gambling buddy Lando Calrissian. Vader then drops in as well, to capture the rebels and to lure Luke into a trap. He succeeds on both counts. Vader tells Luke that he is his father, and invites him to change sides. Luke says he'd rather die and then tries to do so, but Leia and Lando pull off a miracle rescue.

This is the best of the three films; the dialogue is faster and sharper, the romance between Han and Leia is developed, and the lightsaber duel between Luke and Vader is a classic moment in cinema. John Williams contributes the best film score he ever wrote, and the special effects masters improved on the state of their art once again. The "Imperial Walkers" are a particularly ingenious creation. Empire also contains the dreary training sessions with Yoda on Dagobah. Though Yoda is an interesting cross between Master Po from "Kung Fu" and Fozzie Bear, the worst thing this series can do is take itself seriously. Yoda's Zen-like instruction comes the closest.

Return of the Jedi (1983) opened amidst anticipation unheard of for a movie since *Gone With the Wind* (1939) another Civil War story. Luke, now a Jedi Knight, rescues his friends from the slug-like Jabba The Hut. He then returns to Dagobah, where he learns from Yoda and the spirit of Obi-Wan that Leia is his sister. Meanwhile, the Empire is at work on a new, improved Deathstar, and the rebels are at work on blowing it up. Han and Leia lead the ground forces on the forest moon of Endor, while Luke surrenders himself to the Empire and faces Vader once again.

With the Emperor looking on, Luke tries to pull his father back from the dark side of the Force. When Luke appears near death, Vader betrays the Emperor to save his son's life. After Leia and Han complete their mission on Endor, Lando leads a successful attack on the Deathstar, signifying the end of the Empire's rule.

The Deathstar reprise indicates how low originality rates on the priority meter, but once again the action is so intoxicating that it hardly matters. The escape from Jabba's deathtrap is a flawless sequence, and the outer-space battles have developed into lightspeed dogfights of astounding scope and complexity--one can only imagine the number of days required to shoot one minute of footage. The chase through the forest of Endor on airborne scooters is so exciting that you never stop to wonder, as critic Roger Ebert remarked, why they didn't simply fly above the trees.

The Ewoks are funny and cute, but the movie spends too much time with them. The back-and-forth cuts between Luke fighting for the fate of the universe and a race of cuddly teddy bears are ill-conceived.

Further analysis is superfluous. George Lucas went three for three, and even when you know what's coming, it's still fun to watch. However, watching them again I noticed a few things for the first time: in *Star Wars*, Carrie Fisher attempts an English accent in her opening scenes, and abandons it after being rescued by Luke; and in *Return of the Jedi*, did anyone else catch the resemblance between the Emperor and the figure of Death in Ingmar Bergman's *The Seventh Seal* (1957)?

Six more *Star Wars* movies are planned. No one knows when or if they'll be made, but Luke, Han and Leia do not figure in their stories. It will be interesting to see the new heroes Lucas will create to combat new threats to the universe, and if he can recapture the public's imagination.

THE FILMS

Star Wars (20th Century Fox, 1977, 121 minutes)
Directed and written by George Lucas; Produced by Gary Kurtz; Music by John Williams

Cast

MARK HAMILL (LUKE SKYWALKER), Harrison Ford (Han Solo), Carrie Fisher (Princess Leia Organa), Peter Cushing (Grand Moff Tarkin), Alec Guinness

(Obi-Wan Kenobi), Anthony Daniels (C3PO), Kenny Baker (R2D2), Peter Mayhew (Chewbacca), David Prowse (Darth Vader--voice by James Earl Jones)
Rating: *****
Available on Videocassette
Awards: Academy Awards for Best Art Direction-Set Direction, Best Sound, Best Original Score, Best Film Editing, Best Costume Design; nominations for Best Picture, Supporting Actor (Alec Guinness), Direction and Screenplay. Special Achievement Award for Sound Effects (Benjamin Burtt, Jr.)

The Empire Strikes Back (20th Century Fox, 1980, 124 minutes)
Directed by Irvin Kershner; Written by Leigh Brackett and Lawrence Kasdan, based on a story by George Lucas; Produced by Gary Kurtz; Music by John Williams
Cast
MARK HAMILL (LUKE SKYWALKER), Harrison Ford (Han Solo), Carrie Fisher (Princess Leia), Billy Dee Williams (Lando Calrissian), Frank Oz (Yoda)
Rating: *****
Available on Videocassette
Awards: Academy Award for Best Sound; nominations for Best Art Direction, Original Score. Special Achievement Award for Visual Effects.

Return of the Jedi (20th Century Fox, 1983, 133 minutes)
Directed by Richard Marquand; Written by Lawrence Kasdan and George Lucas, based on a story by Lucas; Produced by Howard Kazaijan, Robert Watts and Jim Bloom; Music by John Williams
Cast
MARK HAMILL (LUKE SKYWALKER), Harrison Ford (Han Solo), Carrie Fisher (Princess Leia), Billy Dee Williams (Lando Calrissian), Ian McDiarmid (Emperor Palpatine)
Rating: *****
Available on Videocassette
Awards: Academy Award nominations for Best Art Direction, Sound, Original Score and Sound Effects Editing. Special Achievement Award for Visual Effects.

SPARTACUS

When Hollywood has tried to capture the glory that was ancient Rome, the results have usually been less than glorious. The city that controlled the destiny of all civilization for one thousand years is all too often relegated to being a backdrop for low-budget sword-and-sandal movies. The Romans, in their time unequaled in every field of human endeavor, typically are portrayed as poorly dubbed gladiators or the bad guys in Biblical movies. We won't even discuss *Caligula* (1980).

There are exceptions, but the list is short: *Quo Vadis?* (1951), the 1953 adaptation of Shakespeare's *Julius Caesar*, on the small screen "I, Claudius" and the noblest Roman film of them all, *Spartacus*.

Actually, *Spartacus* is an anti-Roman film, but the momentous and laudable achievements of the ancient republic are evident despite its message.The paradoxes of a city that was so advanced in its political and artistic development and so primitive in its choice of amusements are brilliantly captured in Dalton Trumbo's script, which was based on the equally brilliant novel by Howard Fast.

Fast's novel, like the best historical fiction, stays close to the facts as they are known, but refuses to let history stand in the way of a ripping yarn. A multitude of more factual accounts of Spartacus exists, from ancient Roman texts written by Appian and Cassius Dio to more recent biographies such as J. L. Mitchell's *Spartacus*. Though Fast chose to do so anyway, the actual events do not need embellishment to hold an audience.

HISTORY

A Thracian by birth, Spartacus deserted from the Roman army, but was caught and sold into slavery. This led to a stint at a gladiator-training school in Capua. He led seventy fellow gladiators in a revolt, and they established a camp at Mt. Vesuvius, where other runaway slaves and sympathizers joined the band. Their numbers swelled to anywhere from 10,000 to 140,000, depending on the source, and under Spartacus's leadership they made their way toward the Alps.

Spartacus was an illiterate peasant, not the great political theorist that he is often made out to be. But he did have an instinctive grasp of military strategy, plus the leadership ability to take on the Roman army--the best on the planet at that time--and send them packing in several skirmishes. With many of the legions occupied elsewhere, Spartacus may very well have been able to conquer Rome itself, but that was never his goal. Instead, he just wanted to get the hell out of Italy and return his soldiers to their homelands.

But when arrangements for sea transport fell through, the army was forced back toward Rome anyway, where they were met by eight legions under the command of Marcus Lucinius Crassus, who would later help form the First Triumvirate with Julius Caesar and Gnaeus Pompey. Together they would successfully challenge the authority of the Roman Senate itself. Pompey's army cut off Spartacus' path to the north, and the end of what became known as the Gladiatorial War (73--71 B.C.) was at hand. Spartacus was killed during the battle, and six thousand members of his army were crucified along the Appian Way.

These events rarely merit more than one page in most books about ancient Rome, which isn't much considering what might have happened if Spartacus and company had headed for Rome in the first place. The film and the Howard Fast novel are good history in their essentials: Spartacus's early life, covered in opening narration, is changed (we are told he was sold into slavery at age thirteen, which was not the case), and a love interest was invented for the usual dramatic reasons, but if everything you know about the Gladiatorial War comes from the movie, you're covered.

THE FILMS

After Alex North's overture (a pretentious thing for a movie, but the music is good), the film begins with Spartacus, already a slave, becoming first-round draft choice to a gladiator school run by Batiatus. Slave women are supplied to the trainees, and Spartacus is offered a lovely girl named Varinia, but he refuses to touch her while their captors are watching. Crassus and three others arrive at the school wanting a private show. Spartacus is defeated in the arena, but his opponent refuses to kill him, and is then killed himself. Spartacus and the gladiators break out, and Spartacus is reunited with Varinia. The story then stays relatively true to actual events until the final battle, which in the movie Spartacus survives. He does so, one imagines, so Varinia can show him his freeborn son, just before Spartacus perishes on the cross.

Stick with the 1991 rerelease of *Spartacus*; not for its inclusion of some minor scenes deemed too racy for its original release, but for the pristine quality of the restored print, and for homevideo the opportunity to see the film in a letterboxed format, which is de rigeur` for any Stanley Kubrick film anyway.

There are two more items worth noting on this "uncut" version: first, in the most infamous new scene, in which Crassus makes a homosexual pass at the slave Antoninus, Laurence Olivier's voice was dubbed by Anthony Hopkins, whose abilities at mimicry rival those of Rich Little. [Hopkins does a great John Gielgud too, but that's beside the point.]

Second, although the 1991 model of *Spartacus* earned a PG-13 rating, extremely rare for a film originally released in 1960, it was still not immune to some censor's knife. We have been allowed to see all the bloody carnage in the various battles, but have been protected from a more revealing view of Jean Simmons during Varinia's outdoor bath, which can be seen in the original European cut. This bit of prudishness is hard to understand, considering the PG-13 rating was already in place. It also says something disturbing about what Americans will accept in mainstream movies (violence) and what still makes them nervous (nudity, even when it's as unexploitative as Simmons's skinny-dip).

But enough quibbling. *Spartacus* is an incredible piece of work, a three-hour film that does not feel like one, and an epic that succeeds not only through sheer scope and spectacle but also in its most intimate moments. Three of its four Oscars may have come for technical merit, but my favorite scenes contained no clanging swords, or had any need for the eight thousand extras Kubrick used in the final battle.

Far more memorable is the deft verbal repartee` between Peter Ustinov as Batiatus and Charles Laughton as Gracchus, two charismatic roly-poly stars at their peak. Ustinov received the only acting nomination and deservedly won, but other performances of equal merit were criminally overlooked--Laughton, Olivier as the arrogant Crassus, lovely Jean Simmons and, of course, Kirk Douglas in the title role--and not just for doing his own stunts. Even Woody Strode, who never speaks a line, leaves an indelible impression as the Ethiopian slave who refuses to kill Spartacus in the arena.

Douglas gives us a Thracian who is proud but not patronizing, driven by passion but smart enough to know when to keep his emotions in check. He is branded a barbarian, but longs for the knowledge of art and music possessed by Varinia and Antoninus. Bred for battle, however, he accepts his lot and earns the respect of patricians and slaves alike. Next to *The Bad and the Beautiful* (1952), it is Douglas's best work.

It's interesting how the British members of the cast were given the Roman aristocrat roles (Laughton, Olivier) and the Americans (Douglas and Tony Curtis) play the slaves. Indeed, a Yank cast adrift in a sea of British accents is going to sound flat and uneducated, and the contrast here was clearly a conscious attempt to accentuate the clash of social strata.

Kubrick, whose adroitness with larger-than-life subjects had its first real workout here, replaced original director Anthony Mann at Kirk Douglas's request. Mann's contribution, the gladiator school scenes, are more in line with his expertise, emphasizing the individual as he had done in several above-average fifties Westerns. Kubrick takes over when majestic sweeps across mountains and plains are required. It couldn't have worked out better had they planned it.

Travel tip: those interested in visiting one of the Roman temples used in the movie need not head overseas; the Hearst Castle in San Simeon, California, was used in several establishing shots. It's worth a visit even if you don't see the movie.

Varinia shows the crucified Spartacus his baby son in the film's bittersweet final shot, but who knew that kid would grow up to be Steve Reeves? In *Son of Spartacus* (1963) Reeves leads a slave revolt against Julius Caesar, and carves an "S" in the flesh of his victims (so *that's* where Zorro got the idea!). The film is an example of the kind of gladiator film that is much more prevalent; *Spartacus* took two years to make and cost $12 million in 1960 dollars. The unrelated "sequel" looks like it took two weeks and cost 12 bucks. It is not required viewing for admirers of the original.

The Spartacus name turns up on a handful of other Italian cheapies such as *Spartacus the Gladiator* (1953) and *Spartacus and the 10 Gladiators* (1964), but as these films often turn up as Hercules and Samson movies, depending on who was popular in the country they were exported to, their interchangeable nature disqualifies them as legitimate adaptations.

There was also a silent film called *Spartacus*, made in Italy in 1914. Prints still exist and can be found at video outlets that specialize in the obscure. Historically erroneous and poorly conceived, it is not one of the better examples of silent cinema. Some of the sets, particularly the Circus Maximus, are still impressive, but the performances are atrocious and the fight scenes are laughably stiff. Stick with Kubrick, Trumbo and Douglas.

THE FILMS

Spartacus (Italy, 1914)
No other credits available

Spartacus (Universal, 1960, 196 minutes)
Directed by Stanley Kubrick and (uncredited) Anthony Mann; Written by Dalton Trumbo, based on the novel by Howard Fast; Produced by Edward Lewis; Music by Alex North
Cast
KIRK DOUGLAS (SPARTACUS), Laurence Olivier (Crassus), Tony Curtis (Antoninus), Jean Simmons (Varinia), Charles Laughton (Gracchus), Peter Ustinov (Batiatus), John Gavin (Julius Caesar), Nina Foch (Helena Glabrus), Herbert Lom (Tigranes), John Ireland (Crixus), John Dall (Glabrus), Woody Strode (Draba)
Rating: *****
Available on Videocassette
Awards: Academy Awards for Best Supporting Actor (Peter Ustinov), Best Cinematography, Best Art Direction and Best Costume Design; nominations for Best Score and Editing.

SUPERMAN

Americana. Apple pie and fireworks. Uncle Sam and baseball. And, since June of 1938, Superman. Captain America may wear the flag on his chest, but Superman is a living symbol of the American dream, the strongest man on earth in the strongest nation on earth. Or, as the humble hero himself might say, just another immigrant who arrived in our land with only the cape on his back, and made good.

Comic books were around before Jerry Siegel and Joe Shuster created Superman, but nobody paid attention to them. When Action Comics #1 hit the stands, "the funnies" began their transformation from a poor stepchild of publishing into a force to be reckoned with. Imitators soon materialized, but by then Superman was already the archetypical costumed comic book superhero, and today he is one of the handful of fictional characters recognized around the world.

THE COMICS

From his first appearance more than fifty years ago to this month's issue of Superman Comics, the depiction of the Man of Steel has been remarkably consistent. In 1986 writer-artist John Byrne was at the helm when DC Comics tried to update the legend, but the effects were felt more on Superman's supporting cast than with the hero himself; Lois Lane became an independent, assertive career woman who no longer existed to be rescued. Arch-villain Lex Luthor was transformed from a mad scientist to a corporate raider and, with the arrival of Police Captain Maggie Sawyer, all of a sudden there were gay people in Metropolis.

But Superman was still Superman. He flew in, sized up the situation and dealt with it, without self-doubt or existentialist reflection. He wins, bad guys lose, end of story. There was, however, one trendy refinement that made perfect sense--Clark Kent bought a Nautilus machine to explain his physique to Daily Planet co-workers.

The movies, like the comics, have only so much room for interpretation for the personification of truth, justice and the American way. Unlike Batman, the only other superhero to merit several film adaptations, the idea of a darker, film noir version of Superman ("Feel lucky, Luthor?") or a camp treatment ("Holy Kryptonite!") seems almost sacrilegious. Superman was and always will be a caped boy scout; reliable steadfast and predictable. It's part of his charm, and we wouldn't have it any other way.

THE FILMS

Superman first soared across the movie screen, after a successful radio adventure show and a series of cartoon shorts by the Fleischer brothers (of Betty Boop fame) in a 1948 serial starring Kirk Alyn as Superman and Noel Neill as Lois Lane. By serial standards it ranks well above average, but the pitfalls of the form are also apparent. The story opens with a surprisingly detailed review of Superman's origin, including Krypton's final days and Jor-El's launching of his infant son in an experimental rocket ship toward the planet earth. The baby, Kal-El, is found by the Kents, who adopt the boy and name him Clark. When Clark begins to exhibit incredible powers and abilities, his father tells him that he must use these powers to benefit mankind. Clark creates the alter-ego of Superman, fashions a special costume from the blankets in which he was wrapped as a child, and leaves home to begin a new life.

Superman's first appearance is prompted when Clark's train to Metropolis is nearly derailed. *Daily Planet* reporters Lois Lane and Jimmy Olsen, also passengers on the train, report the incident to their editor, Perry White. Clark is later hired by the *Planet* as well, while the exploits of his heroic counterpart dominate the paper's front page.

The Man of Steel is hired to protect the relativity reducer ray, which is your basic all-powerful new super-weapon that is a staple of serials, and is guaranteed to attract the attention of a dastardly masked villain. Sure enough, the evil Spider Lady sets her sights on the ray, and makes numerous attempts to acquire it. Along the way, she places Lois and Jimmy in danger several times and secures a piece of Kryptonite to deal with Superman. Still unable to steal the ray, the Spider Lady kidnaps a brilliant scientist to build a second weapon. Superman finally wins the day by lining his costume with lead and pretending to collapse after exposure to Kryptonite. He "revives" after being carried back to the villains' secret hideout. The Spider Lady turns the reducer ray on Superman, but is squashed when the beam reflects off his chest.

Superman's film debut is generally a good one. The cast is well chosen and the presence of humor is a welcome departure from most serials. However, audience members who looked forward to the sight of Kirk Alyn flying through Metropolis probably grumbled a bit when their hero suddenly turned into a cartoon every time he left the ground. This not-too-special effect is a letdown, especially to anyone who remembers the still impressive flight sequences in *The Adventures of Captain Marvel*, a serial produced seven years *before Superman*.

But you can't help but like Kirk Alyn. He seems to be having the time of his life playing Superman, or maybe he was just happy to have a job. Either way, his enthusiasm is contagious. Noel Neill is an ideal Lois Lane--sassy, pretty and smart. Tommy Bond disappoints as Jimmy Olsen, but Carol Forman gleefully hams it up as the Spider Lady.

Serials, even the best of them, are difficult to take in one sitting, which of course is not how they were meant to be seen. Problems with repetition and continuity are more obvious when the chapters are watched back to back; when poor Lois is knocked unconscious for the ninth time (a bit much even for the most intrepid reporter), it's hard not to notice a pattern developing. The cast and a couple of unique cliffhangers (personal favorite: episode 5) helps a lot.

Superman was successful enough to spawn a sequel, and two years later *Atom Man vs. Superman* reunited Alyn, Neill and Bond, and introduced Lyle Talbot as Superman's arch enemy Lex Luthor. The story has Luthor developing a matter transmitter, which he uses to commit a variety of crimes. He creates an alter ego known as Atom Man, for reasons that are never made clear. Luthor's schemes are consistently thwarted by Superman, until the evil genius creates synthetic Kryptonite and uses it to force his foe into the matter transmitter. Superman is dispersed into space, but manages to return to earth, albeit in a ghost-like state. He contacts Lois through her typewriter and, with her help, is restored to human form.

Angered by Superman's constant interference and Lois's infiltration into his organization, Luthor takes the gloves off. He creates a series of earthquakes, and launches an atomic missile toward Metropolis. He then blasts off in his homemade spaceship with a captive Lois. Superman blasts off after him and cleans house.

Atom Man vs. Superman is a disappointing follow-up to the first serial. The story runs out of gas before the sixth episode, the characters end up running in circles, and Atom Man is completely forgotten about halfway through the saga. The cliffhangers are dull, and Kirk Alyn's enthusiasm seems to have waned considerably.

On the plus side, brief as it is, Noel Neill remains a delight as Lois, and Luthor's spaceship is good for a laugh. Spread over 252 minutes, though, that's not much to go on. It's a regrettable end to the first chapter in Superman's screen history, but Alyn's tenure in the cape should still be fondly remembered for its blithesome spirit and unpretentious manner.

In 1951, just one year later, Superman leaped from serials to a feature film called *Superman and the Mole Men*. Kirk Alyn was offered the role but declined, so the cape went to George Reeves, a veteran of serials himself and one of Scarlett's throwaways in *Gone With the Wind.* The movie opens with Clark Kent and Lois Lane (Phyllis Coates) on assignment in the town of Silsby, home of the world's largest oil well. The discovery of radioactive soil samples, an oil company watchman frightened to death and possible evidence of life existing at the earth's core has the townspeople nervous. A posse, led by trigger-happy Luke Benson (Jeff Corey) is formed to hunt down any creatures who may have reached the surface.

Superman tries to intervene but is too late to prevent one of the creatures from being shot. But when another "mole man" returns to avenge his comrade with advanced weaponry, the Man of Steel is able to disarm Benson's mob and negotiate a peace. Before returning to their subterranean home, the Mole Men destroy the oil well that opened a passage to their world.

The movie's okay, but deserves our gratitude for inspiring the very popular television series "The Adventures of Superman." Superman and the Mole Men preceded the series by two years, and later turned up during its run as the two-part episode "Unknown People." In his debut outing George Reeves looks the best he ever did as the Man of Steel, but he was still struggling with the character. He had already found Clark Kent's easygoing personality, but Reeves's discomfort in the blue leotard is apparent. He shouts rather than speaks his lines, and does not project the confidence he would show in later episodes of the TV series. To be fair, though, it's hard to be heroic when your opponents are a handful of midgets in ill-fitting skull caps.

Just about any episode of the series is better than the film. Reeves' gradual settling into both Kent and Superman, the replacing of Phyllis Coates with Noel Neill, the addition of Jack Larson as Jimmy Olsen and John Hamilton as Perry White, and the forsaking (at last) of animation for the flight sequences all represent improvements.

"The Adventures of Superman" ran from 1953–57, and is still gaining new fans in syndication. Its most celebrated recurring moments are still fondly remembered, including Superman crashing through styrofoam doors and brick walls, bending gun barrels and jumping out of windows to take to the skies. "Jeepers!" and "Great Caesar's ghost!" and "Don't call me Chief!" became famous lines, and the opening narration ("Faster than a speeding bullet! More powerful than a locomotive!") has emerged as a prominent part of the legend.

It would be two decades before Superman would again go Hollywood, but what a return it was. In 1978, Superman flew first class with a top-dollar epic featuring an all-star cast and special effects that set new standards of excellence. On the day it opened *Superman* became the yardstick by which all film adaptations of comic books and strips can be measured. Only *Superman II* has since risen to its level of quality, grandeur and technical proficiency.

Once again, the origin of Superman is covered, in much greater detail than in previous efforts. With the planet Krypton crumbling around them, Jor-El and his wife Lara place their infant son Kal-El in an experimental rocket ship, and launch it toward earth. The ship reaches its destination and is found by Jonathan and Martha Kent. They adopt its infant passenger and concoct a story to explain his arrival. Growing up, young Clark Kent begins to discover the superhuman abilities that would determine his destiny. Following the death of his father, he is compelled by a mysterious green Kryptonian crystal to head north, where the crystal evolves into a "Fortress of Solitude." For the next five years, Clark investigates his heritage and his powers.

Lessons learned, Clark arrives in Metropolis, where his speed-typing leads to a job at the *Daily Planet.* The first appearance of Superman is prompted by *Planet* reporter Lois Lane, who becomes trapped in a plummeting helicopter. Lex Luthor, a brilliant criminal mastermind, plans to set California adrift with a nuclear missile. He tracks down a fragment of Kryptonite to prevent Superman's inevitable interference. Eve Teschmacher, Luthor's mistress, rescues Superman from the Kryptonite's crippling effects, but he is too late to prevent several disasters, including the death of Lois. Overcome with grief and rage he reverses the rotation of the earth, causing time to regress to the point just before the missile touches down. He then picks up Luthor and drops him in prison, before flying off into the sunset.

The filmmakers gave Marlon Brando three million bucks for about twenty minutes of screen time, but when as Jor-El he bids a tender farewell to his son, it's hard to argue with his pricetag. Brando's presence, along with that of Glenn Ford, Trevor Howard, Gene Hackman and others distinguishes Superman as an important film, as does the writing contributions of Mario Puzo (*The Godfather*) and Robert Benton (*Kramer vs. Kramer*).

Of course, the supporting turns of all these heavyweights would not be money well spent if the guy in the tights didn't command the spotlight. At first, producers considered staying in the superstar mode by wrapping a red cape around a luminary such as Al Pacino, Robert Redford or Sylvester Stallone. Any of these casting disasters would have doomed the film from the start, though if any of these actors actually tested I'd kill to see the footage.

Instead, the role went to unknown Christopher Reeve, who seemed to have walked right off the pages of Action Comics. Fortunately, his dead-on physical resemblance is underscored by a superb performance that has never received enough credit. At the *Daily Planet* Margot Kidder, Jackie Cooper and Marc

McClure couldn't be better as Lois, Perry White and Jimmy Olsen (and look quickly for the cameo appearances of Kirk Alyn and Noel Neill as Lois's parents). Lois's interview and evening flight with Superman are highlights.

Promotional material for the film assured audiences that "You will believe a man can fly," and the special effects masters made good on that promise. Superman's gradual ascent off of Lois's penthouse roof and midair turn still amaze me. John Williams's majestic score is the icing on the cake.

The task of making a sequel to this practically perfect film was indeed formidable. First priority: bring back everyone who made the original a success. So another wonderful script emerged from Puzo and David and Leslie Newman, the cast returned en masse, and although Richard Lester is the director of record, first choice director Richard Donner is credited with doing most of the work before leaving. Lester's subsequent screwing up of *Superman III* would seem to confirm that number *II* is Donner's film.

There was no reason to explain who's who again, so *Superman II* skips the exposition and opens with a marvelous action sequence at the Eiffel Tower, where our hero rescues Lois Lane from a gang of terrorists and hurls their stolen hydrogen bomb into deep space. The resulting blast, however, releases three Kryptonian supercriminals from their Phantom Zone prison--General Zod, Ursa and Non. Lex Luthor, meanwhile, has freed himself from a more conventional prison, and tracks down Superman's Fortress of Solitude. He learns about the bad guys from Superman's hometown and decides to become their earth liaison.

While exposing a honeymoon racket at Niagara Falls, Lois discovers Clark Kent's dual identity. He flies her to the Fortress of Solitude, where after a candlelit dinner and a night of romance Superman sacrifices his powers to live with the woman he loves.

General Zod declares himself ruler of earth, and challenges anyone to question his sovereignty. Using the green crystal that revealed his heritage, Clark is able to reverse the process that negated his powers. After an epic battle over the streets of Metropolis, Superman lures the villains to the Fortress of Solitude, where he is able to drain their powers with the same procedure that he earlier used on himself.

Once again, the guiding principal was to respect the characters and the material and play it straight, and once again the formula worked. The consummation of Superman's romance with Lois attracted the most media attention but, unlike the surrounding publicity, the scene itself was handled with taste and discretion. Too bad they undercut the moment later when Superman erases Lois's memory. But it's a minor hiccup in an otherwise outstanding production. *Superman II* performed very well at the box office, so it was back to the well again for a third installment, in which Superman abandons world-saving to become Richard Pryor's straight man. Bad move.

Pryor plays Gus Gorman, an always-unemployed loser who discovers he has a natural talent for manipulating computers. After landing a job at Webscoe Technologies Gorman begins embezzling thousands of dollars from other employees' paychecks. Webscoe CEO Ross Webster admires Gorman's ingenuity and instructs him to reprogram a weather satellite to destroy the Colombian coffee crop, allowing Webster to control the market. Clark Kent is in Smallville at the time, renewing his friendship with old flame Lana Lang. He takes time out from the reunion to undo the damage caused by the satellite and then returns to Smallville for the birthday of Lana's son Ricky.

An outraged Webster commands Gus to track down a Kryptonite sample in outer space and analyze its chemical components. Webscoe tries to recreate the element in their labs, but Gus's ineptness causes the result to be inexact. As a result, when Superman is exposed to the compound he turns into an outlaw, and ultimately splits into two personas--one good, one evil. The good side wins the fight for control, and a now thoroughly piqued Superman prepares for revenge.

At Ross Webster's desert stronghold, Superman defeats a Gus Gorman--designed super-computer, mops up the other ne'er-do-wells, and flies back to Metropolis in time to welcome Lana Lang to the *Daily Planet* as Perry White's new secretary.

Superman III opens with a series of slapstick vignettes that seem borrowed from a Charlie Chaplin two-reeler, and the comedy cavalcade continues at the *Daily Planet.* Immediately, it becomes apparent that this film was not cut from the same cloth as the previous two. There is a solid action sequence at a toxic chemical plant and some nice moments between Clark Kent and Lana Lang (and give Annette O'Toole a lot of credit for doing her best), but *Superman III* cannot rise above the loss of Margot Kidder to a backstage squabble and the inclusion of Richard Pryor, whose antics dominate much of the film's second half. His partners in crime (Robert Vaughn, Annie Ross and Pamela Stephenson) don't fare any better.

The Man of Steel's winning streak was over, but Christopher Reeve agreed to one more film, motivated primarily by the desire to send a socially relevant message about the arms race. The premise of *Superman IV* (1987), for which Reeve received a story credit, is intriguing, but the film itself lacks the courage of its convictions.

After watching Lex Luthor escape from prison once again, and the *Daily Planet* transform into a sleazy tabloid under new ownership, the movie's central crisis is prompted by a schoolboy's letter to Superman, asking him to rid the world of nuclear weapons. Superman contemplates the possibilities at his Fortress of Solitude, and then announces to the United Nations that he is going to grant the boy's request.

Luthor is busy as well. He steals a strand of Superman's hair from a Metropolis museum and mutates the genes to create Nuclear Man, who will help the world's black market arms dealers keep the war profits rolling, as long as Luthor gets his cut. Inevitably, the battle between Kryptonian and nuclear power is joined, with Superman losing Round 1 and falling victim to radiation poisoning. Round 2, after Superman recharges, is fought on the moon, where Superman deduces that his foe's powers will disappear without exposure to sunlight. He causes an eclipse by pushing the moon in front of the sun, and then drops Nuclear Man down the nearest reactor. After collaring Luthor yet again, he calls a press conference and tells the world's leaders that, "The gift of peace is not mine to give."

The return of Margot Kidder and Gene Hackman elevate this film above *Superman III*, but there are signs everywhere that this was a half-hearted effort at best. At a scant ninety minutes, this film is a half-hour shorter than its three predecessors, and the special effects fall far short of previous installments. The movie's chief sin, however, is the incongruity of its story. The first two *Superman* films had their basis in a very believable reality, which made the fantasy elements more convincing. In *Superman IV* the planet's nuclear arsenal is collected in a big net and tossed into space, and there is no mention of response from various governments. Life simply goes on as usual, and a potentially fascinating predicament is never adequately explored.

Instead, the film plays like an extended rerun. Luthor plots villainy with another bumbling companion (Jon Cryer), Superman takes another romantic flight with Lois Lane, and once again he loses his powers, only to regain them before the final showdown. The cast, for the most part, does rise above these shortcomings, but if Christopher Reeve cared so much about the story he could have hit the gym before donning the uniform. Mariel Hemingway contributes a surprisingly amiable supporting turn as the *Planet*'s new editor, and in its lighter scenes such as Superman's double date with Clark Kent, the film does occasionally recall the magic of earlier series entries. But when Superman flies the film plummets.

Will there be a *Superman V*? It would be inconceivable without Christopher Reeve, and he has agreed to return to the role if the script and the budget are there. But at age forty-two his cape-wearing days are numbered, so that script better materialize soon.

In the meantime, there is "Lois and Clark: The New Adventures of Superman," a splendid TV series that manages to walk the tenuous tightrope between playing the legend straight and playing it for laughs. For once, the mild-mannered reporter gets top-billing over his alterego; the series's strength is the relationship between Clark Kent (Dean Cain) and Lois Lane (Teri Hatcher), which has all the snap and sizzle of a good *Thin Man* movie or a first-season "Moonlighting" episode. Lex Luthor, superbly played by John Shea, is Macbeth in Metropolis; a suave, brilliant, egotistical multimillionaire philantrhropist who is delighted to finally have an opponent worthy of his attention. Smart writing and perceptive performances should keep "Lois and Clark" flying for several seasons.

THE FILMS

Superman (Columbia serial, 1948, 248 minutes)
Directed by Spencer Bennett and Thomas Carr; Written by Arthur Hoerl, Lewis Clay and Royal Cole. Adaptation by George H. Plympton and Joseph F. Poland, based on characters appearing in DC Comics (Superman created by Jerry Siegel and Joe Shuster); Produced by Sam Katzman; Music by Mischa Bakaleinikoff
Cast
KIRK ALYN (SUPERMAN/Clark Kent), Noel Neill (Lois Lane), Tommy Bond (Jimmy Olsen)f, Carol Forman (Spider Lady), Pierre Watkin (Perry White)
Rating: ***
Available on Videocassette

Atom Man vs. Superman (Columbia serial, 1950, 252 minutes)
Directed by Spencer Bennett; Written by George H. Plympton, Joseph F. Poland and David Mathews; Produced by Sam Katzman; Music by Mischa Bakaleinikoff
Cast
KIRK ALYN (SUPERMAN/Clark Kent), Noel Neill (Lois Lane), Lyle Talbot (Lex Luthor), Tommy Bond (Jimmy Olsen), Pierre Watkin (Perry White)
Rating: **
Available on Videocassette

Superman and the Mole Men (Lippert, 1951, 67 minutes)
Directed by Lee Sholem; Written by Richard Fielding and Robert Maxwell; Produced by Robert Maxwell and Barney A. Sarecky; Music by Darrell Calker
Cast
GEORGE REEVES (SUPERMAN/Clark Kent), Phyllis Coates (Lois Lane), Jeff

Corey (Luke Benson), Walter Reed (Bill Corrigan), J. Farrell MacDonald (Pop Shannon)
Rating: ***1/2
Available on Videocassette

Superman (Warner Bros., 1978, 143 minutes)
Directed by Richard Donner; Written by Mario Puzo, David Newman, Leslie Newman and Robert Benton. Story by Mario Puzo; Produced by Pierre Spengler; Music by John Williams
Cast
Marlon Brando (Jor-El), Gene Hackman (Lex Luthor), CHRISTOPHER REEVE (SUPERMAN /Clark Kent), Margot Kidder (Lois Lane), Ned Beatty (Otis), Jackie Cooper (Perry White), Glenn Ford (Jonathan Kent), Valerie Perrine (Eve Teschmacher), Phyllis Thaxter (Martha Kent), Susannah York (Lara), Terence Stamp (General Zod)
Rating: *****
Available on Videocassette
Awards: Special Academy Award for Visual Effects; nominations for Best Sound, Original Score and Editing

Superman II (Warner Bros., 1980, 127 minutes)
Directed by Richard Lester; Written by Mario Puzo, David Newman and Leslie Newman. Story by Mario Puzo; Produced by Pierre Spengler; Music by Ken Thorne, from original material composed by John Williams
Cast
Gene Hackman (Lex Luthor), CHRISTOPHER REEVE (SUPERMAN/Clark Kent), Jackie Cooper (Perry White), Margot Kidder (Lois Lane), Ned Beatty (Otis), Terence Stamp (General Zod), Sarah Douglas (Ursa), Jack O'Halloran (Non), Valerie Perrine (Eve Teschmacher), Susannah York (Lara), Marc McClure (Jimmy Olsen), E.G. Marshall (President)
Rating: *****
Available on Videocassette

Superman III (Warner Bros., 1983, 123 minutes)
Directed by Richard Lester; Written by David & Leslie Newman; Produced by Pierre Spengler; Music by Ken Thorne and John Williams. Songs by Giorgio Moroder
Cast
CHRISTOPHER REEVE (SUPERMAN/Clark Kent), Richard Pryor (Gus Gorman), Jackie Cooper (Perry White), Margot Kidder (Lois Lane), Annette O'Toole (Lana Lang), Annie Ross (Vera Webster), Pamela Stephenson (Lorelei Ambrosia), Robert Vaughn (Ross Webster)
Rating: **1/2
Available on Videocassette

Superman IV (Warner Bros., 1987, 90 minutes)
Directed by Sidney J. Furie; Written by Lawrence Konner and Mark Rosenthal. Story by Konner, Rosenthal and Christopher Reeve; Produced by Menahem Golan and Yoram Globus; Music by John Williams
Cast

CHRISTOPHER REEVE (SUPERMAN/Clark Kent), Gene Hackman (Lex Luthor), Margot Kidder (Lois Lane), Jackie Cooper (Perry White), Marc McClure (Jimmy Olsen), Jon Cryer (Lenny Luthor), Sam Wanamaker (David Warfield), Mark Pillow (Nuclear Man), Mariel Hemingway (Lacy Warfield)
Rating: ***
Available on Videocassette

TELEVISION

"The Adventures of Superman" (syndicated series, 1953-57)
Cast
GEORGE REEVES (SUPERMAN/Clark Kent), Phyllis Coates (Lois Lane, 1953), Noel Neill (Lois Lane, 1954-1957), John Hamilton (Perry White), Jack Larson (Jimmy Olsen), Robert Shayne (Inspector Henderson)
Rating: ***1/2

"Lois and Clark: The New Adventures of Superman" (ABC, 1993)
Cast
DEAN CAIN (SUPERMAN/Clark Kent), Teri Hatcher (Lois Lane), John Shea (Lex Luthor), Tracy Scoggins (Cat), Lane Smith (Perry White)
Rating: ****

TARZAN

Do we really need more than fifty movies about Tarzan? The answer is no, we do not, but it's too late to ask because we've already got them. No disrespect meant to the king of the jungle, but it does seem strange that of all the characters introduced or recreated by Hollywood, the one that inspired the most films wears a loincloth and swings through trees.

You'd think the happiest guy in the world about this turn of events would have been Edgar Rice Burroughs (1875–1950), the creator of Tarzan. He was certainly happy about the money, the primary source of which was the films and not the books they were allegedly based on. But it was a continuing source of frustration to Burroughs that his actual stories were seldom used, and that the Tarzan immortalized by Johnny Weissmuller in a dozen movies was not the half-savage, half-sophisticate he first envisioned in 1911.

Burroughs held an assortment of jobs from accountant to cattle driver, and only turned to writing at age thirty-six as another possible manner of supporting his wife and family. He had no formal training, but after reading a selection of pulp fiction stories he was certain that he could do better. Burroughs's vivid imagination first gave birth to "Dejah Thoris, Princess of Mars" which he sold for $400. His second effort was "Tarzan of the Apes," which sold for $700 and was published by *All-Story Magazine* in 1912.

The concept emerged from Burroughs's questioning of whether heredity or environment is most pervasive in shaping human development and personality. John Clayton, the infant Lord Greystoke, is stranded in the African jungle after the death of his parents and is raised by apes. The apes call him Tarzan, which is ape-talk for "white skin." Its immediate success spawned twenty-five more Tarzan novels, all of which were international bestsellers that were translated into thirty-one languages. The first film adaptation was released in 1918, and just one year later Edgar Rice Burroughs was able to move into a mansion on a 540-acre estate in San Fernando, California. He named the property "Tarzana Ranch," and the city that eventually grew in around the estate became Tarzana.

THE FILMS

Complete details on every Tarzan film would require a separate book. One exists already--*Tarzan of the Movies* by Gabe Essoe, which covers all Tarzan movies in exhaustive detail through 1968. The same level of scrutiny will not be applied here--let's face it, half of the existing Tarzan films have almost exactly the same plot--but fortunately the majority of releases can be neatly and accurately divided into separate eras, which are defined by the actor wearing the loincloth.

The original *Tarzan of the Apes* (1918) was among the most faithful to Burroughs, at least near the beginning; Lord and Lady Greystoke are marooned in Africa after their ship is attacked by pirates. Lady Greystoke dies soon after giving birth, and her husband is killed by apes. Kala, one of the apes who lost her baby, adopts the young Greystoke lord. The boy grows up, finds the books left by his parents and begins to educate himself. What follows is not from the *All-Story Magazine* version. A sailor named Binns who was with the Greystokes when they were attacked returns years later and sees Tarzan. Realizing who the boy is, he continues his education and then leaves Africa to inform the other Greystokes of the surviving heir.

Tarzan of the Apes was one of the first U.S. films to gross more than $1 million, placing it alongside such esteemed company as *Birth of a Nation* (1915). But the truth is that *Tarzan* just doesn't hold up half as well, and really isn't in the same league as *Birth of a Nation* and other landmark silent films. The first screen Tarzan was barrel-chested Elmo Lincoln, who looked twice his age of twenty-eight and every ounce of his two hundred pounds. More than half the film is spent on the young Tarzan, played by Gordon Griffith, a reflection perhaps of the value of keeping Lincoln off-screen. His first appearance, dangling awkwardly from a vine in a bad wig, borders on the pathetic. Enid Markey fits the role of Jane a bit better, and the classical-type score is appealing, but the only reason to see this film today is its curiosity value and minor historical significance.

Lincoln and Markey returned for a sequel, *The Romance of Tarzan*, later that same year. The story is picked up with Tarzan and Jane about to sail for England, when they are separated in an attack by natives. The apeman tracks Jane to San Francisco, but their relationship become conflicted by suspected infidelity. Tarzan returns to the jungle, and Jane soon follows. Getting the primitive Tarzan into the big city was a plot device used over and over by the series, though it doesn't work very well here because the story gets sidetracked into soap-opera-like complications.

As bad as Lincoln was, his first successor was even worse. Gene Pollar inherited the role in the confused, cheaply made *The Revenge of Tarzan* (1920). Pollar, who had even more of a gut than Lincoln, wore an over-the-shoulder leopard skin that made him look like Fred Flintstone. His dreadful performance cannot begin to elevate another film in which Tarzan spends most of his time away from the jungle, rescuing Jane from various lechers. Pollar was gone after one movie, and is better forgotten.

The success of a 1920 serial entitled *The Son of Tarzan*, starring P. Dempsey Tabler, induced Elmo Lincoln to return for *The Adventures of Tarzan*, a fifteen part serial. Queen La of Opar, who loved and hated Tarzan in more than one Burroughs story, is brought to the screen here by Lillian Worth. According to *Tarzan of the Movies* the serial was one of the top five attractions of 1920, along with Charlie Chaplin's *The Kid* and Rudolph Valentino's *The Four Horsemen of the Apocalypse*. Although it is certainly Lincoln's best work in the role and contains a few exciting moments, its overwhelming success seems absolutely inexplicable today.

Tarzan and the Golden Lion (1926) starred Jim Pierce, the first actor who appears to have heard of exercise before taking on the role. The usual story of legendary cities loaded with gold/diamonds/emeralds and bloodthirsty pagan natives is rendered slightly more watchable by Pierce's intense performance and Dorothy Dunbar as Jane. Look fast for Boris Karloff's film debut as a tribal chief.

Frank Merrill, who had been Elmo Lincoln's stand-in during *The Adventures of Tarzan,* landed the role himself for two serials, *Tarzan the Mighty* and *Tarzan the Tiger,* both from 1929. Merrill was both the last of the silent film Tarzans, and the first to be heard. *Tarzan the Tiger* contained a handful of sound sequences, one of which featured the first Tarzan yell, a repetition of the word "yeah!" that in no way resembles the yodeling cry most familiar to audiences today. It can be found in episode 2.

Tarzan the Mighty opens when castaways Mary Trevor and her young brother Bobby are found by Tarzan, who already has his hands full with the pirate king Black John. John becomes aware of Tarzan's aristocratic heritage and impersonates the jungle king to collect the Greystoke family fortune. Tarzan foils the scheme and marries Miss Trevor.

Merrill, like most of his predecessors, did his own stunts, but he was far more graceful and adept at vine-swinging and lion-wrestling than Lincoln, Pollar or Pierce. The costume still recalled Alley Oop more then the Lord of the Apes, and Merrill's resemblance to Buster Keaton doesn't work in his favor, but for the first time Tarzan's adventures are actually more exciting than amusing.

Tarzan the Tiger opens in England, where Tarzan and Jane are living the good life in London (Natalie Kingston, who played Mary Trevor in the last serial, was renamed Jane here). The money starts to run out, and the only way to save the Greystoke estate is by heading back to Africa to find the treasure of Opar. That means tangling with the amorous Queen La again, but Tarzan survives a bout with amnesia to save Jane from slave traders, fight off the queen and a soldier of fortune who also wants the treasure, and rescue Greystoke Manor from the tax man.

In this version Tarzan is almost like a secret identity assumed by Greystoke when needed, something that Edgar Rice Burroughs certainly did not intend. But Merrill, Natalie Kingston and Al Ferguson as the villain of both pieces are all believable, and Lillian Roth provides a link to past projects by again playing Queen La. Both serials were big hits.

The 1930s were Tarzan's Golden Age; a radio show was launched in 1931 and ran for 364 episodes. Carlton Kardell gave Tarzan his first voice. A comic strip drawn by Harold Foster debuted in 1932, and comic books followed in 1936. Burroughs continued to churn out new adventure novels, and in the movies the Johnny Weissmuller era began and rendered all previous incarnations almost obsolete. Weissmuller, then a twenty-eight-year-old Olympic swimmer who broke 174 individual world records during his athletic career, had the face, the physique, the voice and the talent to make the role his own. He also had Maureen O'Sullivan, who played Jane to his Tarzan in six first-rate productions.

British explorers Henry Holt and James Parker are in Africa searching for the elephant's graveyard, where they expect to find a fortune in ivory. Parker's daughter Jane arrives unexpectedly and joins the expedition. Tarzan helps the group navigate a dangerous river, and becomes fascinated with Jane. He whisks her into the treetops for a closer look. She is frightened at first, but as they learn to communicate Jane senses the gentle nature beneath Tarzan's primitive facade. Henry and Jane's father are ready to kill Tarzan for the kidnapping, but when they are abducted themselves by a tribe of dwarves it is Tarzan who leads a herd of elephants to the rescue. They find the elephant's graveyard, but Parker doesn't survive the trip. Henry returns to England, but Jane decides to remain with Tarzan.

The script, loosely adapted by Cyril Hume and Ivor Novello, uses only bits and pieces of Edgar Rice Burroughs's story. The Jane Porter from Baltimore in

Burroughs becomes Jane Parker of London, but that's nothing compared to the makeover done on Tarzan. The origin story is deleted entirely, and the often erudite, civilized man among beasts described by his creator became a primitive man-ape with no knowledge of the world outside his jungle. Burroughs complained vigorously, but the film was a huge hit and Weissmuller was dubbed the perfect Tarzan by critics and audiences. His interpretation became the official one, and a prototype for all future attempts. And so the character who spoke in complete sentences in twenty-six novels would be forever identified on screen with such grammar violations as "Me Tarzan, You Jane." Even worse, the line is misquoted, as most famous movie lines are.

Within these parameters Weissmuller's performance seems just right. I could be reading more into his acting inexperience than was actually intended, but let's give him the benefit of the doubt and say that his confused look upon first seeing Jane was a conscious decision. Delightful Maureen O'Sullivan plays Jane as a giggling, giddy schoolgirl who matures over the course of six films into a capable young woman who stands by her man. She is sweet and funny and very sexy, and when Tarzan and Jane get acquainted up in the trees the steam on screen isn't all jungle humidity.

A programmer at other studios, *Tarzan* was a priority film at MGM and was launched with style and class. The strong supporting performances from Neil Hamilton, the future Commissioner Gordon, and Hollywood's favorite stuffy Brit C. Aubrey Smith, set a precedent for keeping the quality high in cast, and each film was budgeted at a minimum of $1 million, which ensured top-flight production values. There are some technical flaws--interaction between actors and some old stock African footage is poor, some of the apes are obviously guys in suits, and Weissmuller is clearly swinging on a trapeze instead of a vine--but it was 1931 so let's cut them some slack. This is the first Tarzan classic, with more to come.

Tarzan and His Mate (1934) was hailed as that rarest of sequels that improves on the original, and despite the lavish *Greystoke* (1984) it is still considered the best Tarzan movie ever. The story opens one year later, with Henry Holt returning to Africa for another run at the ivory in the elephant's graveyard, and another chance at wooing Jane away from Tarzan. The expedition is decimated by a tribe of cannibals, but Harry and his partner Martin Arlington manage to escape and are reunited with the first couple of the jungle. The explorers reach the graveyard despite Tarzan's objections, but the cannibals block the exit and trap Henry and Martin, along with Jane. Once again its Tarzan and his elephants to the rescue, but not before Henry and Martin are killed.

After the success of the first film, MGM built a twelve-acre outdoor jungle complete with a lake. Weissmuller and O'Sullivan look right at home leading a herd of pachyderms through this elaborate set, and from here on they owned the roles of Tarzan and Jane. The plot of Henry Holt's second ivory quest takes a backseat to their relationship, and how it's progressed since their first meeting. He's learned a few words and phrases, she's learned the famous yell and how to swing through the trees. They are never officially married, but their obvious mutual affection, trust and respect would be the envy of most husbands and wives.

Tarzan and His Mate is also remembered for the daring costume worn by O'Sullivan, and a romantic swim in which Jane appears nude. The latter scene was spliced after a protest by the almighty Hays Code, but has since been restored on homevideo versions. There is also a lot of blood and gore that was equally shocking for its time. The series then took a turn towards family entertainment, making this the last "adult" Tarzan film until Bo Derek played Jane.

O'Sullivan was more demurely covered in *Tarzan Escapes* (1936), and even Weissmuller had brown BVDs on under his loincloth. Tarzan's education and domestication continues, but he is hunted like a wild animal by the awful Captain Fry. After luring Jane away with promises of a family fortune that was hers to claim, Fry then goes after her mate with both barrels, but Tarzan exacts his revenge on the hunter in gruesome fashion. The famous Tarzan treehouse makes its first appearance here, complete with elephant-driven elevator. These scenes are among the few that survived early screenings, in which horrified young viewers saw scenes of torture and murder that sent parents on the warpath. These scenes were then toned down or excised completely, signaling the end of the "PG" era for Tarzan. All of the cuts forced the producers to reuse the sequence from *Tarzan and His Mate* in which Tarzan wrestles an alligator.

The Tarzan family grew by one in *Tarzan Finds a Son* (1939), featuring the debut of Johnny Sheffield as Boy. The infant is the only survivor of a plane crash, and is adopted by Tarzan and Jane. The character had to be introduced this way and not as Tarzan's natural child with Jane, as that would have ticked off the Hays Office again. Five years later, relatives of Boy's biological parents turn up in the jungle to investigate the crash. When Jane learns that a large inheritance is involved, she admits that Boy was found at the crash site. But the relatives only want the money for themselves, and they'd have got it too if it weren't for those ever-present cannibals. The greedy outsiders are killed, and Boy remains in the jungle.

With a mate, a house and now a family, Tarzan's transition from savage jungle lord to Ozzie Nelson is complete. His table manners are still a bit crude, and his manner shocks the veddy proper relatives of Boy's actual parents, but when their true colors are revealed it is obvious that Boy is better off swinging on vines with his dad than attending Eton. The running theme of many Tarzan films--the so-called "civilized" people acting more uncivilized than Tarzan--is first used here. By now, Maureen O'Sullivan had grown tired of the jungle and feared typecasting, even though she worked steadily between Tarzan films, including notable performances in *The Thin Man* (1934) and *David Copperfield* (1935). She wanted out of the series, and MGM planned to kill off Jane at the end of the film. The studio didn't care when Burroughs objected, but when the fans got wind of the plan, the public outcry forced a change that allowed Jane to survive and (after a hefty raise) swing again.

She was worth every penny. Weissmuller and O'Sullivan are the main reasons to tune in, and their relationship is still a joy to watch. Amidst the obligatory scenes of Weissmuller cavorting with turtles (he spent as much time underwater as Esther Williams), there are some exciting action scenes and some very sad moments as well. When Tarzan restrains a baby elephant from following its wounded mother to the elephant's graveyard, it is unexpectedly moving.

Gold is discovered on Tarzan's land by a scientific expedition in *Tarzan's Secret Treasure* (1941). Greed brings out the worst in certain members of the team, and Jane and Boy are kidnapped when Tarzan starts causing trouble. There is more humor and less drama this time, and the elephant stampede finale is starting to get old, but the ever-likable leads plus a supporting performance by Barry Fitzgerald make this a typically solid entry. At the end Tarzan and Jane adopt a black orphan boy, but the character is written out of future entries.

Maureen O'Sullivan makes her final appearance as Jane in *Tarzan's New York Adventure* (1942), and the series was never quite the same after her departure.

If she was fed up with the role by now, it never showed. The story opens with circus owners landing in Tarzan's neighborhood to trap a few lions. They are amazed to see Boy taming elephants, and after Tarzan and Jane are believed killed by cannibals they take the kid back to New York to join the circus. Of course, our favorite couple survives and learn what happened from Cheeta. They follow Boy to New York, where Tarzan feels very out of place. But the jungle king gets his day in court, and wins back custody of his adopted son.

The idea was a natural, and it's incredible that it took them this long to try it. Tarzan being fitted for a suit, and his first encounters with opera, indoor plumbing and a smoke-filled nightclub ("Smells like Swahili swamp") are priceless. There's a little too much Cheeta for my taste, but the change of locale injected new life into a series that was already healthy.

The series moved from MGM to RKO for *Tarzan Triumphs* (1943). Jane's absence is explained in a letter from London, where she is visiting relatives. It's just as well that she's not around because the Nazis have invaded Africa to stock up on tin and oil reserves for their war machine. Though it is obvious propaganda, *Tarzan Triumphs* is also the best Weissmuller film without O'Sullivan, and its thrilling conclusion, in which Tarzan uses guerrilla tactics to wipe out a battalion of goosesteppers, is as good as anything in the series. O'Sullivan's absence is balanced somewhat by Frances Gifford as Zandra, princess of something-or-other, who helps Tarzan defend democracy. Gifford was known to audiences as Nyoka, another Edgar Rice Burroughs creation, in one of the best serials ever made.

Tarzan's Desert Mystery, also from 1943, was a sequel of sorts. This time we learn early on that Jane is nursing British soldiers back home--apparently the studio still wanted to leave the door open for O'Sullivan's return. Tarzan cleans out the last few Nazis still in the jungle. RKO finally gave up and recast the Jane role in 1945's *Tarzan and the Amazons*. Blond Brenda Joyce was as beautiful as O'Sullivan but not as vivacious, though coming in late puts her at an insurmountable disadvantage. No matter how many times Tarzan calls her Jane, it seems like he's cheating on his wife. The usual lost city plot is played out again, and is helped along by Maria Ouspenskaya, who was so memorable as the gypsy in *The Wolf Man* (1941).

Tarzan and the Leopard Woman (1946) represents the low point for Weissmuller's tenure, but it still ranks above the best efforts of other screen Tarzans. A leopard cult is on a sacrificing spree, and it's up to Tarzan and Boy to put them out of business. Johnny Sheffield makes his last series appearance in *Tarzan and the Huntress* (1947). Two years later he would start an eleven-film run as Bomba the Jungle Boy. The war has caused a shortage of animals in U.S. zoos, so a team of trainers is sent to Africa to restock. There are a couple of troublemakers in the group, of course, who round up too many jungle inhabitants, and Tarzan leads in the elephants to change their behavior.

The Weissmuller era ended in 1948 with *Tarzan and the Mermaids*--just as we're getting used to Brenda Joyce! Another twisted high priest is loose in the jungle, chasing native babes and sacrificing everyone else. Tarzan puts the kibosh on that. George Zucco is an effective villain, and Linda Christian is beguiling as the object of Zucco's affections. Weissmuller, who still looked marvelous seventeen years after his first Tarzan film, later began a seven-year stint as Jungle Jim. The series was similar in style to Tarzan, but never rose above mediocre.

Four other Tarzan projects were made in the years that Weissmuller owned the role, and none achieved anywhere near the same level of quality or popularity.

From 1933, *Tarzan the Fearless* was a twelve-part serial starring Buster Crabbe, who like Weissmuller was an Olympic gold-medal swimmer. He cut a dashing figure in his speedo loincloth, his athletic prowess was evident, and he was the best vine-swinger to ever play Tarzan, but his performance was atrocious.

The story had Tarzan aiding the daughter of a missing explorer, and fighting off two turncoat trappers trying to collect a price on his head. There is no Jane, but Jacqueline Wells, who plays the explorer's daughter, remains in the jungle with Tarzan at the finale. Crabbe laughs like a dimwit through all twelve episodes, and would prove much better as Flash Gordon. The serial was greeted with derision by audiences, for the cheapness of its production and the weakness of Crabbe and Wells in the leads. The first four episodes were released under the same title as a feature film, but the lack of an ending made for an unsatisfying ninety minutes.

With the full support of Edgar Rice Burroughs, Olympian Herman Brix threw his loincloth into the ring in the serial *The New Adventures of Tarzan* (1935). Burroughs hoped that this version, over which he could exercise more creative control, would finally capture the flavor of his literary sagas. The finished product would later be released as two separate feature movies, one with the same title, the other entitled *Tarzan and the Green Goddess.*

The action was set in Guatemala, where Tarzan arrived after learning that an old friend named D'Arnot had disappeared. From there its the usual lost city (Mayan this time), sacred idols and buried treasure. Brix was actually rather good, and his would be the only portrayal of Tarzan as Burroughs intended--soft spoken, intelligent, multilingual, and without the yodels and grunts of past incarnations. For that alone it's worth seeing, but the absence of Jane or any love interest is regrettable.

The Olympics had by now become a breeding ground for Tarzans, so it was 1936 Olympic decathlon champion Glenn Morris who starred in *Tarzan's Revenge* (1938). Wonder how Bruce Jenner missed out in 1976? Morris's greatest contribution to the series was proving that it's not as easy to play a monosyllabic apeman as it might seem, and that Weissmuller never received enough credit. The story dealt with a rich American couple out to bag some big game on the dark continent. Their daughter Eleanor is then bagged by Ben Aleu Bey, who sets her up as his 101st wife. Tarzan springs her from the harem. Famed gossip columnist Hedda Hopper played Eleanor's mother, but she never penned a line about Glenn Morris. After *Tarzan's Revenge* he disappeared, never to surface on a movie screen again.

Lex Barker, who bore a strong resemblance to Johnny Weissmuller, starred in the next five Tarzan films. He had gone to prep school and Princeton, which hardly seem the right qualifications for the role, and even worse he had no Olympic medals. However, Barker was always the best reason to watch any of his entries, which rarely rose above programmer status. He debuted in *Tarzan's Magic Fountain* (1949), a fountain of youth story with *Lost Horizon* overtones. Brenda Joyce's appearance provided some continuity with the previous era, plus there's a cameo by original Tarzan Elmo Lincoln.

Vanessa Brown became the best of Barker's many Janes in 1950's *Tarzan and the Slave Girl.* She is kidnapped by a lion-worshipping tribe (wonder if they knew the leopard-worshippers in the 1946 film?), and is of course rescued by Tarzan, who as might be expected has to fight a few extra lions this time. Brown had quite a bit of Maureen O'Sullivan's class and charm, but she was replaced anyway by Virginia Houston in *Tarzan's Peril* (1951). The change of lead actress in all five films prevented Barker from building the type of screen relationship Weissmuller had with O'Sullivan, and was just one more problem that he did not need in trying to salvage his five outings. The opposition is provided by gunrunners this time, who try to incite a war between two tribes. Dorothy Dandridge was still in the "anything to get a resume` credit" stage of her career, which explains her appearance as Queen Melmendi. Her performance helps make *Tarzan's Peril* Barker's best.

From 1952, *Tarzan's Savage Fury* had the apeman unwittingly helping and then shutting down crooks who were after a diamond mine. Dorothy Hart played Jane, and Tommy Carlton played Joey, who was to be the new Boy. Barker ended his run in 1953's *Tarzan and the She-Devil,* another ivory-hunting tale buoyed by Raymond Burr as the heavy (and I do mean heavy), and Monique Van Vooren as the seductive Lyra. She couldn't act, but at the time no one really cared. Joyce MacKenzie played Jane.

Muscleman Gordon Scott began his six-film run in *Tarzan's Hidden Jungle* (1955), a poor debut for the charismatic actor who earns the silver medal behind Weissmuller as the movie's best Tarzan. Vera Miles played Jill, not Jane, and became Mrs. Gordon Scott after the film was completed. An overzealous hunter played by veteran screen nasty Jack Elam is tamed by Tarzan. *Tarzan and the Lost Safari* (1958) was something of a series milestone; it was the first Tarzan movie in color, the first in Cinemascope, and the first to be fully made on location in Africa. The story was nothing new--Tarzan leads survivors of a plane crash to safety, but the pumped up production values were undeniably welcome.

Three separate pilots for a Tarzan TV series were edited together for the TV movie "Tarzan and the Trappers" (1958). Black and white and studio bound, it was Scott's poorest outing. The story had Tarzan kicking some animal trappers out of his jungle. From 1959, *Tarzan's Fight for Life* was a return to form. There are hints of an actual new plot in a nasty witch doctor's conflict with a medical doctor over the welfare of his tribe, and though made on the cheap there is evidence of renewed life for the series that would fully blossom in the next installment. Eva Brent plays Jane.

Tarzan's Greatest Adventure (1959), while not fully living up to its title, is the only post-Weissmuller film until *Greystoke* with a classy reputation. The plot is nothing new--unscrupulous diamond searchers have a series of run-ins with Tarzan--but its production values, mature approach to conflict and violence, and supporting appearances by Sean Connery and Anthony Quayle make for a wholly unexpected return to the "A" list for a series that had long since grown tired. Too bad it didn't last very long. *Tarzan the Magnificent* (1960) is a capable end to Scott's tenure, but comes as a disappointment after *Greatest Adventure*. Scott's successor Jock Mahoney appears as the bad guy whom Tarzan escorts through the jungle. Worst oversight--for the first time since the silent era, Tarzan doesn't let loose with one trademark yell.

While Scott was trying to pull the character off the critical list, a 1959 remake of *Tarzan, the Ape Man* was bad enough to pull the plug on all future jungle epics. The project's utter lack of skill and ambition is evidenced in its lifting and tinting of several scenes from its 1931 predecessor, including Weissmuller's yell, vine-swinging and the oft-repeated alligator fight from *Tarzan and His Mate*. Blond apeman Dennis Miller plays Tarzan, and he's just awful. Joanna Barnes plays Jane, and Cesare Danova and Robert Douglas play the roles first essayed by Neil Hamilton and C. Aubrey Smith. There have been worse Tarzan films, but none showed less effort in even trying to be different.

Jock Mahoney was up next with two adequate Tarzan films set outside of Africa.*Tarzan Goes to India* (1962) featured a score by Ravi Shankar, and introduced Mahoney as a tall, slender and wiry jungle-man, older than all his predecessors at forty-three and sans Jane and Cheeta. By now loyalty to both Burroughs and earlier screen versions was out the window, but Mahoney's brief era has its moments. Filmed in India, this old-hat story about an elephant herd's being threatened by construction of a dam is agreeable family entertainment. *Tarzan's Three Challenges* (1963) moved the setting to Thailand and closed Mahoney's brief reign. He became ill during production and lost thirty pounds. Somehow he finished the film, but his condition was evident in the finished product. You wouldn't have bet on Mahoney to beat Woody Strode in the last reel, but the script told him to win so he did. Despite the setback *Tarzan's Three Challenges* is the better of Mahoney's efforts.

Football star Mike Henry, the most buffed Tarzan in history, was top billed in the next three films. But the inherent limitations of the character had been obvious for years, and even if Henry were a first-rate Tarzan, which he wasn't, there was nothing he could do that hasn't been seen before. Realizing this, the producers tried to update the character by giving him a gun and a few extra I.Q. points. It was different, all right, but it also wasn't Tarzan. *Tarzan and the Valley of Gold* (1966) showcases the 1960s model, if you're curious. *Tarzan and the Great River* (1967) has an interesting supporting cast--comedian Jan Murray, Olympian Rafer Johnson as the villain and Diana Millay, one of the busiest and most reliable character actresses of the decade. Rafer Johnson returned, but as a different character, in *Tarzan and the Jungle Boy* (1968), in which Tarzan helps a lady reporter follow up rumors of a wild jungle boy. If you're compelled to sample at least one Tarzan film from every era, let Mike Henry be represented by *Valley of Gold*.

Henry had been slated to star in a Tarzan TV series, but illness forced him to withdraw. His replacement was Ron Ely, who romped through the jungle foliage from 1966 to 1969. The only other series regular was Manuel Padilla, Jr., as the orphan boy Jai, who accompanied Tarzan on many adventures. Ely was the closest in approach to the literary Tarzan since Herman Brix, but the most enjoyable aspect of the series was its guest stars. Among the visitors to Ely's Africa were Julie Harris, Ethel Merman, Helen Hayes and--believe it or not--Diana Ross and the Supremes, as three traveling nuns. Two feature films were patched together from the series, *Tarzan's Jungle Rebellion* and *Tarzan's Deadly Silence*, both released in 1970. Jock Mahoney plays the villain in the latter film.

Even the oldest cliches` might seem fresh again if they are given a rest for awhile, but the steady stream of Tarzan projects from 1918 to 1970 left little time to catch one's breath. So it was with renewed enthusiasm that viewers in 1981 awaited the first Tarzan film in more than a decade. Even more exciting was its revival of the Tarzan-Jane relationship, which had not figured in a movie since the Gordon Scott era. But *Tarzan, the Ape Man* turned out the be the worst Tarzan film since the first remake of the original story in 1959.

Set in West Africa circa 1910, the story begins with Jane Parker setting out to find the father she never knew. After an uneasy reunion Jane joins Henry Parker's expedition to the elephant graveyard. When they hear Tarzan's yell (Weissmuller's is still being used), Henry vows to kill the apeman and mount the carcass on his wall. Jane will have none of that. From there it's similar to previous versions--Tarzan kidnaps Jane and they get to know each other, then a nasty local tribe abducts her and Tarzan leads the elephants to the rescue.

The film was produced by its leading lady, Bo Derek, and was directed and photographed by her husband John. Four jobs held by two people, and not one of them was handled well. Bo Derek may be one of the ten most beautiful women ever to step before a movie camera, but she is also the only one on that list without talent. The film tells Jane's story more than Tarzan's, and she is incapable of carrying the story.

Tarzan is played by Miles O'Keeffe, whose fourth-billing indicates how important he was to the project. Returning the character to his strong, silent roots was a good idea, but O'Keeffe doesn't even speak one word in the entire film. Considering the quality of the script, he got off lucky. Tarzan and Jane connect on a sexual level, but there is no emotional bond between them. Thus the relationship becomes a one night stand and not the beginning of a beautiful friendship. But the character most changed in this distorted adaptation is Jane's father, played by Richard Harris as a wife-deserter, a drunk egotist and a borderline raving lunatic who cannot mask incestuous feelings toward his daughter.

The Edgar Rice Burroughs had plenty of reasons to sue, but the one they chose regarded Bo's nude scenes, which to be fair were not that explicit and were tastefully done. In fact, they were probably the one aspect of the film which turned out well, and the only reason to watch at all. Seems the Burroughs descendants are more prudish than Edgar, who didn't seem to mind when Maureen O'Sullivan went skinny-dipping in *Tarzan and His Mate*.

Such a misfire could have kept Tarzan on the inactive list in Hollywood for decades, but just three years after Bo's African beach party another film emerged, eight years in the making, that erased all memory of the Dereks' debacle. *Greystoke: The Legend of Tarzan, Lord of the Apes* was the most lavish, most expensive, and most faithful adaptation of Burroughs' creation yet. It is a film of epic proportions, but only adequate substance.

The origin of Tarzan is still a fascinating account, and because of this the film's first hour is often compelling entertainment. Lord Jack Clayton and his pregnant wife, Lady Alice, are shipwrecked off the African coast. Both soon perish, Alice by disease and her husband in an attack by a fierce ape colony. One of the apes, having lost her own baby, adopts the Claytons' child and raises him to manhood. These scenes of young Tarzan developing both human and simian abilities are among the finest in the film. As an adult, Tarzan rules the ape colony that nurtured him. His first encounter with another human occurs when members of a British expedition are massacred by pygmies, leaving only one survivor, Belgian explorer Phillip d'Arnot. He discovers Tarzan's heritage through a locket found near the shipwreck, and begins educating his discovery in the ways of civilization. Having learned to mimic any animal to perfection, the ape man quickly learns the basics of English, and is soon on his way to Greystoke Manor.

It is here that *Greystoke* runs out of steam, though much is salvaged by an excellent cast, specifically Sir Ralph Richardson as the Earl of Greystoke, and newcomer Christopher Lambert, who is the best Tarzan since Johnny Weissmuller. A budding romance with American Jane Porter (Andie MacDowell, whose voice is dubbed by Glenn Close) is introduced, but takes a backseat to Tarzan's personal problems of adjustment. This is unfortunate, because an uncommon love story could have provided the necessary spark to support the last reel.

Forty million dollars was poured into *Greystoke*, making it the best-looking

Tarzan film in history. Director Hugh Hudson (*Chariots of Fire*) and cinematographer John Alcott have brought dignity and grandeur back to a character that had become unaccustomed to such treatment. Breathtaking location footage of Cameroon, West Africa, is flawlessly mixed with shooting on remarkable indoor sets. Oscar winner Rick Baker's ape costumes are light years ahead of the Halloween variety. Storywise the film sets some very high goals, and achieves most of them. The problem, ironically, may be that *Greystoke* lacks the one element that more shabby, earlier treatments had in abundance--action. *Greystoke* takes a "Masterpiece Theater" approach to a character more suited to the Saturday matinee. Tarzan has become one of the most durable myths of the twentieth century, but its roots are in pulp fiction with characters like Conan and Doc Savage, not classic literature. The stories were propelled by fortune-seeking hunters and loopy tribal chiefs, who were defeated by Tarzan with strength, guile and a fired-up herd of elephants. A sequel may have given Lambert's Tarzan a chance to swing, but it was not to be.

The most recent Tarzan project was the TV series pilot "Tarzan in Manhattan" (1989). Tarzan, played by Joe Lara, leaves the jungle for New York when Cheeta is apenapped by deranged vivisectionists. A cab driver named Jane becomes his guide and translator in the big city. The influence of *Greystoke* is evident in Lara's long-haired look and brooding characterization, but Anna Sandor's and William Gough's script can't decide if it wants to be a straightforward or comic treatment of its subject. Based on the pilot, no tears need be shed for the series that did not follow.

Gabe Essoe's book *Tarzan of the Movies* mentions a few other unauthorized versions, most produced overseas. Among these are *The Adventures of Chinese Tarzan* (1940), the Soviet-made *Tarzan Des Mers* (1964) and ten quickies made in India between 1963 and 1965. You might also check out *Trading Places* (1983), in which the old nature-vs.-nurture debate is revived. Rich yuppie executive Dan Aykroyd is abandoned in the urban jungle of New York, but does not fare as well as Tarzan. And don't forget George, George, George of the Jungle, easily the best Tarzan parody ever--watch out for that tree!

THE FILMS

Tarzan of the Apes (National Film Corp. of America, 1918, 51 minutes)
Directed by Scott Sidney; Written by William E. Wing
Cast
ELMO LINCOLN (TARZAN), Enid Markey (Jane)
Rating: **

The Romance of Tarzan (National Film, 1918, 60 minutes)
Directed by Wilfred Lucas; Written by Bess Meredyth
Cast
ELMO LINCOLN (TARZAN) Enid Markey (Jane)
Rating: **

The Revenge of Tarzan (Numa Pictures, 1920)
Directed by Harry Revier; Written by Robert Saxmar; Produced by the Weiss Brothers
Cast
GENE POLLAR (TARZAN), Karla Schramm (Jane)

Rating: 1/2*

The Adventures of Tarzan (Numa Pictures serial, 1921)
Directed by Robert F. Hill; Written by Lillian Valentine and Robert F. Hill; Produced by the Weiss Brothers
Cast
ELMO LINCOLN (TARZAN), Louise Lorraine (Jane), Lillian Worth (Queen La of Opar)
Rating: **

Tarzan and the Golden Lion (R-C Pictures, 1926)
Directed by J.P. McGowan; Written by William E. Wing; Produced by Edwin C. King
Cast
JIM PIERCE (TARZAN), Dorothy Dunbar (Jane) Edna Murphy (Flora Hawks)
Rating: *1/2

Tarzan the Mighty (Universal serial, 1929)
Directed by Jack Nelson and Ray Taylor; Written by Ian McClosky Heath
Cast
FRANK MERRILL (TARZAN), Natalie Kingston (Jane), Bobby Nelson (Boy)
Rating: **

Tarzan the Tiger (Universal serial, 1929)
Directed by Henry MacRae; Written by Ian McCloskey Heath; Music by Burt Fiske
Cast
FRANK MERRILL (TARZAN), Natalie Kingston (Jane), Al Ferguson (Albert Werper)
Rating: **

Tarzan, the Ape Man (MGM, 1932, 99 minutes)
Directed by W.S. Van Dyke; Written by Cyril Hume and Ivor Novello; Produced by Irving Thalberg
Cast
JOHNNY WEISSMULLER (TARZAN) Maureen O'Sullivan (Jane), Neil Hamilton (Harry Holt), C. Aubrey Smith (James Parker)
Rating: ****
Available on Videocassette

Tarzan the Fearless (Lesser/Principal serial, 1933)
Directed by Robert Hill; Written by Basil Dickey, George Plympton, Ford Beebe and Walter Anthony; Produced by Sol Lesser; Music by Sam K. Wineland
Cast
BUSTER CRABBE (TARZAN), Jacqueline Wells (Mary Brooks)
Rating: * 1/2

Tarzan and His Mate (MGM, 1934, 105 minutes)
Directed by Cedric Gibbons; Written by Howard Emmett Rogers and Leon Gordon, based on a story by J. Kevin McGuinness; Produced by Bernard H. Hyman

Cast
JOHNNY WEISSMULLER (TARZAN), Maureen O'Sullivan (Jane), Neil Hamilton (Harry Holt), Paul Cavanagh (Martin Arlington)
Rating: ****1/2
Available on Videocassette

The New Adventures of Tarzan (Burroughs-Tarzan serial, 1935)
AKA Tarzan and the Green Goddess
Directed by Edward Kull and W.F. McGaugh; Written by Charles F. Royal and Edwin Blum; Produced by Ben S. Cohen, Ashton Dearholt and Edgar Rice Burroughs; Music by Abe Meyer
Cast
HERMAN BRIX (TARZAN), Ula Holt (Ula Vale)
Rating: **1/2

Tarzan Escapes (MGM, 1936, 95 minutes)
Directed by Richard Thorpe; Written by Cyril Hume, John Farrow and Karl Brown; Produced by Sam Zimbalist
Cast
JOHNNY WEISSMULLER (TARZAN), Maureen O'Sullivan (Jane), John Buckler (Captain Fry)
Rating: ***1/2

Tarzan's Revenge (20th Century Fox, 1938, 70 minutes)
Directed by D. Ross Lederman; Written by Robert Lee Johnston and Jay Vann; Produced by Sol Lesser; Music by Hugo Riesenfeld
Cast
GLENN MORRIS (TARZAN), Eleanor Holm (Eleanor), Hedda Hopper (Penny)
Rating: *

Tarzan Finds a Son (MGM, 1939, 90 minutes)
Directed by Richard Thorpe; Written by Cyril Hume; Produced by Sam Zimbalist
Cast
JOHNNY WEISSMULLER (TARZAN), Maureen O'Sullivan (Jane), John Sheffield (Boy)
Rating: ****
Available on Videocassette

Tarzan's Secret Treasure (MGM, 1941, 81 minutes)
Directed by Richard Thorpe; Written by Myles Connolly and Paul Gangelin; Produced by B.P. Fineman
Cast
JOHNNY WEISSMULLER (TARZAN), Maureen O'Sullivan (Jane), John Sheffield (Boy), Barry Fitzgerald (O'Doul)
Rating: ***1/2
Available on Videocassette

Tarzan's New York Adventure (MGM, 1942, 70 minutes)
Directed by Richard Thorpe; Written by Myles Connolly and William R. Lipman; Produced by Frederick Stephani; Music by David Snell

Cast
JOHNNY WEISSMULLER (TARZAN), Maureen O'Sullivan (Jane), John Sheffield (Boy), Virginia Grey (Connie Beach), Elmo Lincoln (Roustabout)
Rating: ****
Available on Videocassette

Tarzan Triumphs (RKO, 1943, 78 minutes)
Directed by William Thiele; Written by Carroll Young and Roy Chanslor; Producer by Sol Lesser; Music by Paul Sawtell
Cast
JOHNNY WEISSMULLER (TARZAN), Johnny Sheffield (Boy), Frances Gifford (Zandra), Sig Rumann (Sergeant)
Rating: ***
Available on Videocassette

Tarzan's Desert Mystery (RKO, 1943, 70 minutes)
Directed by William Thiele; Written by Edward T. Lowe, based on a story by Carroll Young; Produced by Sol Lesser; Music by Paul Sawtell
Cast
JOHNNY WEISSMULLER (TARZAN), Johnny Sheffield (Boy), Nancy Kelly (Connie Bryce)
Rating: ***

Tarzan and the Amazons (RKO, 1945, 76 minutes)
Directed by Kurt Neumann; Written by Hans Jacoby and Marjorie L Pfaelzer; Produced by Sol Lesser; Music by Paul Sawtell
Cast
JOHNNY WEISSMULLER (TARZAN), Brenda Joyce (Jane), Johnny Sheffield (Boy), Maria Ouspenskaya (Amazon Queen)
Rating: ***1/2

Tarzan and the Leopard Woman (RKO, 1946, 72 minutes)
Directed by Kurt Neumann; Written by Carroll Young; Produced by Sol Lesser; Music by Paul Sawtell
Cast
JOHNNY WEISSMULLER (TARZAN), Brenda Joyce (Jane), Johnny Sheffield (Boy), Acquanetta (Lea)
Rating: **1/2

Tarzan and the Huntress (RKO, 1947, 72 minutes)
Directed by Kurt Neumann; Written by Jerry Gruskin and Rowland Leigh; Produced by Sol Lesser; Music by Paul Sawtell
Cast
JOHNNY WEISSMULLER (TARZAN), Brenda Joyce (Jane), Johnny Sheffield (Boy)
Rating: **1/2

Tarzan and the Mermaids (RKO, 1948, 68 minutes)
Directed by Robert Florey; Written by Carroll Young; Produced by Sol Lesser; Music by Dimitri Tiomkin

Cast
JOHNNY WEISSMULLER (TARZAN), Brenda Joyce (Jane), Linda Christian (Mara)
Rating: **

Tarzan's Magic Fountain (RKO, 1949, 73 minutes)
Directed by Lee Sholem; Written by Curt Siodmak and Harry Chandlee; Produced by Sol Lesser
Cast
LEX BARKER (TARZAN), Brenda Joyce (Jane)
Rating: **

Tarzan and the Slave Girl (RKO, 1950, 74 minutes)
Directed by Lee Sholem; Written by Hans Jacoby and Arnold Belgard; Produced by Sol Lesser; Music by Paul Sawtell
Cast
LEX BARKER (TARZAN), Vanessa Brown (Jane), Robert Alda (Neil)
Rating: **1/2

Tarzan's Peril (RKO, 1951, 79 minutes)
Directed by Byron Haskin and Phil Brandon; Written by Samuel Newman, Francis Swann and John Cousins; Produced by Sol Lesser; Music by Michel Michelet
Cast
LEX BARKER (TARZAN), Virginia Huston (Jane)
Rating: **

Tarzan's Savage Fury (RKO, 1952, 80 minutes)
Directed by Cyril Endfield; Written by Cyril Hume, Hans Jacoby and Shirley White; Produced by Sol Lesser; Music by Paul Sawtell
Cast
LEX BARKER (TARZAN), Dorothy Hart (Jane)
Rating: *1/2

Tarzan and the She-Devil (RKO, 1953, 76 minutes)
Directed by Kurt Neumann; Written by Karl Lamb and Carroll Young; Produced by Sol Lesser; Music by Paul Sawtell
Cast
LEX BARKER (TARZAN), Joyce MacKenzie (Jane), Monique Van Vooren (Lyra), Raymond Burr (Vargo)
Rating: **1/2

Tarzan's Hidden Jungle (RKO, 1955, 73 minutes)
Directed by Harold Schuster; Written by William Lively; Produced by Sol Lesser; Music by Paul Sawtell
Cast
GORDON SCOTT (TARZAN), Vera Miles (Jill Hardy)
Rating: *1/2

Tarzan and the Lost Safari (Solar/MGM, 1958, 84 minutes)
Directed by Bruce Humberstone; Written by Montgomery Pittman and Lillie

Hayward; Produced by John Croydon; Music by Clifton Parker
Cast
GORDON SCOTT (TARZAN), Wilfrid Hyde-White (Doodles Fletcher)
Rating: **1/2

Tarzan's Fight For Life (MGM, 1958, 86 minutes)
Directed by Bruce Humberstone; Written by Thomas Hal Phillips; Produced by Sol Lesser; Music by Ernest Gold
Cast
GORDON SCOTT (TARZAN), Eva Brent (Jane)
Rating: **1/2

Tarzan's Greatest Adventure (Solar/Paramount, 1959, 88 minutes)
Directed by John Guillermin; Written by John Guillermin and Berne Giler, based on a story by Les Crutchfield; Produced by Sy Weintraub and Harvey Hayutin; Music by Douglas Camley
Cast
GORDON SCOTT (TARZAN), Anthony Quayle (Slade), Niall MacGinnis (Kruger), Sara Shane (Angie), Sean Connery (O'Bannion)
Rating: ***

Tarzan, the Ape Man (MGM, 1959, 82 minutes)
Directed by Joseph Newman; Written by Robert Hill; Produced by Al Zimbalist; Music by Shorty Rogers
Cast
DENNIS MILLER (TARZAN), Joanna Barnes (Jane), Cesare Danova (Holt), Robert Douglas (Col. Parker)
Rating: 1/2 *

Tarzan the Magnificent (Solar/Paramount, 1960, 82 minutes)
Directed by Robert Day; Written by Berne Giler and Robert Day; Produced by Sy Weintraub; Music by Ken Jones
Cast
GORDON SCOTT (TARZAN), Jock Mahoney (Coy Banton), John Carradine (Abel Banton)
Rating: **

Tarzan Goes to India (Solar/MGM, 1962, 88 minutes)
Directed by John Guillermin; Written by Robert Hardy Andrews and John Guillermin; Produced by Sy Weintraub; Music by Ken Jones, Ravi Shankar and Panchal Jaikishan
Cast
JOCK MAHONEY (TARZAN)
Rating: **

Tarzan's Three Challenges (Banner/MGM, 1963, 92 minutes)
Directed by Robert Day; Written by Berne Giler and Robert Day; Produced by Sy Weintraub; Music by Joseph Horovitz
Cast
JOCK MAHONEY (TARZAN), Woody Strode (Khan)

Rating: **

Tarzan and the Valley of Gold (Banner-Allfin/AIP, 1966, 90 minutes)
Directed by Robert Day; Written by Clair Huffaker; Produced by Sy Weintraub; Music by Van Alexander
Cast
MIKE HENRY (TARZAN), Nancy Kovack (Sophia Renault)
Rating: **1/2

Tarzan and the Great River (Banner-Allfin/Paramount, 1967, 88 minutes)
Directed by Robert Day; Written by Bob Barbash, based on a story by Barbash and Lewis Reed; Produced by Sy Weintraub; Music by William Loose
Cast
MIKE HENRY (TARZAN), Jan Murray (Capt. Sam Bishop), Diana Millay (Dr. Ann Phillips), Rafer Johnson (Chief Barcuna)
Rating: **

Tarzan and the Jungle Boy (Banner-Allfin/Paramount, 1968, 90 minutes)
Directed by Robert Gordon; Written by Stephen Lord; Produced by Robert Day; Music by William Loose
Cast
MIKE HENRY (TARZAN), Rafer Johnson (Nagambi)
Rating: *

Tarzan the Ape Man (MGM, 1981, 112 minutes)
Directed by John Derek; Written by Tom Rowe and Gary Goddard; Produced by Bo Derek; Music by Perry Botkin
Cast
Bo Derek (Jane), Richard Harris (Parker), John Phillip Law (Holt), MILES O'KEEFFE (TARZAN)
Rating: *1/2
Available on Videocassette

Greystoke: The Legend of Tarzan, Lord of the Apes (Warner Bros. 1984, 129 minutes)
Directed by Hugh Hudson; Written by Robert Towne and Michael Austin; Produced by Hugh Hudson and Stanley S. Canter; Music by John Scott
Cast
Ralph Richardson (Earl of Greystoke), Ian Holm (Phillippe D'Arnot), CHRISTOPHER LAMBERT (TARZAN), Andie MacDowell (Jane Porter)
Rating: ****
Available on Videocassette
Awards: Academy Award nominations for Best Supporting Actor (Richardson), Screenplay and Makeup

TELEVISION

"Tarzan" (NBC unreleased pilots, 1958)
AKA Tarzan and the Trappers (theatrical release)
Directed by Bruce Humberstone; Written by Thomas Hal Phillips; Produced by Jack Denove

Cast
GORDON SCOTT (TARZAN)
Rating: **

"Tarzan" (NBC series, [1966-68], CBS [1969])
AKA "Tarzan's Jungle Rebellion," "Tarzan's Deadly Silence" (theatrical releases)
Cast
RON ELY (TARZAN), Manuel Padilla, Jr. (Jai)
Rating: **

"Tarzan in Manhattan" (CBS movie, 1989, 90 minutes)
Directed by Michael Schultz; Written by Anna Sandor and William Gough; Produced by Charles Hairston; Music by Charles Fox
Cast
JOE LARA (TARZAN), Kim Crosby (Jane)
Rating: *1/2

DICK TRACY

THE COMICS

As a kid I never really got the appeal of the Dick Tracy comic strip. Compared to Spider-Man and the other crimefighters in the Sunday funnies, Tracy didn't have much sparkle and flash, and the cops and robbers stories seemed a bit dated. Sure, the rogues' gallery was colorful, and the two-way wrist radio probably looked pretty neat to Depression-era tykes, but the drawing was stiff, and who had the patience to wait three months for a story to be resolved?

It was only later, when I happened upon a book of collected Tracy strips, that I began to appreciate the talents of Chester Gould and discovered that those who didn't mind a storyline that gradually unfolded three panels at a time were richly rewarded. His stories were unpredictable--Gould had no compunctions about killing beloved characters to keep the reader guessing, and his manner of disposal for villains was always ingeniously gruesome. Who could forget when The Brow, a Nazi spy, is impaled on a flagpole as Old Glory waves proudly?

There was humor as well, beyond just the habitual use of such names as B.O. Plenty. This was Pat Patton's department--Tracy's somewhat inept partner was always being amusingly hoodwinked by minor-league bad guys whom Tracy could have for lunch.

The artwork I once found so lifeless is actually capable of conveying great drama. The death of Model, Tracy Jr.'s first love, is heartbreaking. When Bonnie Braids, the daughter of Tracy and Tess Trueheart, is kidnapped, the emotion Gould communicates with simple line drawings is exceptional. The detective didn't change expression much in sixty years, but his despair when learning of her abduction is clearly registered, as is Tracy's joy at her return. You grow up, you learn a lot.

Unlike the other comics-based heroes in this volume, Dick Tracy remained under the aegis of his creator for more than forty years. The strip debuted in 1931, which was a big year for gangsters; Al Capone was busted for income tax evasion, while *Public Enemy* and *Little Caesar* were packing movie theaters. Tracy's "origin," presented in the opening days of the strip, is likewise gangster related: Tess Trueheart's father is murdered by an underworld leader known as Big Boy. Tracy swears vengeance and joins the police force. Surprisingly, this story has never been adapted for any of Tracy's film appearances, though Big Boy did appear in the 1990 movie.

Gould continued to guide Tracy through wartime adventures, marriage, fatherhood, and encounters with the likes of Steve the Tramp, Stooge Viller, Pruneface, Flattop and the Blank. In the 1960s Tracy even went to the moon, in a story that didn't jibe with many longtime fans. After Gould's death, Max Allen Collins became Tracy's second scribe in 1977. His strips show a profound attempt to carry on the Gould traditions of malformed evildoers, two-fisted action and appropriately messy demises for the bad guys.

Those who know Dick Tracy only from his film appearances are also seeing a fairly accurate portrait of Gould's original concept--an impeccably honest, business-before-pleasure police detective, who ends up killing more bad guys than he apprehends, but always in self-defense. On the screen, as in the strip, we see his fellow officers in awe of Tracy's deductive skills, and his girlfriend demonstrating eternal patience.

THE FILMS

The character made his debut in the 1937 Republic serial *Dick Tracy*. Republic was the Rolls Royce of serial producers; its standards in performance, writing and particularly special effects were consistently higher than its competitors', as demonstrated in two of the best serial adaptations of comic heroes, *The Adventures of Captain Marvel* (1941) and *Captain America* (1944). *Dick Tracy* and the three successive Tracy serials rank with Republic's best work. However, the storylines sometimes stray into science fiction and fantasy, and feature the usual hooded serial menaces. At times Tracy is more reminiscent of Indiana Jones than a downtown detective, but you can't fill fifteen chapters with fingerprint dusting. Ralph Byrd, who played Dick Tracy, helped keep the stories grounded even in the most outlandish moments. His portrayal represents one of the best marriages of actor and role in the comic movie genre.

Sadly, the regular supporting cast that lent some consistency to the later series of Tracy movies, such as Tess and Pat Patton, are not part of the serials. However, some of the names and faces that turn up in the supporting casts will amuse film buffs; in *Dick Tracy* alone cowboy hero Smiley Burnette and silent film star Francis X. Bushman appear. The story begins when Tracy's brother Gordon is kidnapped by the notorious Spider Gang. To secure his release, the detective must ground the Spider's Flying Wing, a futuristic aircraft armed with a powerful death ray. This is the weakest of the four serials, but the scenes with Byrd and Burnette are fun.

In *Dick Tracy Returns* (1938) the action moves west as Tracy and new police recruit Ron Merton set out to end the crime spree of the Stark family. One by one, the family members fall, until Tracy squares off against Pa Stark, the last survivor, in a thrilling aerial confrontation. Ralph Byrd becomes Dick Tracy with this serial, which features plenty of battles on land, sea and air. Charles Middleton, best known for his superb portrayal of Ming the Merciless in the *Flash Gordon* serials, appears as Pa Stark.

Tracy takes on a spy ring in *Dick Tracy's G-Men* (1939). The ringleader, Zarnoff, is captured and executed, but his body is stolen and revived with strange drugs. Tracy is able to recapture Zarnoff after an aerial chase that leaves them both stranded in the desert. A great late-plot twist and many fine touches make this the best of the Tracy serials. The stunning Jennifer Jones, who at this point was still billed as Phyllis Isley, plays Tracy's girlfriend Gwen. Four years later she would win the Academy Award for *Song of Bernadette*.

The final serial, *Dick Tracy Vs. Crime, Inc.* (1941), does not end the series on a high note. It's the most "serial-ish" of the quartet, with Tracy battling a mysterious master criminal known only as The Ghost. The detective deduces that The Ghost is actually a member of a crimefighting organization known as the "Council of Eight." When members of the Council begin dying Tracy centers his investigation on the survivors. The villain, however, is killed before he can be apprehended (which is pretty standard when Tracy takes the case), this time resulting from electrocution. You can almost forecast the entire story from the first episode.

Morgan Conway replaced Ralph Byrd in *Dick Tracy, Detective* (1945), the first of four "B" movies that were quickly churned out over the next two years. Unlike the serials, where stories are dragged out to an absurd length, the films are tightly paced crime dramas that tell their tales in sixty minutes, and not one minute is wasted. Considering their programmer status, all four films hold up surprisingly well.

Detective opens with a schoolteacher being slashed to death with a surgical knife. A note signed "Splitface" is found in her purse, demanding $500. Tracy and Pat Patton are assigned to take the case, which heats up when the mayor receives a similar note from the slasher. Tess Trueheart nearly becomes Splitface's next victim, but Tracy intervenes in time, and follows the killer to the rooftop apartment of Professor Starling, an occult scientist. Finding a surgical knife under the professor's bed, he takes Starling in for questioning, but not before hearing Starling's prediction that fourteen people will be killed before the slasher's reign of terror ends. After being released from custody, Starling is murdered by Splitface.

Back at police headquarters, Tracy deduces that Starling was an acquaintance of Splitface, and the extortionist behind the notes. The professor knew the victims would be killed anyway, so he tried to take advantage of the situation. The detective also figured out the meaning of Starling's prediction--the fourteen intended victims were all members of the jury that convicted Splitface years ago. Splitface, knowing he has been discovered, kidnaps Tess. Tracy Jr. rides on the bumper of the getaway car and leads the police to the slasher's waterfront hideout. After a fierce struggle, Splitface is apprehended by Tracy and Patton.

Ralph Byrd is sorely missed. Morgan Conway does not possess either Byrd's sense of humor or his physical resemblance to the comic strip Tracy. His performance is adequate, though, and *Dick Tracy, Detective* offers his best work in the role. Supporting performances (as they are throughout the series) are top-notch. Joseph Crehan (Chief Brandon) and Lyle Latell (Patton) are joined here by Anne Jeffreys, the first of three Tess Truehearts. For classic movie aficionados, the name that jumps off the cast list is Jane Greer, the seductive femme fatale who would later star opposite Robert Mitchum is Jacques Tourneur's landmark film noir, *Out of the Past* (1947). As the nightclub owner's high-strung daughter, her work here is not indicative of things to come. But then, Morgan Conway is no Robert Mitchum.

Conway's second and final outing is *Dick Tracy vs. Cueball* (1946), arguably the worst film in the series. This film has also earned the singular honor of inclusion in a ranking of "The 50 Worst Films of All Time" by *Golden Turkey Awards* authors Harry Medved and Randy Dreyfuss. Come on, guys, it's not that bad.

Cueball, the title troublemaker, is hired to steal a shipment of diamonds from the S.S. *Palomar*. He kills the courier and completes his mission. After looking into the case Tracy is able to establish a connection between the murderer and Percival Priceless's Antique Shop. Cueball, meanwhile, spots a newspaper story listing the value of the diamonds (which he still possesses) at $300,000, and suddenly his $10,000 cut doesn't seem big enough. Cueball demands more money from Priceless, the brains behind the heist. After spotting Tracy, still hot on his trail, Cueball strangles Priceless and escapes. The murder weapon, a leather strap, provides Tracy with his first solid clue.

The strap itself is found beside Cueball's landlord, who attempts to steal the diamonds and becomes the killer's next victim. From the files of the strap's manufacturer Tracy learns the identity of the murderer. He recruits Tess to pose as a buyer for the diamonds. Cueball discovers the set-up, and reaches for the strap. Tracy arrives with seconds to spare, rescues Tess and pursues Cueball to a railroad yard. Fleeing, the villain traps his foot between two rails. Tracy arrives too late to save Cueball from becoming flattened.

Once again, part of the fun is lost without Byrd, but the Tracy stock company (Latell, Jeffreys, Crehan) is back in force, this time joined by Ian Keith as Vitamin Flintheart. Keith gives a grandiose scenery-chewing performance of the type that Peter O'Toole would later perfect, and his antics tend to undercut the film's attempts at establishing an atmosphere of genuine danger. Dick Wessel as Cueball is another liability--would it have been too much trouble to actually hire a bald actor? Wessel's skull cap looks like it was borrowed from the aliens in *Superman and the Mole Men* (1951) and his one-note performance falls way short of suggesting any real menace. The story moves right along, though, and packs plenty of twists and turns. *Cueball* is not exactly a feast of thrills but for Tracy fans it is still a satisfying snack, and for a low point in a low rent series, that's high praise.

Things pick up considerably with *Dick Tracy Meets Gruesome* (1947), thanks to Byrd's return and the powerful presence of Boris Karloff, who is the perfect personification of a ruthless and ugly Chester Gould–type villain. Gruesome and his gang rob a bank using a strange gas that renders both tellers and customers immobile. Tess, who is in the bank when the gas is released, avoids becoming frozen by stepping in a phone booth. She fakes immobility until the gang leaves, and then calls Tracy.

Later, reporter Dan Sterne overhears Tracy discussing the case in his office, and announces his intention to run the story in the afternoon edition. Tracy, fearing a run on the city's banks, asks him to hold off until the next day, but is forced to settle for a 2 a.m. deadline, which gives Sterne time to make the evening edition. Tracy visits Dr. A. Tomic to see if he can identify the gas, but learns from Dr. I. M. Learned, his assistant, that the doctor has disappeared. When Tracy tells Learned of the robbery, she becomes agitated. That night, Tracy and Patton track Gruesome to a waterfront bar. A car chase ensues in which Melody, one of Gruesome's gang, is injured. The others manage to escape. Tracy leaks a phony news bulletin stating that Melody is alive and talking, which lures Gruesome to the hospital. When he arrives he is captured by the police, just minutes before reporter Sterne's deadline.

The appearance of Karloff opens the door to some wonderful inside jokes--I defy anyone not to think of *Frankenstein* during an early scene in which Gruesome rises slowly from a slab in the morgue. The Tracy name game (I. Stuffum, taxidermist) injects an additional dose of humor.

Anne Gwynne is the best and prettiest Tess in the series, and this time she's actually given something to do besides (1) complain about missed dinner reservations, (2) get kidnapped and rescued, and (3) stamp her foot just before the closing credits as her all-work-no-play boyfriend abandons her again. The lesser character roles are all filled effectively, particularly Jim Nolan as Sterne. Look quickly for Lex (Tarzan) Barker as an ambulance driver.

The animosity between Tracy and Gruesome builds convincingly, and the knock-down drag out conclusion is worthy of its set-up. John Rawlins's direction successfully traverses a limited budget and production values. If you only see one of the Tracy movies, make it this one.

The final entry, *Dick Tracy's Dilemma* (1947) ends the series on a high note. This time, Tracy's nemesis is The Claw, a vicious but ignorant thug with a steel hook for a right hand. He steals a shipment of furs, but is later berated by his partners for killing a night watchman during the crime. Tracy gets a tip on The Claw's gang from Sightless, one of his informants. He follows it up and captures the fence for the stolen merchandise, but is too late to nab The Claw. When Sightless returns home, he is murdered. Tracy and Patton later discover that the fur theft was arranged by their owner, who hoped to sell them to a fence and still collect the insurance money. Tracy concocts a plan to trap the crooks and their boss.

After The Claw murders his partners for double-crossing him, Tracy pursues the killer to a junkyard. The Claw lifts his arm to strike yet another killing blow, but his metal appendage touches a high-voltage fence, and he is electrocuted.

Under John Rawlins's reliable direction, *Dilemma* comes the closest the series ever gets to establishing a genuine film noir atmosphere, complete with snappy Raymond Chandleresque dialogue, rain-soaked nighttime cityscapes and no-nonsense violence resulting in a surprisingly high body count. Still, it's hard to take things too seriously with Vitamin Flintheart around and typical Tracy characters like Peter Premium from the Honesty Insurance Company.

As The Claw (no jokes, Maxwell Smart fans!), Jack Lambert is a truly frightening villain who meets an appropriately nasty end. Kay Christopher takes over as Tess Trueheart, who is once again reduced to cheering on the sidelines. 'B' movie veterans Jimmy Conlin and Bernadene Hayes, among others, round out a solid cast.

Fast forward forty-three years now to the Dick Tracy film that is now most familiar to current audiences. It was a dream project for producer/director/star Warren Beatty, possibly the last actor you'd expect to be inspired by a comic strip. Be thankful he was, for only someone on his star-power level could have put together such a boldly unique treatment, and recruited such a pantheon of creative and technical talent. The result, quite simply, is one of the most visually arresting films ever made.

The story had to be a huge treat for fans of the strip, as it resurrects the first Tracy nemesis, Big Boy, as the leader of an underworld organization comprised of Gould's most infamous rogues. As the film opens, Big Boy takes over the Ritz Club from Lips Manlis, who is given a complimentary cement bath. Tracy is unable to pin the murder on Big Boy, even after grilling Mumbles and Flattop, two of his lieutenants. Tracy is sure that singer Breathless Mahoney witnessed the crime, but she refuses to cooperate.

Breathless later visits Tracy in his office, and tries to seduce him, but all he wants from her is her testimony. Big Boy hears about Tracy's informal adoption of a street urchin, and sends two cronies to his apartment posing as representatives from the orphanage. Tracy is kidnapped and offered a bribe to switch sides. He refuses, and is tied to a chair next to a furnace that is rigged to explode. After the crooks leave, the Kid breaks in and frees Tracy just in time. Later, Breathless again offers herself to Tracy in exchange for her help in building a case against Big Boy. Outside the door, Tess Trueheart sees her boyfriend succumb briefly, and tells him that she's leaving town.

The police plant a bug in the Ritz Club, which temporarily threatens to put the underworld out of business. When the device is discovered, Big Boy uses it to frame Tracy, with the help of a mysterious figure known as The Blank. With Tracy in jail, the mob returns with a vengeance. The Blank kidnaps Tess and takes her to the attic of the Ritz Club, hoping to frame Big Boy for her abduction. The Kid, now in an orphanage, is allowed to accompany Tracy on his journey from city to county jail, but the detective's friends on the force decide to take a detour to the Ritz. There they find Tess and arrest Big Boy's gang. Big Boy himself grabs Tess and gets away. Tracy follows, as does The Blank, and in the ensuing melee` The Blank is fatally shot and Big Boy falls to his death. Tracy rescues Tess and then removes The Blank's cowl to reveal the face of Breathless Mahoney.

The release of *Dick Tracy* just one year after *Batman*, another megahit (and megahyped) comic adaptation, made comparisons inevitable. Although *Tracy* is a far superior film in almost every way, the similarities between the two stretch far beyond their source material. Both movies are unabashed triumphs of style over substance. However, while *Batman* was brought to life amidst the nightmarish urban cesspool envisioned by Anton Furst, the world of *Dick Tracy* is much simpler and brighter, though just as surreal.

The film's astonishing look is the result of the vision and talents of Warren Beatty, production designer Richard Sylbert, cinematographer Vittorio Storaro, costumer Milena Canorero and dozens of skilled craftspeople. Vivid primary comic strip colors are used without blending or dilution. Imagine Ted Turner going nuts on a copy of *Little Caesar*, and you'll begin to grasp the wonders of *Dick Tracy*'s world (which can only be fully appreciated on a theater screen). Bright red Studebakers and bright blue Cords are parked along streets that glow in reflected green and gold hues. Only in a setting like this could Tracy's traditional Easter egg yellow trenchcoat not look overpowering. An unparalleled use of mattes and miniatures further enhance the visual feast. At times the scenery is so intoxicating that the characters almost seem intrusive; unwanted distractions in an iridescent wonderland.

Another parallel with *Batman* is the threatened dominance of the villain over the hero. But while Jack Nicholson blew Michael Keaton off the screen, Warren Beatty does manage to hold his own against Al Pacino's blustery Big Boy Caprice and his gang of misshaped mobsters. Beatty has no choice but to underplay amidst such characters, and to his credit he does so without fading into the background.

Madonna, as both hero and villain, delivers her finest performance to date (some would say her only performance to date) in a role that is perfectly suited to her talent and persona. The Material Girl also does justice to several terrific Stephen Sondheim tunes. Glenne Headly smartly contrasts Madonna's flash with quietly effective tenderness as Tess Trueheart. Several other cast members deserve credit for turning bit parts into memorable appearances. Displaying a refreshing lack of ego, leading actors such as James Caan and Henry Silva turn up for one scene or sometimes one line, and make it count. Dustin Hoffman in particular is hilarious as Mumbles, and William Forsythe plays Flattop with inspired nastiness. The only deterrents to an otherwise unfaultable production are an occasionally meandering script (from Top Gun writers Jim Cash and Jack Epps, Jr.) which is a bit slow out of the gate, and a typically overblown score by Danny Elfman.

Dick Tracy made money, but don't expect a sequel. Beatty's not the type to repeat himself, and the possibility of getting Pacino and Hoffman and the rest back together is minimal, especially if they all demand a slice of the profits.

THE FILMS

Dick Tracy (Republic serial, 1937, 250 minutes)
Directed by Ray Taylor and Alan James; Written by Barry Shipman, Winston Miller, Morgan Cox and George Morgan; Produced by Nat Levine; Music by Harry Grey
Cast
RALPH BYRD (DICK TRACY), Kay Hughes (Gwen), Smiley Burnette (Mike McGurk), Lee Van Alta (Junior), John Piccori (Moloch), Francis X. Bushman (Anderson)
Rating: ***
Available on Videocassette

Dick Tracy Returns (Republic serial, 1938, 250 minutes)
Directed by William Witney and John English; Written by Barry Shipman, Franklyn Adreon, Ronald Davidson, Rex Taylor and Sol Shor; Produced by Robert Beche; Music by Harry Grey
Cast
RALPH BYRD (DICK TRACY), Lynn Roberts (Gwen), Charles Middleton (Pa Stark), Jerry Tucker (Junior), Lee Ford (Mike McGurk), David Sharpe (Ron Merton)
Rating: ***
Available on Videocassette

Dick Tracy's G-Men (Republic serial, 1939, 250 minutes)
Directed by William Witney and John English; Written by Ronald Davidson, Norman Hall, William Lively, Joe O'Donnell and Joe Polan; Produced by W.J. O'Sullivan; Music by Cy Feuer
Cast
RALPH BYRD (DICK TRACY), Irving Pichel (Zarnoff), Ted Pearson (Steve), Phyllis Isley [Jennifer Jones] (Gwen), Walter Miller (Robal)
Rating: ***
Available on Videocassette

Dick Tracy vs. Crime, Inc. (Republic serial, 1941, 250 minutes)
Directed by William Witney and John English; Written by Barry Shipman, Franklyn Adreon, Ronald Davidson, Rex Taylor and Sol Shor; Produced by Robert Beche; Music by William Lava
Cast
RALPH BYRD (DICK TRACY), Michael Owen (Billy Carr), Jan Wiley (June Chandler), John Davidson (Lucifer)
Rating: **1/2
Available on Videocassette

Dick Tracy, Detective (RKO, 1945, 61 minutes)
Directed by William Berke; Written by Eric Taylor; Produced by Herman Schlom; Music by Roy Webb
Cast
MORGAN CONWAY (DICK TRACY), Anne Jeffreys (Tess Trueheart), Mike Mazurki (Splitface), Jane Greer (Judith Owens), Lyle Latell (Pat Patton), Joseph Crehan (Chief Brandon), Mickey Kuhn (Tracy Jr.)

Rating: ***
Available on Videocassette

Dick Tracy Vs. Cueball (RKO, 1946, 62 minutes)
Directed by Gordon M. Douglas; Written by Dane Lossier and Robert E. Kent. Story by Luci Ward; Produced by Herman Schlom; Music by Constantin Bakaleinikoff
Cast
MORGAN CONWAY (DICK TRACY), Anne Jeffreys (Tess Trueheart), Lyle Latell (Pat Patton), Rita Corday (Mona Clyde), Ian Keith (Vitamin Flintheart), Dick Wessel (Cueball), Douglas Watson (Priceless), Esther Howard (Filthy Flora), Joseph Crehan (Chief Brandon)
Rating: **
Available on Videocassette

Dick Tracy Meets Gruesome (RKO, 1947, 65 minutes)
Directed by John Rawlins; Written by Robertson White and Eric Taylor, based on a story by William H. Graffis and Robert E. Kent; Produced by Herman Schlom; Music by Paul Sawtell
Cast
RALPH BYRD (DICK TRACY), Boris Karloff (Gruesome), Anne Gwynne (Tess Trueheart), Edward Ashley (L.E. Thal), June Clayworth (Dr. I.M. Learned), Lyle Latell (Pat Patton), Tony Barrett (Melody), Joseph Crehan (Chief Brandon), Jim Nolan (Dan Sterne)
Rating: ***1/2
Available on Videocassette

Dick Tracy's Dilemma (RKO, 1947, 60 minutes)
Directed by John Rawlins; Written by Robert Stephen Brode; Produced by Herman Schlom; Music by Paul Sawtell
Cast
RALPH BYRD (DICK TRACY), Kay Christopher (Tess Trueheart), Lyle Latell (Pat Patton), Jack Lambert (The Claw), Ian Keith (Vitamin Flintheart), Bernadene Hayes (Longshot Lillie), Jimmy Conlin (Sightless)
Rating: ***
Available on Videocassette

Dick Tracy (Touchstone, 1990, 103 minutes)
Directed and produced by Warren Beatty; Written by Jim Cash and Jack Epps, Jr.; Music by Danny Elfman, songs by Stephen Sondheim
Cast
WARREN BEATTY (DICK TRACY), Charlie Korsmo (Kid), Glenne Headly (Tess Trueheart), Madonna (Breathless Mahoney), Al Pacino (Big Boy Caprice), Dustin Hoffman (Mumbles), William Forsythe (Flattop), Charles Durning (Chief Brandon), Mandy Patinkin (88 Keys), Paul Sorvino (Lips Manlis), R.G. Armstrong (Pruneface), Dick Van Dyke (D.A. Fletcher)
Rating: ****1/2
Available on Videocassette

Zorro

Johnston McCulley's novel *The Curse of Capistrano* was not a bestseller upon its publication in 1919 and its reputation has not improved since. Even the most dedicated fans of Western fiction have probably never penciled it onto their reading lists. However, this undistinguished story by an unheralded author introduced the world to a character who has thrilled generations of moviegoers--Zorro, the fox.

McCulley (1883-1958) deserves credit for creating the character, but Hollywood is entirely responsible for Zorro's enduring popularity. Even the author did not think he was anything special at first; *The Curse of Capistrano* was just one of dozens of stories that the prolific McCulley churned out over more than fifty years. He concentrated mostly on Westerns, though he also wrote crime fiction and the odd detective story. His interest in the California mission system of the early Spanish settlers provided the background for *Capistrano*, which was first published in the pulp magazine *All Star Weekly*.

In reading the tale today one cannot detect a creative high point for the author or the seeds of a legend that would outlive its creator. If anything, Zorro seemed an ebony-garbed knock-off of the Scarlet Pimpernel, who first appeared in 1905. But it didn't take Hollywood long to recognize Zorro's potential, and in 1920 Douglas Fairbanks starred in *The Mark of Zorro*, his best film and one of the greatest silents ever made. McCulley then published *The Curse of Capistrano* in book form and retitled the story after the film. He wrote *The Further Adventures of Zorro* in 1926, but would pen only three more Zorro stories in the next twenty years, which brought him some fortune but zero fame.

From the moment Douglas Fairbanks unsheathed his sword and slashed his first "Z," Zorro belonged to the movies. Had McCulley known his creation would appear in two classic Hollywood adventures, several lesser but appealing films, a hit television series and some of the best serials ever produced, he would certainly have cut a better deal. Such are the benefits of hindsight.

THE FILMS

Start with *The Mark of Zorro*, a lavish, thrilling high-energy showcase for Fairbanks's charisma and athletic prowess. Very little was adapted from *The Curse of Capistrano* outside of the look and style of the Zorro character; in old California, the local government, led by the corrupt Sergeant Gonzalez, is soaking the citizens with exorbitant taxes. If they can't pay, they are tossed in jail. Enter Don Diego Vega, a foppish college boy who is branded a coward by the community. Vega falls for the lovely Lolita, but she has fallen in love with the mysterious masked avenger known as Zorro. After running circles around Gonzalez and his troops, Zorro removes his mask and, to Lolita's astonishment, reveals himself to be Vega.

This was the first of many swashbuckler roles for Douglas Fairbanks and, amazingly, he wasn't sure if the part was right for him, or if he would be accepted by the audience. Today anyone else would be inconceivable in the role, and even though the film was successfully remade more than once the original has never been topped. The comedic skills for which the actor was wellknown are apparent in his portrayal of Don Diego, but the magic begins when he dons the cape and mask of Zorro. Fairbanks had demonstrated his acrobatic skills in several Westerns, but he really cuts loose here--the final twenty minutes of *The Mark of Zorro* rank with the best extended action sequences ever captured on film.

Marguerite de la Motte is a charming leading lady, and Noah Beery blusters through a series of embarrassing defeats as Sergeant Gonzalez. One of the film's best moments is when Gonzalez, tired of losing, just gives up and changes sides. So successful was *The Mark of Zorro* that Fairbanks continued in the genre, playing both Robin Hood and D'Artagnan with equal zest. In 1925, he picked up a sword again for *Don Q, Son of Zorro.* Although he was forty-two years old, Fairbanks played both Zorro and his dashing son Don Cesar de Vega with undiminished energy.

Sent by his father to Spain, Don Cesar becomes a popular figure at the royal court, but is later accused of murder. He fakes his own death and then begins investigating as Zorro. The odds are stacked a bit too high this time, though, but when the original Zorro arrives to help his son the tide is turned. Clever camerawork and the use of a double create the illusion of two dueling Dougs, which amounts to twice the action. There is a wonderful scene in which father and son casually converse while dispatching fifteen foes. The swordplay is expert and the bullwhip, another weapon associated with Zorro by McCulley, is first used on film here. Fairbanks's deadeye proficiency with the lash makes Indiana Jones look like a dime store dominatrix. The outstanding supporting cast included Mary Astor, Donald Crisp, Warner Oland (the movies' best Charlie Chan) and Jean Hersholt.

The Bold Caballero (1936) is quite a step down, but is nonetheless a rousing film which packs a lot into its sixty minute running time. Zorro again leads a revolt against the Spanish government, becoming a hero to the locals. He is then framed for the murder of the governor, whose daughter Isabel vows to see the vigilante hanged. As Don Diego he woos the daughter, while trying to prove the innocence of his alterego.

The film is worth seeing, but not because of Zorro--the character makes three brief, not very exciting appearances in a baggy mask and ill-fitting costume. It's the performances that register, particularly Sig Rumann as the tyrannical commandante and Heather Angel as the lovely and very liberated Isabel. Bob Livingston is an amusing Don Diego, and his attempts to play Cyrano for the portly Rumann are among the film's best moments. *The Bold Caballero* was one ofRepublic Pictures' first attempts at color moviemaking, but today it's tough to find even a black and white copy.

Half the entries in the Zorro filmography would be eliminated if restricted only to appearances of the actual character created by McCulley. Case in point--*Zorro Rides Again* (1937), the first of five Zorro serials by Republic, and the most unsatisfying. Here James Vega is a descendent of the original who swings into action in modern times when tensions erupt between the United States and Mexico.

The construction of the California-Yucatan railroad is hampered by the ruthless El Lobo and his gang, who want to snag control of the project for the corrupt robber baron J. A. Marsden. Vega and his friend Renaldo mount the opposition.

As in the first Lone Ranger serial, Zorro's mask is a bandana that covers his entire face, which hampers the performance of John Carroll. In this case though maybe it helped, as Carroll is an uncharismatic hero with a Frito Bandito accent who does not inspire much excitement. Not much swordplay here either--whips and guns are the weapons of choice.

The portrait of Vega's "great-grandfather Zorro" looks suspiciously like Douglas Fairbanks, which makes for a nice inside joke, as does the appearance of Noah Beery as Marsden--Beery menaced Fairbanks in his first Zorro film as well. But the sight of Zorro being chased by automobiles, swinging through cities with high-rise buildings, and dodging bombs dropped by a World War I fighter jet don't do anything for the character, and the terrible pseudo cowboy ballads that underscore the action are simply awful.

Most of these problems were corrected in *Zorro's Fighting Legion* (1939), in which the character is returned to his proper environment, working with Benito Juarez to keep Mexico free. The new republic is struggling from the loss of several gold shipments. Don Del Oro, the legendary God of Gold, has appeared to incite the Yaqui Indians into robbing the shipments. Don Diego joins the council of Mexican leaders after his uncle is murdered, and suspects one of the councilmen of masquerading as Don Del Oro. Diego begins investigating, while Zorro leads the fighting legion created by his uncle to turn away the Yaqui. Zorro finally convinces the tribe that their god is a fake, and exposes the council's scheme to turn Mexico back into a brutal empire.

Reed Hadley is obviously not an experienced swordsman, but he is excellent as Don Diego and still holds his own in the action scenes. William Carson is an able villain, but a stronger female lead would have helped--getting kidnapped in episode 6 about sums up the extent of Sheila Darcy's contribution. Don Del Oro is one of those hysterically hokey serial villains with a boxy tin suit, a booming voice and a well-protected secret identity. Every time he emerges from behind the elevator doors in his cave to address his followers, the image gets funnier.

The creators of the Indiana Jones trilogy must have watched this serial--*Temple of Doom* borrowed the suspension bridge cliffhanger from episode 4, and in episode 8, Zorro does a 360-degree rotation around a moving stagecoach in the same way that Indy played ring-around-the-truck in *Raiders of the Lost Ark*. The highlight is episode 3, in which Diego is forced into action, and manages to defeat his enemies while preserving his cover as a wimp. There's also a good cliffhanger at the bottom of a mineshaft. Only major complaint--Zorro on a white horse just doesn't look right.

In 1940, a remake of *The Mark of Zorro* starring Tyrone Power actually gave the Fairbanks original a serious run for its money. Actually they're too close to call; Fairbanks is more athletic, but Power's expert fencing skills are shown to full advantage. The climactic duel with Basil Rathbone is the best sword fight in movies.

It's the same story--Don Diego returns to California and learns that the people are under the corrupt rule of Don Luis Quintero. He becomes a symbol of the resistance as Zorro, while playing the fool by day. Only the mission priest, Father Felipe, knows Diego's secret. The cast is outstanding; Power, Rathbone in his usual heartless villain mode, and Linda Darnell as the senorita attracted to Zorro but promised by her parents to the dullard Diego are expertly led through their paces by director Rouben Mamoulian. Like Fairbanks, Power embarked on a series of swashbucklers after the film's success, including *The Black Swan* and *Captain From Castile*, but never again approached the sheer joy and exuberance of his performance here. Zorro, likewise, was never again handled this well in the movies.

Back to the serials for *Zorro's Black Whip* (1944), which is not about Zorro but a character called the Black Whip, who fights cruelty and injustice in Idaho, of all places. The state is trying to join the union, but the territorial government is cleaning up through corruption and works to keep Idaho independent. The Black Whip is killed in action, and his sister Barbara assumes the identity and fulfills her brother's mission.

A female action hero was a novel twist that was rarely used in the 1940s, except in serials. From *The Perils of Pauline* to the Nyoka stories, ladies were doing it for themselves, and Linda Stirling was a charter member in the club. As the Black Whip she high-kicks villains into submission twenty years before Emma Peel, and makes *Zorro's Black Whip*, despite its in-name-only status, an action-packed treat worth checking out.

The Zorro serials peaked two years later with *Son of Zorro*, set in the post-Civil War south. Captain Jeff Stewart returns to his Box County home, only to find that while the troops were away a group of crooked politicians have taken over and are taxing the locals into bankruptcy. At the urging of his friend Pancho, Jeff reluctantly dons the mask of his ancestor Zorro to clean up the county. *Son of Zorro* wastes no time getting started--Jeff reins in a runaway horse buggy less than one minute into the first of thirteen episodes, and with veteran serial director Spencer Bennet pushing the pace more than usual the story seldom slows down after that.

Performances are well above serial standards, especially by George Turner as Jeff/Zorro and Peggy Stewart as his ally and future wife. There's a nice dichotomy with Jeff trying to beat the crooks legally by cutting off their ill-gotten profits, instead of feigning cowardice a la Don Diego, and also beating them back as the vigilante Zorro. With the Spanish influence removed, however, our hero favors the gun over the blade, and a Zorro story without a few good duels just doesn't have the same delights. But by any other yardstick *Son of Zorro* is first-rate.

Ghost of Zorro (1949) is nearly as good, if only to see star Clayton Moore wear a different mask than that of the Lone Ranger. The setting this time is the newly opened New Mexico territory, where the discovery of gold has attracted a powerful lawless element. The Pioneer Telegraph Company plans to establish communication lines all the way to the Pacific, but the criminal cartel would rather have their activities go unreported, and try to shut the company down. Ken Mason, a new engineer, is sent from the east to oversee operations. Together with Rita White, the daughter of Pioneer Telegraph's murdered founder, they try to get thesystem operational. Mason, the grandson of the legendary Zorro, revives his ancestor's alterego to lend a hand.

If anyone can explain how a guy named Ken Mason can be a direct descendent of a guy named Don Diego Vega, I'd love to hear it. It's amusing to watch Moore speak in his normal voice as Mason and adopt an accent when he dons the mask. There's not as much action as in previous serials, but the performances are above average.

After Walt Disney had a hit with the Davy Crockett series on television, it tried to duplicate this popularity with a series based on Zorro. Black capes never outsold coonskin caps, but looking back now it seems clear that "Zorro" was a much better series and ranks with the best of Disney's live-action television. The format was borrowed from Crockett, in that each story was comprised of three or four episodes, and the Disney Zorro followed Davy to the big screen in *Sign of Zorro* (1960) and others, but did not survive the conversion as well.

Guy Williams played Don Diego/Zorro, wisely with just a hint of a Spanish accent, and he's a made-to-order hero for the family-values audience. He is dashing, brave, smart and grins from ear to ear whether clashing swords with soldiers or communicating with his deaf-mute manservant Bernardo (Gene Sheldon). The army that was so ruthless and vicious in other versions has been Disney-fied into bumbling clowns. It's possible that the antics of Britt Lomond as the manic Captain Monastario and Henry Calvin as the plump Sergeant Garcia were the models for Colonel Klink and Sergeant Schultz from "Hogan's Heroes." Other villains and supporting characters came and went during the series' two-year run, including Annette Funicello as a singing senorita and George J. Lewis as Zorro's dad. Lewis had previously played the Black Whip in the 1944 serial.

Another connection to the Republic serials is William Lava's music, used both in *Zorro's Fighting Legion* and in the series. The familiar theme song, however, was written by Norman Foster and George Burns. It didn't become a standard like the Davy Crockett theme, but did hit the charts in a cover version by The Chordettes.

In 1962 another film entitled *The Mark of Zorro* turned up, but its original title was *Duel at the Rio Grande*. The story concerns a young man returning home to Mexico and finding his parents murdered by a dictator. He leads a band of revolutionaries and exacts revenge. This reworking of the Zorro theme starred Errol Flynn's son Sean, which is all that's noteworthy about the film today. Of course, had Sean done a better job, the movie would be a lot better known.

Hollywood forgot about Zorro for awhile after the serials, but his sword was picked up in Europe, resulting in a series of wholly forgettable films that were the swashbuckling equivalents of the Italian muscleman genre featuring Hercules and Samson. For the record, the cycle began (if we don't start with the Flynn film, which was also made overseas) with the Spanish-made *Zorro the Avenger* (1963), which retold the same origin story, this time with Frank Latimore in the title role. The Italians then rode in with *Zorro and the Three Musketeers*, also from 1963. One-time Hercules Gordon Scott starred in this team-up tale set in the seventeenth century. That same year Zorro was played by Pierre Brice in *Samson and the Slave Queen*, the unlikely story of a Biblical strongman and a hero of eighteenth century California joining forces to fight an evil king in the fifteenth century. The sheer stupidity of the premise is undeniably intriguing, and Brice is better than you might expect.

Back to Spain for what is probably the most watchable of the EuropeanZorros, 1963's *The Three Swords of Zorro*. At least they got the time and place almost right; the story is set in 1830 Mexico, where a predictably tyrannical local government is opposed by the hero dressed in black. After ten years the vigilante is captured and thrown in jail. While his legend grows Diego, a young infant who was saved by the soldiers when his village was destroyed, assumes the identity of Zorro and renews the people's fight. By day, Diego makes time with Virginia, the governor's attractive young fiancee`. When the governor gets wise he sets a trap which works--Diego is thrown in the same cell as his predecessor. They discover during their incarceration that they are father and son. Meanwhile, Diego's step-sister Maria helps them both escape, and the three of them, garbed in Zorro's guise, crash the governor's wedding and end his reign of terror. Diego and Virginia are married.

As with all entries in this series the editing is choppy and the dubbing poor, and there are the obligatory Ay-yi-yi-yi musical interludes at the local cantina. But the screenplay at least tries to introduce some novel ideas, the action scenes are frequent and the episodes you can't avoid in a Zorro movie, such as when the foppish Diego is ridiculed by soldiers ("Him? Zorro? Ha-ha-ha") are gamely played by Guy Stockwell, with good support from Gloria Milan as lady Zorro. The three swords in the title only appear together for the final five minutes, which was a mistake, but it's not a chore to get there.

Three more interchangeable Italian films close out this phase--*Zorro the Rebel* (1966) with Howard Ross as the hero who assists a beautiful girl being forced to marry the governor's dopey son; *Zorro in the Court of Spain* (1968), another *Mark of Zorro* knock-off with George Ardisson, and *Zorro, Marquis of Navarra* (1971), in which the masked man (Nadior Moretti) works with the Spanish king and army for a change, to drive out the French.

The nadir for the character came with two unrelated soft-porn spoofs, *The Naked Sword of Zorro* in 1969 and *The Erotic Adventures of Zorro* in 1974. Like *Flesh Gordon* (1974), the most famous (infamous?) of this gone and better forgotten genre, half-hearted attempts at humor and action are uncomfortably blended with X-rated material. You really have to wonder who the audience was for these movies--the raincoat crowd would have no interest in the lame comedy that interrupts the sex scenes, and audiences who thrilled to Fairbanks and Power would be shocked to see how Zorro uses his bullwhip here.

The Mark of Zorro was adapted for television in 1974 with a lackluster Frank Langella as Zorro and the excellent Gilbert Roland as Don Diego's father. Some good people in small roles, especially Anne Archer and Louise Sorel, but after two bona-fide classic screen renderings of this tale, one more became as superfluous as the Catherine Oxenberg-Tom Conti TV version of *Roman Holiday* (1987). Never heard of it? I rest my case.

But the character could still be turned loose in other adventures with success, as evidenced by Alain Delon's surprisingly spirited turn in a 1975 French-Italian production simply titled *Zorro*. A quantum leap above the programmers of ten years earlier, the film has an entirely different flavor from any previous or subsequent release. Delon masquerades as the wimpy governor of Nuova Aragon, while taking on the cruel military chief Huerta as Zorro. The South American locations, the strange, radio jingle-like music and the action scenes that at times resemble a cartoon come to life make this a hard film to get a bead on. Primarily it's aimed at kids, with the army acting as dumb and clumsy as in the Disney version, and the scenes that show Zorro's closest allies as the children of the town. TheFairbanks influence is also evident, with Delon bounding off awnings, and eluding dozens of men with carefree abandon. Nice to see the usually serious star of *The Leopard* (1963) having such fun. The final duel to the death, which starts with swords and progresses to axes, spears and torches, is impressively directed and choreographed, but the film should also have wrapped up its romantic subplot before fading out.

The most recent theatrical attempt is *Zorro, The Gay Blade* (1981), an all-out parody composed of equal amounts of hits and misses. The film opens with Don Diego Vega, in Madrid fifty years A. Z. (After Zorro) returning to California to find conditions changed for the worse. He learns from a note left by his late father that it is the destiny of Vega men to fight tyranny as Zorro. He tries, but sprains his ankle in his first appearance. Fortunately, his gay brother Bunny Wigglesworth returns from his stint in the Royal Navy in time to continue the tradition--with a few changes. Garbed in a lavender variation of the Zorro outfit, he carries out the family tradition until Vega can recover.

George Hamilton, who plays both brothers in a dual role, could conceivably have played the role straight in a version with different intentions. Give credit where it's due for creating two very different characters, but no points for the generally low level of humor. Hamilton and costar Lauren Hutton revive the Ricky Ricardo Latino accent jokes, a poor running gag, as is the scenes with Zorro's deaf sidekick (a spoof of the Disney series). There's nothing wrong with humor in bad taste as long as its funny; the film shoots at all the usual targets, especially homosexuals, as the title implies, but can do no better than phrases like "sissy boy," which if it was ever funny was so a good forty years ago.

But to be fair, there are also some amusing jabs at the legend, such as the masked ball where *everyone* comes as Zorro, and some inspired scene-stealing from Brenda Vaccaro as the oversexed wife of overbearing head bad guy Ron Leibman. Lauren Hutton is ravishing as Diego's lady, the set design is elaborate and unique, and the music is memorable. Still, dedicating this film to Rouben Mamoulian is like dedicating *Blood Feast* to Alfred Hitchcock. Not quite that bad, but close.

After the success of their original "Zorro" television series, Disney tried again with "Zorro and Son" (1983), but this time it came up short. It's a sequel of sorts, with the revival of the setting and the Bernardo character (now played by Bill Dana), but the tone has shifted away from adventure and toward lowbrow comedy. It is twenty years since Zorro first appeared to clean up California, but injustice still exists and Don Diego (Henry Darrow) is getting too old to leap in the saddle. He asks his son Don Carlos (Paul Regina) to return from Spain and continue the crusade. Zorro, Jr., agrees, but makes a few changes in the hero's tactics. As Don Carlos, he continues to gamble and chase the ladies, much to his father's chagrin. Bad puns and silly jokes punctuate almost every scene and, as in *The Gay Blade*, it seems a waste of a talented cast who could have played the material straight and made it work.

In recent years Steven Spielberg has talked about reviving Zorro once again, and one need only look at the Indiana Jones trilogy to realize that no one could better take the helm.

THE FILMS

The Mark of Zorro (Douglas Fairbanks/United Artists, 1920, 90 minutes)
Directed by Fred Niblo; Written and produced by Douglas Fairbanks; Music by William Perry
Cast
DOUGLAS FAIRBANKS (ZORRO/Don Diego), Noah Beery (Sgt. Gonzalez), Marguerite de la Motte (Lolita)
Rating: *****
Available on Videocassette

Don Q, Son of Zorro (Elton/United Artists, 1925, 100 minutes)
Directed by Donald Crisp; Written by Jack Cunningham, based on a story by Hesketh and Kate Prichard; Music by Mortimer Wilson
Cast
DOUGLAS FAIRBANKS (ZORRO, Don Cesar), Mary Astor (Dolores de Muro), Donald Crisp (Don Sebastian), Warner Oland (Archduke Paul of Austria) Jean Hersholt (Don Fabrique)
Rating: ****
Available on Videocassette

The Bold Caballero (Republic, 1936, 60 minutes)
Directed and written by Wells Root; Produced by Nat Levine; Music by Harry Grey
Cast
ROBERT LIVINGSTON (ZORRO), Heather Angel (Isabella) Sig Rumann (Commandante), Ian Wolfe (Priest)
Rating: ***

Zorro Rides Again (Republic serial, 1937, 213 minutes)
Directed by William Witney and John English; Written by Barry Shipman, Franklyn Adreon, John Rathmell, Ronald Davidson and Morgan Cox; Produced by Sol Siegel; Music by Alberto Colombo
Cast
JOHN CARROLL (ZORRO), Noah Berry (J.A. Marsden), Richard Alexander (El Lobo), Helen Christian (Joyce), Duncan Renaldo (Renaldo)
Rating: **
Available on Videocassette

Zorro's Fighting Legion (Republic serial, 1939, 211 minutes)
Directed by William Witney and John English; Written by Ronald Davidson, Franklyn Adreon, Morgan Cox, Sol Shor and Barney A. Sarecky; Produced by Hiram S. Brown, Jr.; Music by William Lava
Cast
REED HADLEY (ZORRO/Don Diego), Sheila Darcy (Volita), William Carson (Ramon)
Rating: ***1/2
Available on Videocassette

The Mark of Zorro (20th Century Fox, 1940, 93 minutes)
Directed by Rouben Mamoulian; Written by John Tainton Foote, Garrett Fort and Bess Meredyth; Produced by Raymond Griffith; Music by Alfred Newman
Cast
TYRONE POWER (ZORRO/Don Diego), Linda Darnell (Lolita Quintero), Basil Rathbone (Capt. Esteban Pasquale) Gale Sondergard (Inez Quintero), Eugene Pallette (Fra Felipe)
Rating: *****
Available on Videocassette
Awards: Academy Award nomination for Best Score

Zorro's Black Whip (Republic serial, 1944, 182 minutes)
Directed by Spencer Gordon Bennett and Wallace Grissell; Written by Basil

Dickey, Jesse Duffy, Grant Nelson and Joseph Poland; Produced by Ronald Davidson; Music by Richard Cherwin
Cast
Linda Stirling (Black Whip), George J. Lewis (Vic Gordon), Lucien Littlefield (Hammon)
Rating: ***1/2
Available on Videocassette

Son of Zorro (Republic serial, 1947, 250 minutes)
Directed by Spencer Bennett and Fred C. Bannon; Written by Franklyn Adreon, Basil Dickey, Jesse Duffy and Sol Shor; Produced by Ronald Davidson; Music by Mort Glickman
Cast
GEORGE TURNER (ZORRO/Jeff Stewart), Peggy Stewart (Kate), Roy Bancroft (Boyd)
Rating: ***1/2
Available on Videocassette

Ghost of Zorro (Republic serial, 1949, 250 minutes)
Directed by Fred C. Bannon; Written by Royal Cole, William Lively and Sol Shor; Produced by Franklyn Adreon; Music by Stanley Wilson
Cast
CLAYTON MOORE (ZORRO/Ken Mason), Pamela Blake (Rita White)
Rating: ***1/2

Zorro the Avenger (Spain, 1963, 90 minutes)
Directed by Joaquin Luis Romero Marchent; Produced by Norberto Solino
Cast
FRANK LATIMORE (ZORRO), Mary Anderson, Howard Vernon
Rating: **

Zorro and the Three Musketeers (Golden Era, 1962, 99 minutes)
Directed by Marino Vacca
Cast
GORDON SCOTT (ZORRO), Jose Greci, Giacomo Rossi Stuart
Rating: **

The Three Swords of Zorro (Hispamer/Rodes, 1963, 88 minutes)
Directed by Richard Blasco
Cast
GUY STOCKWELL (ZORRO), Gloria Milan (Virginia)
Rating: **1/2

Zorro Against Maciste (Romana/AIP, 1963, 86 minutes)
AKA Samson and the Slave Queen
Directed by Umberto Lenzi; Written by Guido Malatesta; Produced by Fortunato Misiano; Music by Angelo Francesco Lavagnino
Cast
PIERRE BRICE (ZORRO/Ramon), Alan Steel (Samson), Moira Orfei (Malva)
Rating: ***

Zorro the Rebel (Romana, 1966, 90 minutes)
Directed and written by Pierro Pierotti
Cast
HOWARD ROSS (ZORRO)
Rating: *1/2

Zorro in the Court of Spain (Italian, 1968, 90 minutes)
Directed by Guido Zurli
Cast
GEORGE ARDISSON (ZORRO)
Rating: *1/2

The Naked Sword of Zorro (1969)
Other credits unavailable

Zorro, Marquis of Navarra (Romana, 1971, 91 minutes)
Directed by Jean Monty
Cast
NADIOR MORETTI (ZORRO)
Rating: 1/2 *

The Erotic Adventures of Zorro (1974, 102 minutes)
Directed by Robert Freeman; Written by Mona Lott, Joy Boxe and David F. Friedman; Produced by David F. Friedman; Music by Billy Allen and William Loose
Cast
DOUGLAS FREY (ZORRO), Robyn Whitting (Maria), Penny Boran (Helena)
Rating: zero

Zorro (Allied Artists, 1975, 100 minutes)
Directed by Duccio Tessari; Written by Giorgio Arlorio; Produced by Luciano Martino; Music by Guido and Maurizio De Angelis
Cast
ALAIN DELON (ZORRO), Stanley Baker (Huerta), Ottavia Piccolo (Hortensia), Moustache (Sergeant), Adrianna Asti (Countess)
Rating: ***1/2

Zorro, the Gay Blade (Melvin Simon/20th Century Fox, 1981, 93 minutes)
Directed by Peter Medak; Written by Hal Dresner, based on a story by Dresner, Greg Alt, Don Moriarty and Bob Randall; Produced by George Hamilton and C.O. Erickson; Music by Ian Frazer
Cast
GEORGE HAMILTON (ZORRO/Bunny Wigglesworth), Lauren Hutton (Charlotte), Brenda Vaccaro (Florinda), Rob Leibman (Esteban)
Rating: **
Available on Videocassette

TELEVISION
"Zorro" (ABC series, 1957-1959)
Cast

GUY WILLIAMS (ZORRO), George J. Lewis (Don Alejandro), Gene Sheldon (Bernardo), Henry Calvin (Sgt. Garcia)
Rating: ***

"The Mark of Zorro" (ABC movie, 1974, 74 minutes)
Directed by Don McDougall; Written by Brian Taggert, Music by Alfred Newman
Cast
FRANK LANGELLA (ZORRO/Don Diego), Ricardo Montalban, Gilbert Roland, Yvonne De Carlo
Rating: **

"Zorro and Son" (CBS series, 1983)
Cast
HENRY DARROW (ZORRO, SR./Don Diego), PAUL REGINA (ZORRO, JR./Don Carlos), Gregory Sierra (Commandante Paco Pico), Bill Dana (Bernardo)
Rating: *

FOR MORE INFORMATION

I began my research for *Hollywood's Heroes* at the good old reliable *Encyclopedia Britannica* (15th Edition, Encyclopedia Britannica Inc., 1980). The following books were also very helpful and are recommended as sources for additional information on the heroes chronicled in the preceding pages.

KING ARTHUR
Le Morte Darthur (Edited by R.M. Lumiansky, Collier Books, New York, 1982)

King Arthur (Norma Goodrich, F. Watts, New York, 1986)

BATMAN
The Encyclopedia of Comic Book Heroes, Vol. 1 (Michael L. Fleisher, Collier Books, New York, 1976)

JAMES BOND
The Incredible World of 007 (Lee Pfeiffer and Philip Lisa, Citadel Press, New York, 1992)

DAVY CROCKETT
Davy Crockett: the man, the legend, the legacy, 1786-1986 (Edited by Michael A. Lofaro, University of Tennessee Press, Knoxville, 1985)

WYATT EARP
The Earps of Tombstone (*Tombstone Epitaph* newspaper files, Tombstone,1880-1882)

The Earps Talk (Edited by Alford E. Turner, Creative Publishing Co., College Station, Texas, 1980)

HENRY V
The Riverside Shakespeare (Edited by G. Blakemore Evans, Houghton Mifflin Company, Boston, 1974)

HERCULES
Bullfinch's Mythology (Thomas Bullfinch, Mentor, New York, 1962)

JASON
Bullfinch's Mythology (Thomas Bullfinch, Mentor, New York, 1962)

JOAN OF ARC
Joan of Arc in History, Literature, and Film (Nadia Margolis, Garland Publishing, New York, 1990)

BRUCE LEE
Bruce Lee (various authors, Rainbow Publishing, Los Angeles, 1974)

AUDIE MURPHY
To Hell and Back (Audie Murphy, Holt, New York, 1949)

No Name on the Bullet (Don Graham, Viking, New York, 1989)

ELIOT NESS
Torso: The Story of Eliot Ness (Steven Nickel, Blair, Winston-Salem, North Carolina, 1989)

GENERAL GEORGE S. PATTON
War as I Knew It (George S. Patton, Houghton Mifflin Company, Boston, 1947)

The Last Days of Patton (Ladislas Farago, McGraw-Hill, New York, 1981)

ROBIN HOOD
Outlaws of Medieval Legend (Maurice Keen, University of Toronto Press, Toronto, 1977)

SAMSON
The Good News Bible (Thomas Nelson Publishers, Nashville, 1976)

SINBAD
Tales From the Thousand and One Nights (translated by N. J. Dawood, Penguin Books, London, 1973)

SPARTACUS
From the Gracchi to Nero (H.H. Scullard, Methuen & Co., Ltd., London, 1959)

SUPERMAN
The Great Superman Book (Michael L. Fleisher, Warner Books, New York, 1978)

TARZAN
Tarzan of the Movies (Gabe Essoe, Citadel Press, New Jersey, 1968)

MOVIE SOURCES

To locate some of the movies not listed as available on videocassette, you might try one of the following sources:

Captain Bijou
Post Office Box 87
Toney, AL 35773

Eddie Brandt's Saturday Matinee
6310 Colfax Avenue
North Hollywood, CA 91606

Sinister Cinema
Post Office Box 4369
Medford, OR 97501

Stokey's Serials
P.O. Box 426
Selden, NY 11784

<u>INDEX</u>